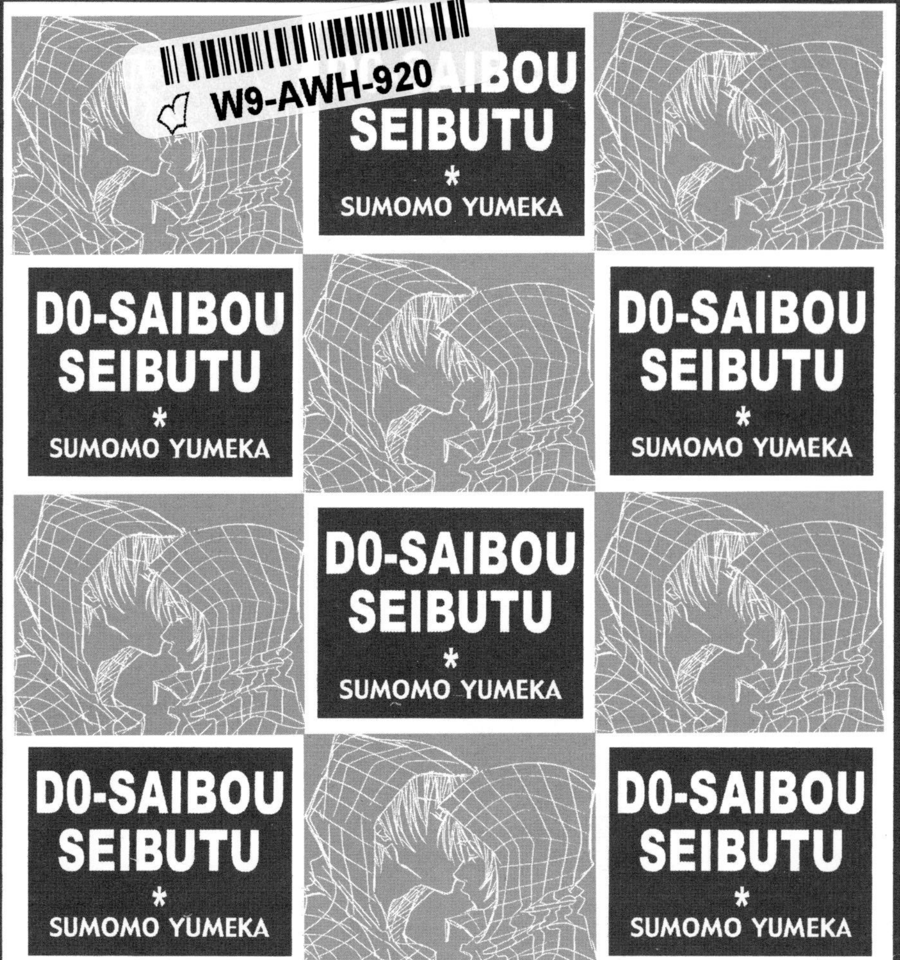
SAIBOU
SEIBUTU
*
SUMOMO YUMEKA
DO-SAIBOU
SEIBUTU
*
SUMOMO YUMEKA
DO-SAIBOU
SEIBUTU
*
SUMOMO YUMEKA
DO-SAIBOU
SEIBUTU
*
SUMOMO YUMEKA
DO-SAIBOU
SEIBUTU
*
SUMOMO YUMEKA
DO-SAIBOU
SEIBUTU
*
SUMOMO YUMEKA
DO-SAIBOU
SEIBUTU
*
SUMOMO YUMEKA

同細胞生物
SAME-CELL ORGANISM

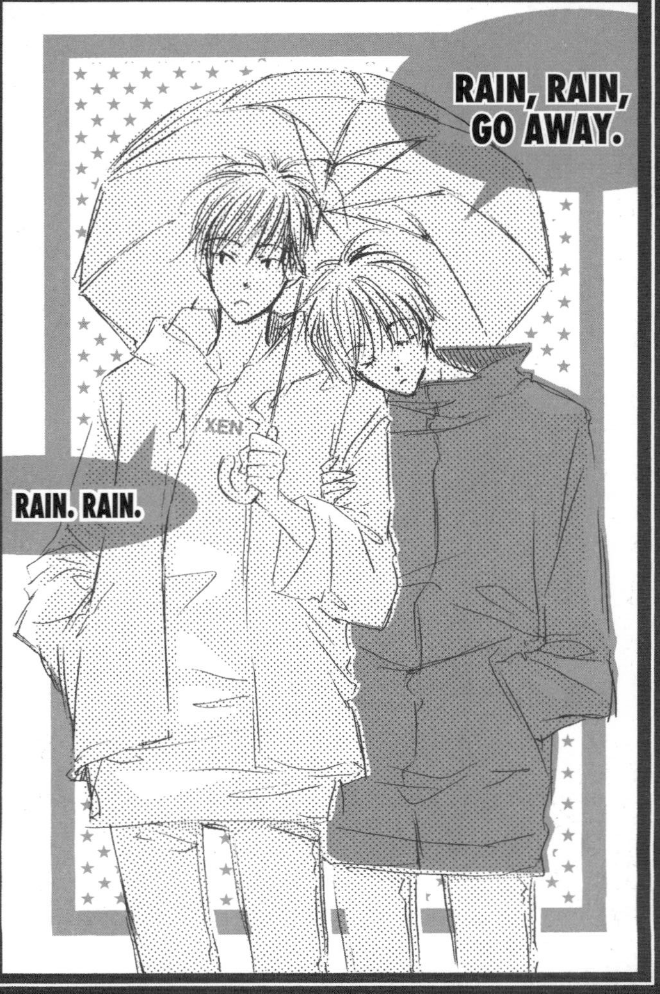
RAIN, RAIN,
GO AWAY.
RAIN. RAIN.

SAME-CELL ORGANISM

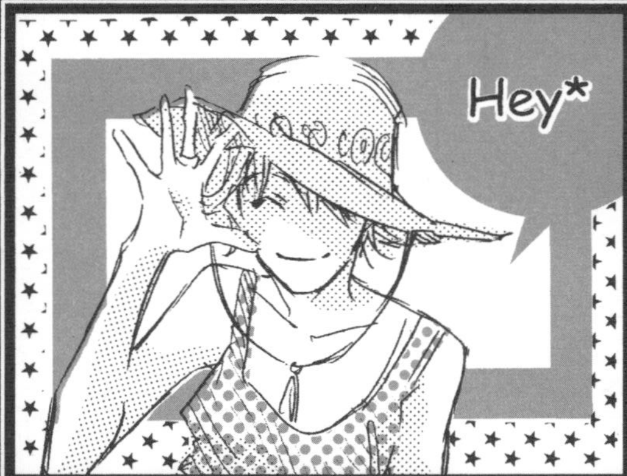
Hey*

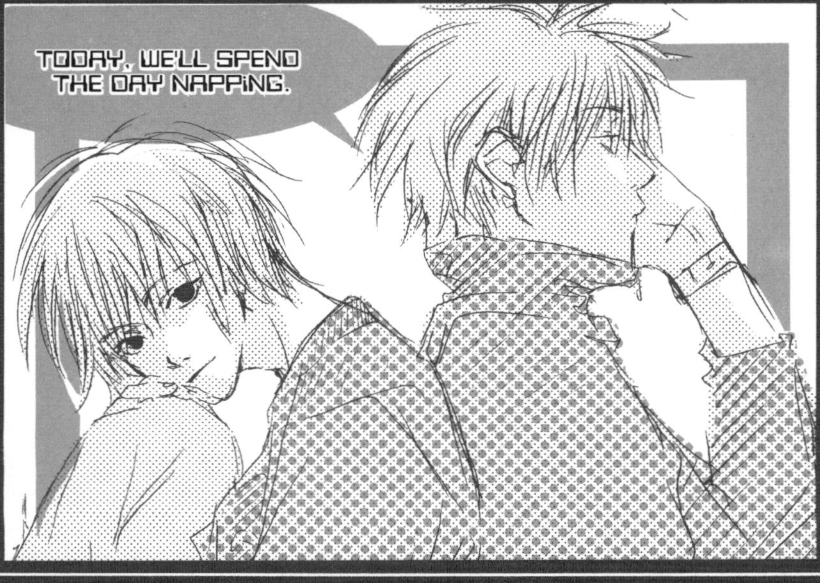
TODAY, WE'LL SPEND
THE DAY NAPPING.

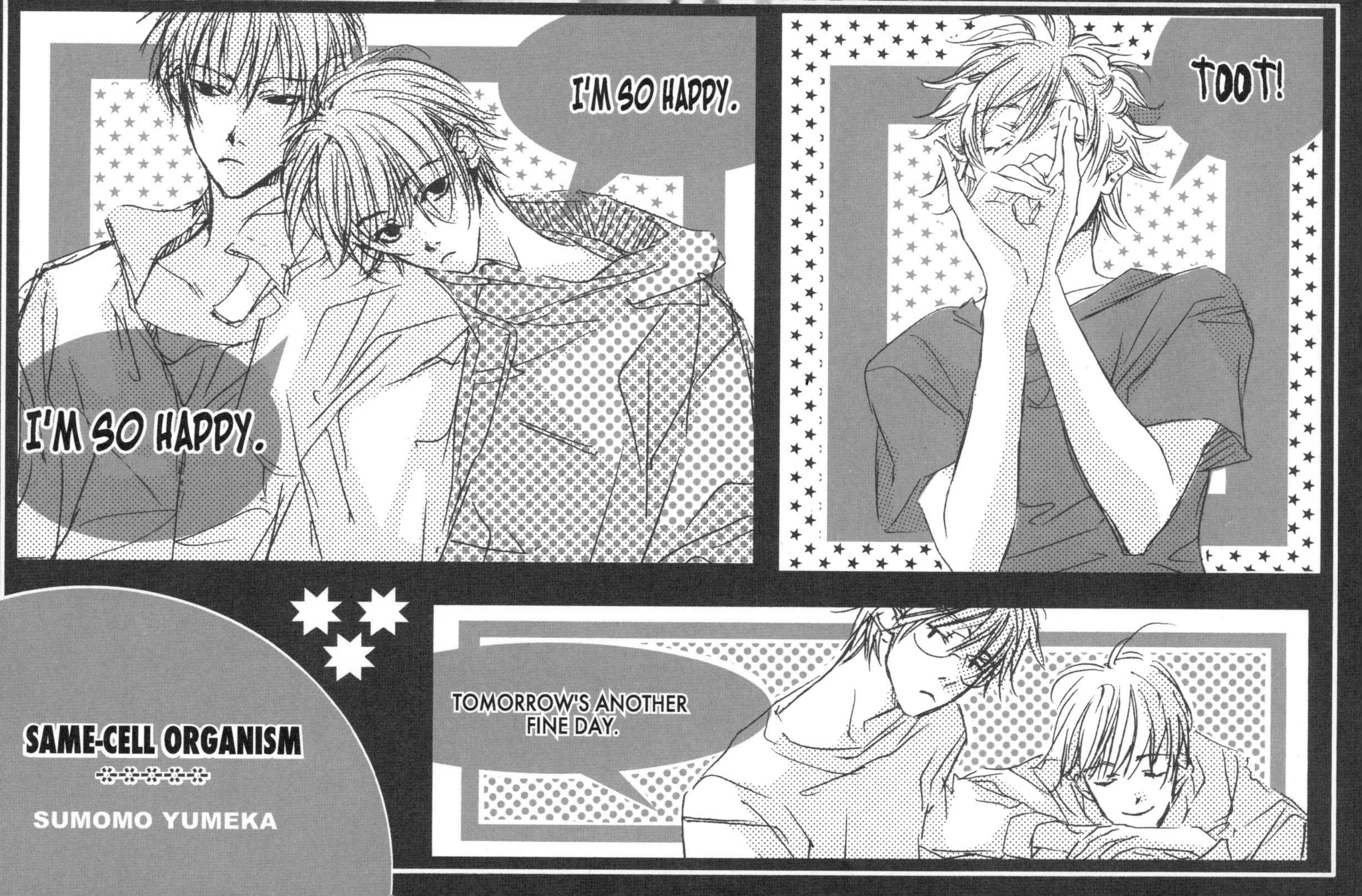
TOOT!
I'M SO HAPPY.
I'M SO HAPPY.
TOMORROW'S ANOTHER FINE DAY.

SAME-CELL ORGANISM

SUMOMO YUMEKA

SAME-CELL ORGANISM

SAME-CELL ORGANISM...007
I LOVE YOU...035
LULLABY IN MY HAND...039
THE LETTER IN THE ATTIC...057
TO MAKE AN ANGEL (PT.1)...085
TO MAKE AN ANGEL (PT.2)...119
WE SELFISH TWO...141

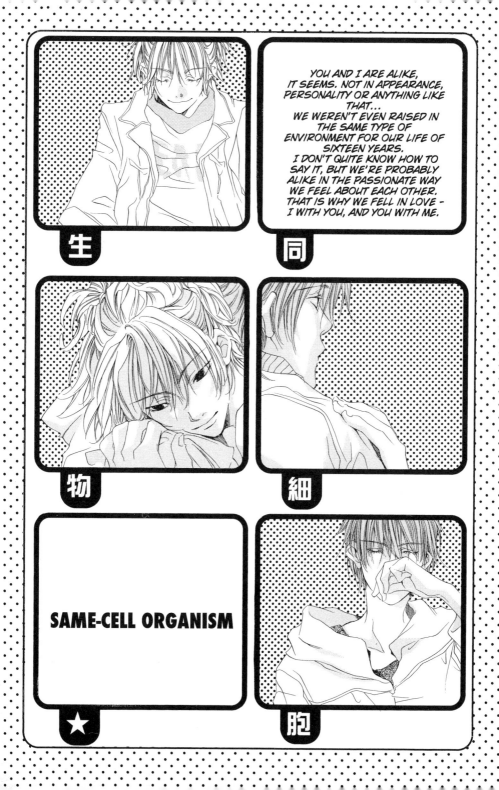

YOU AND I ARE ALIKE,
IT SEEMS. NOT IN APPEARANCE,
PERSONALITY OR ANYTHING LIKE
THAT...
WE WEREN'T EVEN RAISED IN
THE SAME TYPE OF
ENVIRONMENT FOR OUR LIFE OF
SIXTEEN YEARS.
I DON'T QUITE KNOW HOW TO
SAY IT, BUT WE'RE PROBABLY
ALIKE IN THE PASSIONATE WAY
WE FEEL ABOUT EACH OTHER.
THAT IS WHY WE FELL IN LOVE -
I WITH YOU, AND YOU WITH ME.

SAME-CELL ORGANISM

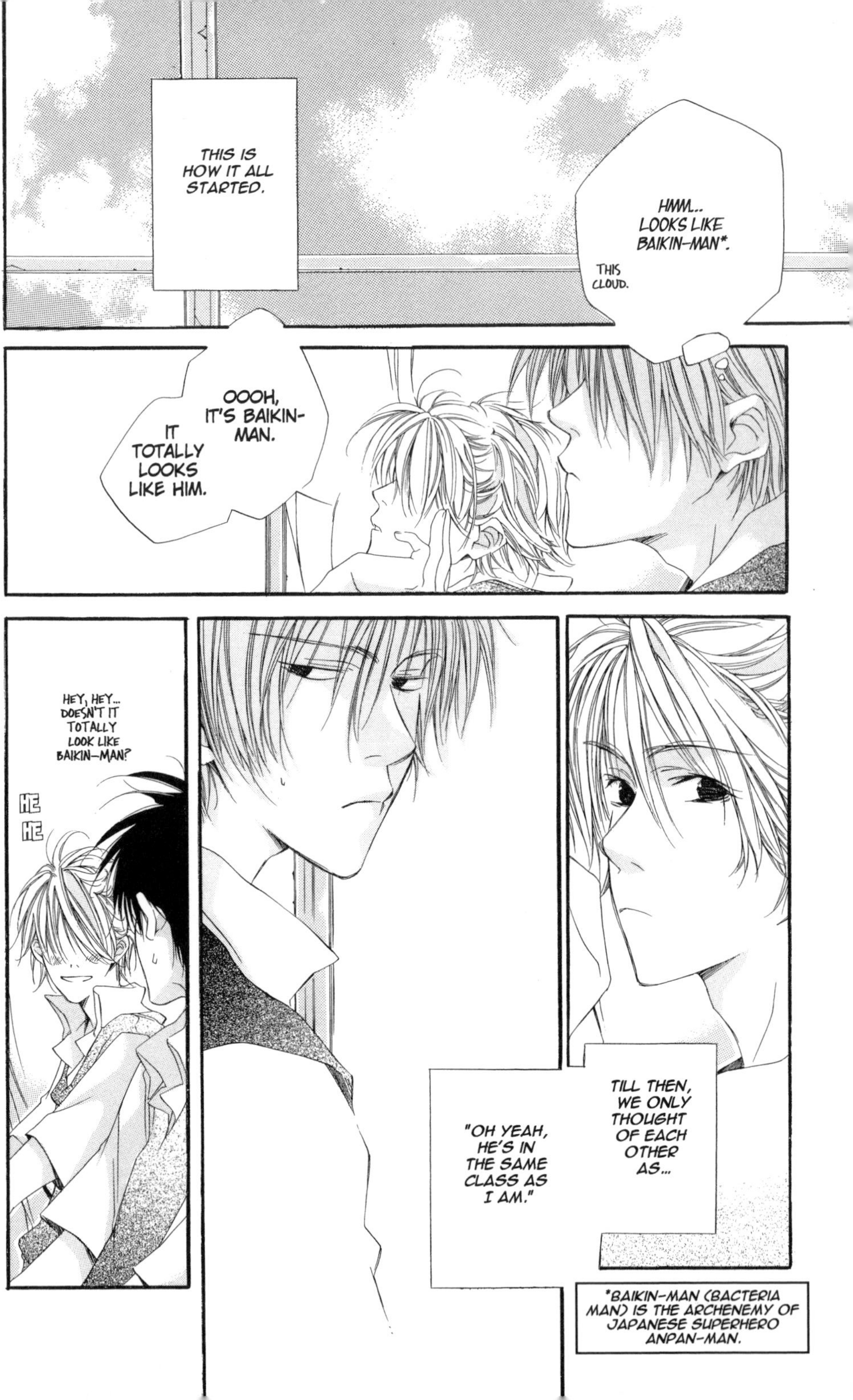
HMM... LOOKS LIKE BAIKIN-MAN*.
THIS CLOUD.
THIS IS HOW IT ALL STARTED.
OOOH, IT'S BAIKIN-MAN.
IT TOTALLY LOOKS LIKE HIM.
TILL THEN, WE ONLY THOUGHT OF EACH OTHER AS...
"OH YEAH, HE'S IN THE SAME CLASS AS I AM."
HEY, HEY... DOESN'T IT TOTALLY LOOK LIKE BAIKIN-MAN?
HE HE

*BAIKIN-MAN (BACTERIA MAN) IS THE ARCHENEMY OF JAPANESE SUPERHERO ANPAN-MAN.

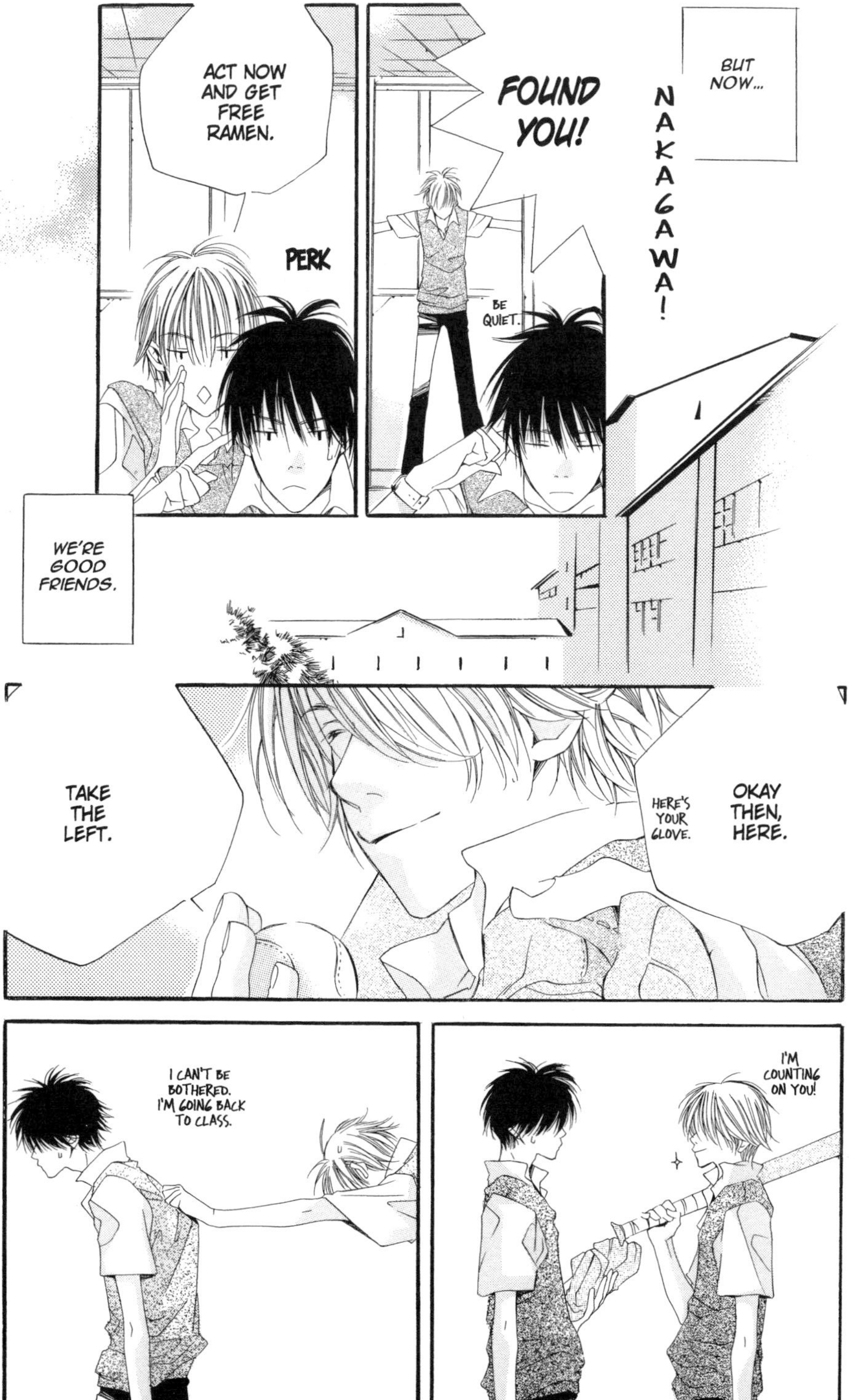
BUT NOW...
NAKAGAWA!
FOUND YOU!
BE QUIET.
ACT NOW AND GET FREE RAMEN.
PERK
WE'RE GOOD FRIENDS.
OKAY THEN, HERE.
HERE'S YOUR GLOVE.
TAKE THE LEFT.
I'M COUNTING ON YOU!
I CAN'T BE BOTHERED. I'M GOING BACK TO CLASS.

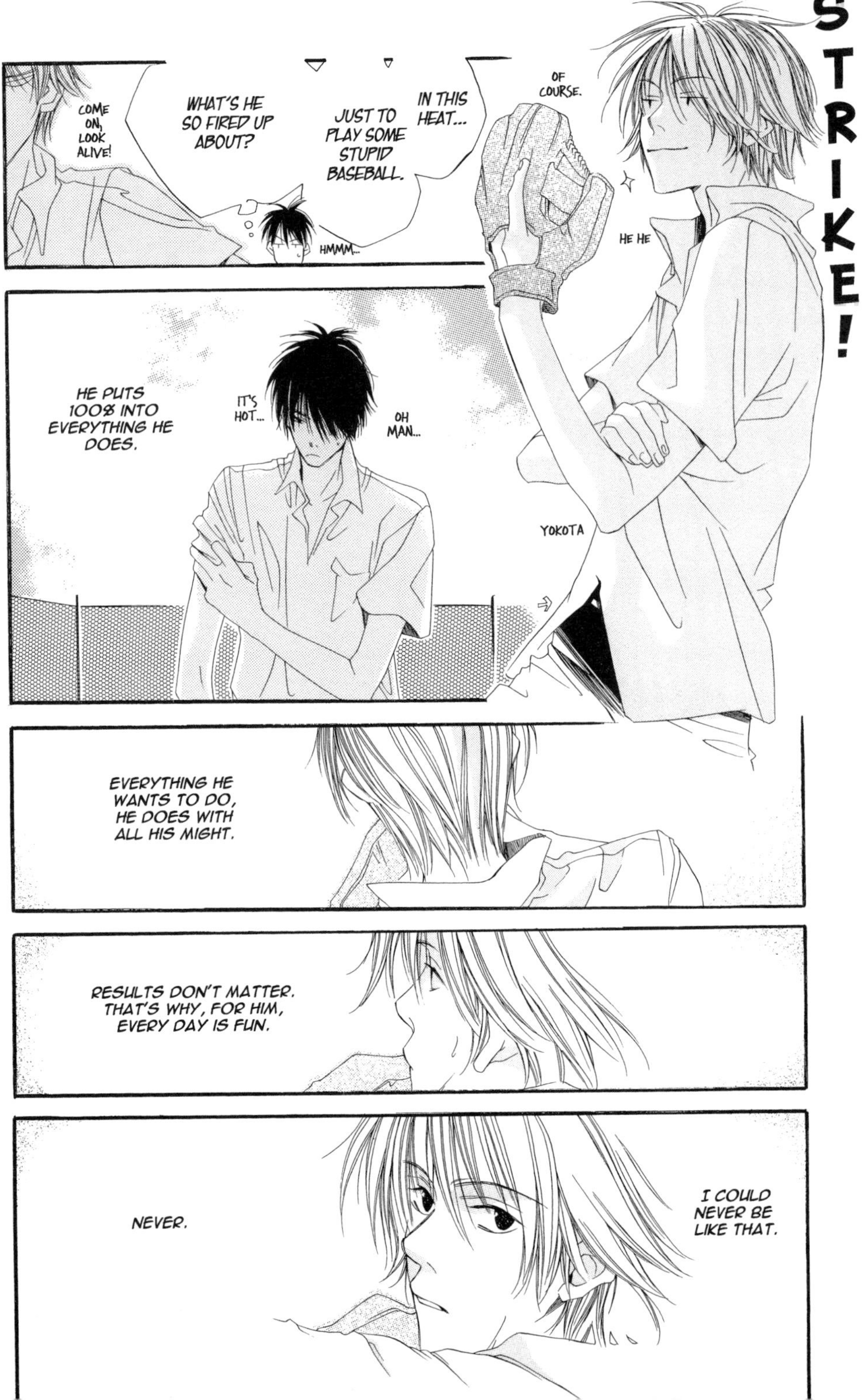
STRIKE!
OF COURSE.
HE HE
YOKOTA
IN THIS HEAT...
JUST TO PLAY SOME STUPID BASEBALL.
WHAT'S HE SO FIRED UP ABOUT?
COME ON, LOOK ALIVE!
HMMM...
OH MAN...
IT'S HOT...
HE PUTS 100% INTO EVERYTHING HE DOES.
EVERYTHING HE WANTS TO DO, HE DOES WITH ALL HIS MIGHT.
RESULTS DON'T MATTER. THAT'S WHY, FOR HIM, EVERY DAY IS FUN.
I COULD NEVER BE LIKE THAT.
NEVER.

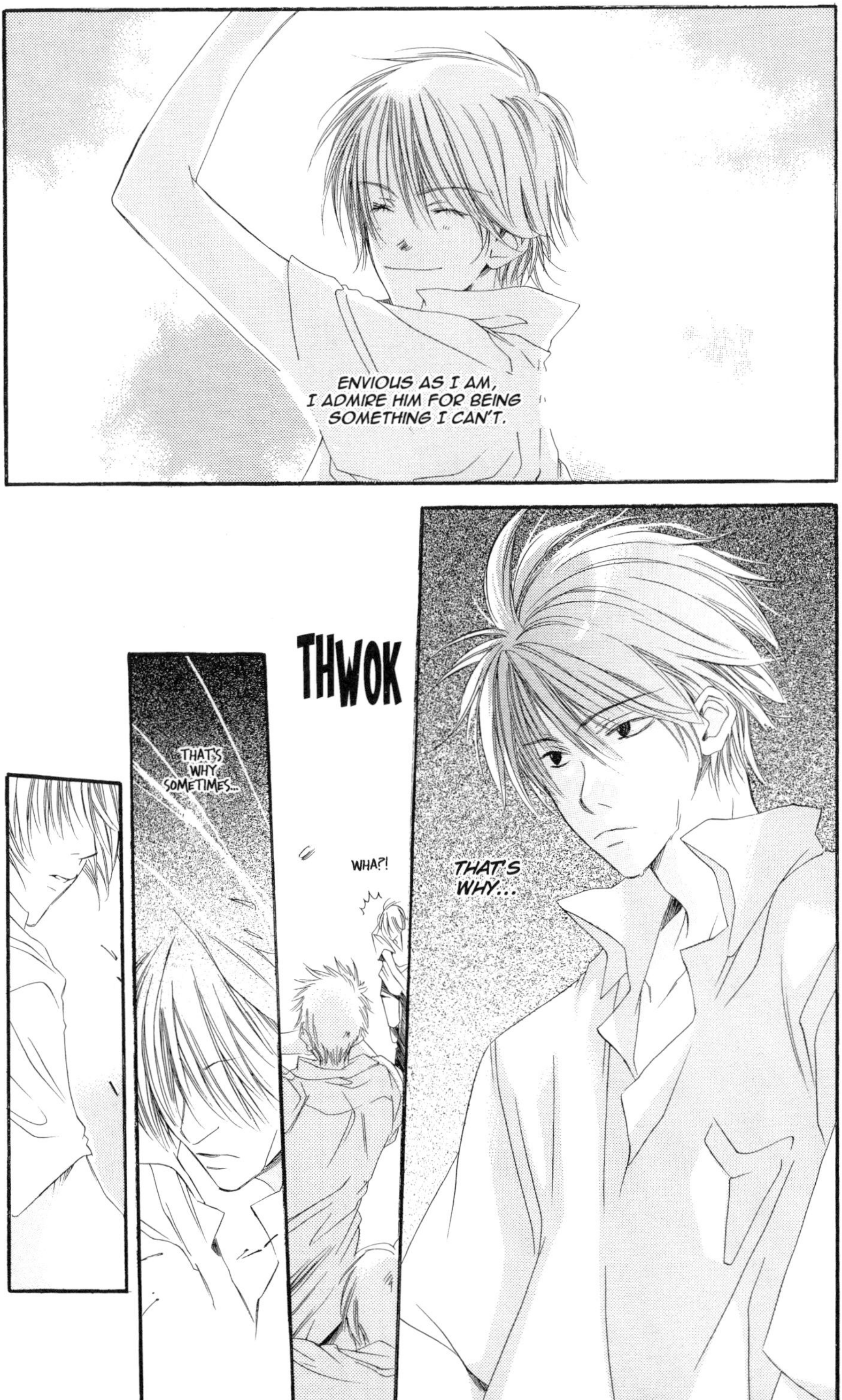
ENVIOUS AS I AM, I ADMIRE HIM FOR BEING SOMETHING I CAN'T.
THAT'S WHY...
THWOK
WHA?!
THAT'S WHY SOMETIMES...

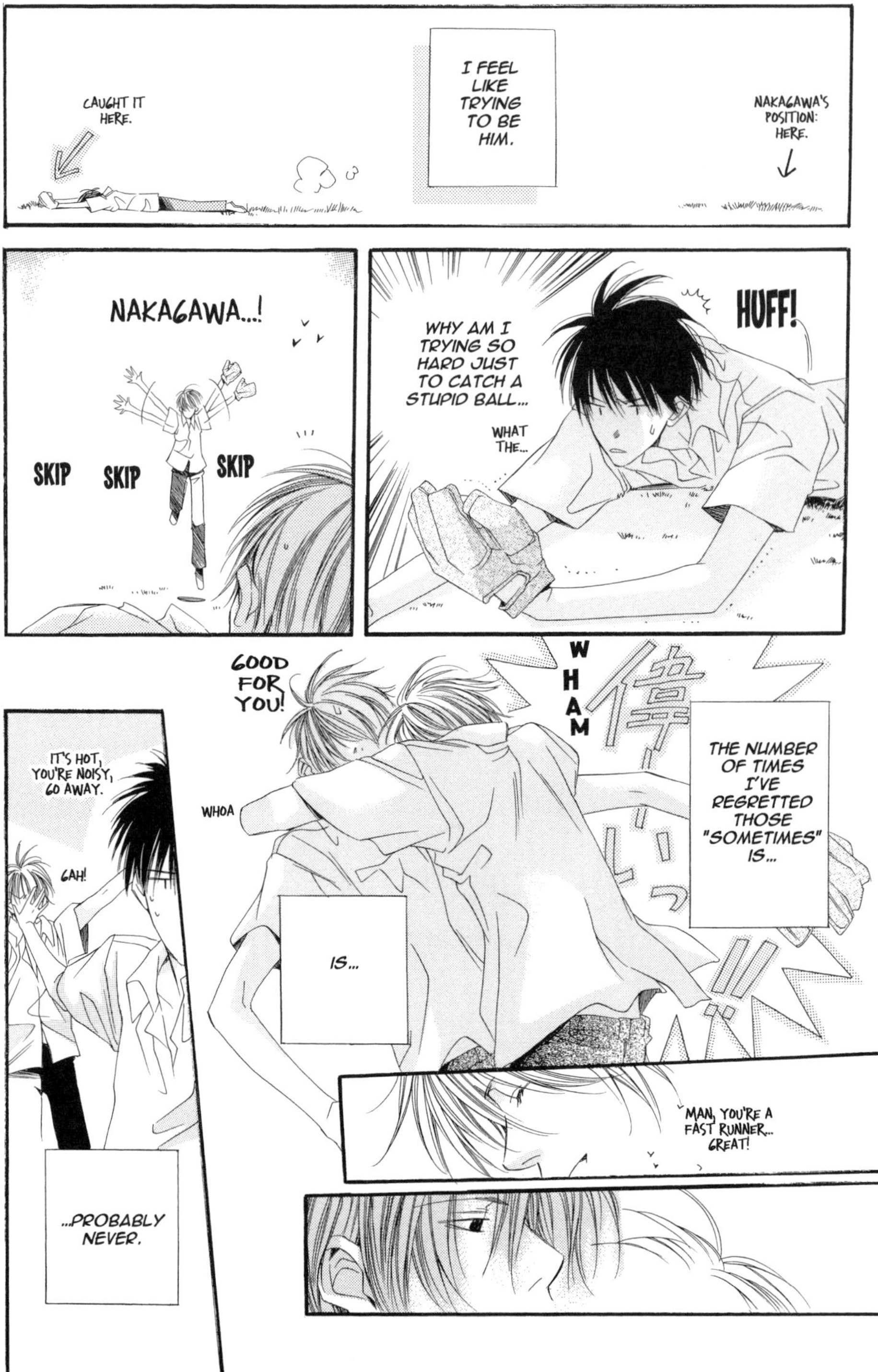
NAKAGAWA'S POSITION: HERE.
I FEEL LIKE TRYING TO BE HIM.
CAUGHT IT HERE.
HUFF!
WHY AM I TRYING SO HARD JUST TO CATCH A STUPID BALL...
WHAT THE...
NAKAGAWA...!
SKIP
SKIP
SKIP
THE NUMBER OF TIMES I'VE REGRETTED THOSE "SOMETIMES" IS...
WHAM
GOOD FOR YOU!
WHOA
IS...
MAN, YOU'RE A FAST RUNNER... GREAT!
IT'S HOT, YOU'RE NOISY, GO AWAY.
GAH!
...PROBABLY NEVER.

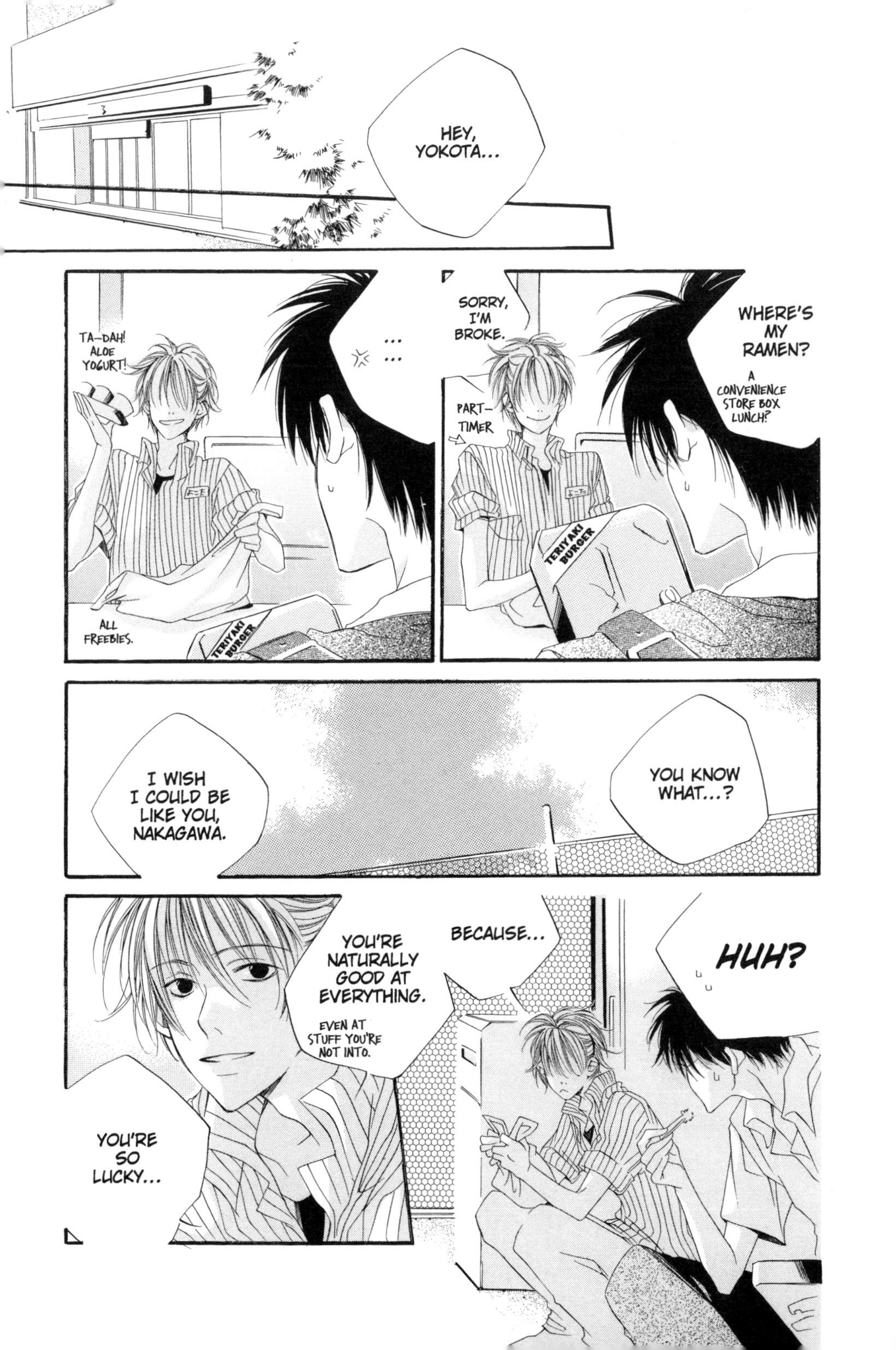
HEY, YOKOTA...
WHERE'S MY RAMEN?
A CONVENIENCE STORE BOX LUNCH?
SORRY, I'M BROKE.
PART-TIMER
TERIYAKI BURGER
...
...
TA-DAH! ALOE YOGURT!
ALL FREEBIES.
TERIYAKI BURGER
YOU KNOW WHAT...?
I WISH I COULD BE LIKE YOU, NAKAGAWA.
HUH?
BECAUSE...
YOU'RE NATURALLY GOOD AT EVERYTHING.
EVEN AT STUFF YOU'RE NOT INTO.
YOU'RE SO LUCKY...

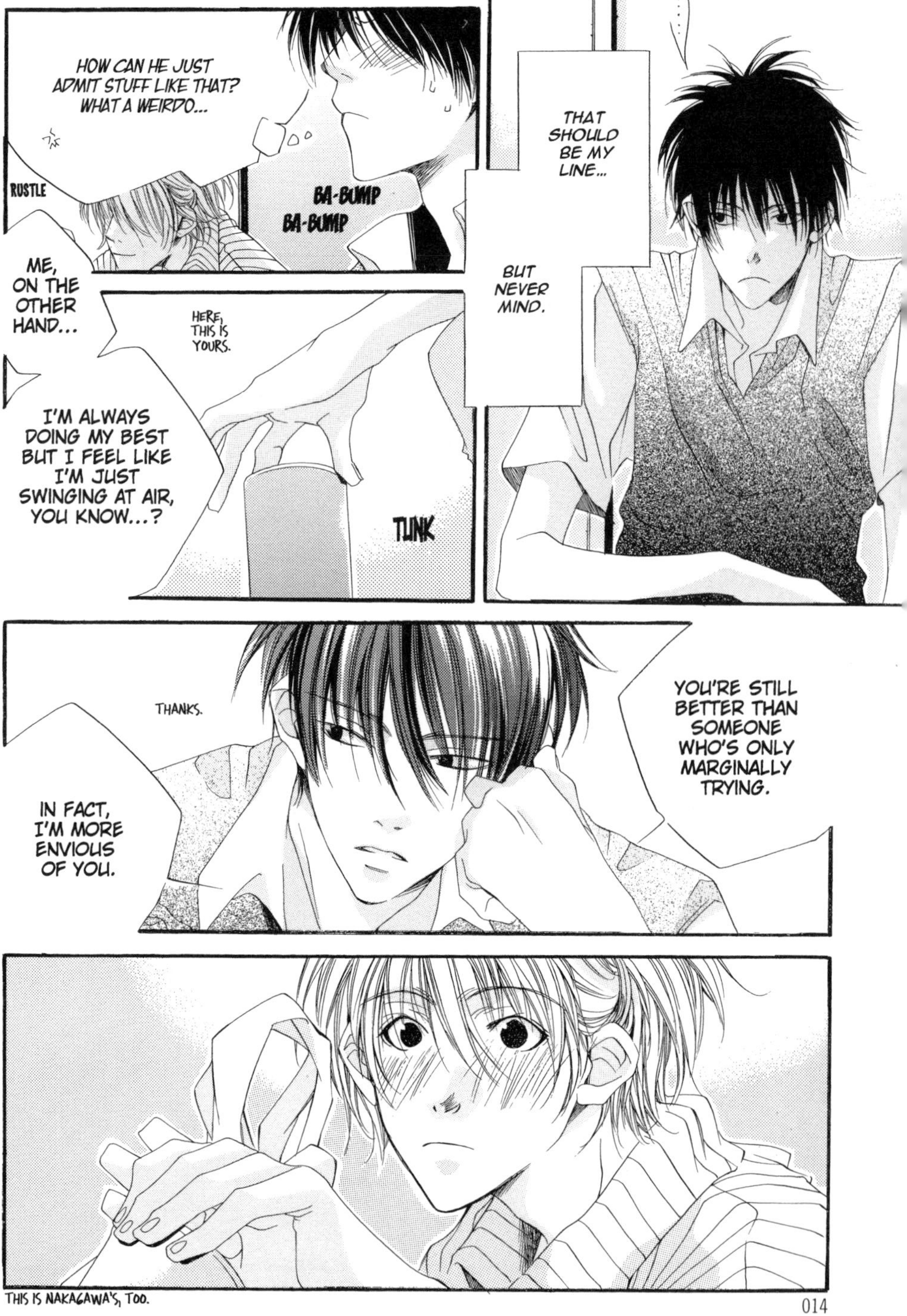
THAT SHOULD BE MY LINE...
BUT NEVER MIND.
HOW CAN HE JUST ADMIT STUFF LIKE THAT? WHAT A WEIRDO...
RUSTLE
BA-BUMP
BA-BUMP
ME, ON THE OTHER HAND...
HERE, THIS IS YOURS.
I'M ALWAYS DOING MY BEST BUT I FEEL LIKE I'M JUST SWINGING AT AIR, YOU KNOW...?
TUNK
YOU'RE STILL BETTER THAN SOMEONE WHO'S ONLY MARGINALLY TRYING.
THANKS.
IN FACT, I'M MORE ENVIOUS OF YOU.

THIS IS NAKAGAWA'S, TOO.

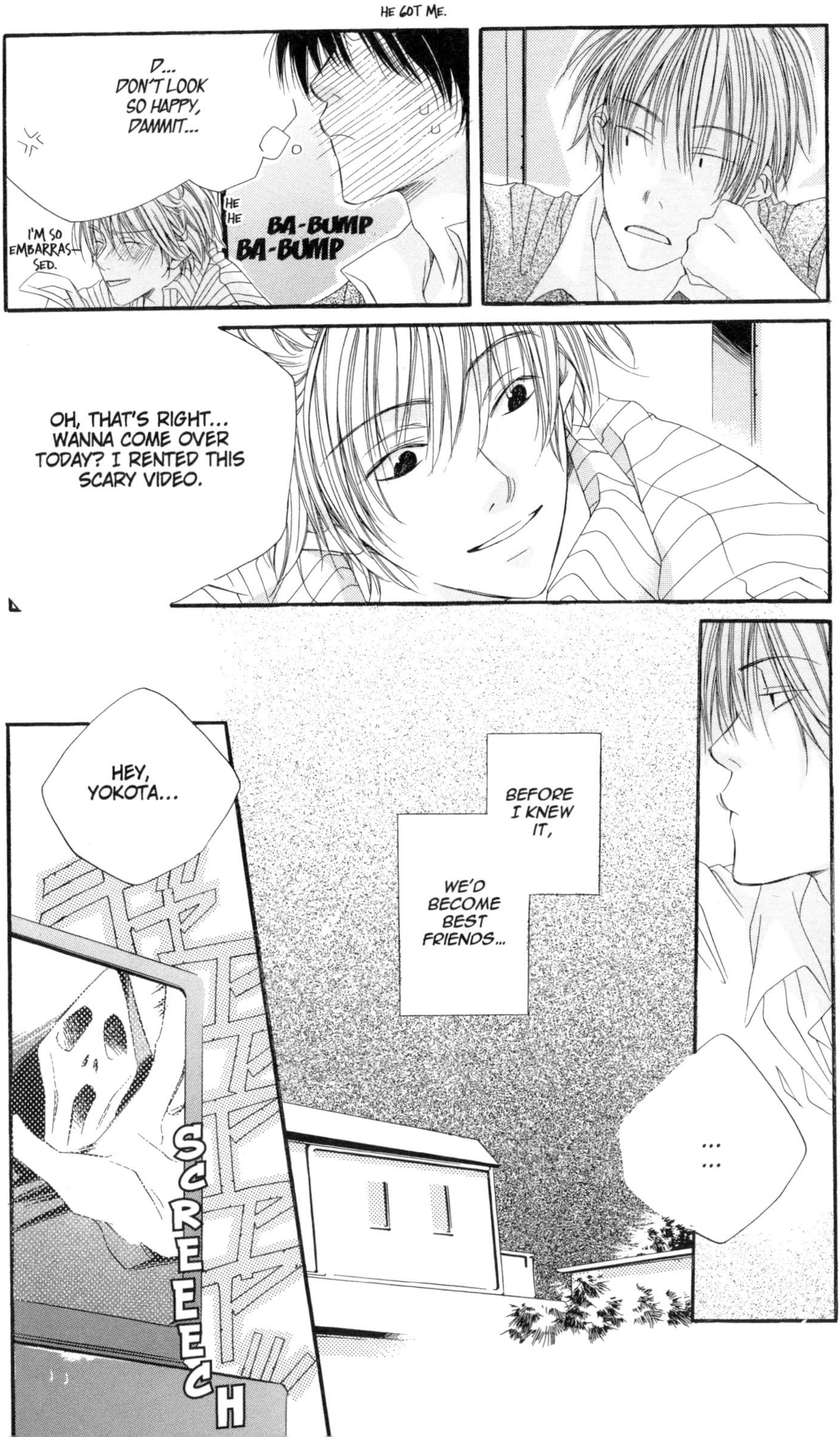
HE GOT ME.
D... DON'T LOOK SO HAPPY, DAMMIT...
HE HE
BA-BUMP BA-BUMP
I'M SO EMBARRAS-SED.
OH, THAT'S RIGHT... WANNA COME OVER TODAY? I RENTED THIS SCARY VIDEO.
... ...
BEFORE I KNEW IT,
WE'D BECOME BEST FRIENDS...
HEY, YOKOTA...
SCREECH

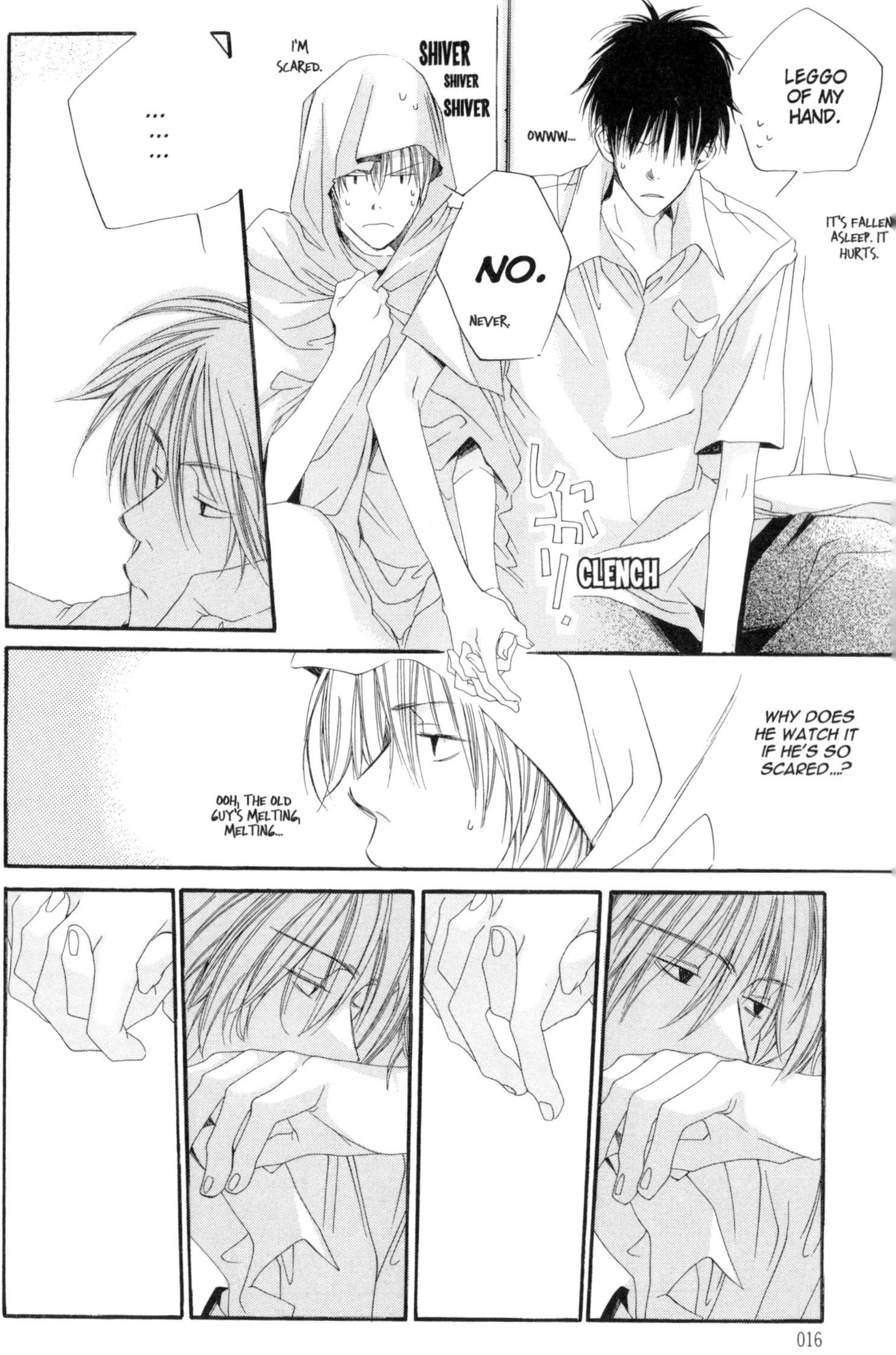
LEGGO OF MY HAND.
OWWW...
IT'S FALLEN ASLEEP. IT HURTS.
NO.
NEVER.
I'M SCARED.
SHIVER
SHIVER
SHIVER
しっかり!
CLENCH
...
...
...
WHY DOES HE WATCH IT IF HE'S SO SCARED...?
OOH, THE OLD GUY'S MELTING, MELTING...

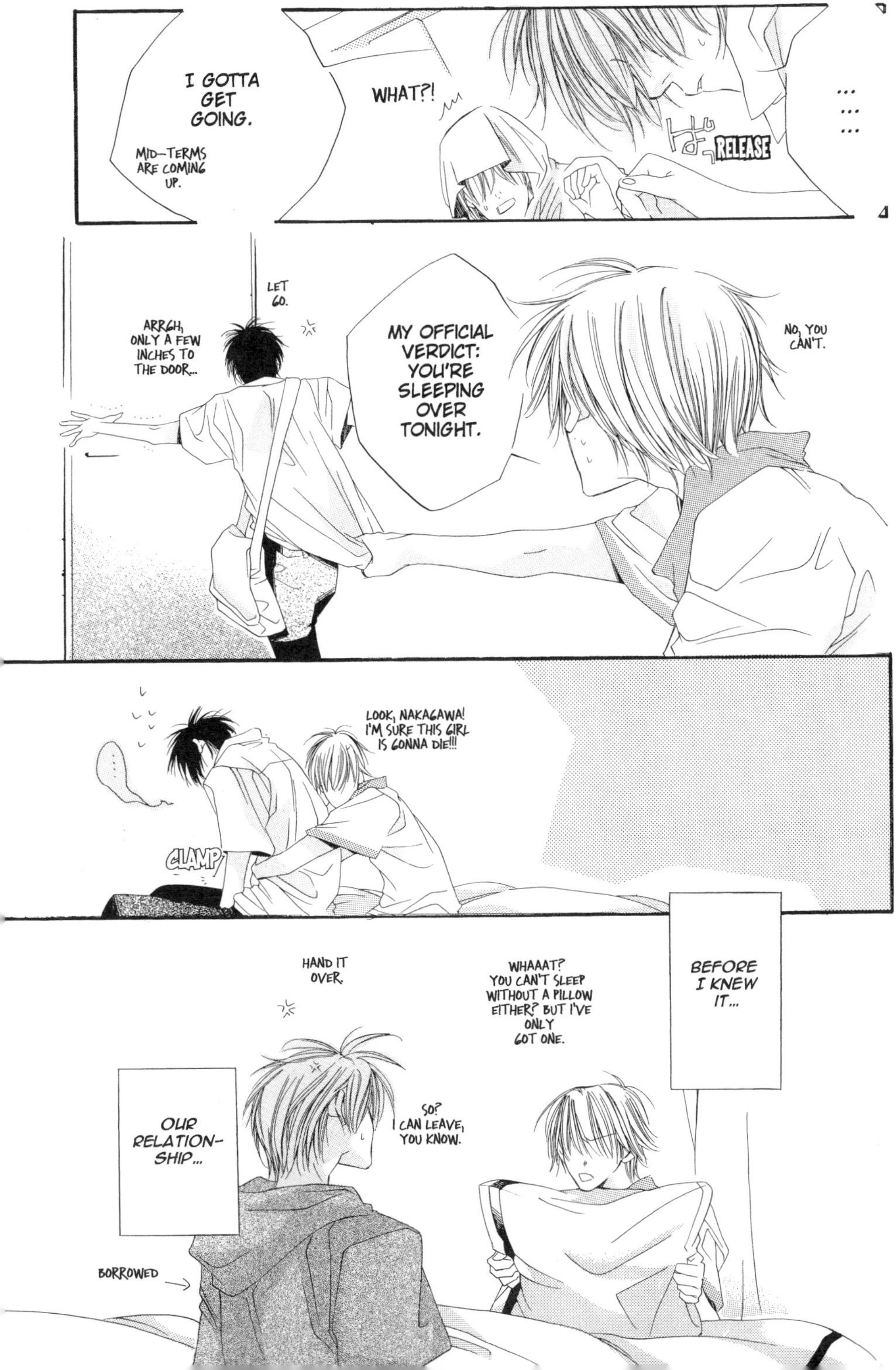
...
...
...
WHAT?!
はっ RELEASE
I GOTTA GET GOING.
MID-TERMS ARE COMING UP.
NO, YOU CAN'T.
MY OFFICIAL VERDICT: YOU'RE SLEEPING OVER TONIGHT.
LET GO.
ARRGH, ONLY A FEW INCHES TO THE DOOR...
LOOK, NAKAGAWA! I'M SURE THIS GIRL IS GONNA DIE!!!
...
CLAMP
BEFORE I KNEW IT...
WHAAAT? YOU CAN'T SLEEP WITHOUT A PILLOW EITHER? BUT I'VE ONLY GOT ONE.
HAND IT OVER.
SO? I CAN LEAVE, YOU KNOW.
OUR RELATION-SHIP...
BORROWED

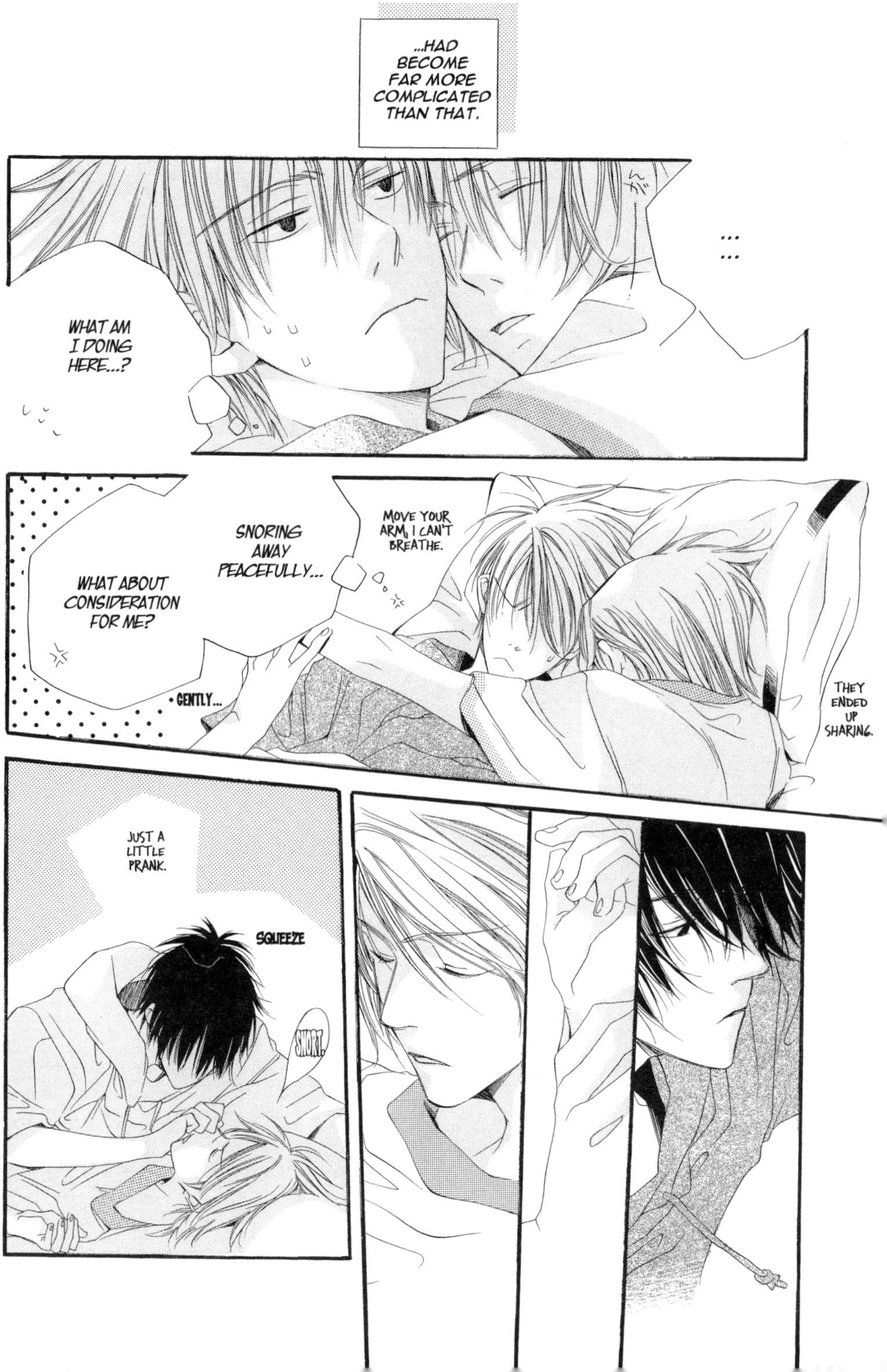
...HAD BECOME FAR MORE COMPLICATED THAN THAT.
...
...
WHAT AM I DOING HERE...?
THEY ENDED UP SHARING.
MOVE YOUR ARM, I CAN'T BREATHE.
SNORING AWAY PEACEFULLY...
WHAT ABOUT CONSIDERATION FOR ME?
GENTLY...
JUST A LITTLE PRANK.
SQUEEZE
SNORT.

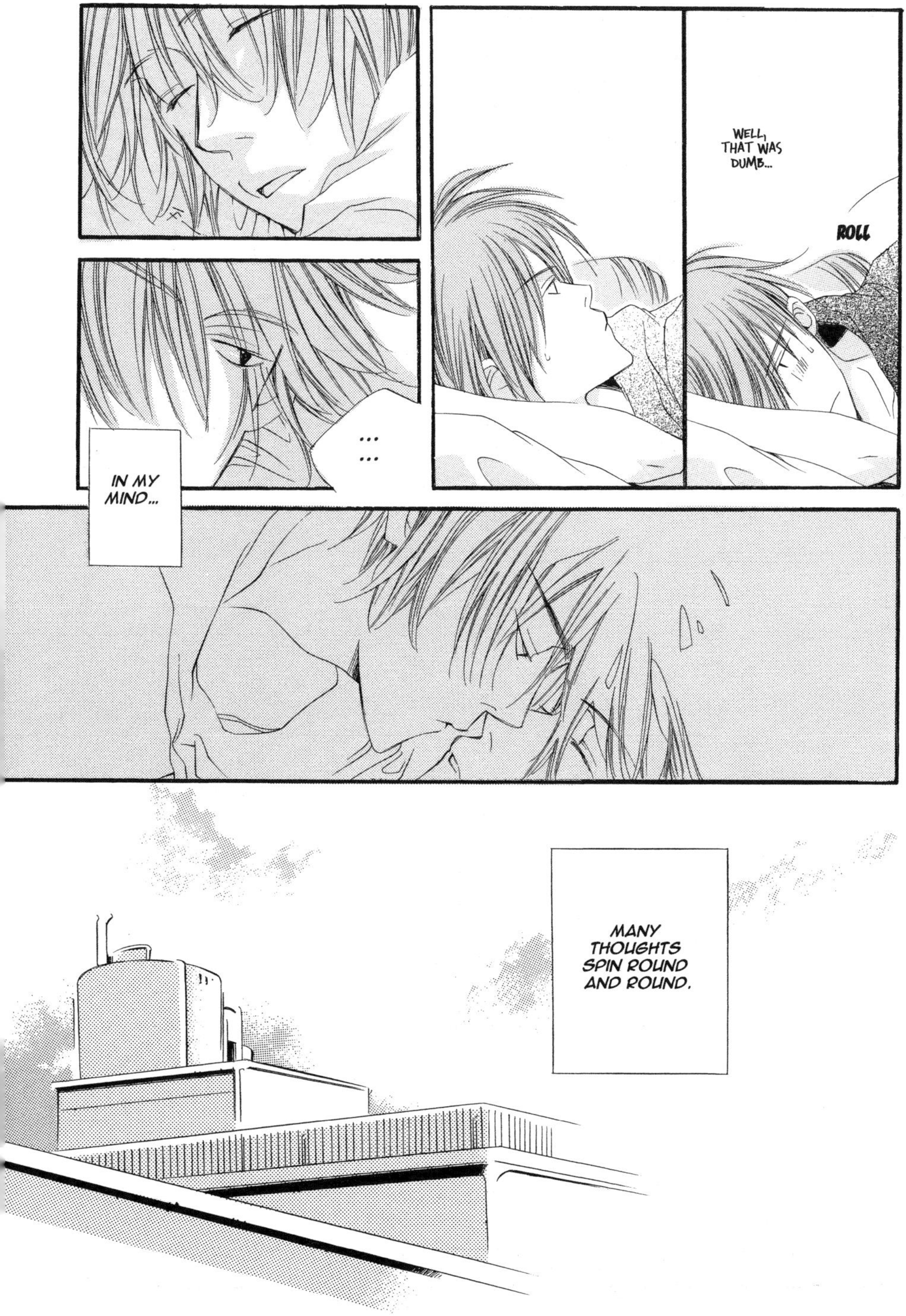
WELL, THAT WAS DUMB...
ROLL
...
...
IN MY MIND...
MANY THOUGHTS SPIN ROUND AND ROUND.

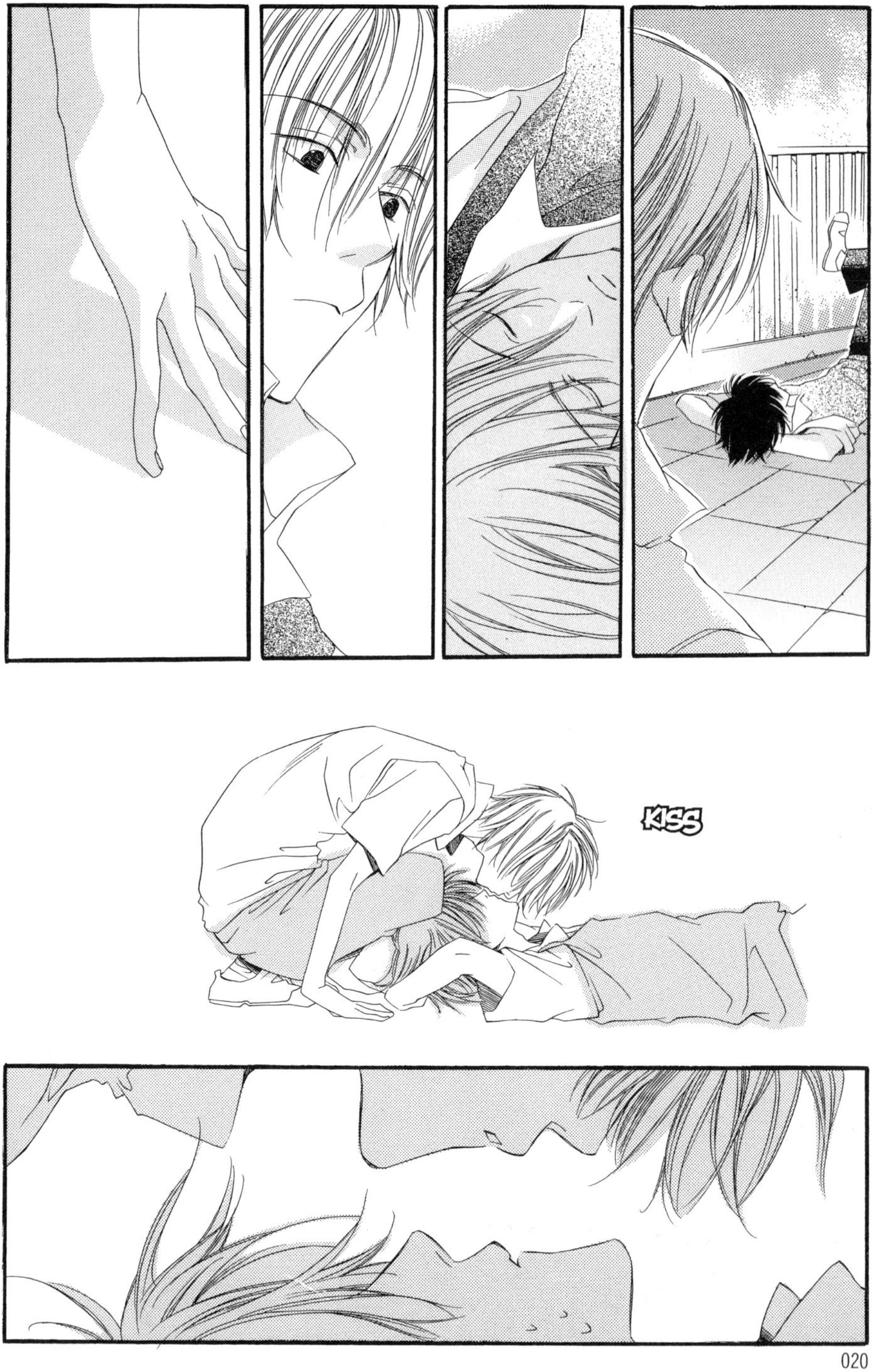
KISS

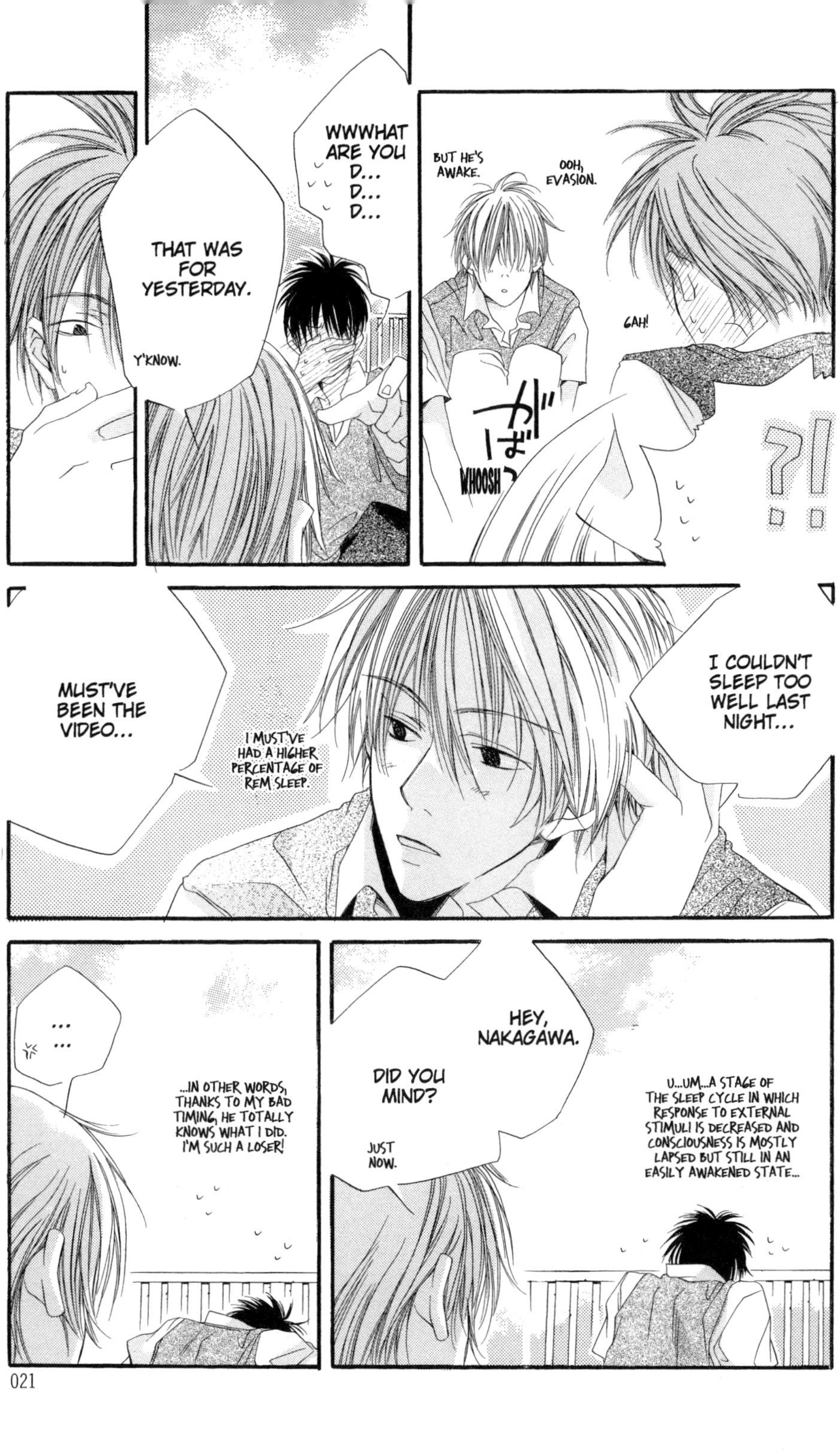
?!
GAH!
OOH, EVASION.
BUT HE'S AWAKE.
がばっ
WHOOSH
WWWHAT ARE YOU D... D... D...
THAT WAS FOR YESTERDAY.
Y'KNOW.
I COULDN'T SLEEP TOO WELL LAST NIGHT...
I MUST'VE HAD A HIGHER PERCENTAGE OF REM SLEEP.
MUST'VE BEEN THE VIDEO...
HEY, NAKAGAWA.
DID YOU MIND?
JUST NOW.
U...UM...A STAGE OF THE SLEEP CYCLE IN WHICH RESPONSE TO EXTERNAL STIMULI IS DECREASED AND CONSCIOUSNESS IS MOSTLY LAPSED BUT STILL IN AN EASILY AWAKENED STATE...
... ...
...IN OTHER WORDS, THANKS TO MY BAD TIMING, HE TOTALLY KNOWS WHAT I DID. I'M SUCH A LOSER!

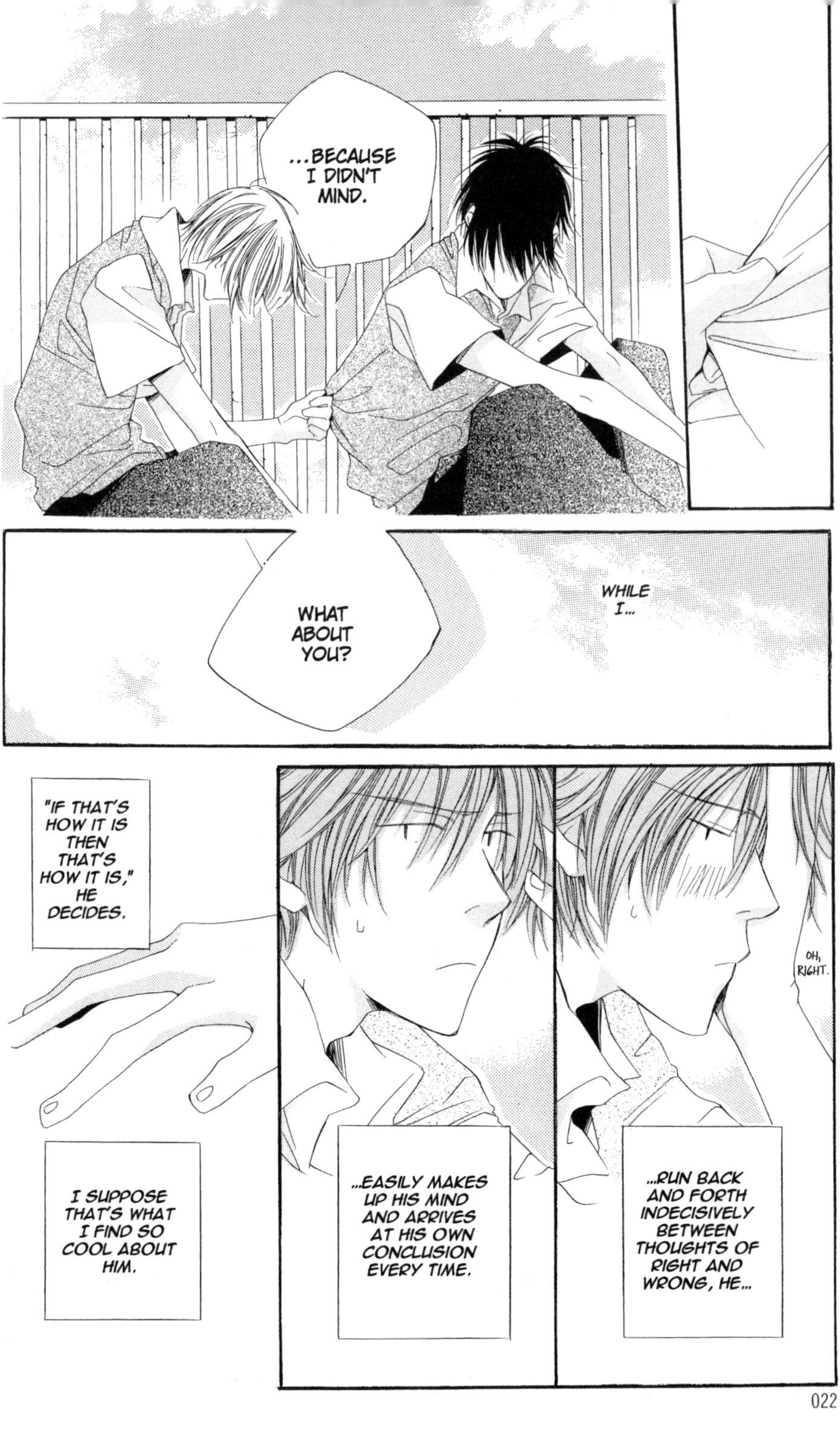
...BECAUSE I DIDN'T MIND.
WHILE I...
WHAT ABOUT YOU?
OH, RIGHT.
...RUN BACK AND FORTH INDECISIVELY BETWEEN THOUGHTS OF RIGHT AND WRONG, HE...
...EASILY MAKES UP HIS MIND AND ARRIVES AT HIS OWN CONCLUSION EVERY TIME.
"IF THAT'S HOW IT IS THEN THAT'S HOW IT IS," HE DECIDES.
I SUPPOSE THAT'S WHAT I FIND SO COOL ABOUT HIM.

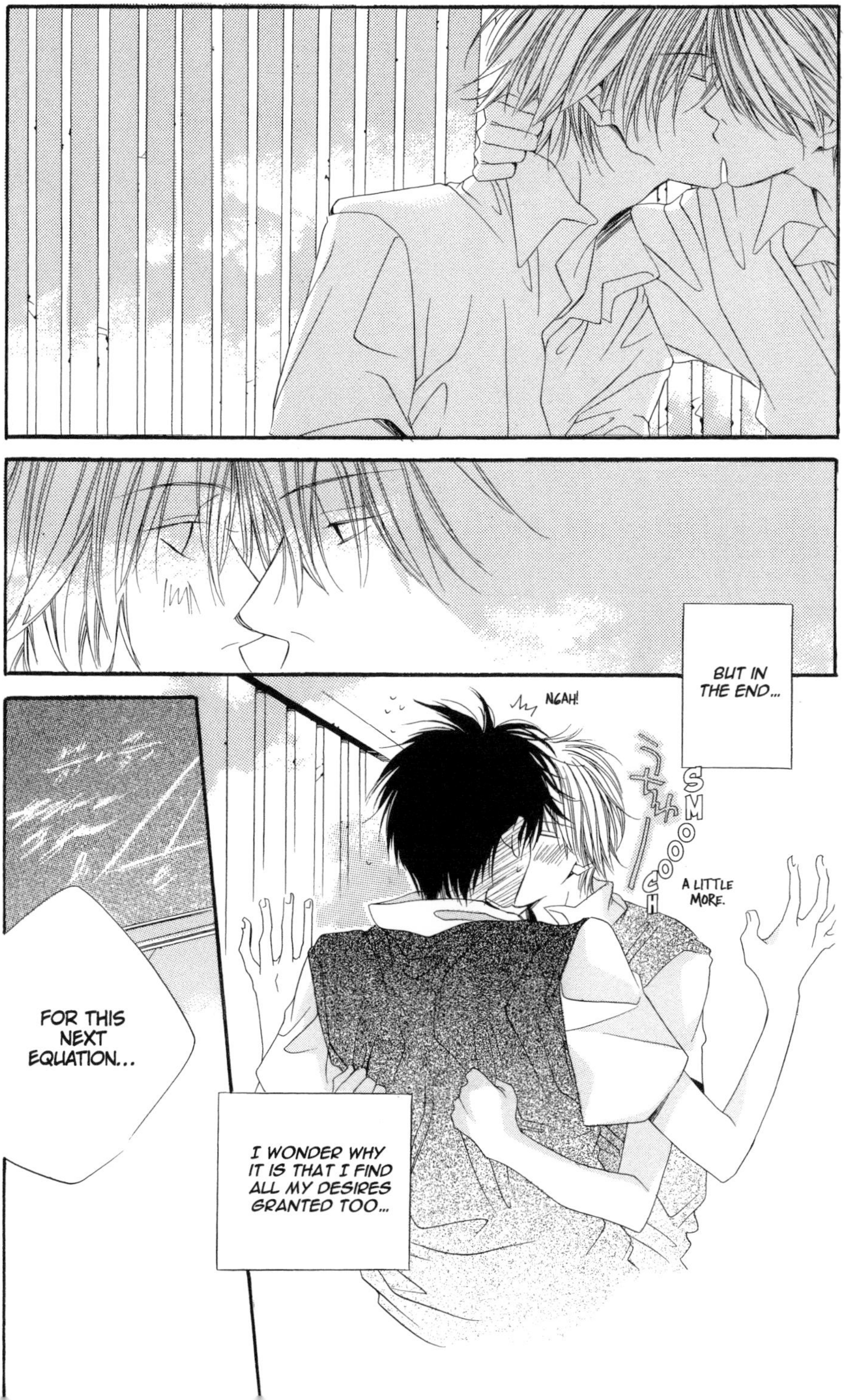

BUT IN THE END...
NGAH!
SMOOOCH
A LITTLE MORE.
I WONDER WHY IT IS THAT I FIND ALL MY DESIRES GRANTED TOO...
FOR THIS NEXT EQUATION...

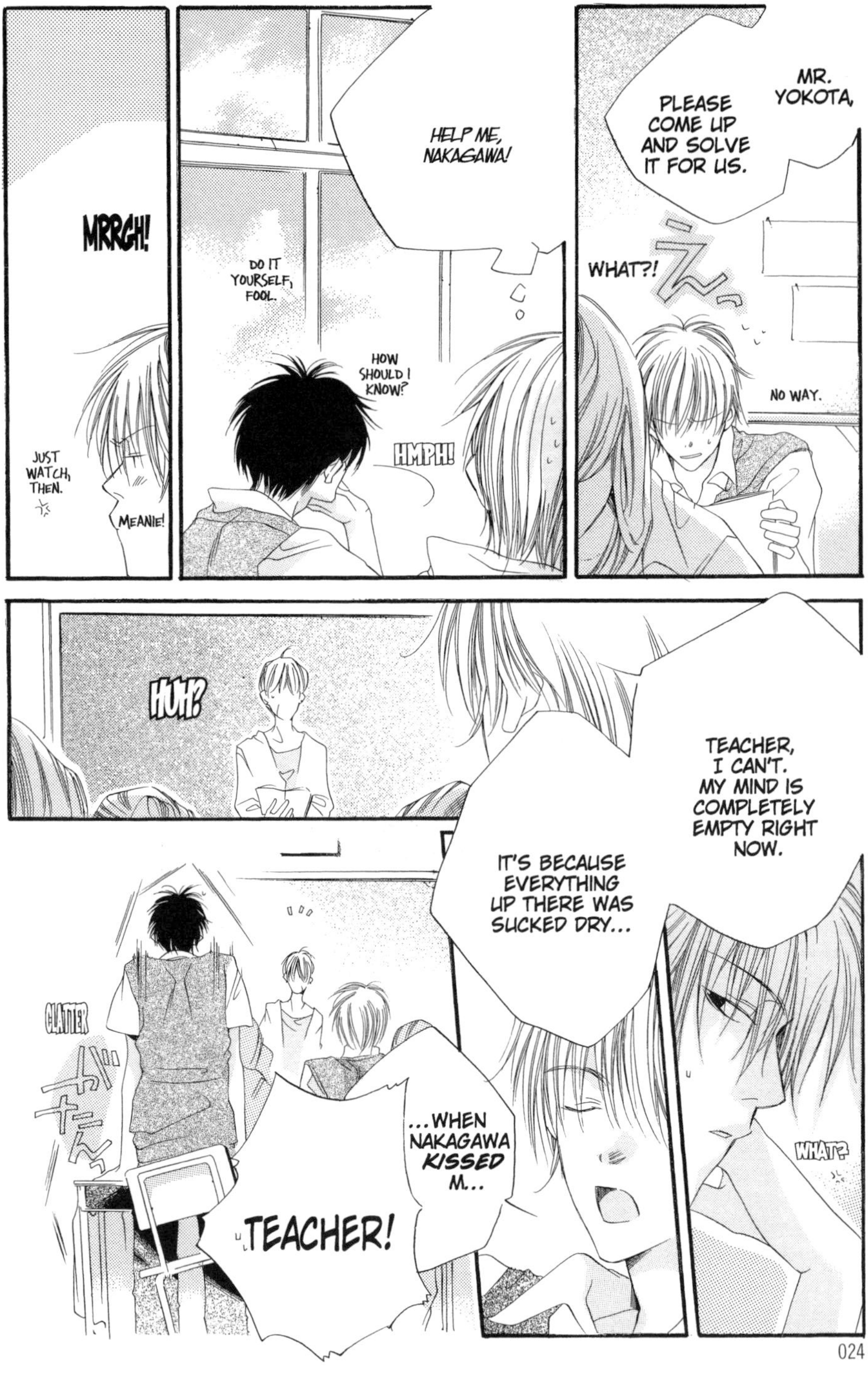
MR. YOKOTA,
PLEASE COME UP AND SOLVE IT FOR US.
WHAT?!
NO WAY.
HELP ME, NAKAGAWA!
HOW SHOULD I KNOW?
HMPH!
DO IT YOURSELF, FOOL.
MRRGH!
JUST WATCH, THEN.
MEANIE!
HUH?
TEACHER, I CAN'T. MY MIND IS COMPLETELY EMPTY RIGHT NOW.
IT'S BECAUSE EVERYTHING UP THERE WAS SUCKED DRY...
WHAT?
...WHEN NAKAGAWA KISSED M...
TEACHER!
CLATTER

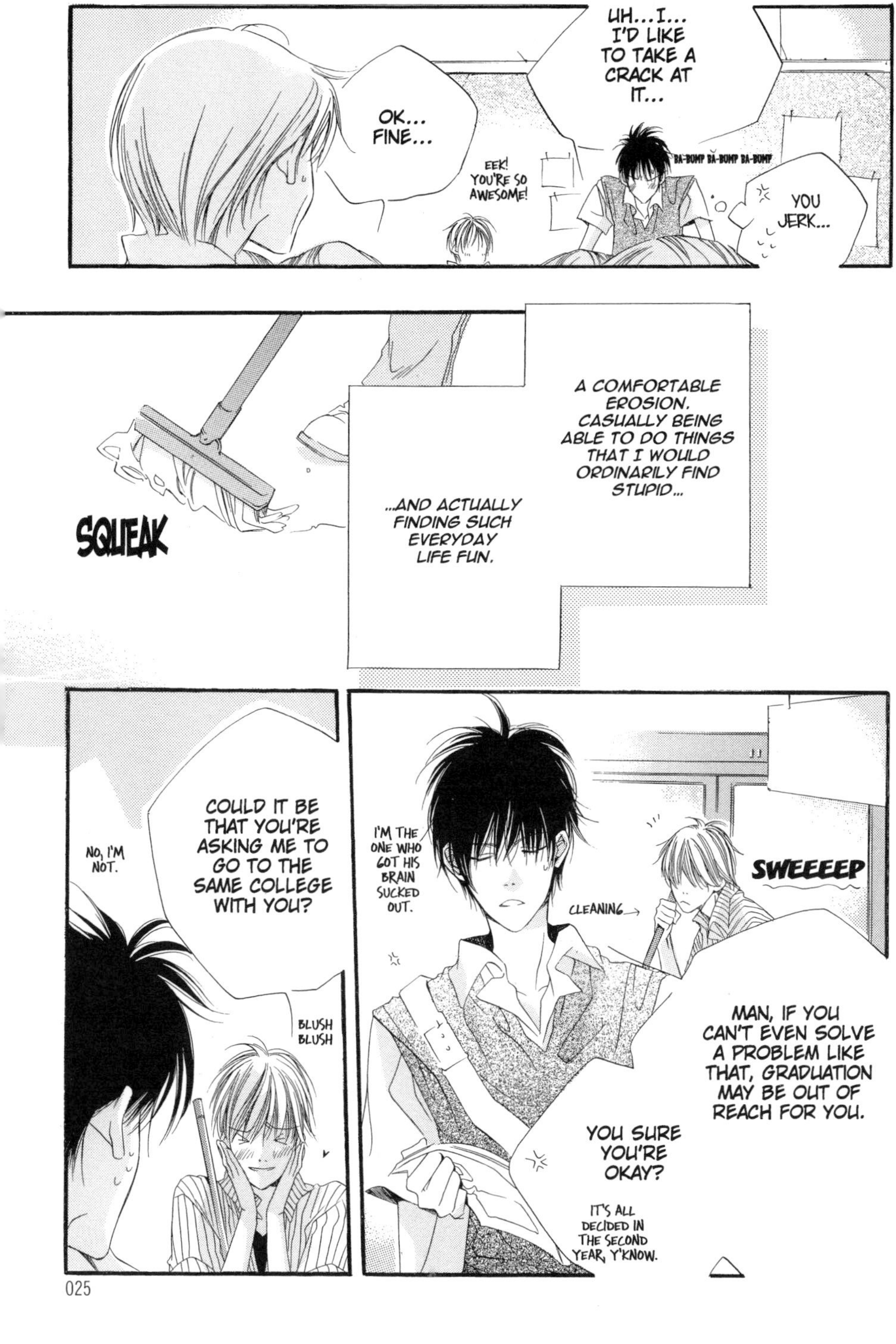
UH...I... I'D LIKE TO TAKE A CRACK AT IT...
BA-BUMP BA-BUMP BA-BUMP
YOU JERK...
OK... FINE...
EEK! YOU'RE SO AWESOME!
A COMFORTABLE EROSION. CASUALLY BEING ABLE TO DO THINGS THAT I WOULD ORDINARILY FIND STUPID...
...AND ACTUALLY FINDING SUCH EVERYDAY LIFE FUN.
SQUEAK
SWEEEEP
MAN, IF YOU CAN'T EVEN SOLVE A PROBLEM LIKE THAT, GRADUATION MAY BE OUT OF REACH FOR YOU.
CLEANING
I'M THE ONE WHO GOT HIS BRAIN SUCKED OUT.
YOU SURE YOU'RE OKAY?
IT'S ALL DECIDED IN THE SECOND YEAR, Y'KNOW.
COULD IT BE THAT YOU'RE ASKING ME TO GO TO THE SAME COLLEGE WITH YOU?
NO, I'M NOT.
BLUSH BLUSH

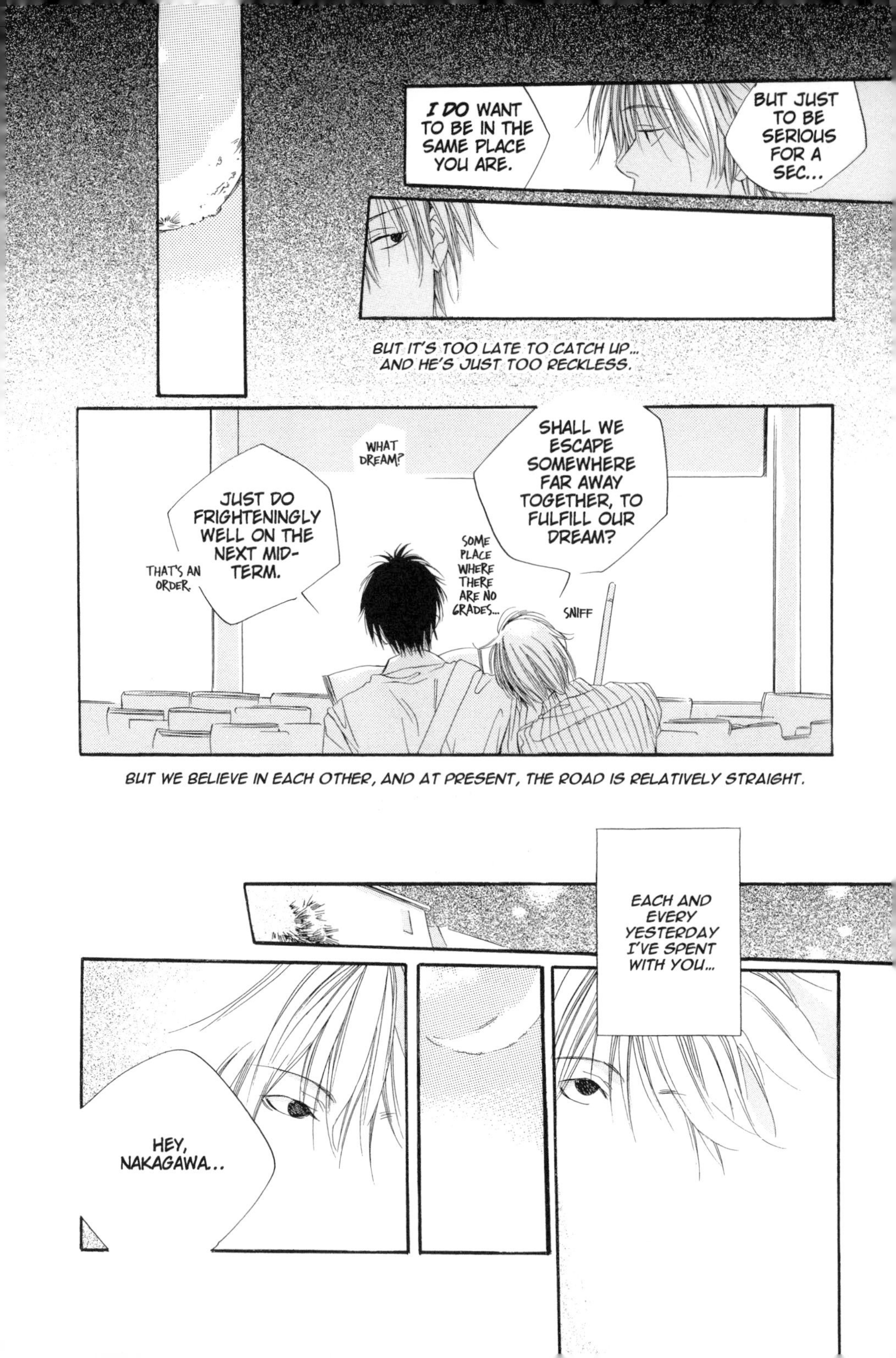
BUT JUST TO BE SERIOUS FOR A SEC...
I DO WANT TO BE IN THE SAME PLACE YOU ARE.
BUT IT'S TOO LATE TO CATCH UP... AND HE'S JUST TOO RECKLESS.
SHALL WE ESCAPE SOMEWHERE FAR AWAY TOGETHER, TO FULFILL OUR DREAM?
SNIFF
SOME PLACE WHERE THERE ARE NO GRADES...
WHAT DREAM?
JUST DO FRIGHTENINGLY WELL ON THE NEXT MID-TERM.
THAT'S AN ORDER.
BUT WE BELIEVE IN EACH OTHER, AND AT PRESENT, THE ROAD IS RELATIVELY STRAIGHT.
EACH AND EVERY YESTERDAY I'VE SPENT WITH YOU...
HEY, NAKAGAWA...

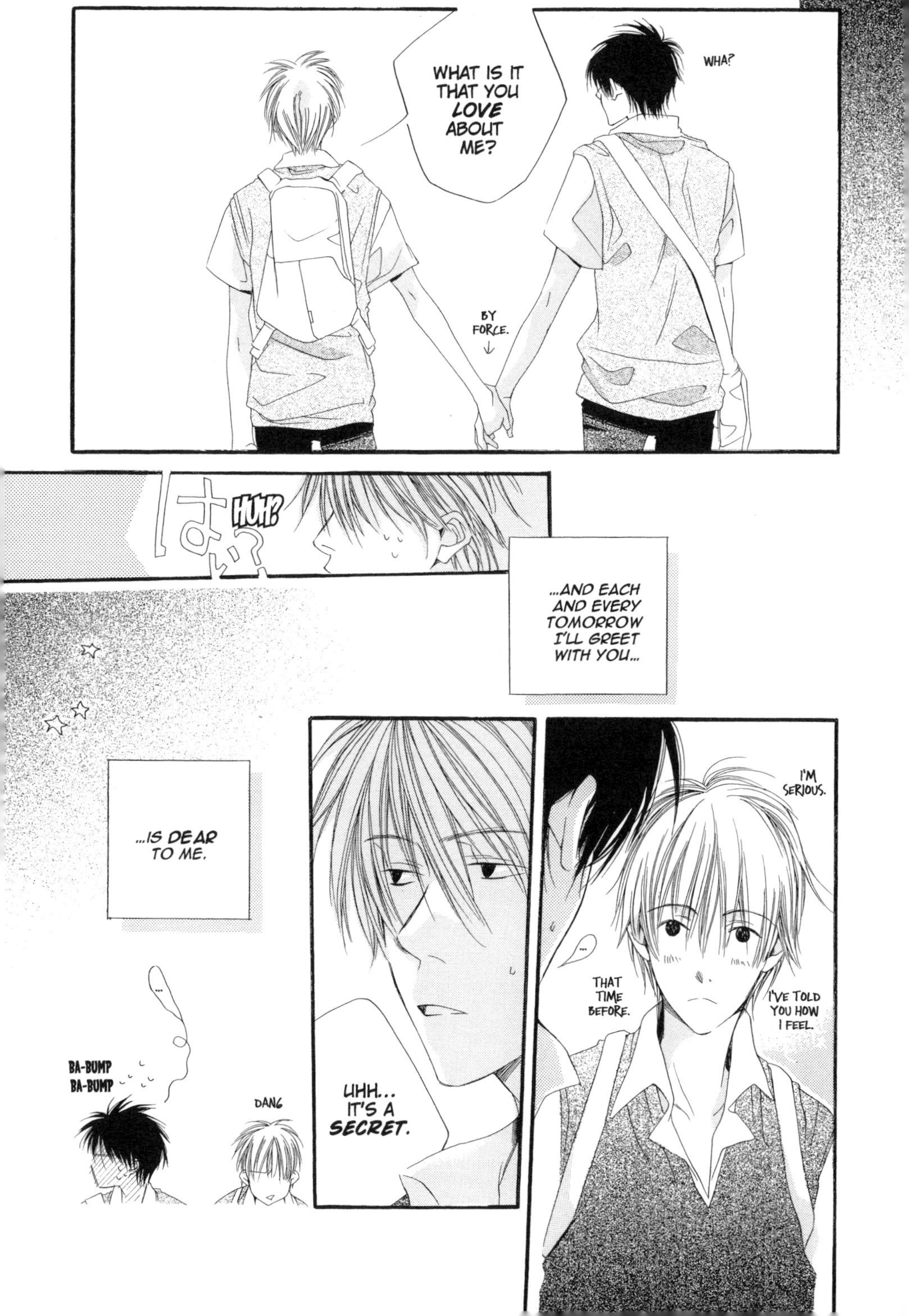
WHA?
WHAT IS IT THAT YOU LOVE ABOUT ME?
BY FORCE.
はぁ？
HUH?
...AND EACH AND EVERY TOMORROW I'LL GREET WITH YOU...
I'M SERIOUS.
I'VE TOLD YOU HOW I FEEL.
THAT TIME BEFORE.
...
UHH... IT'S A SECRET.
...IS DEAR TO ME.
...
BA-BUMP BA-BUMP
DANG

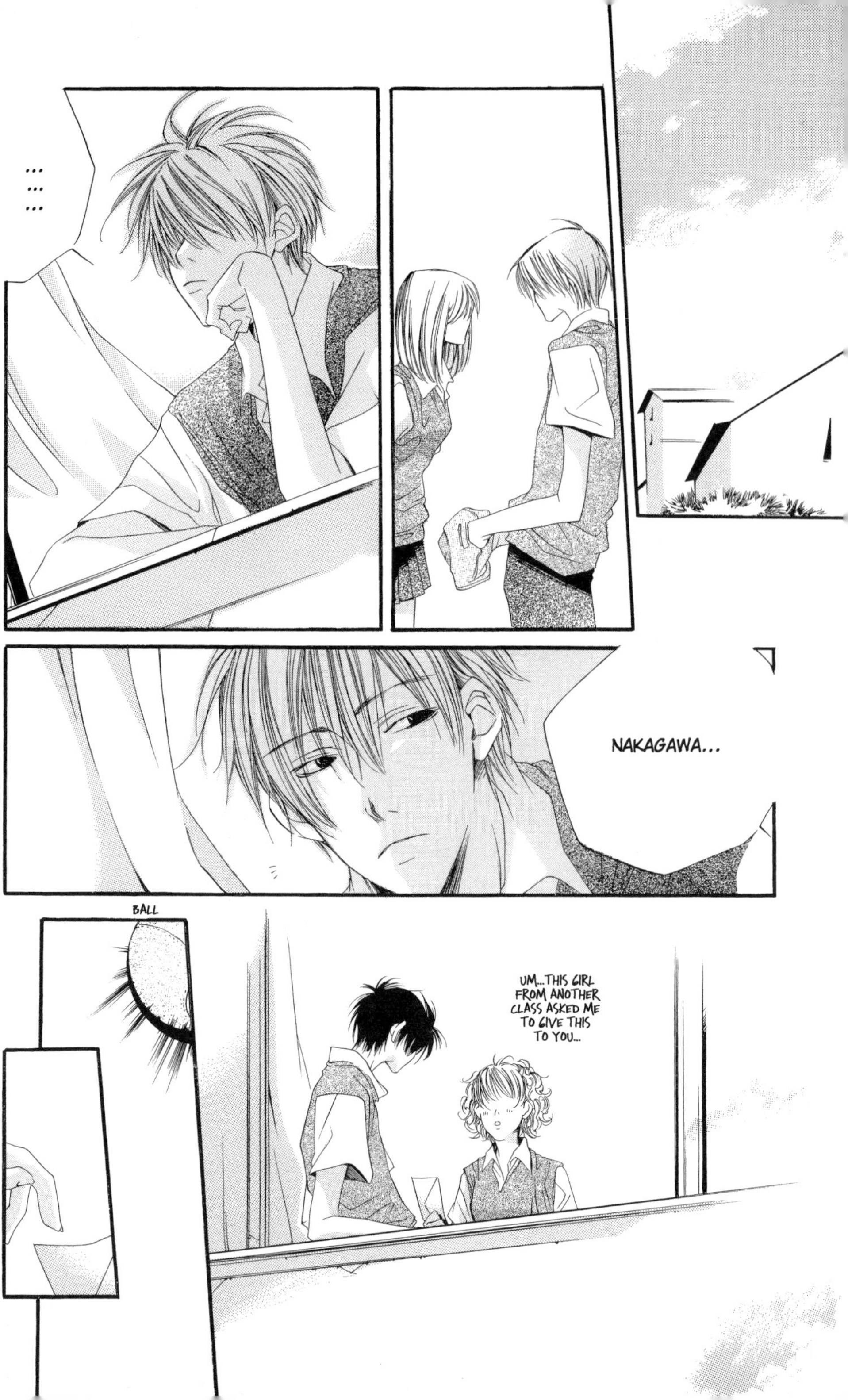
...
...
...
NAKAGAWA...
UM...THIS GIRL FROM ANOTHER CLASS ASKED ME TO GIVE THIS TO YOU...
BALL

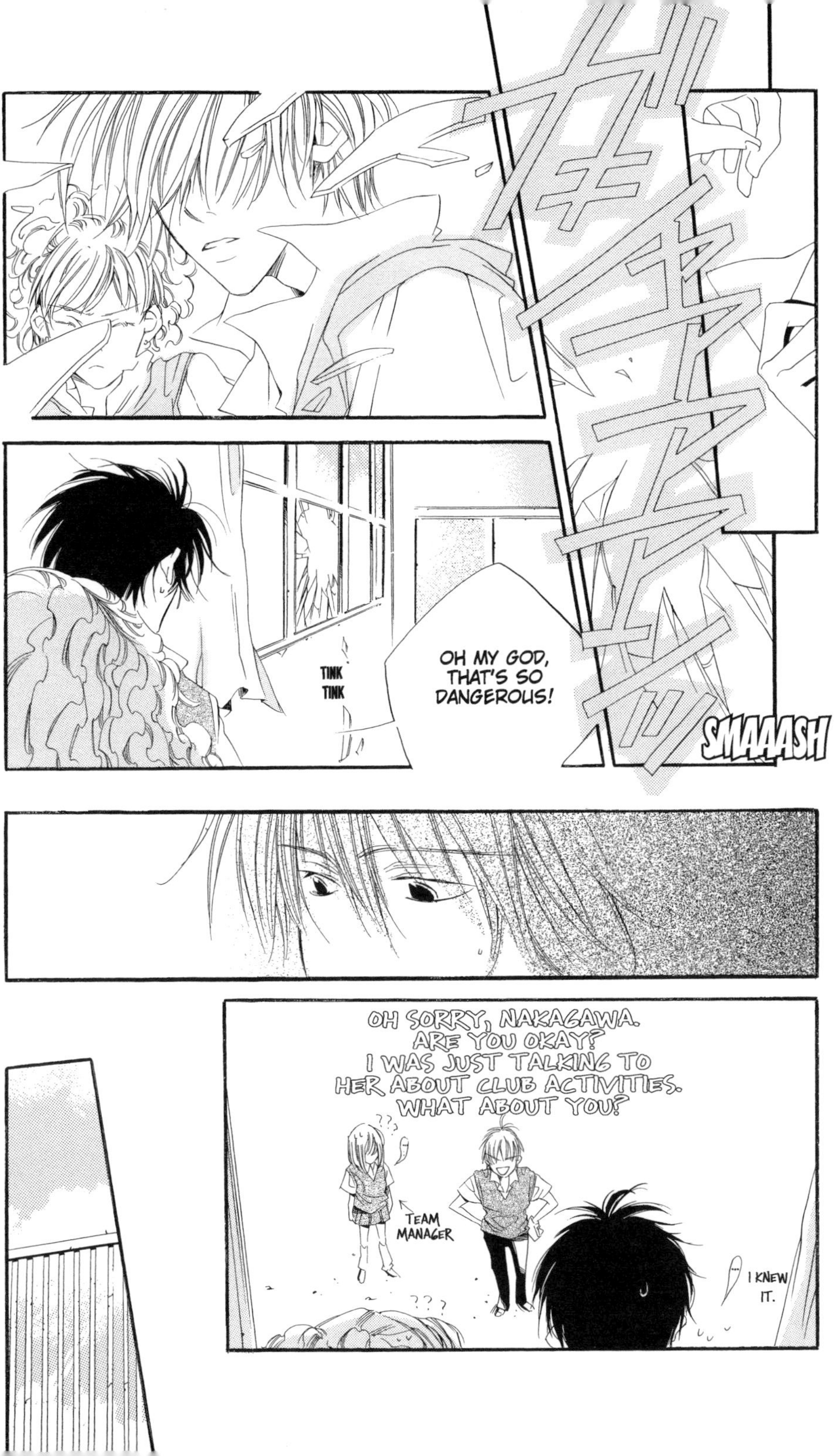
SMAAASH
OH MY GOD, THAT'S SO DANGEROUS!
TINK TINK
OH SORRY, NAKAGAWA. ARE YOU OKAY? I WAS JUST TALKING TO HER ABOUT CLUB ACTIVITIES. WHAT ABOUT YOU?
I KNEW IT.
TEAM MANAGER

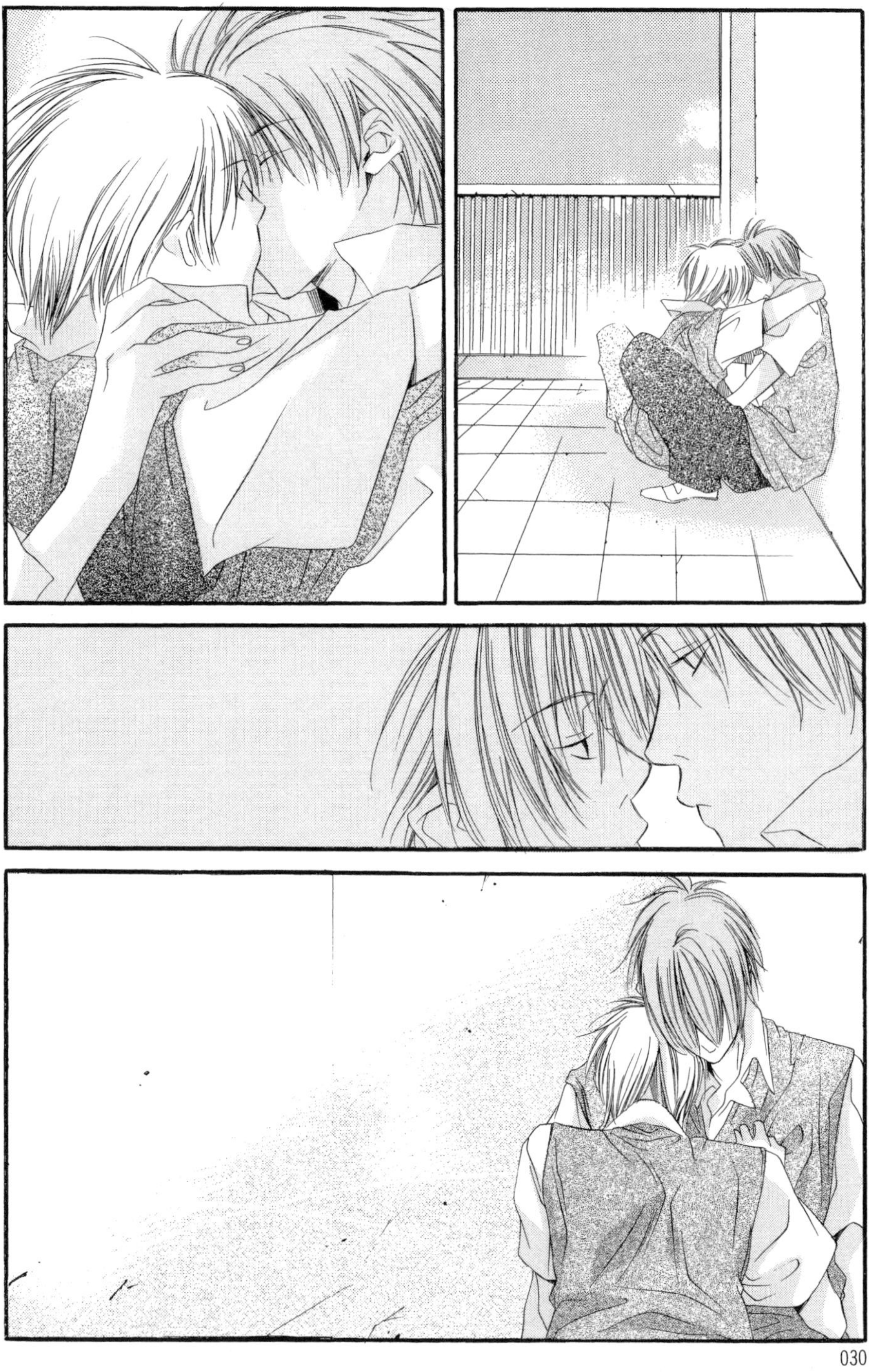

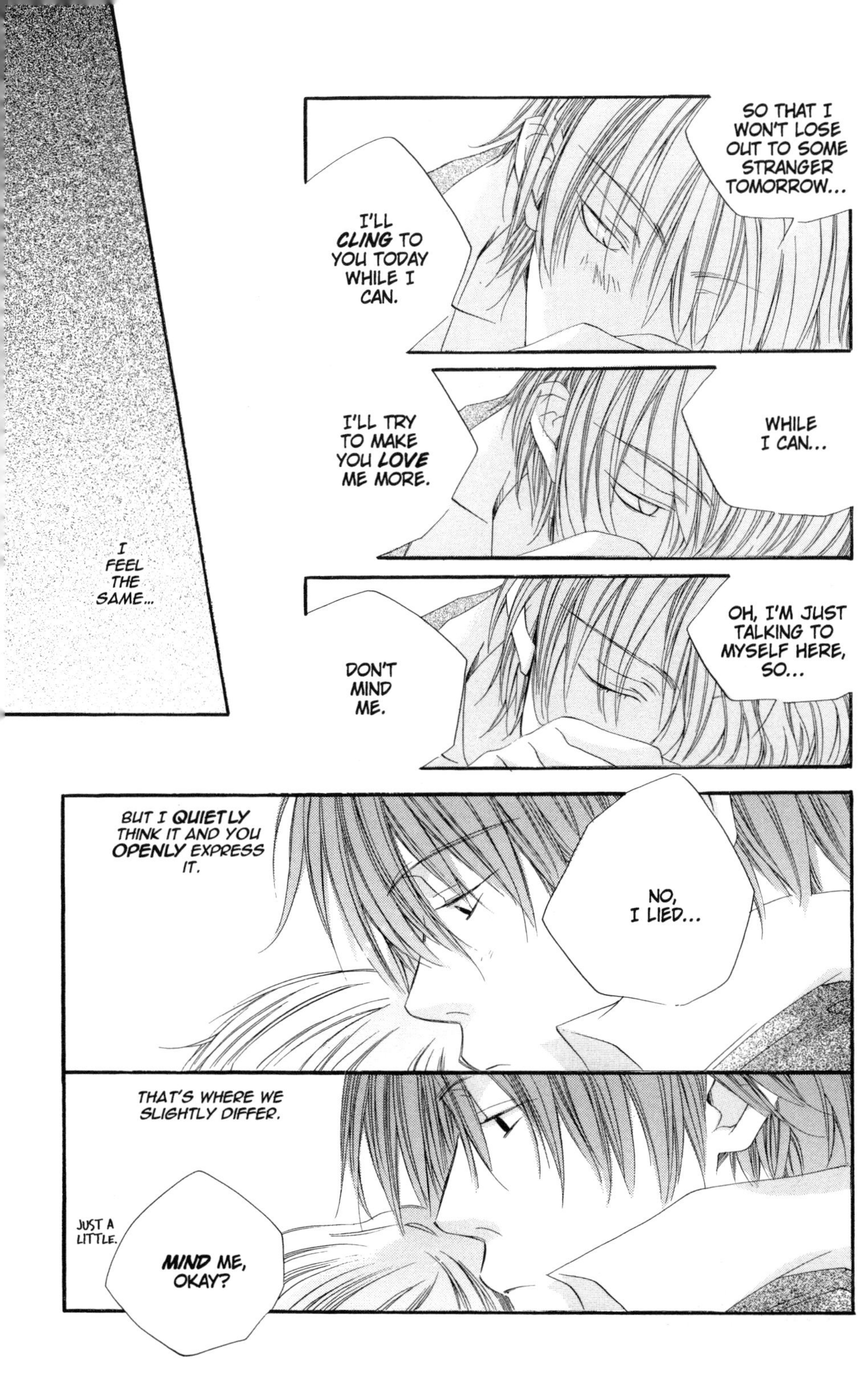
SO THAT I WON'T LOSE OUT TO SOME STRANGER TOMORROW...
I'LL CLING TO YOU TODAY WHILE I CAN.
WHILE I CAN...
I'LL TRY TO MAKE YOU LOVE ME MORE.
OH, I'M JUST TALKING TO MYSELF HERE, SO...
DON'T MIND ME.
I FEEL THE SAME...
NO, I LIED...
BUT I QUIETLY THINK IT AND YOU OPENLY EXPRESS IT.
THAT'S WHERE WE SLIGHTLY DIFFER.
MIND ME, OKAY?
JUST A LITTLE.

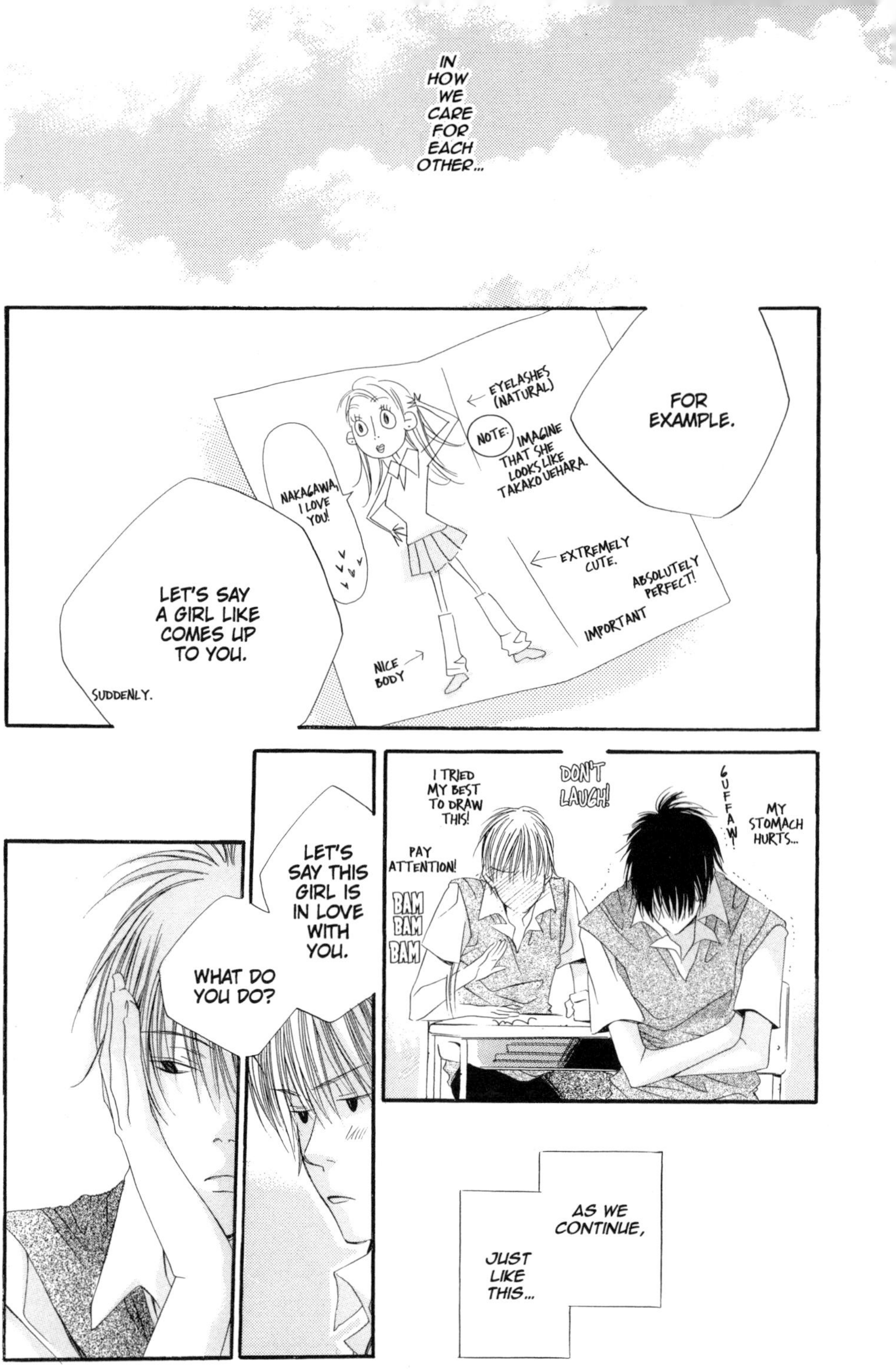
IN HOW WE CARE FOR EACH OTHER...
FOR EXAMPLE.
EYELASHES (NATURAL)
NOTE: IMAGINE THAT SHE LOOKS LIKE TAKAKO UEHARA.
NAKAGAWA, I LOVE YOU!
EXTREMELY CUTE.
ABSOLUTELY PERFECT!
IMPORTANT
NICE BODY
LET'S SAY A GIRL LIKE COMES UP TO YOU.
SUDDENLY.
MY STOMACH HURTS...
GUFFAW!
DON'T LAUGH!
I TRIED MY BEST TO DRAW THIS!
PAY ATTENTION!
BAM BAM BAM
AS WE CONTINUE,
JUST LIKE THIS...
LET'S SAY THIS GIRL IS IN LOVE WITH YOU.
WHAT DO YOU DO?

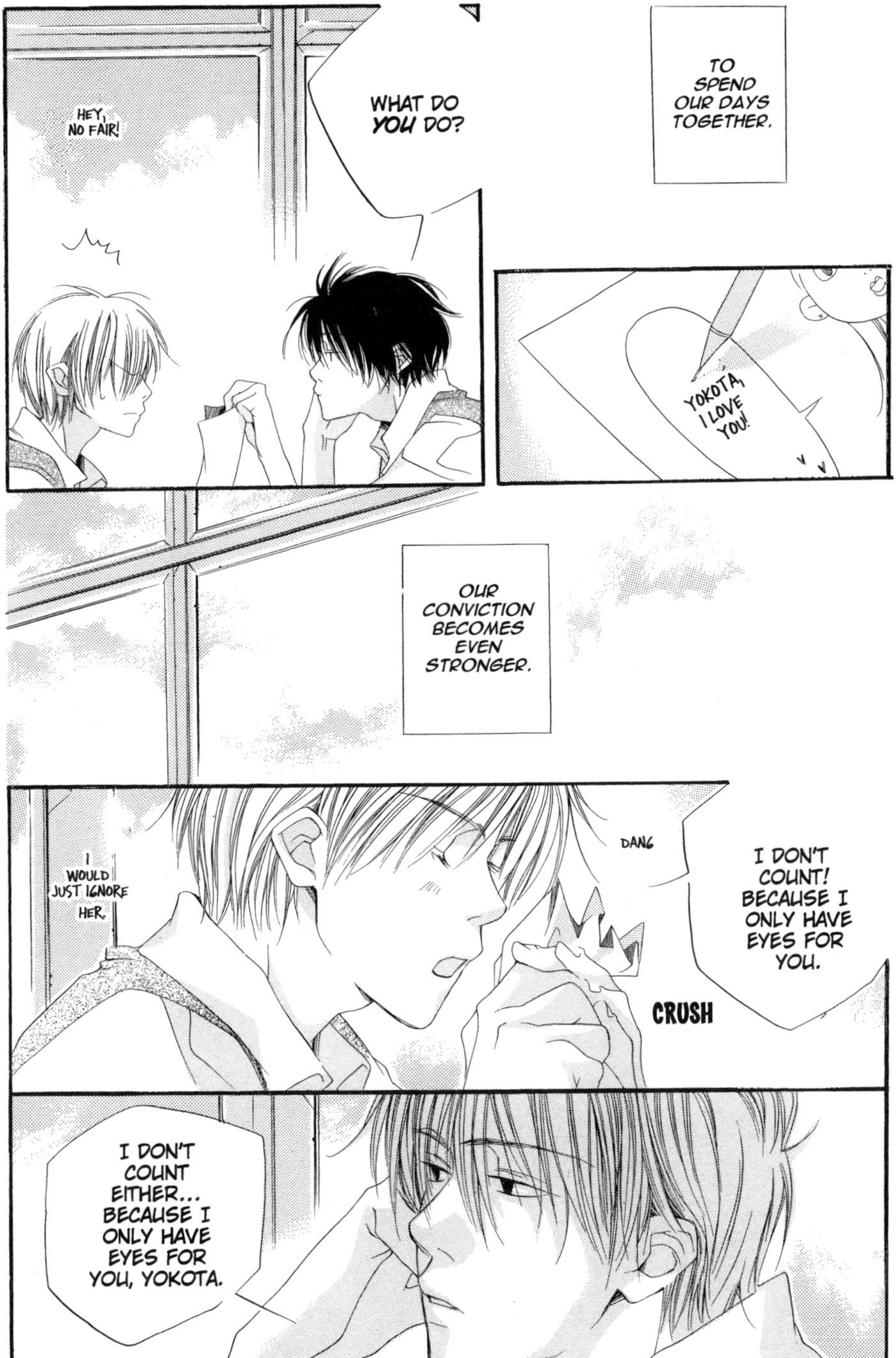
TO SPEND OUR DAYS TOGETHER.
YOKOTA, I LOVE YOU!
WHAT DO *YOU* DO?
HEY, NO FAIR!
OUR CONVICTION BECOMES EVEN STRONGER.
I DON'T COUNT! BECAUSE I ONLY HAVE EYES FOR YOU.
DANG
CRUSH
I WOULD JUST IGNORE HER.
I DON'T COUNT EITHER... BECAUSE I ONLY HAVE EYES FOR YOU, YOKOTA.

HUH?! WHY?! WHY ARE YOU RUNNING AWAY?
YOU MADE ME HAPPY, REALLY HAPPY!!!
HEY
EMBAR-RASSED
CAUGHT
YOU'RE REALLY A SHY PERSON, AREN'T YOU? SO CUTE.
OHHH MAN! MORE AND MORE OF ME IS EXPOSED...WHAT DID I SAY THAT FOR... I'M SUCH AN IDIOT.
WISHES HE'D NEVER SAID ANYTHING.

THE CELLULAR STRUCTURE OF THE LOVE IN OUR HEARTS MUST BE ONE AND THE SAME.

SAME-CELL ORGANISM / END

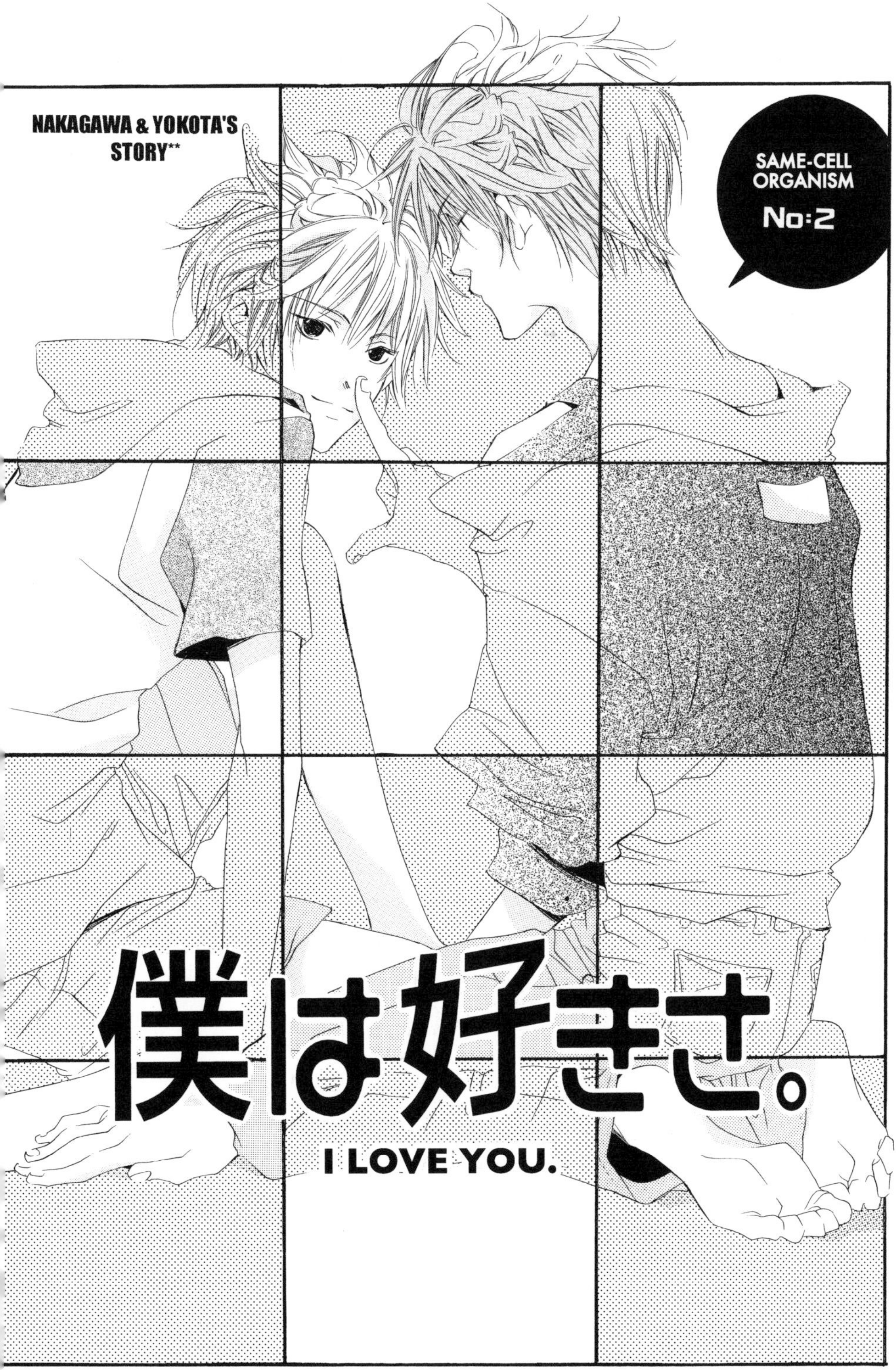
SAME-CELL ORGANISM
No:2
NAKAGAWA & YOKOTA'S STORY**
僕は好きさ。
I LOVE YOU.

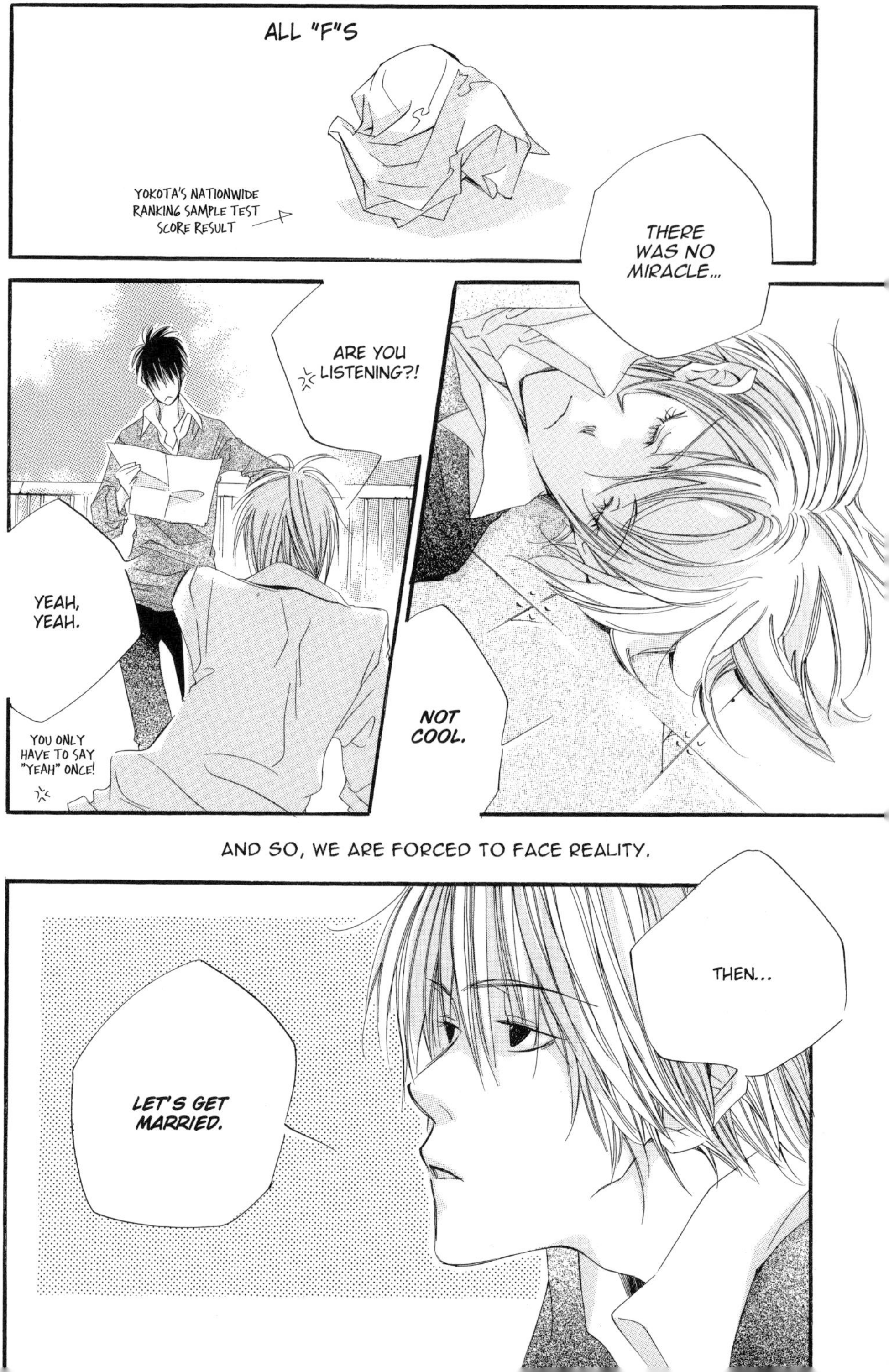
ALL "F"S
YOKOTA'S NATIONWIDE RANKING SAMPLE TEST SCORE RESULT
THERE WAS NO MIRACLE...
NOT COOL.
ARE YOU LISTENING?!
YEAH, YEAH.
YOU ONLY HAVE TO SAY "YEAH" ONCE!
AND SO, WE ARE FORCED TO FACE REALITY.
THEN...
LET'S GET MARRIED.

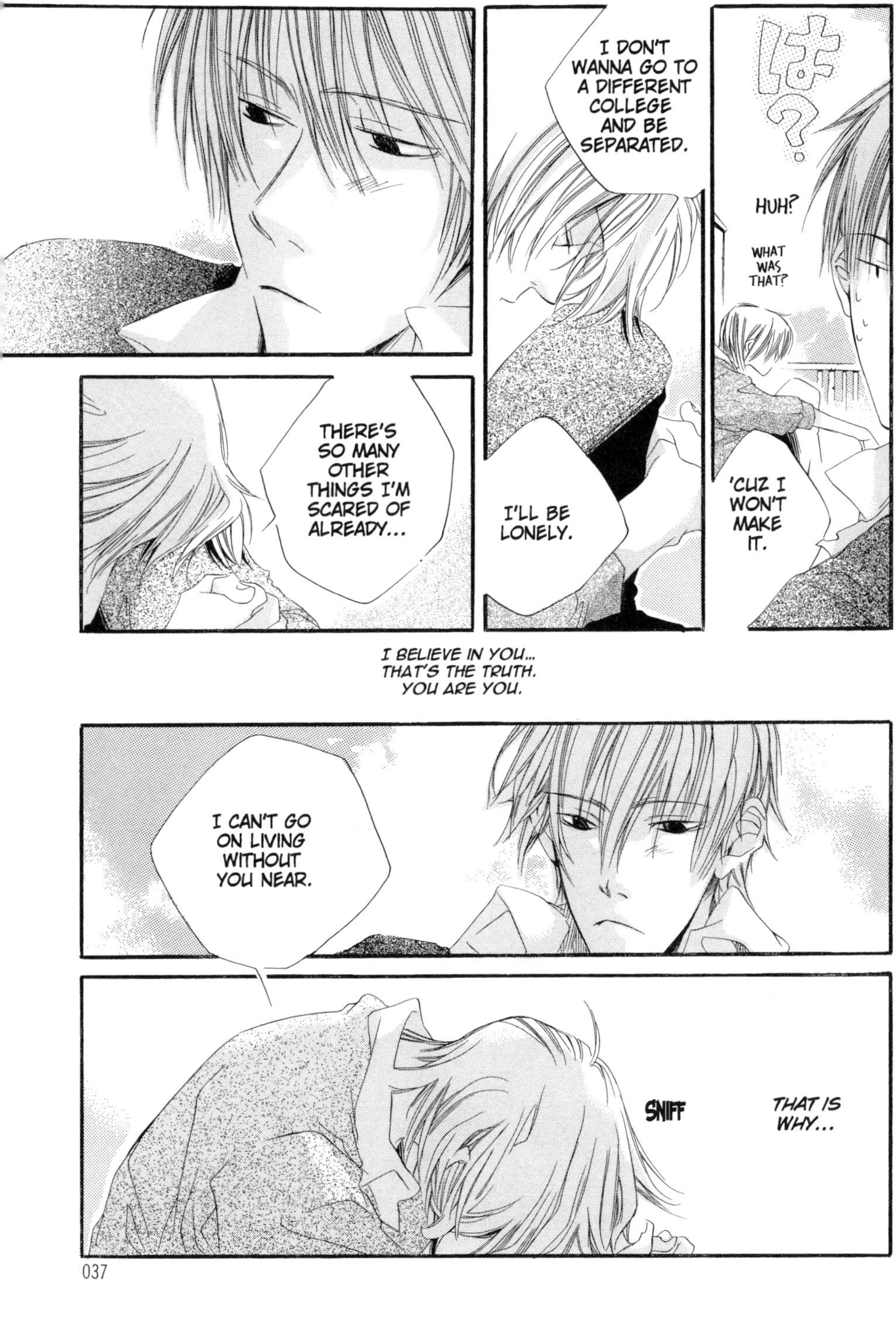

は？
HUH?
WHAT WAS THAT?
'CUZ I WON'T MAKE IT.
I DON'T WANNA GO TO A DIFFERENT COLLEGE AND BE SEPARATED.
I'LL BE LONELY.
THERE'S SO MANY OTHER THINGS I'M SCARED OF ALREADY...
I BELIEVE IN YOU... THAT'S THE TRUTH. YOU ARE YOU.
I CAN'T GO ON LIVING WITHOUT YOU NEAR.
THAT IS WHY...
SNIFF

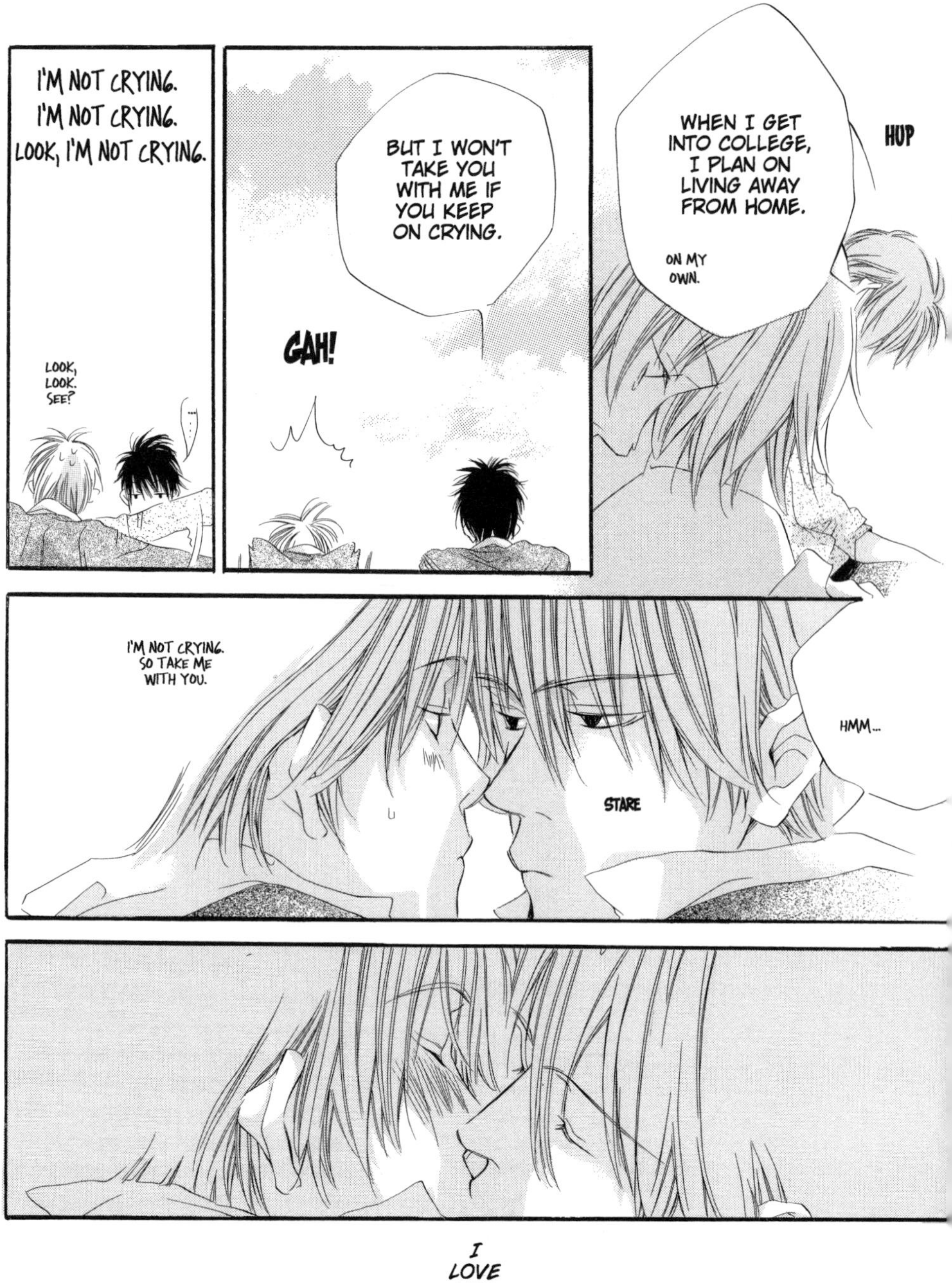
HUP
WHEN I GET INTO COLLEGE, I PLAN ON LIVING AWAY FROM HOME.
ON MY OWN.
BUT I WON'T TAKE YOU WITH ME IF YOU KEEP ON CRYING.
GAH!
I'M NOT CRYING. I'M NOT CRYING. LOOK, I'M NOT CRYING.
...
LOOK, LOOK. SEE?
HMM...
STARE
I'M NOT CRYING. SO TAKE ME WITH YOU.
I LOVE YOU.

I LOVE YOU. / END

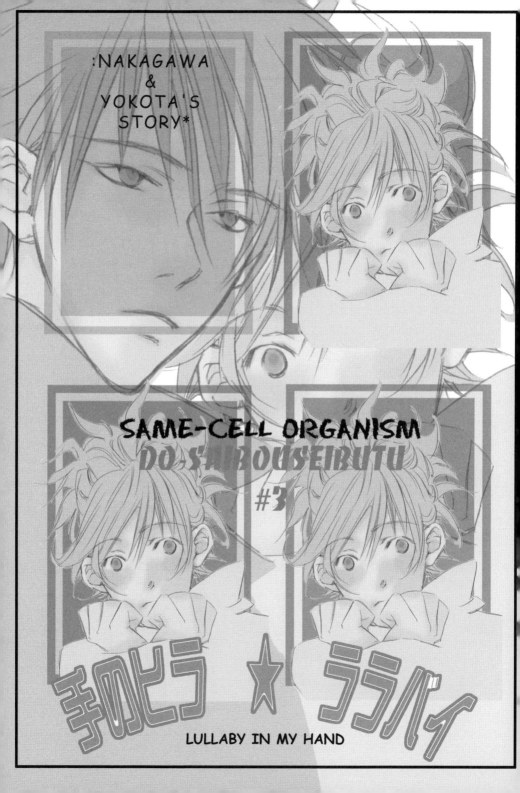

:NAKAGAWA & YOKOTA'S STORY*

SAME-CELL ORGANISM
DO-SAIBOUSEIBUTU
#3

LULLABY IN MY HAND

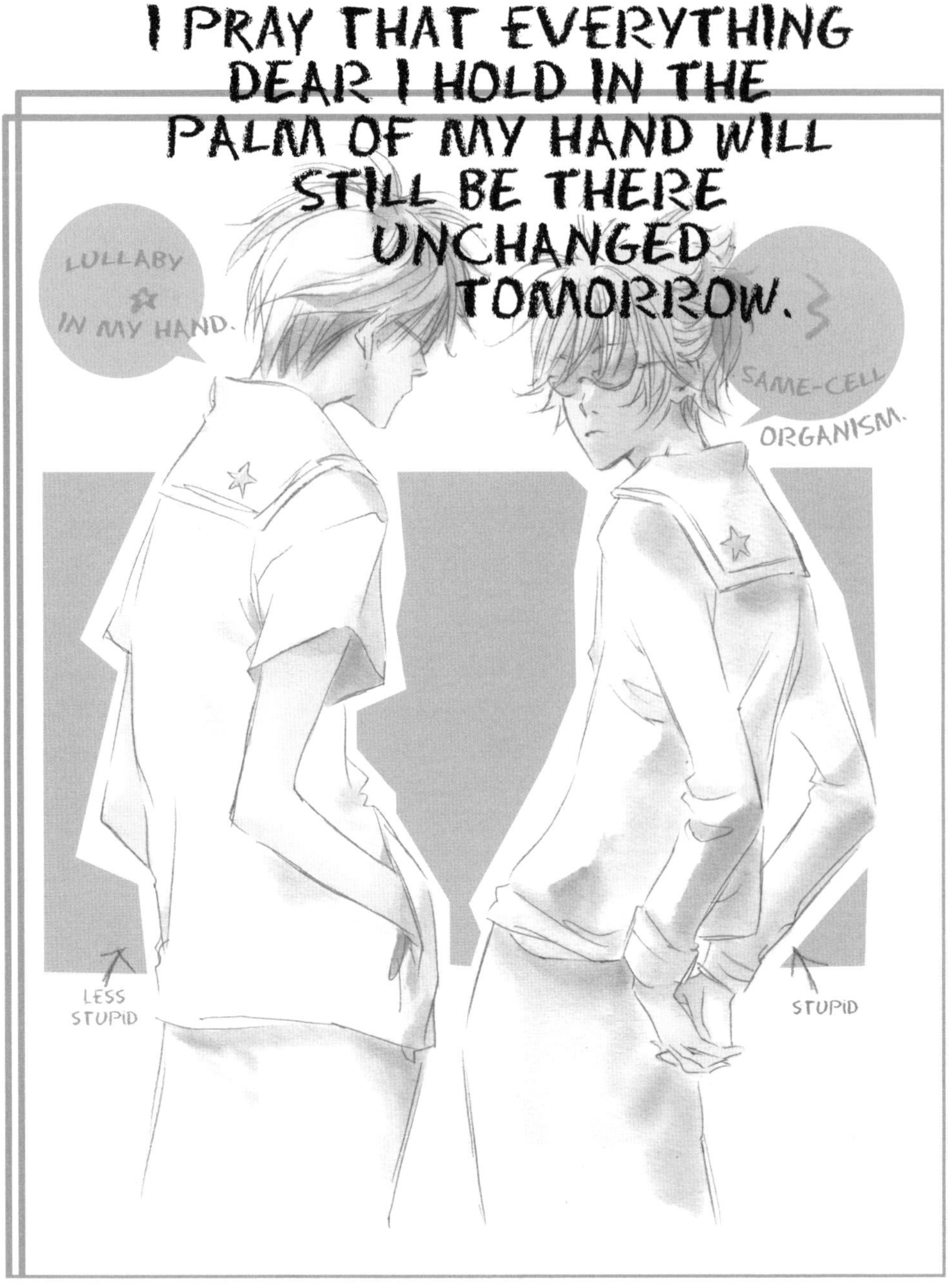
I PRAY THAT EVERYTHING DEAR I HOLD IN THE PALM OF MY HAND WILL STILL BE THERE UNCHANGED TOMORROW.
SAME-CELL ORGANISM.
LULLABY ☆ IN MY HAND.
STUPID
LESS STUPID

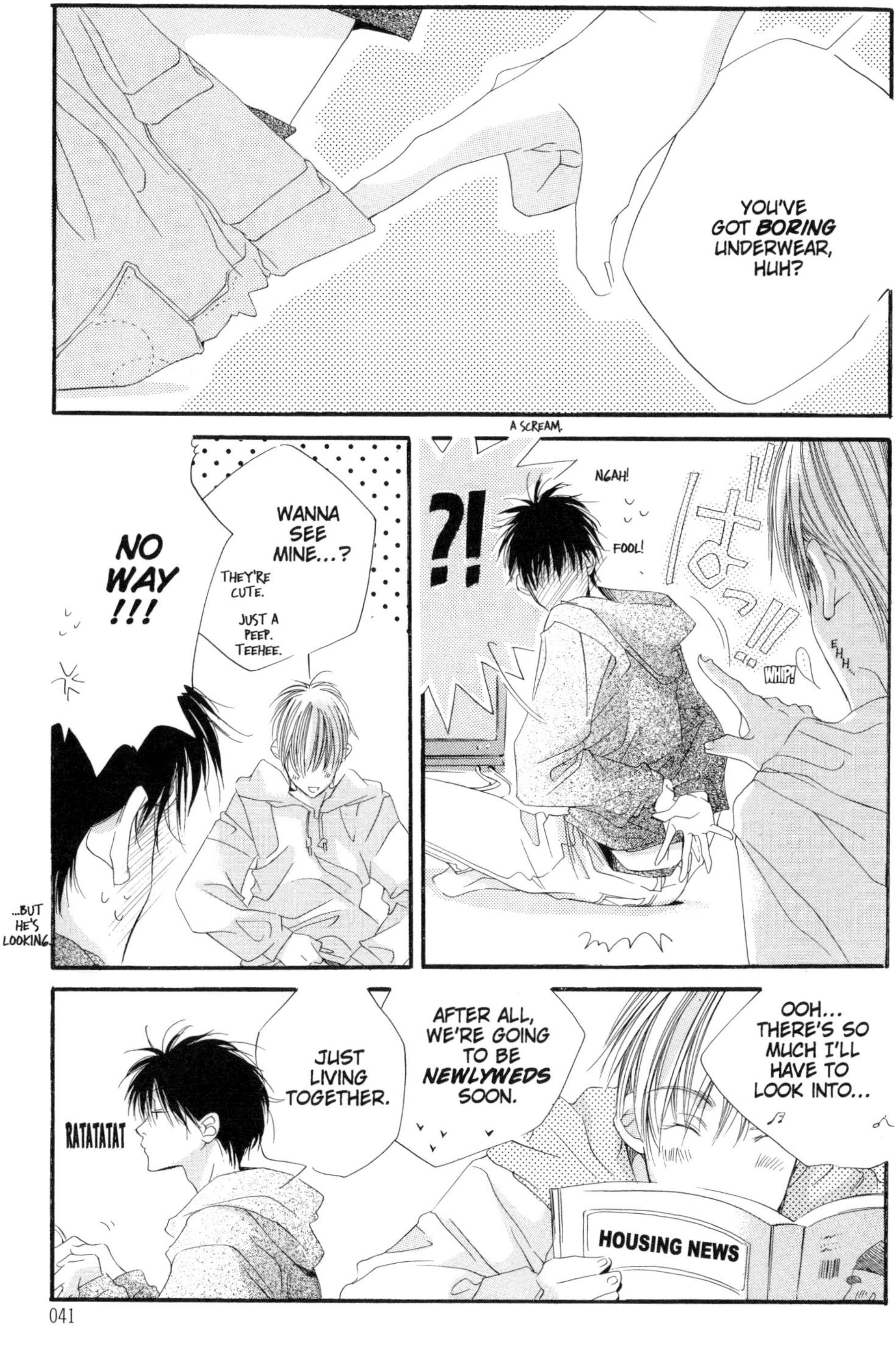
YOU'VE GOT BORING UNDERWEAR, HUH?
A SCREAM.
NGAH!
FOOL!
?!
WHIP!
EHH...
WANNA SEE MINE...?
THEY'RE CUTE.
JUST A PEEP. TEEHEE.
NO WAY!!!
...BUT HE'S LOOKING.
OOH... THERE'S SO MUCH I'LL HAVE TO LOOK INTO...
HOUSING NEWS
AFTER ALL, WE'RE GOING TO BE NEWLYWEDS SOON.
JUST LIVING TOGETHER.
RATATATAT

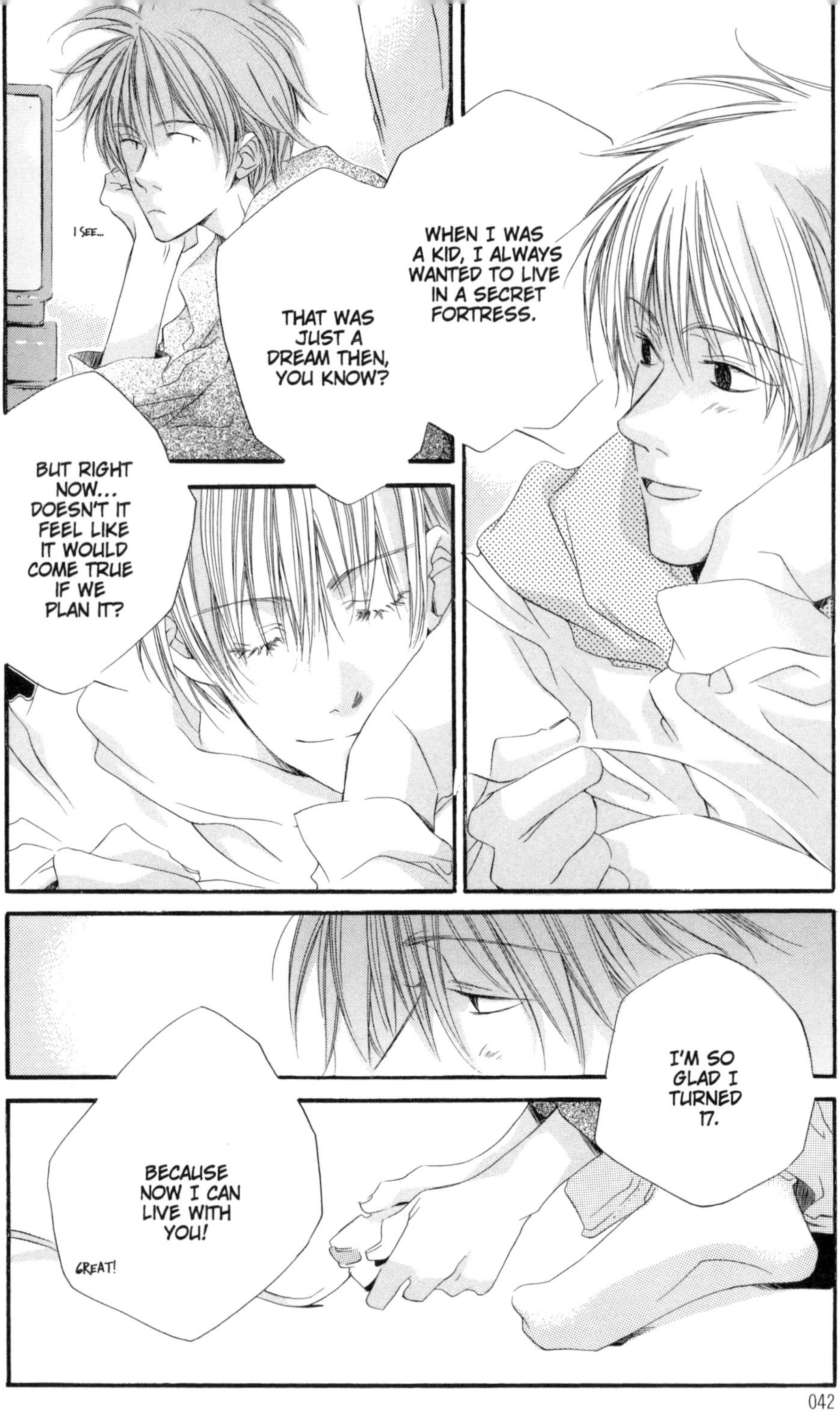
WHEN I WAS A KID, I ALWAYS WANTED TO LIVE IN A SECRET FORTRESS.
THAT WAS JUST A DREAM THEN, YOU KNOW?
I SEE...
BUT RIGHT NOW... DOESN'T IT FEEL LIKE IT WOULD COME TRUE IF WE PLAN IT?
I'M SO GLAD I TURNED 17.
BECAUSE NOW I CAN LIVE WITH YOU!
GREAT!

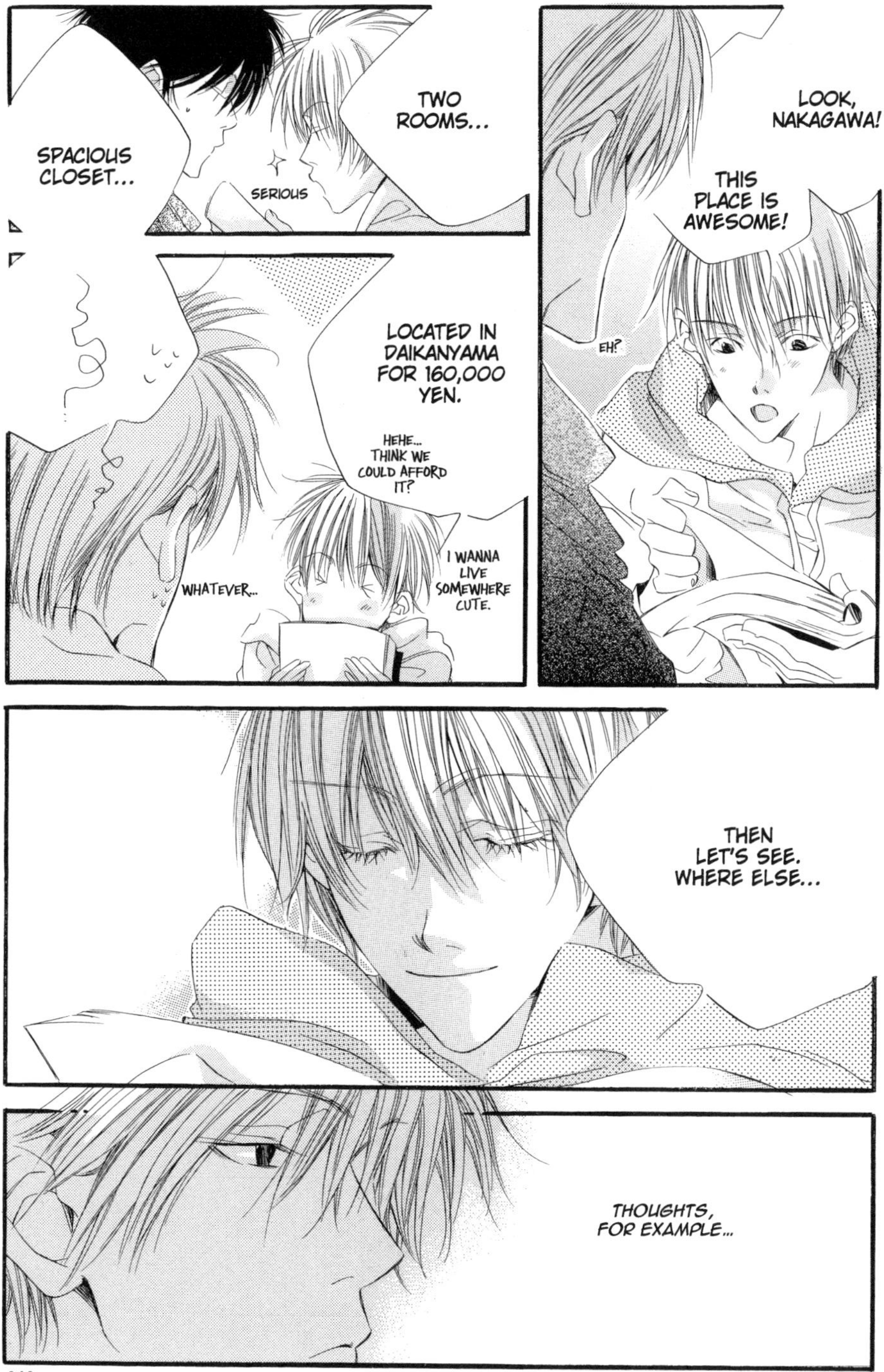
LOOK, NAKAGAWA!
THIS PLACE IS AWESOME!
EH?
TWO ROOMS...
SPACIOUS CLOSET...
SERIOUS
LOCATED IN DAIKANYAMA FOR 160,000 YEN.
HEHE... THINK WE COULD AFFORD IT?
I WANNA LIVE SOMEWHERE CUTE.
WHATEVER...
THEN LET'S SEE. WHERE ELSE...
THOUGHTS, FOR EXAMPLE...

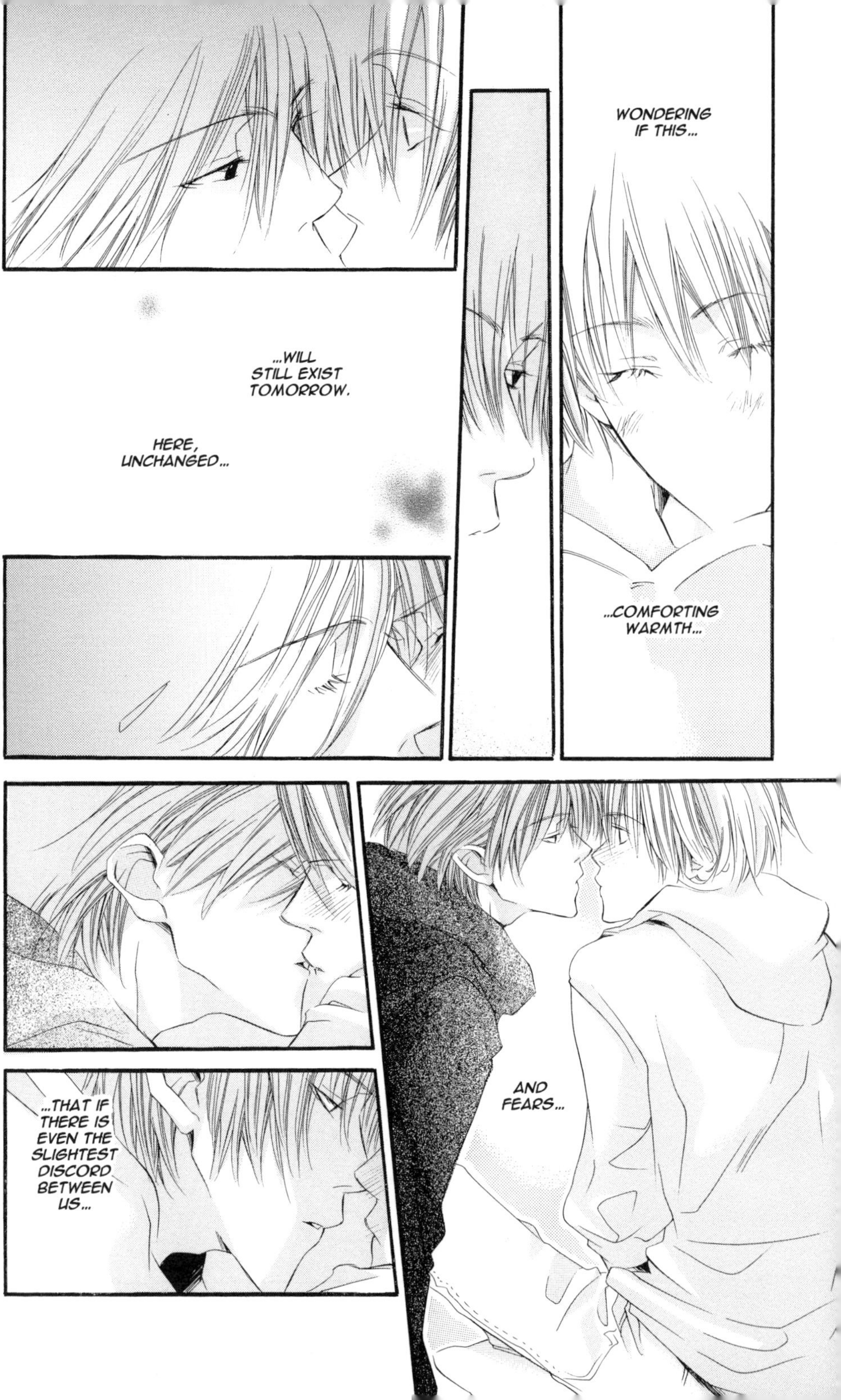
WONDERING IF THIS...
...COMFORTING WARMTH...
...WILL STILL EXIST TOMORROW.
HERE, UNCHANGED...
AND FEARS...
...THAT IF THERE IS EVEN THE SLIGHTEST DISCORD BETWEEN US...

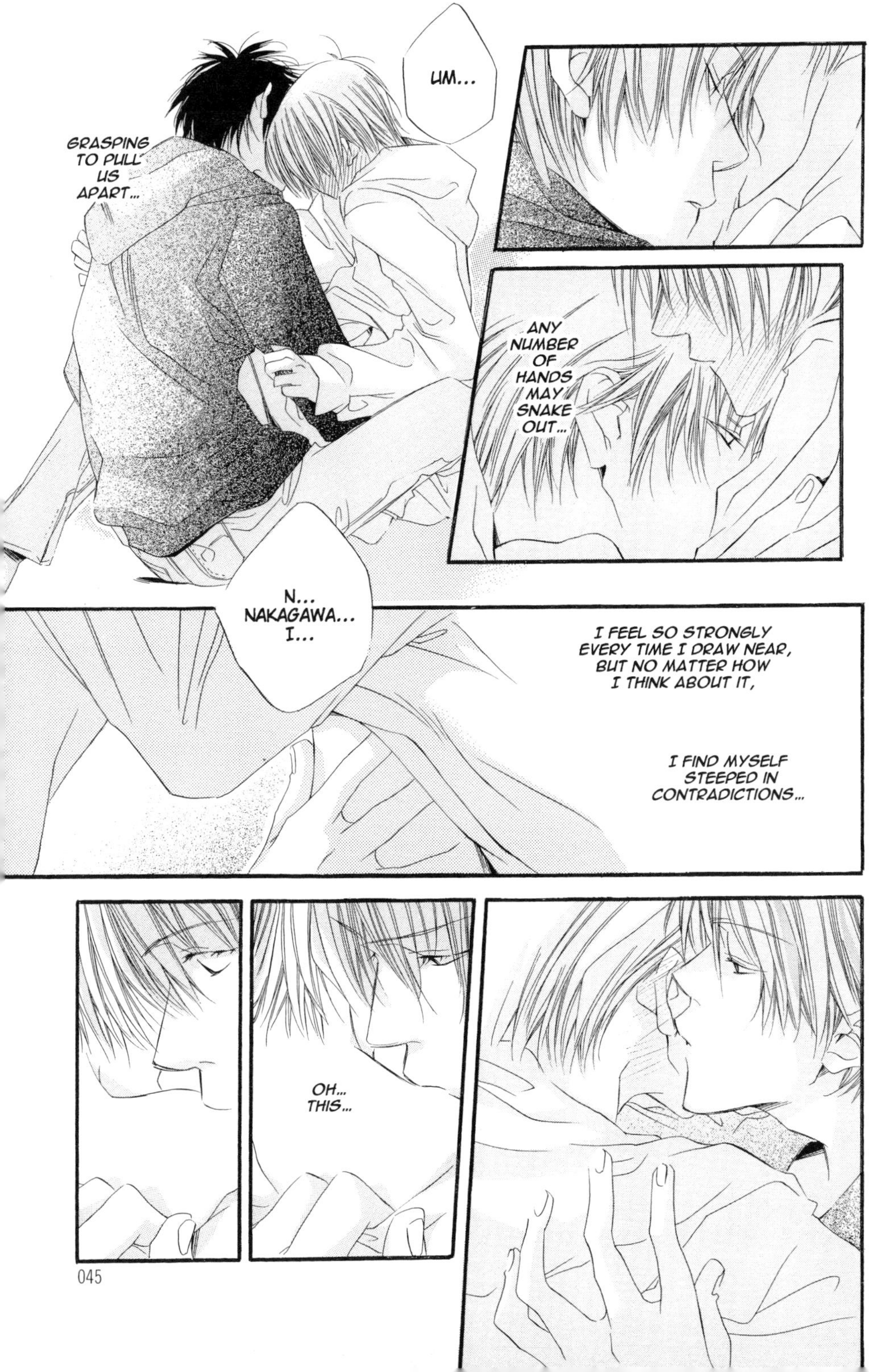
UM...
ANY NUMBER OF HANDS MAY SNAKE OUT...
GRASPING TO PULL US APART...
N... NAKAGAWA... I...
I FEEL SO STRONGLY EVERY TIME I DRAW NEAR, BUT NO MATTER HOW I THINK ABOUT IT,
I FIND MYSELF STEEPED IN CONTRADICTIONS...
OH... THIS...

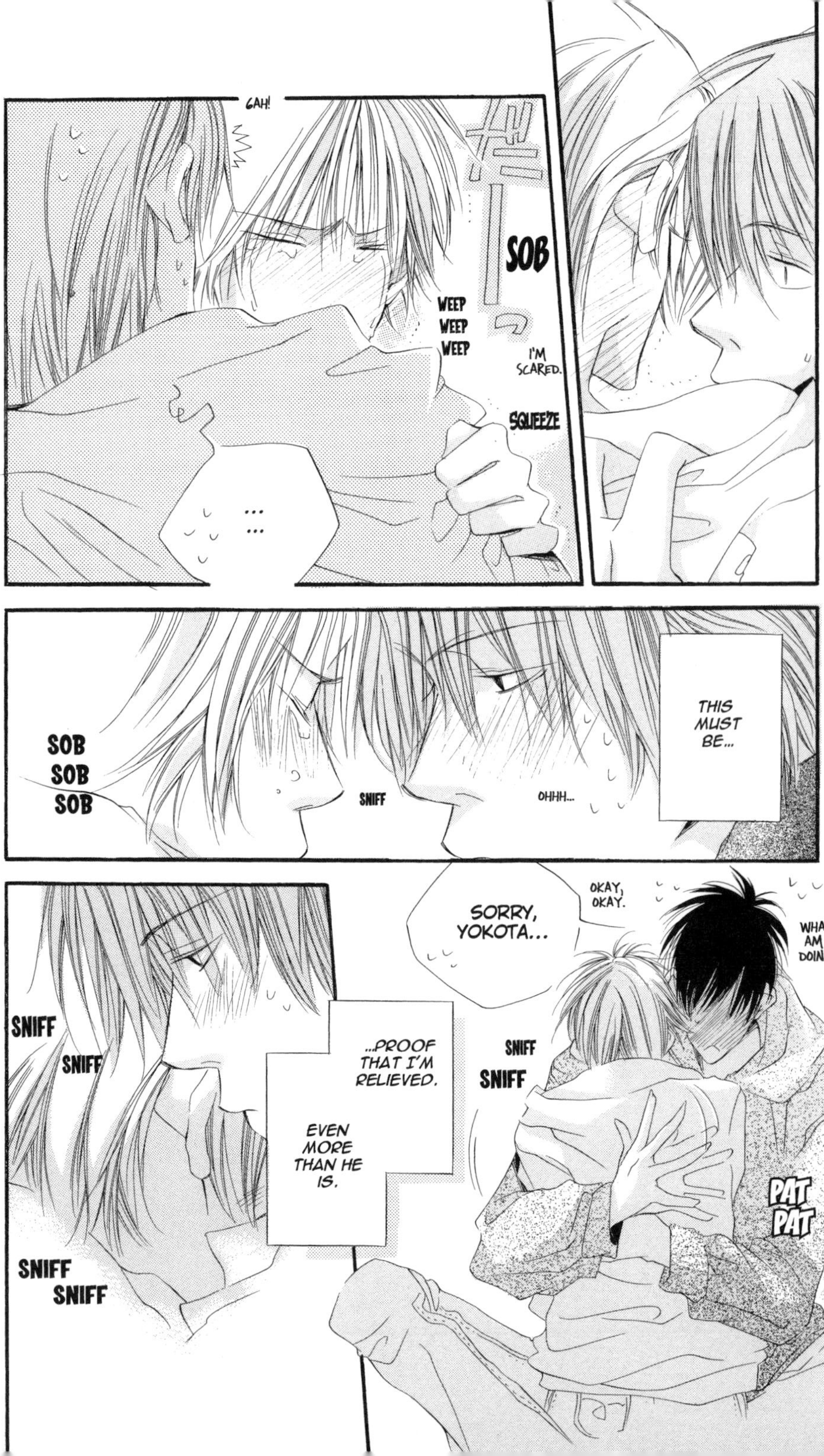
SOB
GAH!
I'M SCARED.
WEEP
WEEP
WEEP
SQUEEZE
...
...
THIS MUST BE...
OHHH...
SNIFF
SOB
SOB
SOB
WHAT AM I DOING...
OKAY, OKAY.
SORRY, YOKOTA...
SNIFF
SNIFF
PAT PAT
...PROOF THAT I'M RELIEVED.
EVEN MORE THAN HE IS.
SNIFF
SNIFF
SNIFF
SNIFF

I'M SORRY...

THERE, THERE.

THAT I'M ABLE TO FEEL THIS WAY...

MR. YOKOTA, ARE YOU COLD?

THAT SCARF...

I'M COLD.

YOU DON'T LOOK IT.

REALLY?

BEET RED.

BLUSH

...

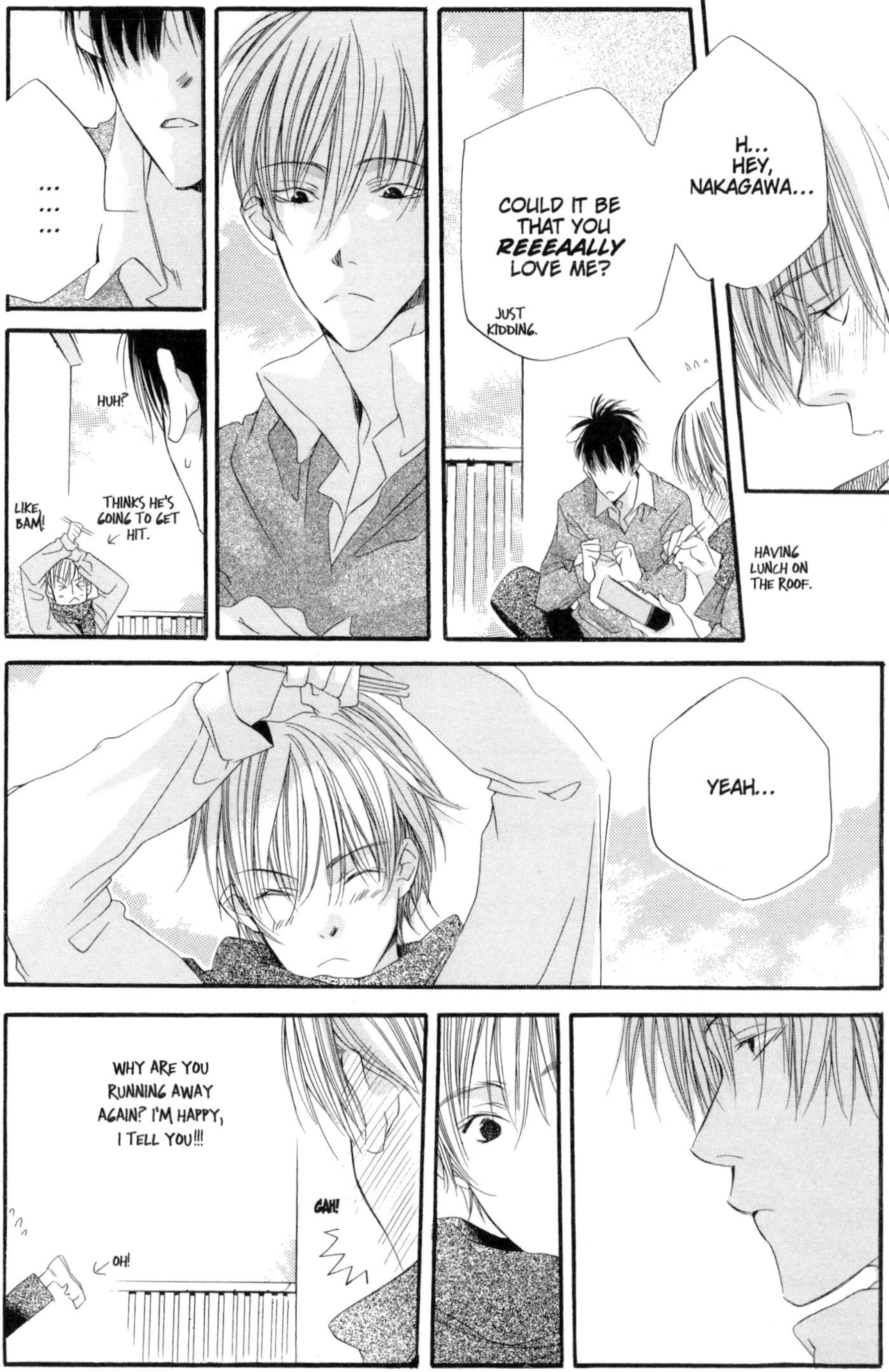
H... HEY, NAKAGAWA...
COULD IT BE THAT YOU REEEAALLY LOVE ME?
JUST KIDDING.
HAVING LUNCH ON THE ROOF.
...
...
...
HUH?
THINKS HE'S GOING TO GET HIT.
LIKE, BAM!
YEAH...
GAH!
WHY ARE YOU RUNNING AWAY AGAIN? I'M HAPPY, I TELL YOU!!!
OH!

STILL EMBARRASSED.

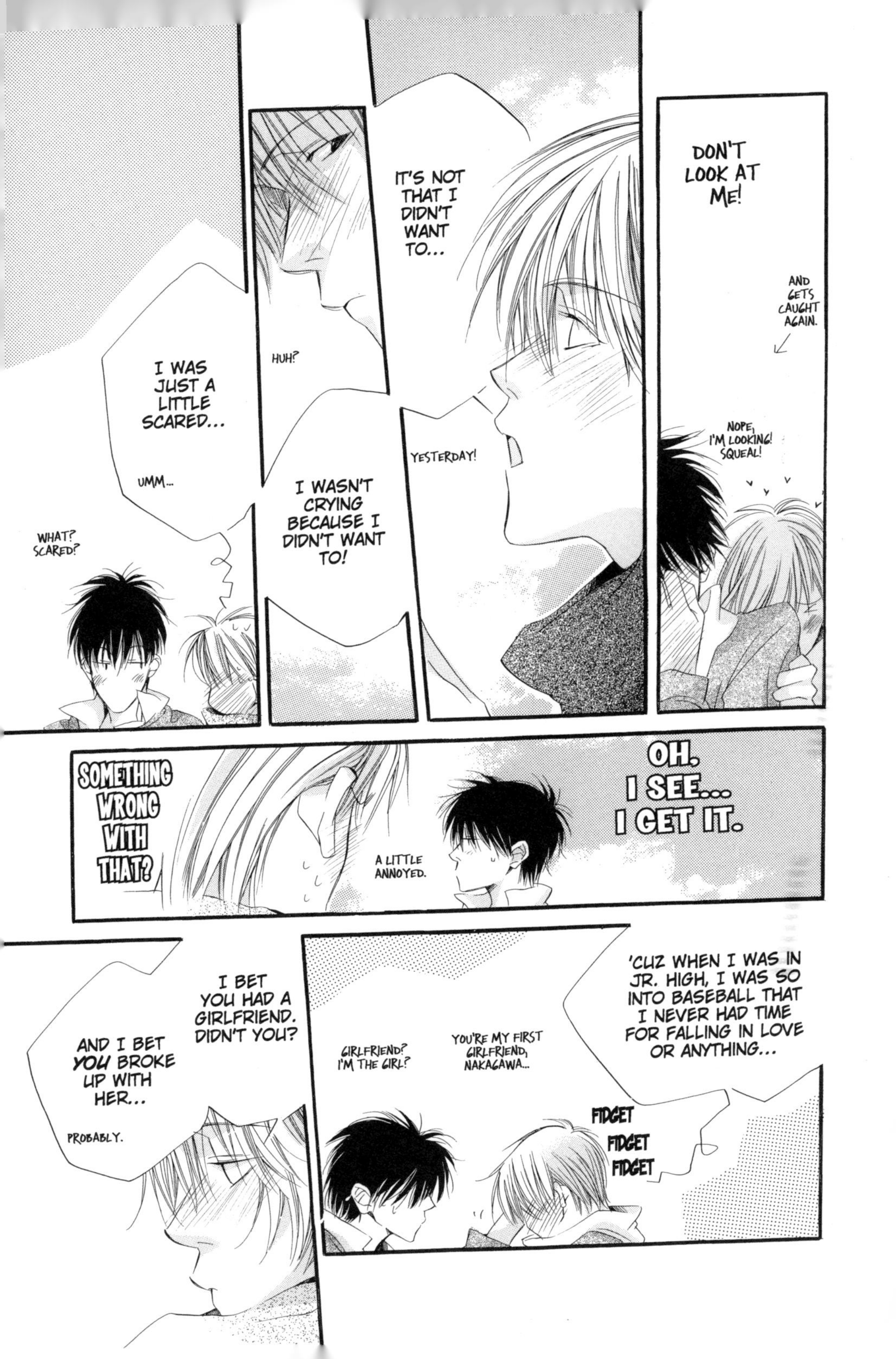

DON'T LOOK AT ME!
AND GETS CAUGHT AGAIN.
NOPE, I'M LOOKING! SQUEAL!
IT'S NOT THAT I DIDN'T WANT TO...
YESTERDAY!
HUH?
I WASN'T CRYING BECAUSE I DIDN'T WANT TO!
I WAS JUST A LITTLE SCARED...
UMM...
WHAT? SCARED?
OH. I SEE... I GET IT.
A LITTLE ANNOYED.
SOMETHING WRONG WITH THAT?
'CUZ WHEN I WAS IN JR. HIGH, I WAS SO INTO BASEBALL THAT I NEVER HAD TIME FOR FALLING IN LOVE OR ANYTHING...
YOU'RE MY FIRST GIRLFRIEND, NAKAGAWA...
GIRLFRIEND? I'M THE GIRL?
FIDGET
FIDGET
FIDGET
I BET YOU HAD A GIRLFRIEND. DIDN'T YOU?
AND I BET YOU BROKE UP WITH HER...
PROBABLY.

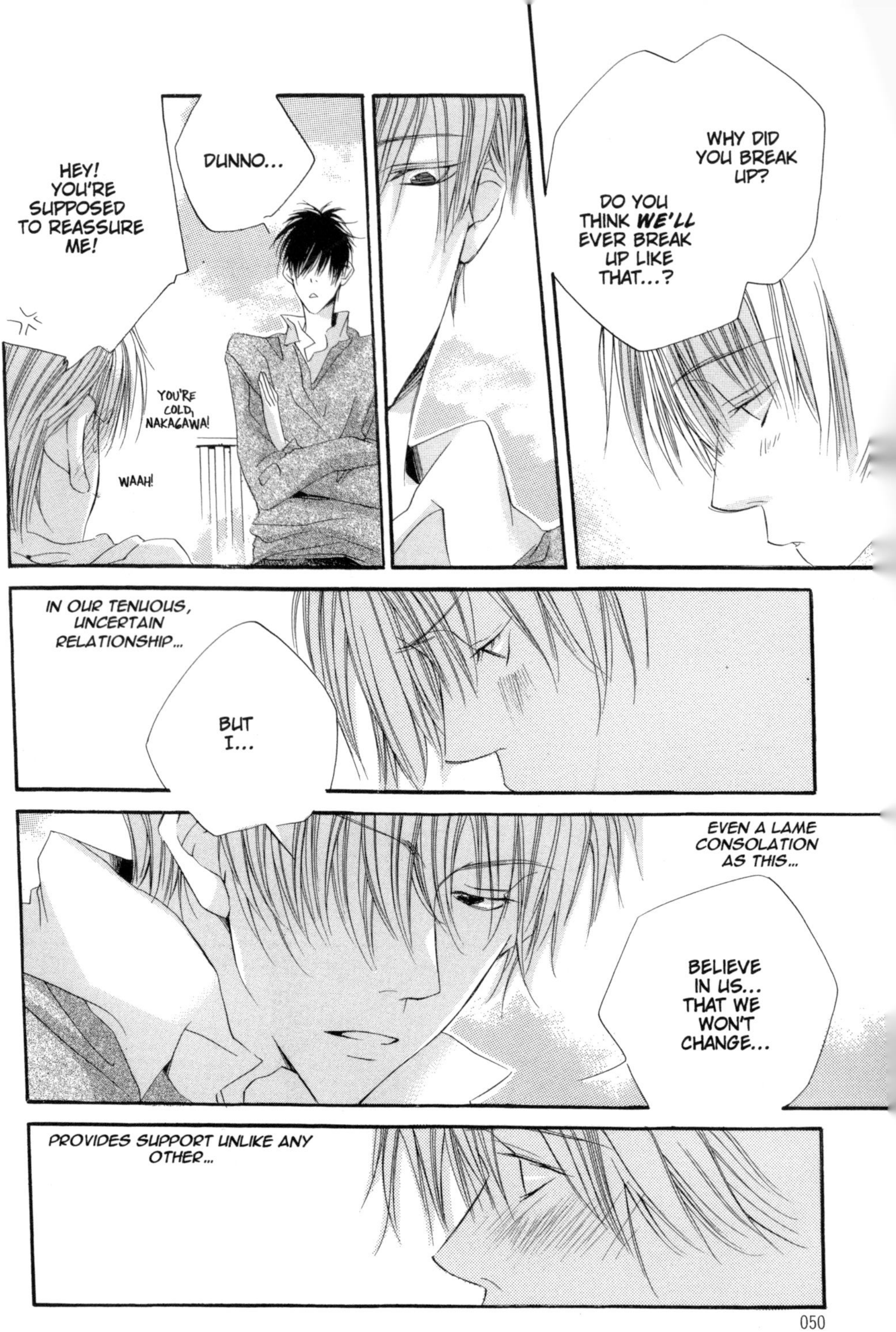
WHY DID YOU BREAK UP?
DO YOU THINK WE'LL EVER BREAK UP LIKE THAT...?
DUNNO...
HEY! YOU'RE SUPPOSED TO REASSURE ME!
YOU'RE COLD, NAKAGAWA!
WAAH!
IN OUR TENUOUS, UNCERTAIN RELATIONSHIP...
BUT I...
EVEN A LAME CONSOLATION AS THIS...
BELIEVE IN US... THAT WE WON'T CHANGE...
PROVIDES SUPPORT UNLIKE ANY OTHER...

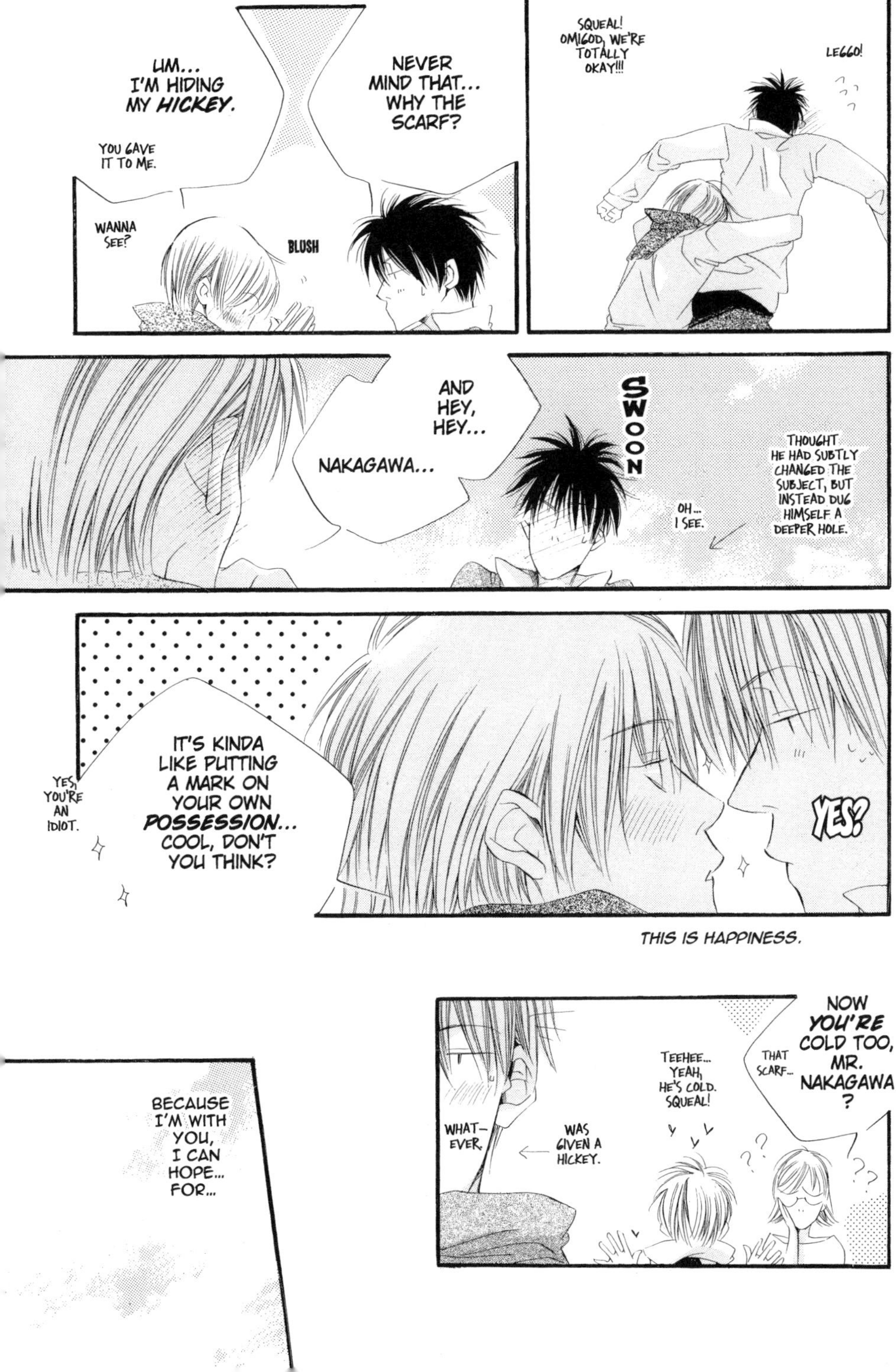
NO!
SQUEAL! OMIGOD, WE'RE TOTALLY OKAY!!!
LEGGO!
NEVER MIND THAT... WHY THE SCARF?
UM... I'M HIDING MY ***HICKEY***.
YOU GAVE IT TO ME.
BLUSH
WANNA SEE?
THOUGHT HE HAD SUBTLY CHANGED THE SUBJECT, BUT INSTEAD DUG HIMSELF A DEEPER HOLE.
SWOON
OH... I SEE.
AND HEY, HEY...
NAKAGAWA...
YES?
IT'S KINDA LIKE PUTTING A MARK ON YOUR OWN ***POSSESSION***... COOL, DON'T YOU THINK?
YES, YOU'RE AN IDIOT.
THIS IS HAPPINESS.
NOW ***YOU'RE*** COLD TOO, MR. NAKAGAWA?
THAT SCARF...
TEEHEE... YEAH, HE'S COLD. SQUEAL!
WAS GIVEN A HICKEY.
WHAT-EVER.
BECAUSE I'M WITH YOU, I CAN HOPE... FOR...

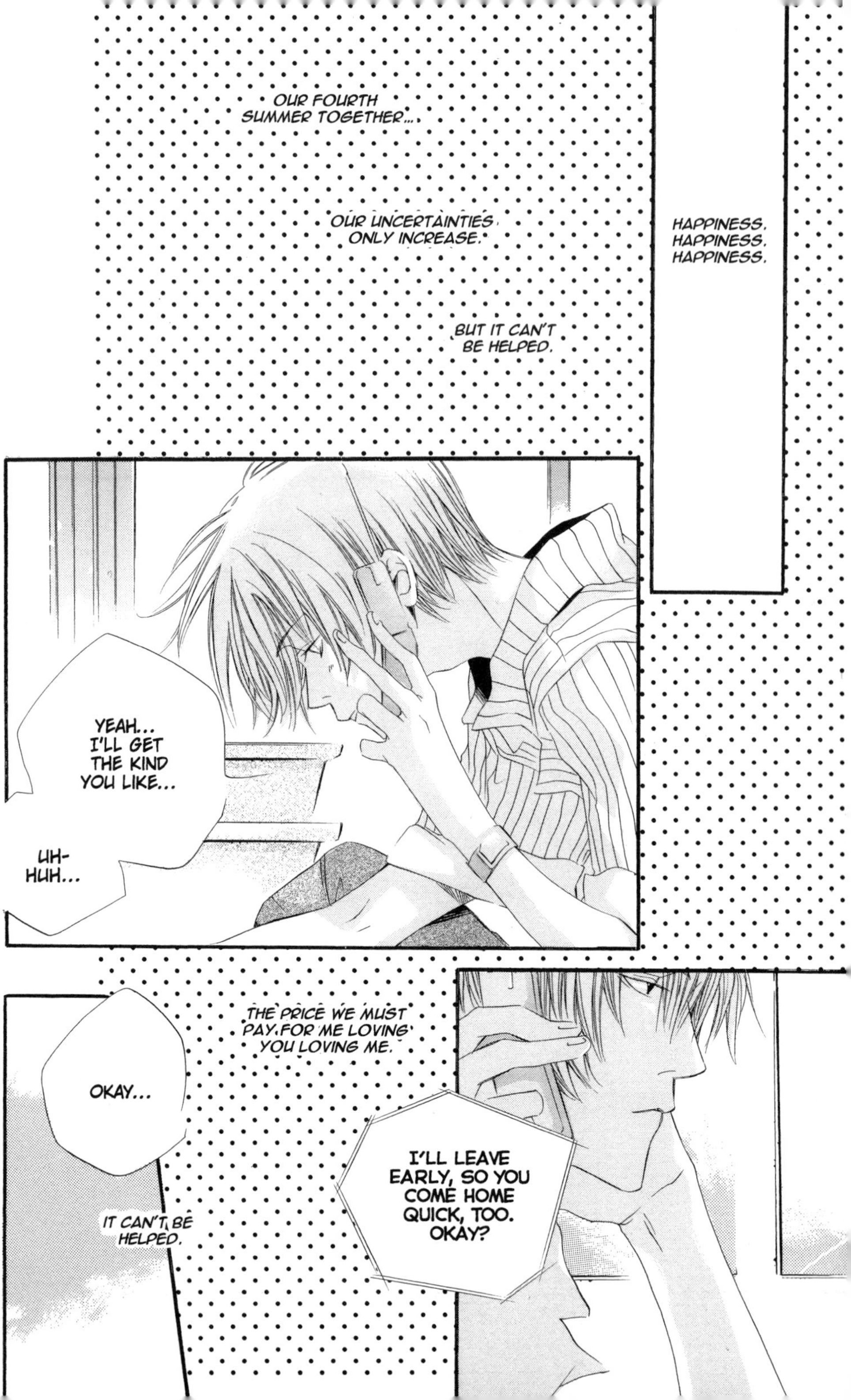
HAPPINESS. HAPPINESS. HAPPINESS.
OUR FOURTH SUMMER TOGETHER...
OUR UNCERTAINTIES ONLY INCREASE.
BUT IT CAN'T BE HELPED.
YEAH... I'LL GET THE KIND YOU LIKE...
UH-HUH...
I'LL LEAVE EARLY, SO YOU COME HOME QUICK, TOO. OKAY?
THE PRICE WE MUST PAY FOR ME LOVING YOU LOVING ME.
OKAY...
IT CAN'T BE HELPED.

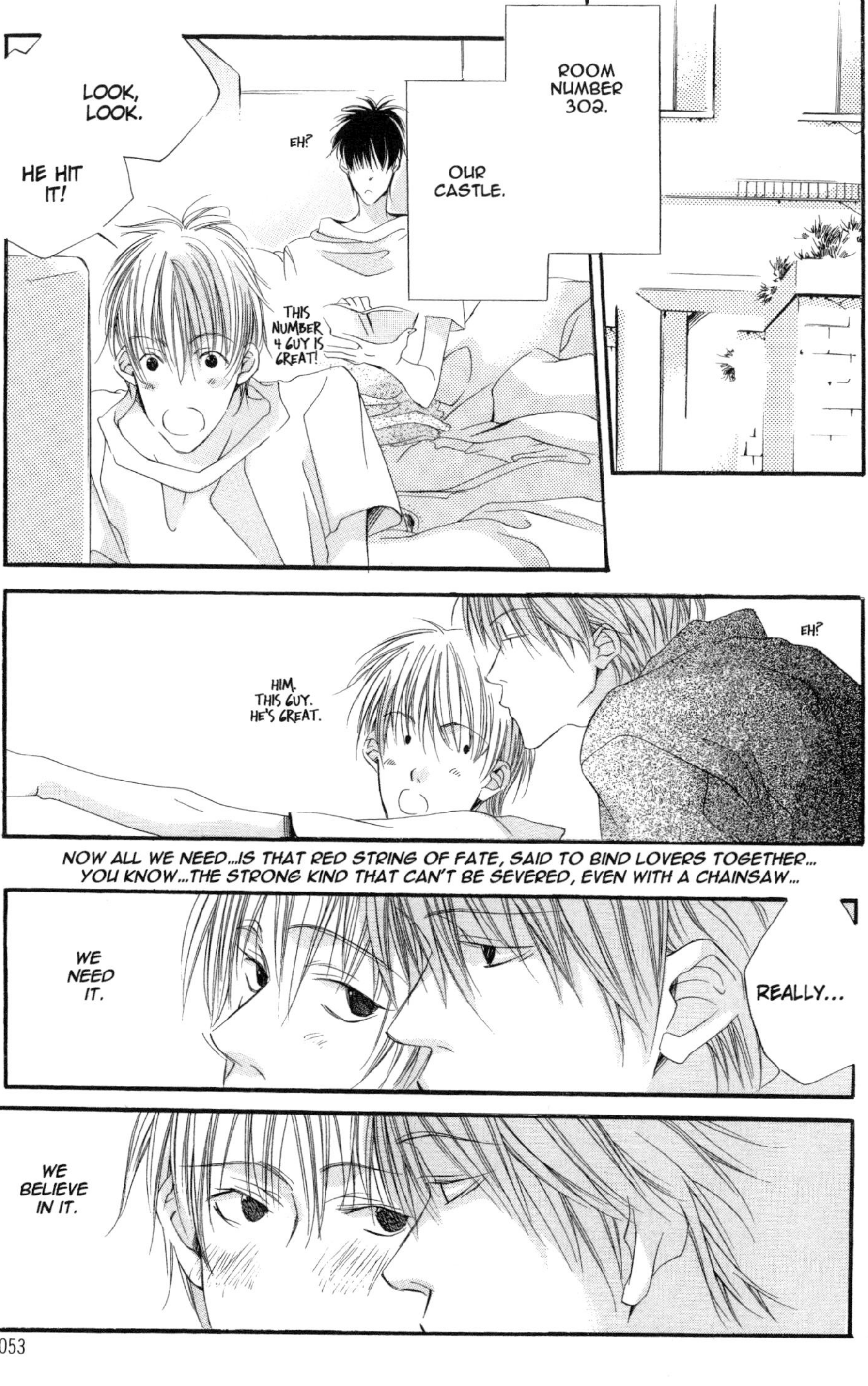
ROOM NUMBER 302.
OUR CASTLE.
LOOK, LOOK.
HE HIT IT!
EH?
THIS NUMBER 4 GUY IS GREAT!
EH?
HIM. THIS GUY. HE'S GREAT.
NOW ALL WE NEED...IS THAT RED STRING OF FATE, SAID TO BIND LOVERS TOGETHER... YOU KNOW...THE STRONG KIND THAT CAN'T BE SEVERED, EVEN WITH A CHAINSAW...
REALLY...
WE NEED IT.
WE BELIEVE IN IT.

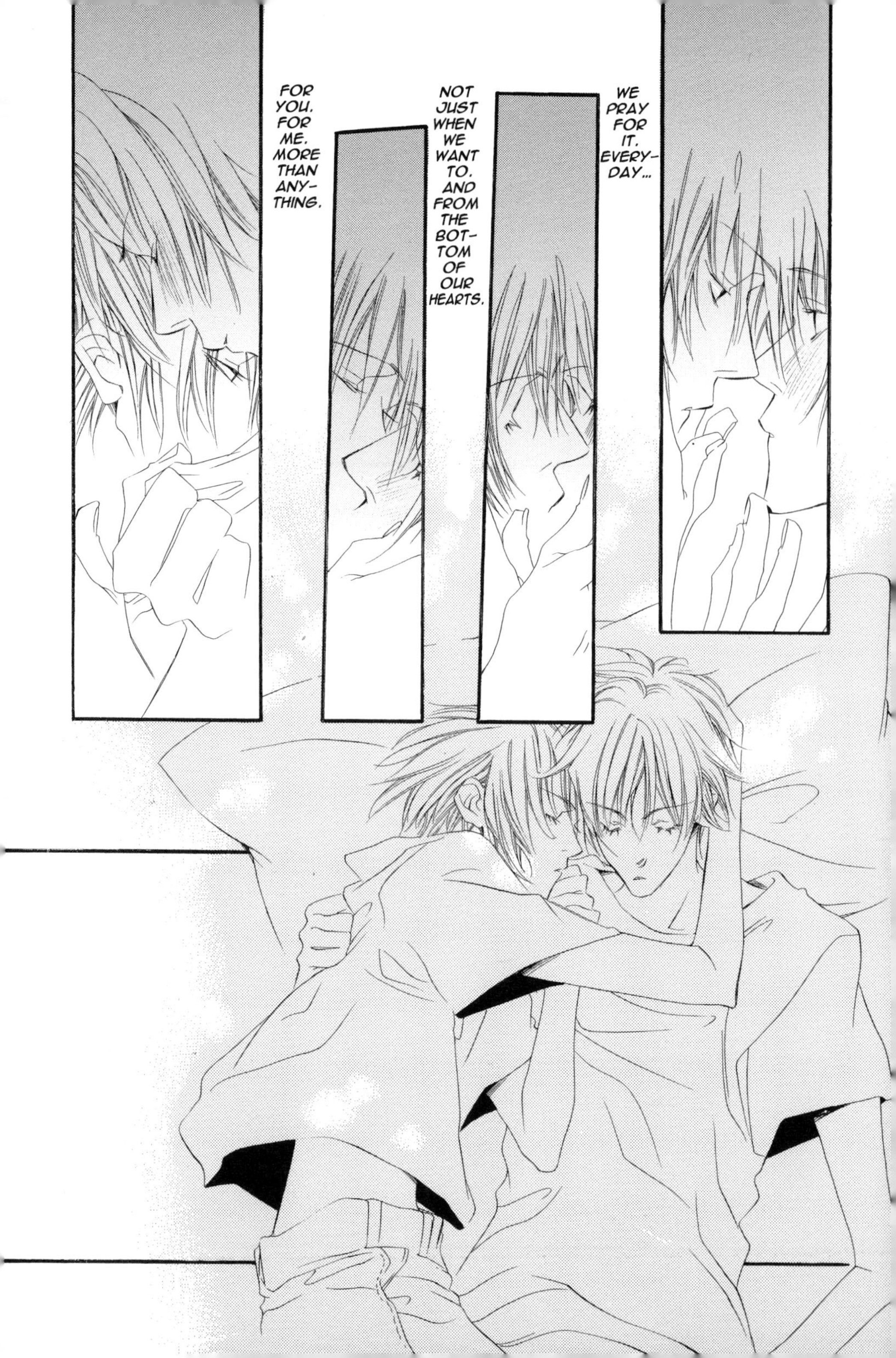
WE PRAY FOR IT. EVERY-DAY...
NOT JUST WHEN WE WANT TO. AND FROM THE BOT-TOM OF OUR HEARTS.
FOR YOU. FOR ME. MORE THAN ANY-THING.

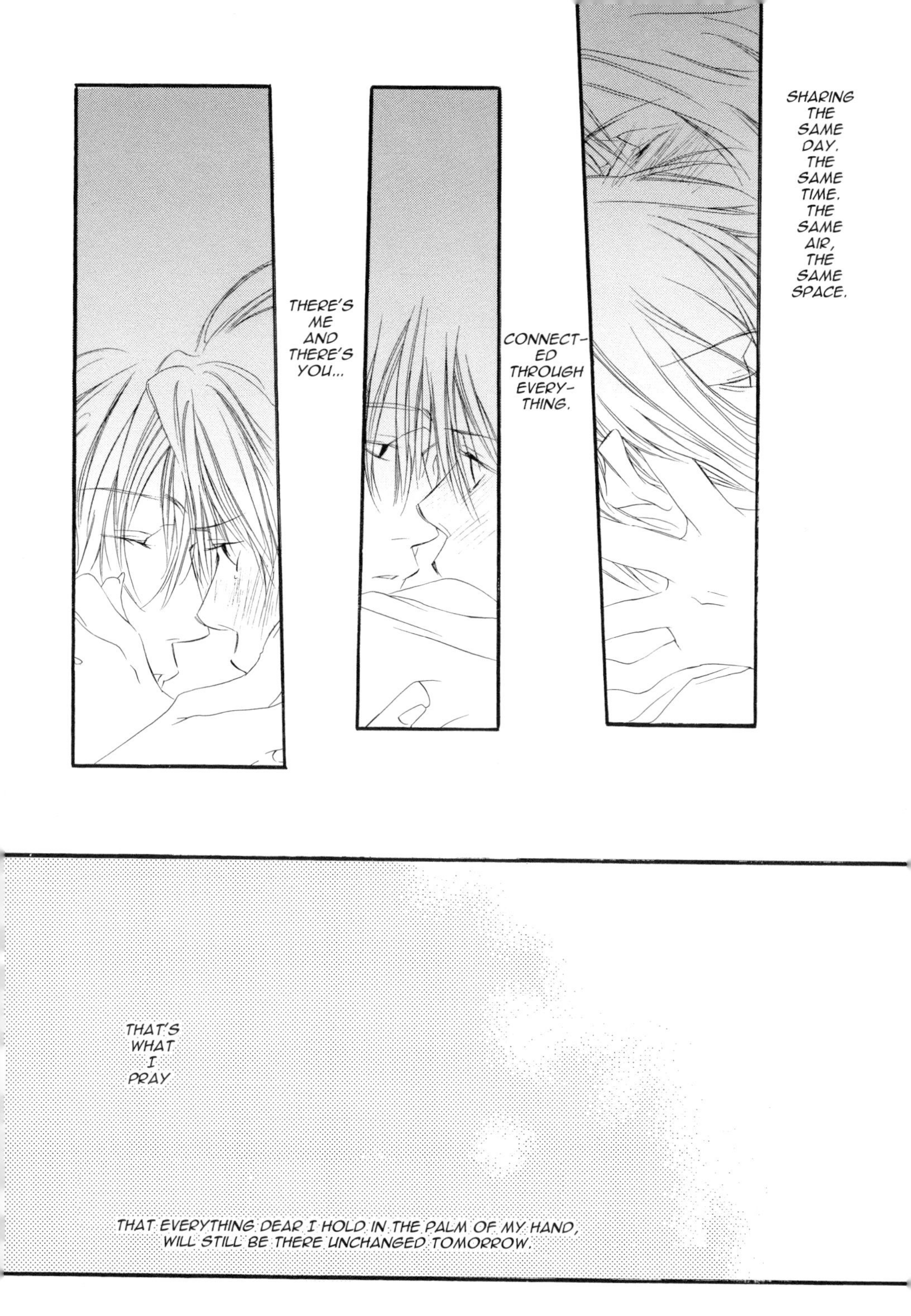
SHARING THE SAME DAY. THE SAME TIME. THE SAME AIR, THE SAME SPACE.
CONNECTED-ED THROUGH EVERY-THING.
THERE'S ME AND THERE'S YOU...
THAT'S WHAT I PRAY
THAT EVERYTHING DEAR I HOLD IN THE PALM OF MY HAND,
WILL STILL BE THERE UNCHANGED TOMORROW.

TODAY,
THE SAME SKY.
THE SAME PALM
OF MY HAND.

LULLABY
IN MY HAND / END

THE LETTER IN THE ATTIC

屋根裏郵便物語

WE TWO DIFFER FROM EVERYBODY ELSE... BUT YOU AND I ARE MUCH ALIKE...

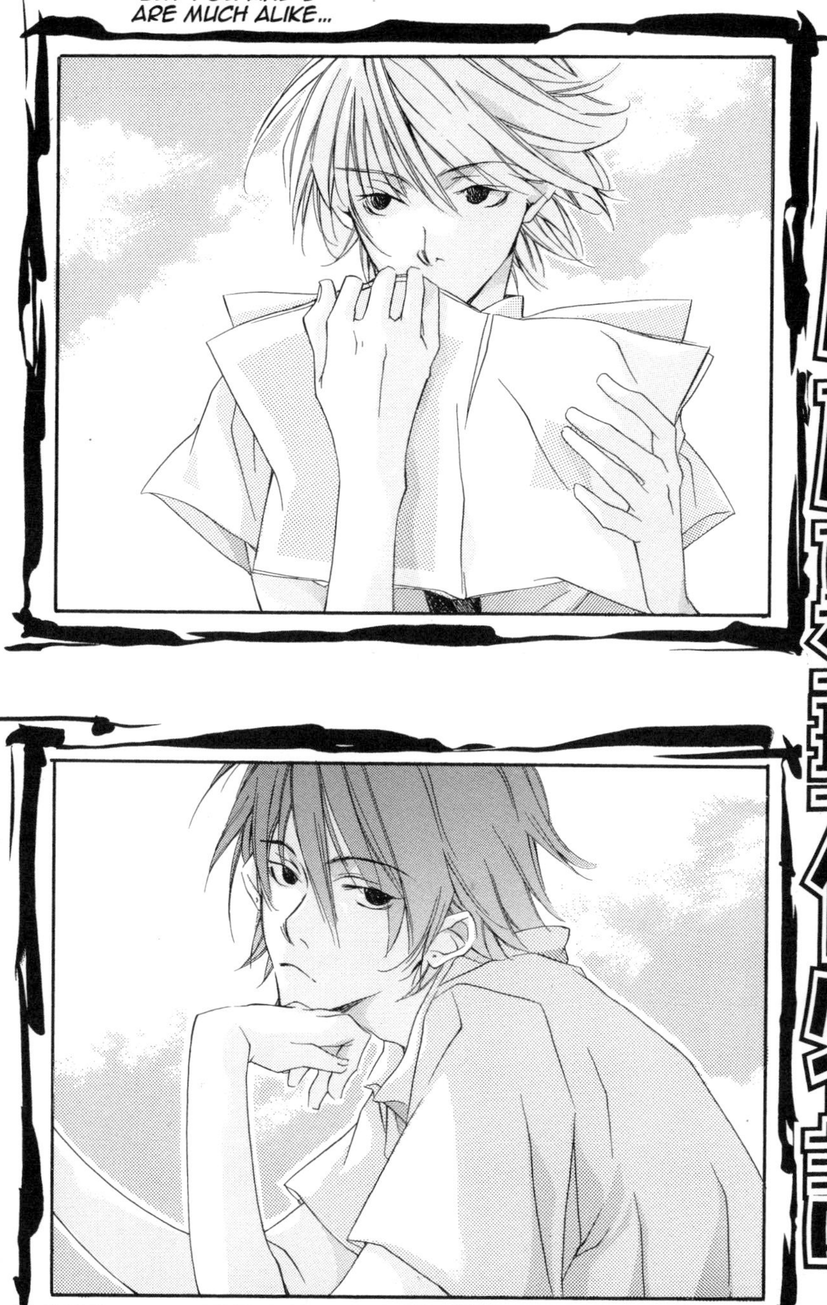

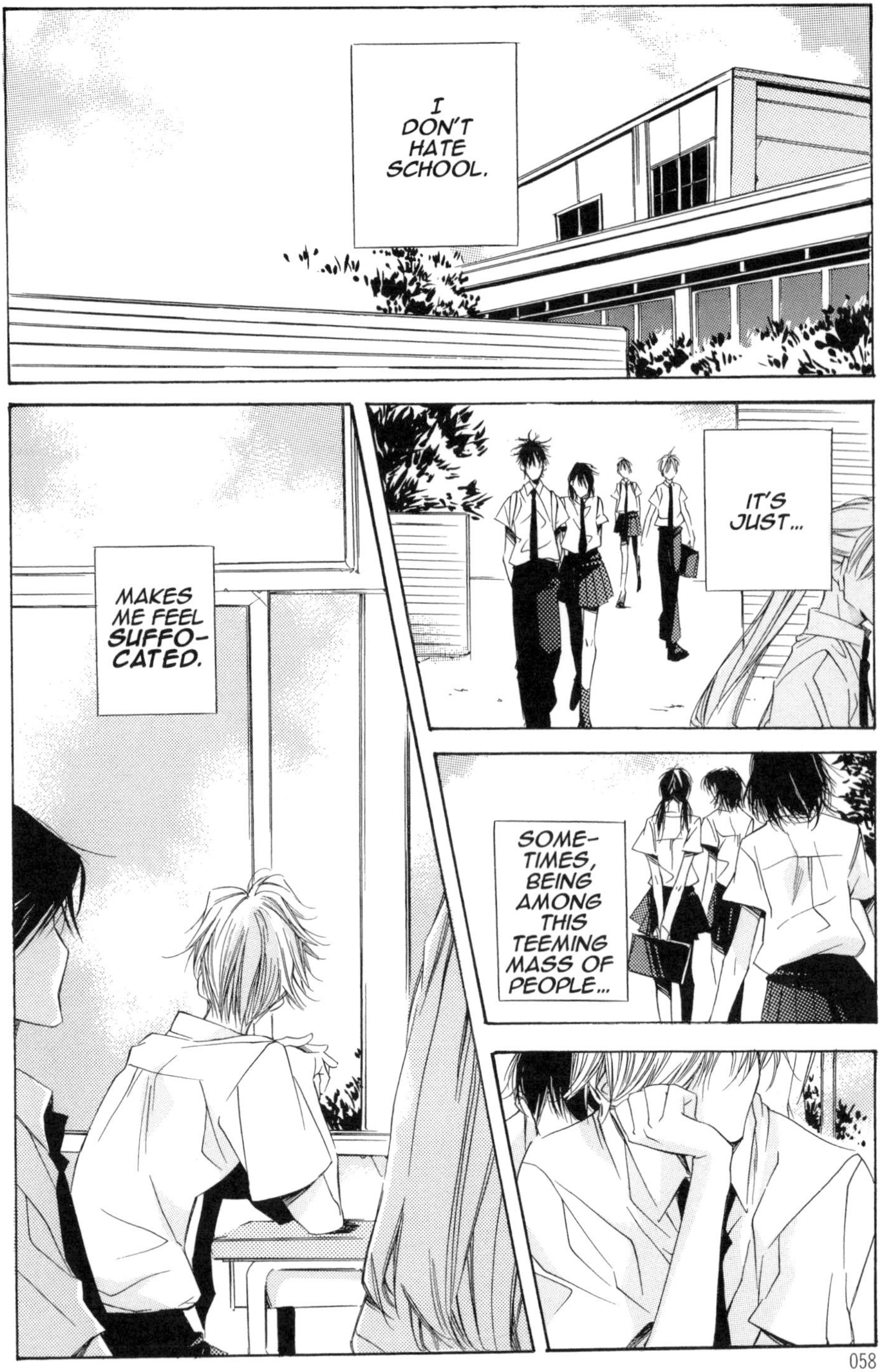
I DON'T HATE SCHOOL.
IT'S JUST...
SOME-TIMES, BEING AMONG THIS TEEMING MASS OF PEOPLE...
MAKES ME FEEL SUFFO-CATED.

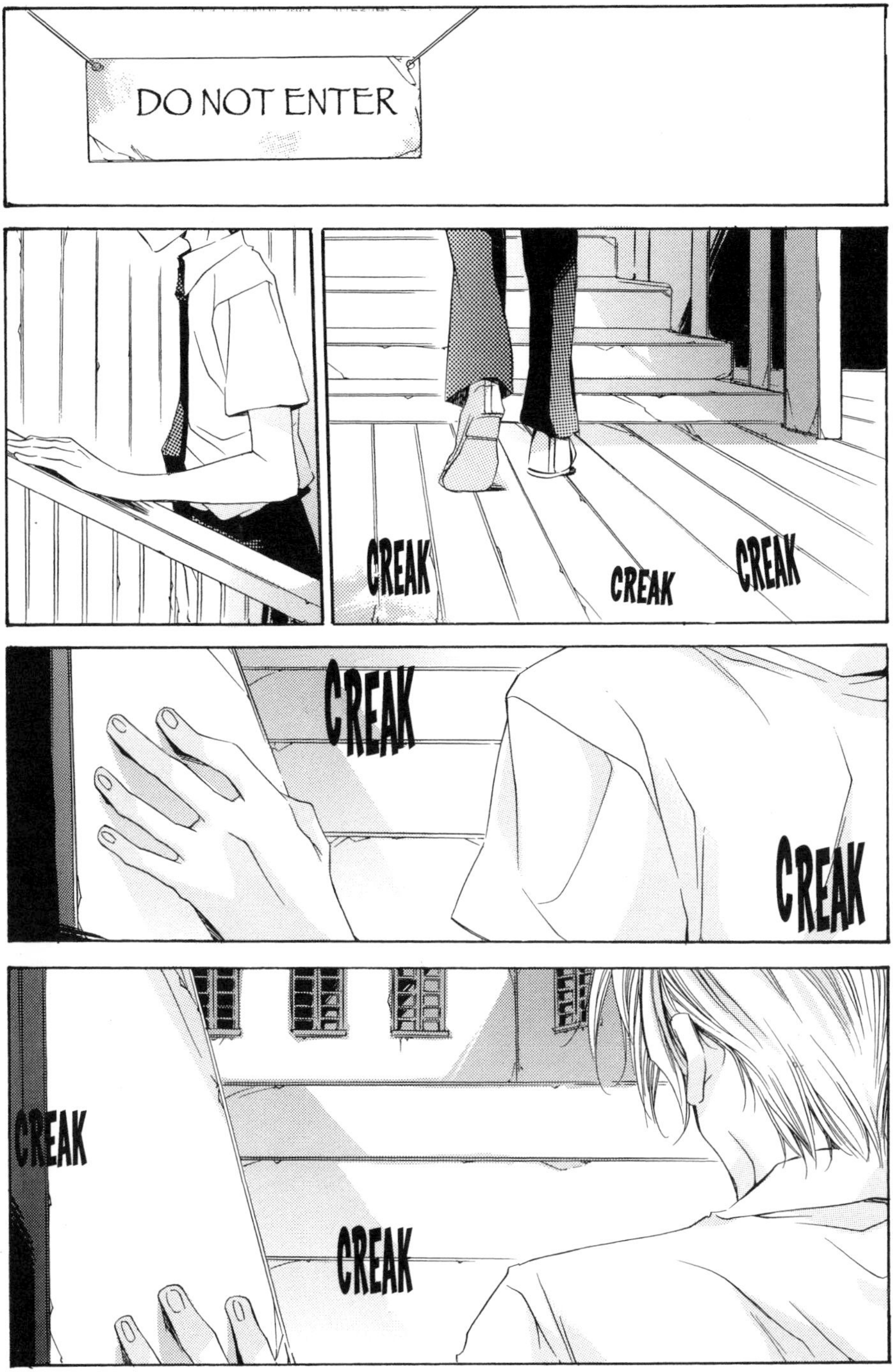
DO NOT ENTER
CREAK
CREAK
CREAK
CREAK
CREAK
CREAK
CREAK

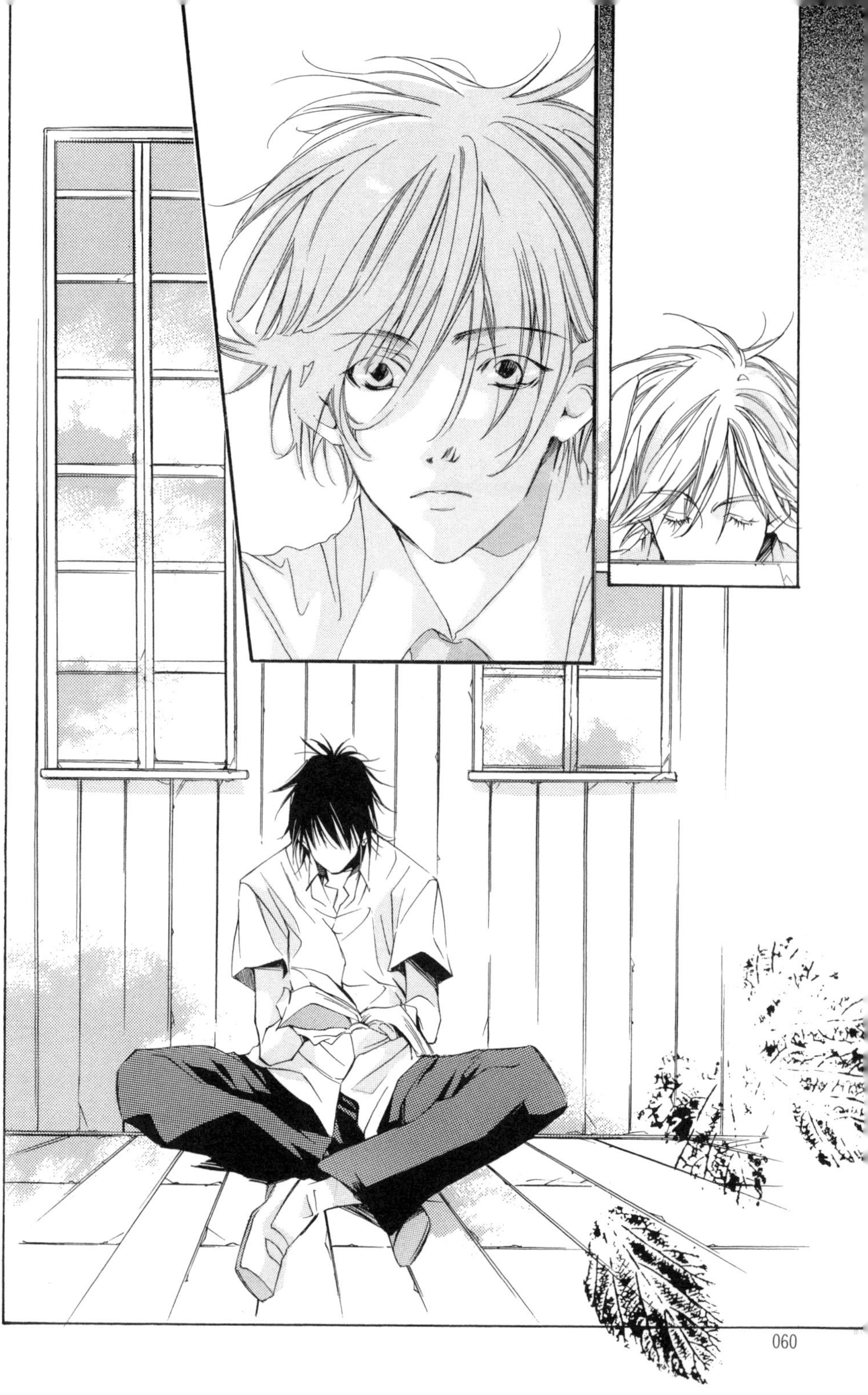

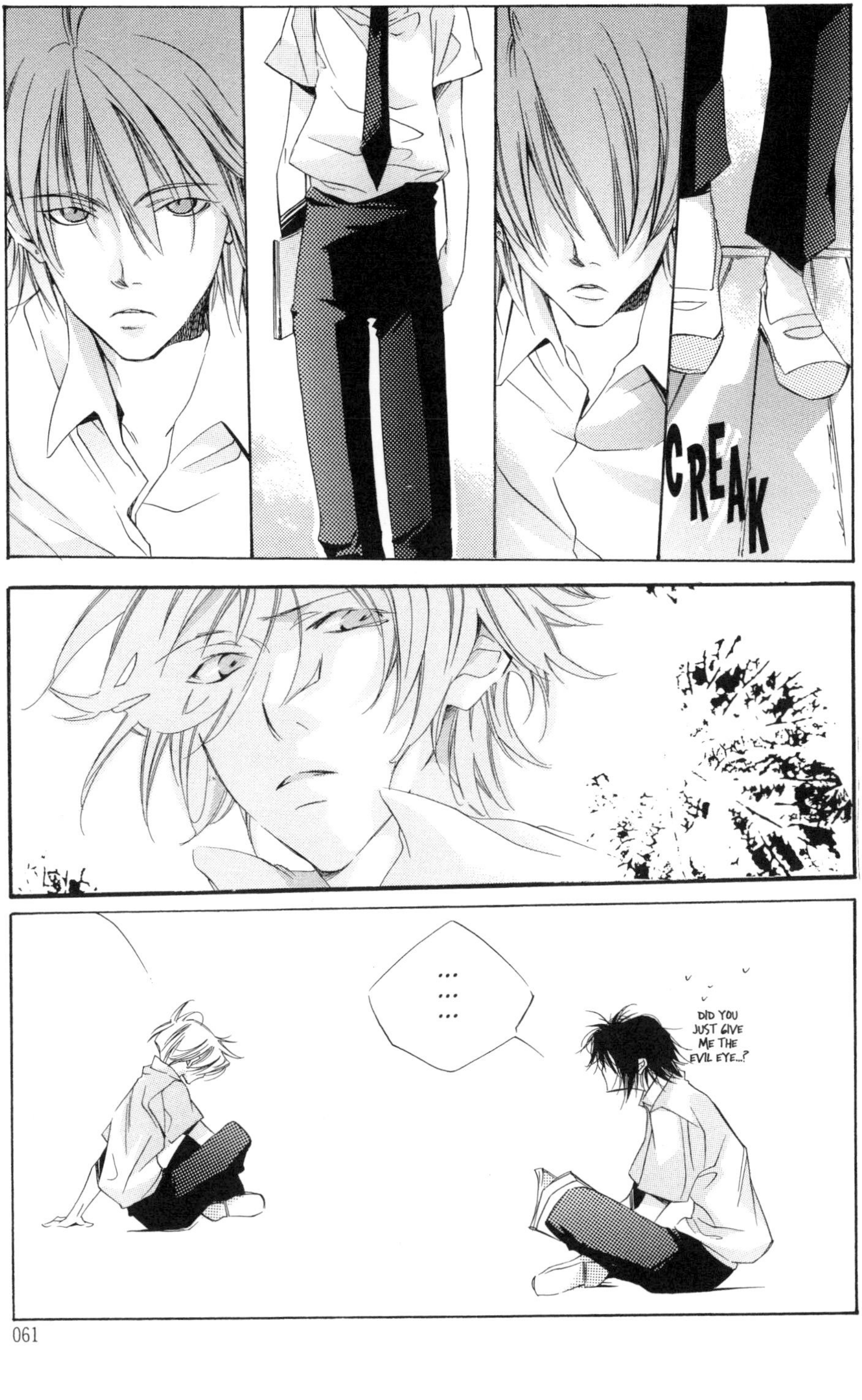
CREAK
DID YOU JUST GIVE ME THE EVIL EYE...?
...
...
...

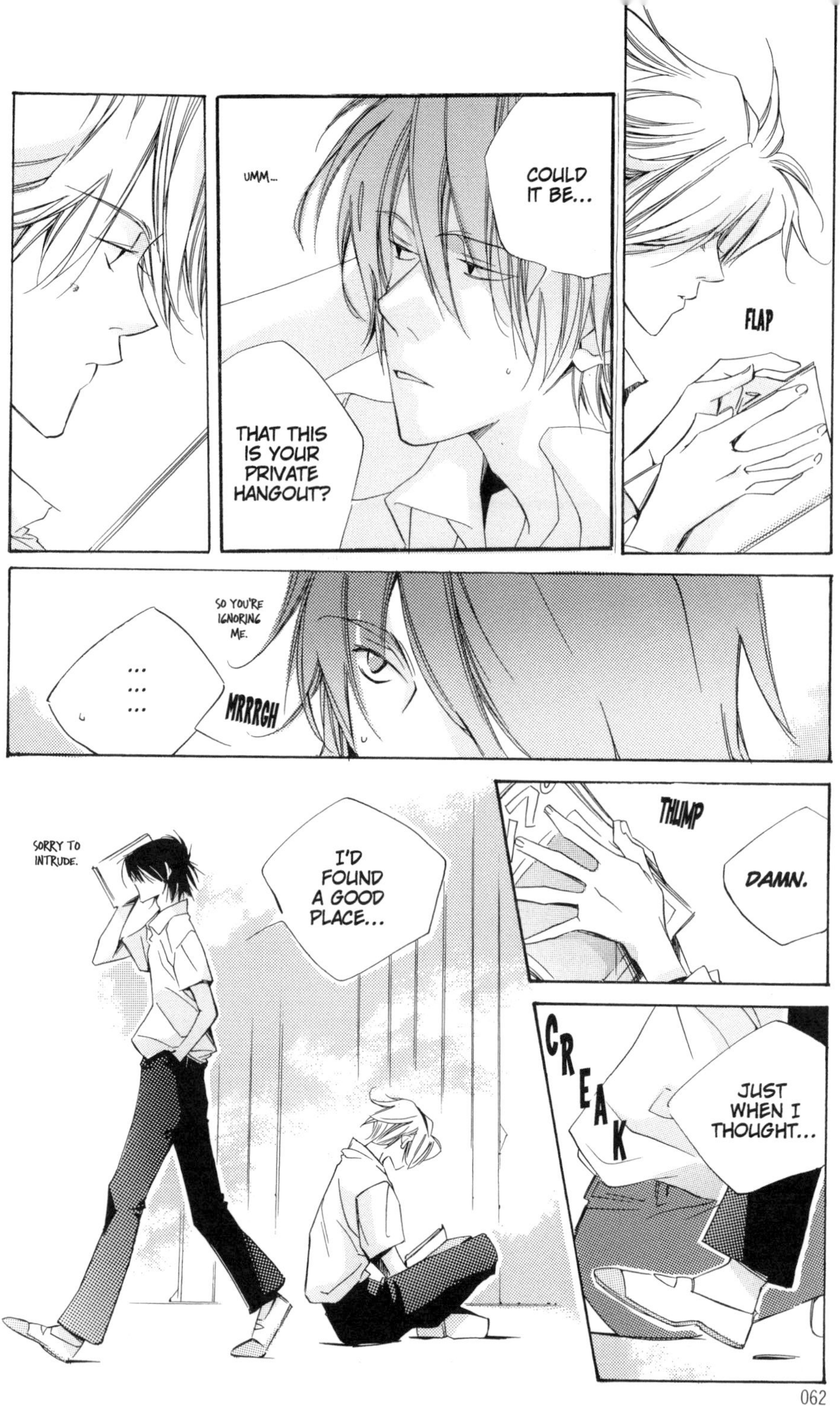
FLAP
COULD IT BE...
UMM...
THAT THIS IS YOUR PRIVATE HANGOUT?
SO YOU'RE IGNORING ME.
...
...
...
MRRRGH
THUMP
DAMN.
CREAK
JUST WHEN I THOUGHT...
I'D FOUND A GOOD PLACE...
SORRY TO INTRUDE.

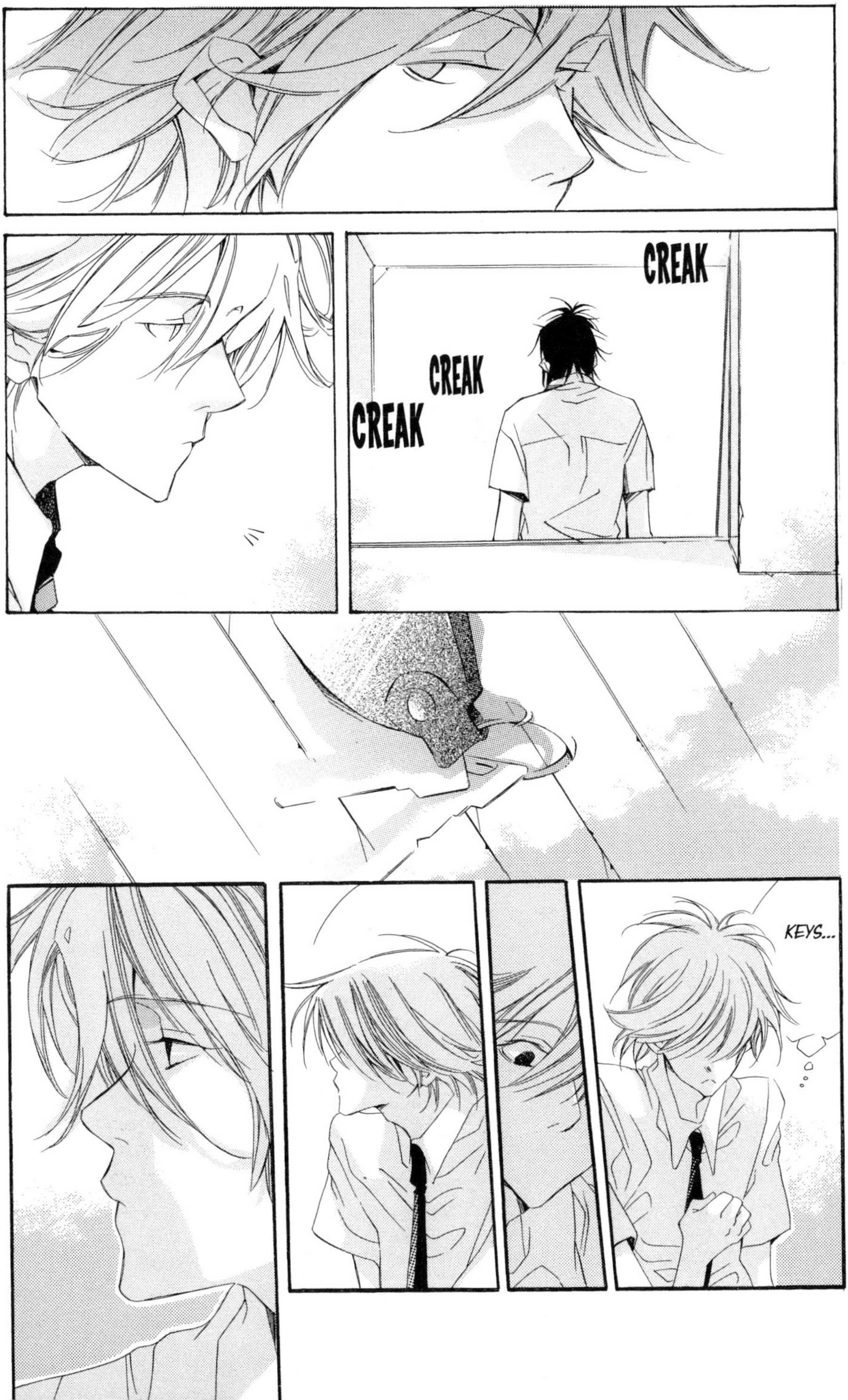
CREAK
CREAK
CREAK
KEYS...

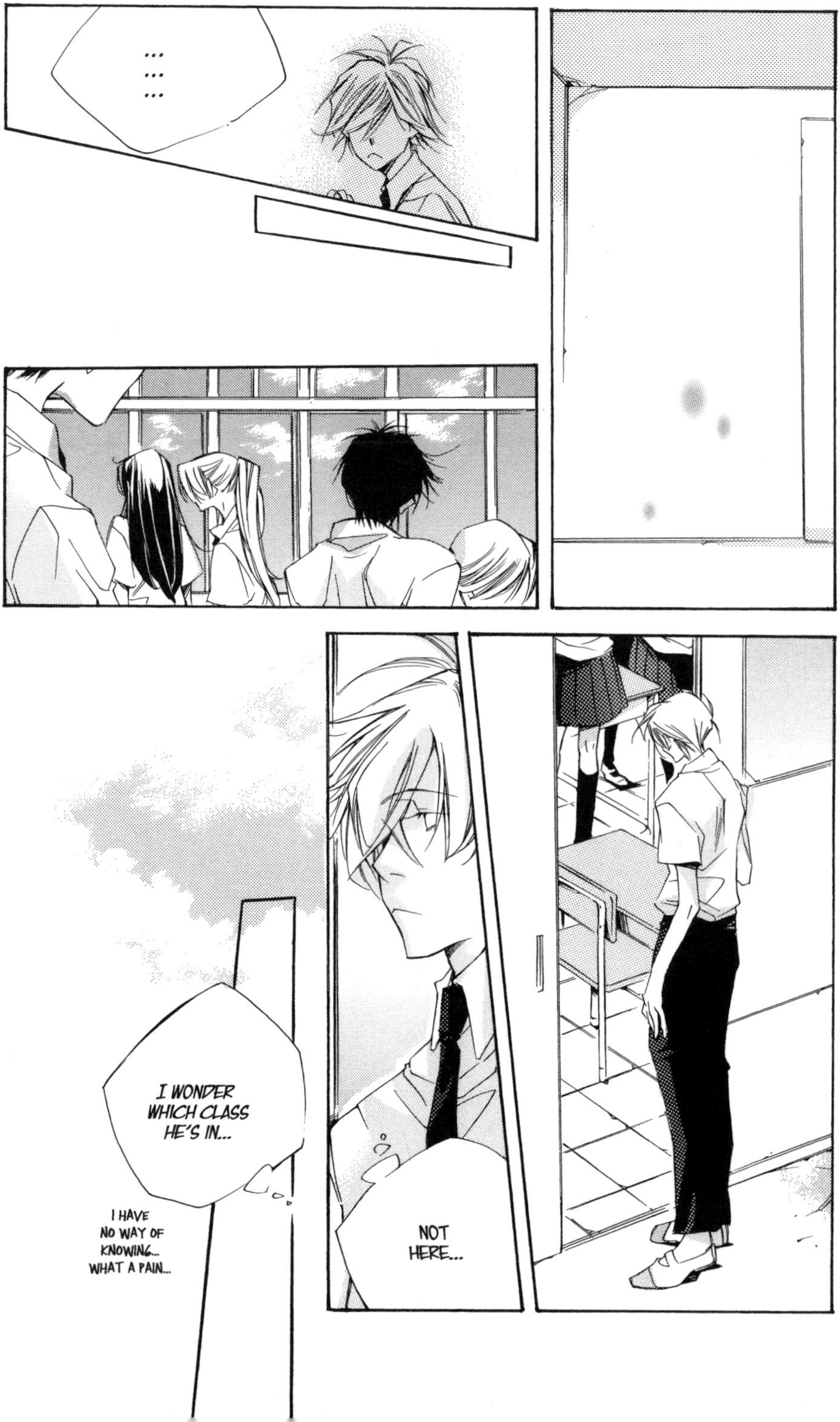
...
...
...
NOT HERE...
I WONDER WHICH CLASS HE'S IN...
I HAVE NO WAY OF KNOWING... WHAT A PAIN...

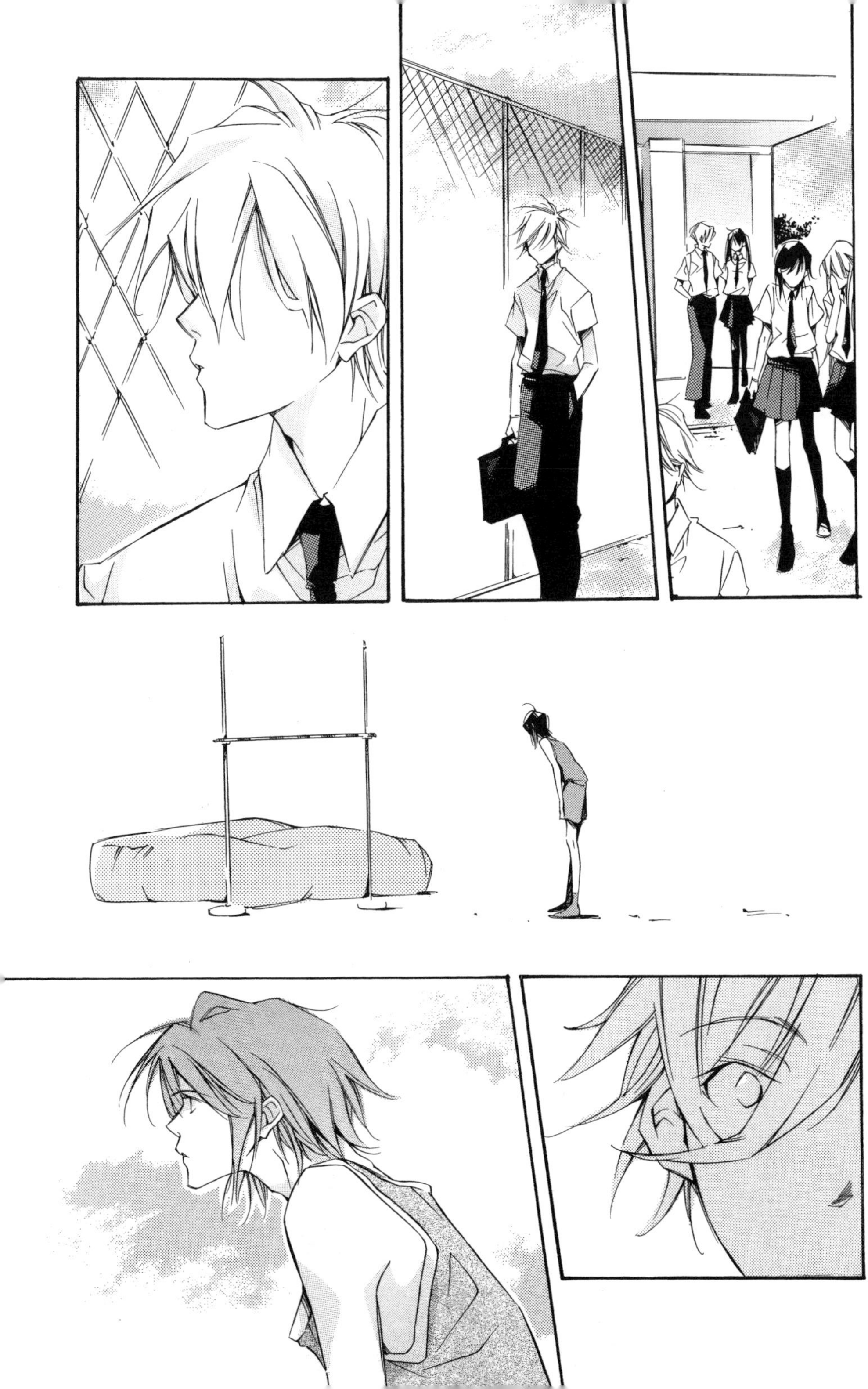

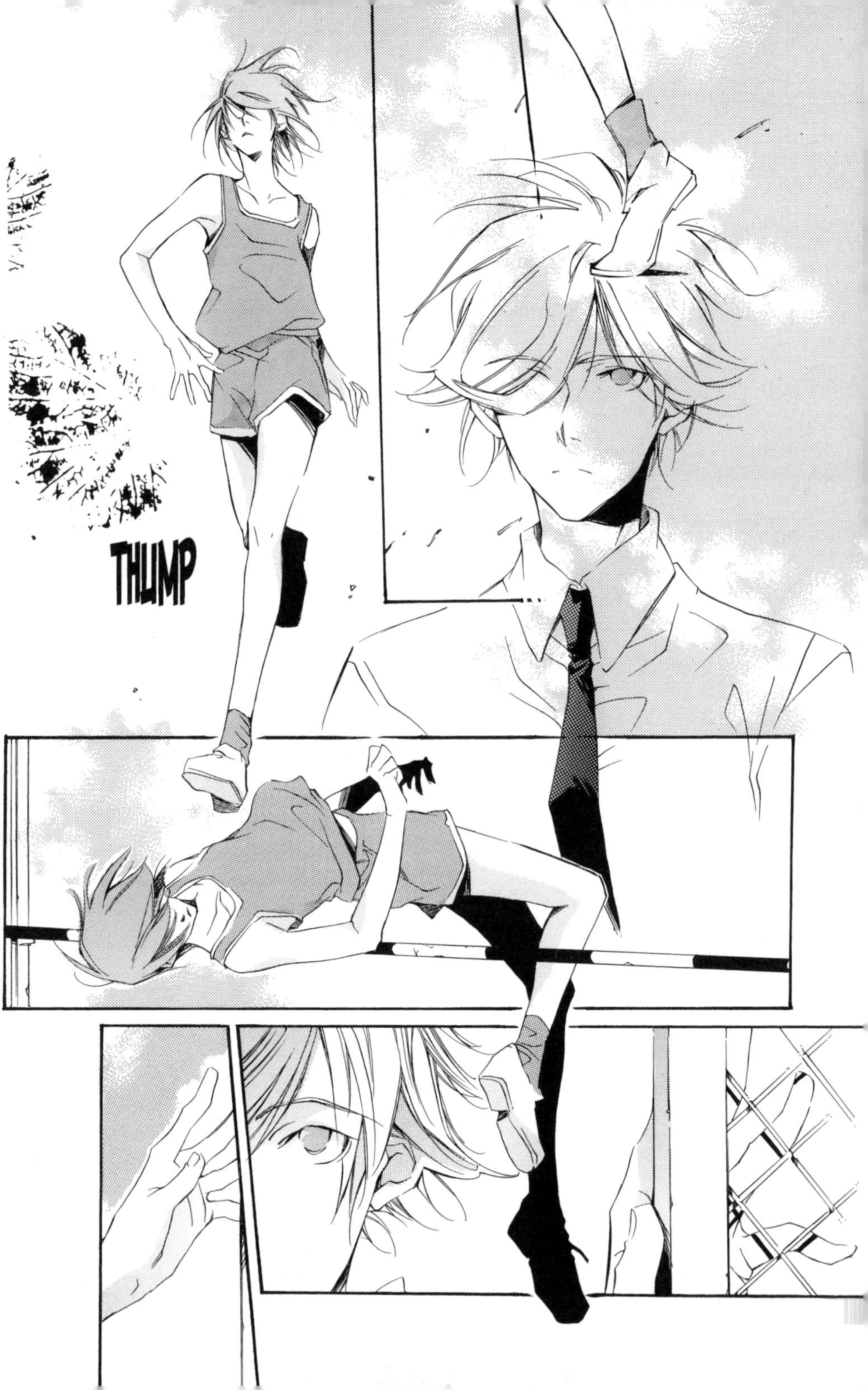
THUMP

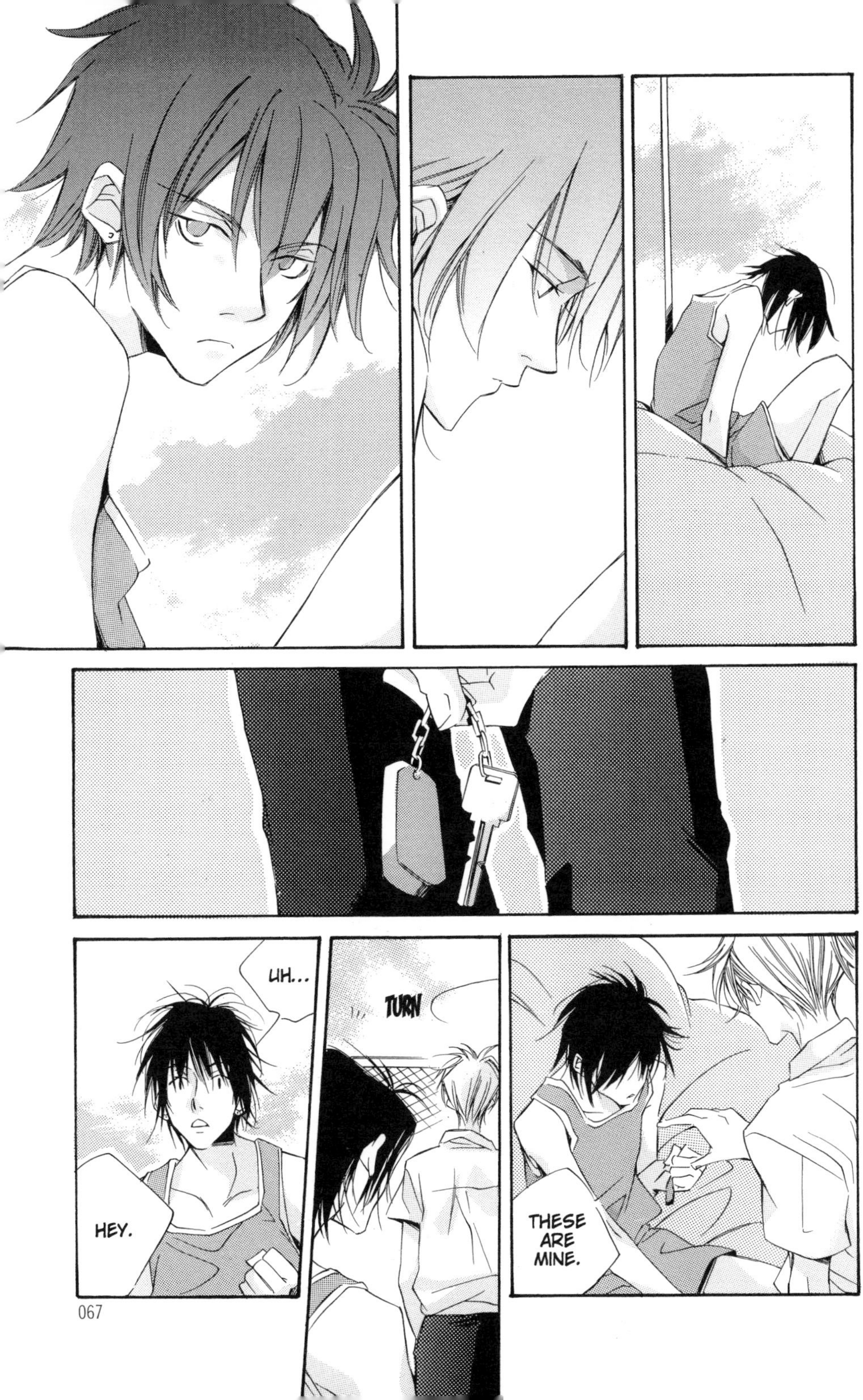
THESE ARE MINE.
TURN
UH...
HEY.

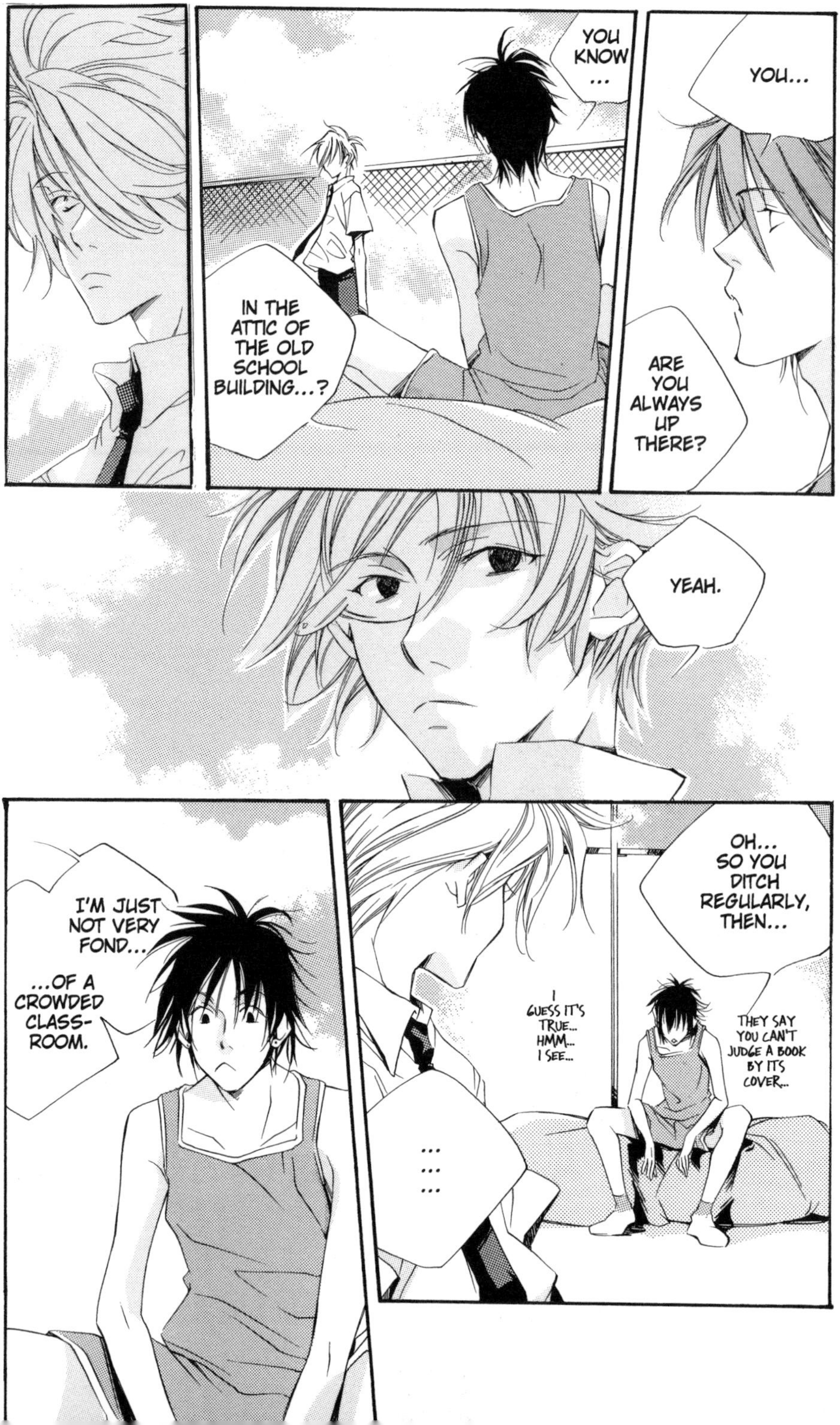
YOU...
ARE YOU ALWAYS UP THERE?
YOU KNOW ...
IN THE ATTIC OF THE OLD SCHOOL BUILDING...?
YEAH.
OH... SO YOU DITCH REGULARLY, THEN...
THEY SAY YOU CAN'T JUDGE A BOOK BY ITS COVER...
I GUESS IT'S TRUE... HMM... I SEE...
... ...
I'M JUST NOT VERY FOND...
...OF A CROWDED CLASS-ROOM.

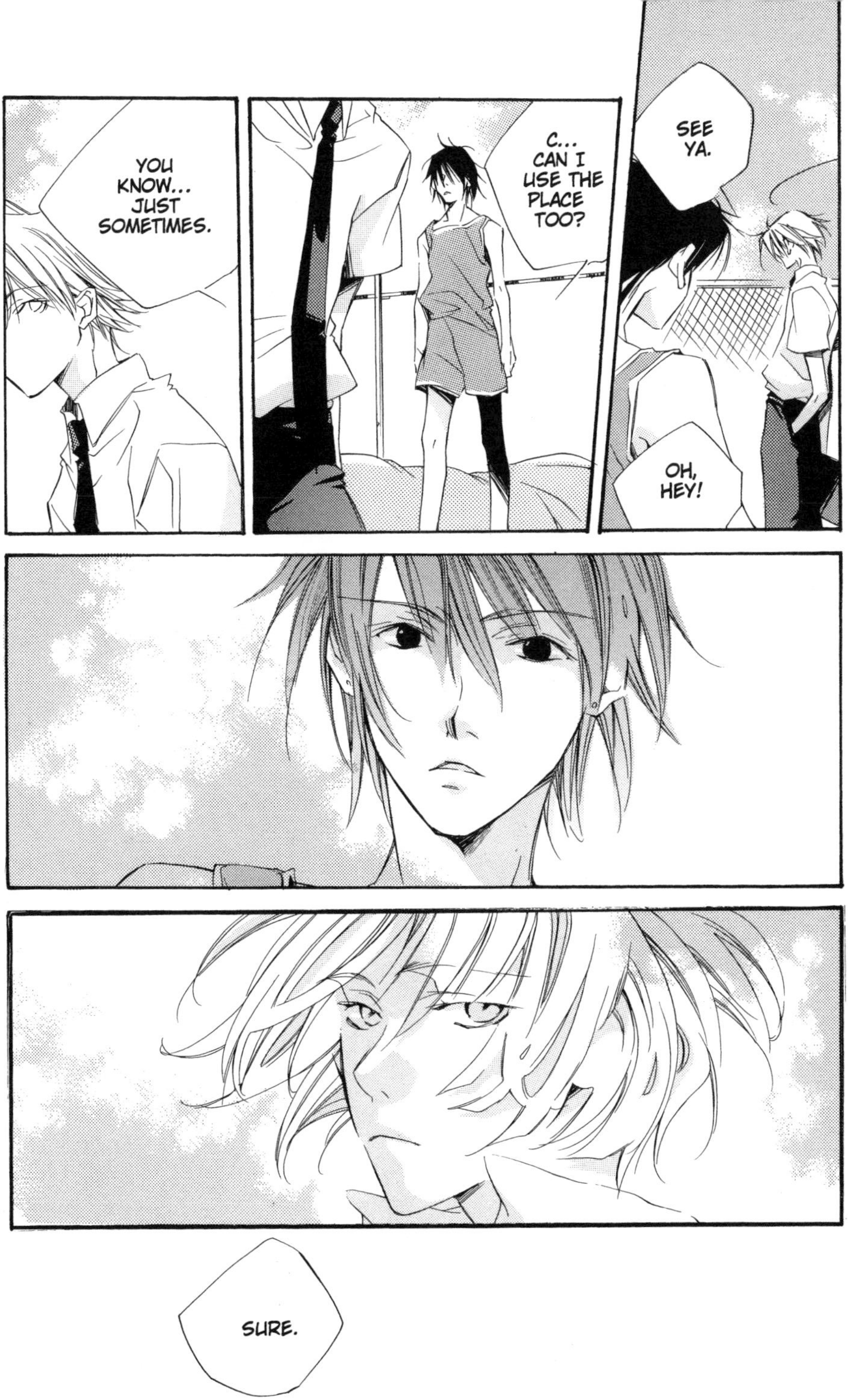
SEE YA.
OH, HEY!
C... CAN I USE THE PLACE TOO?
YOU KNOW... JUST SOMETIMES.
SURE.

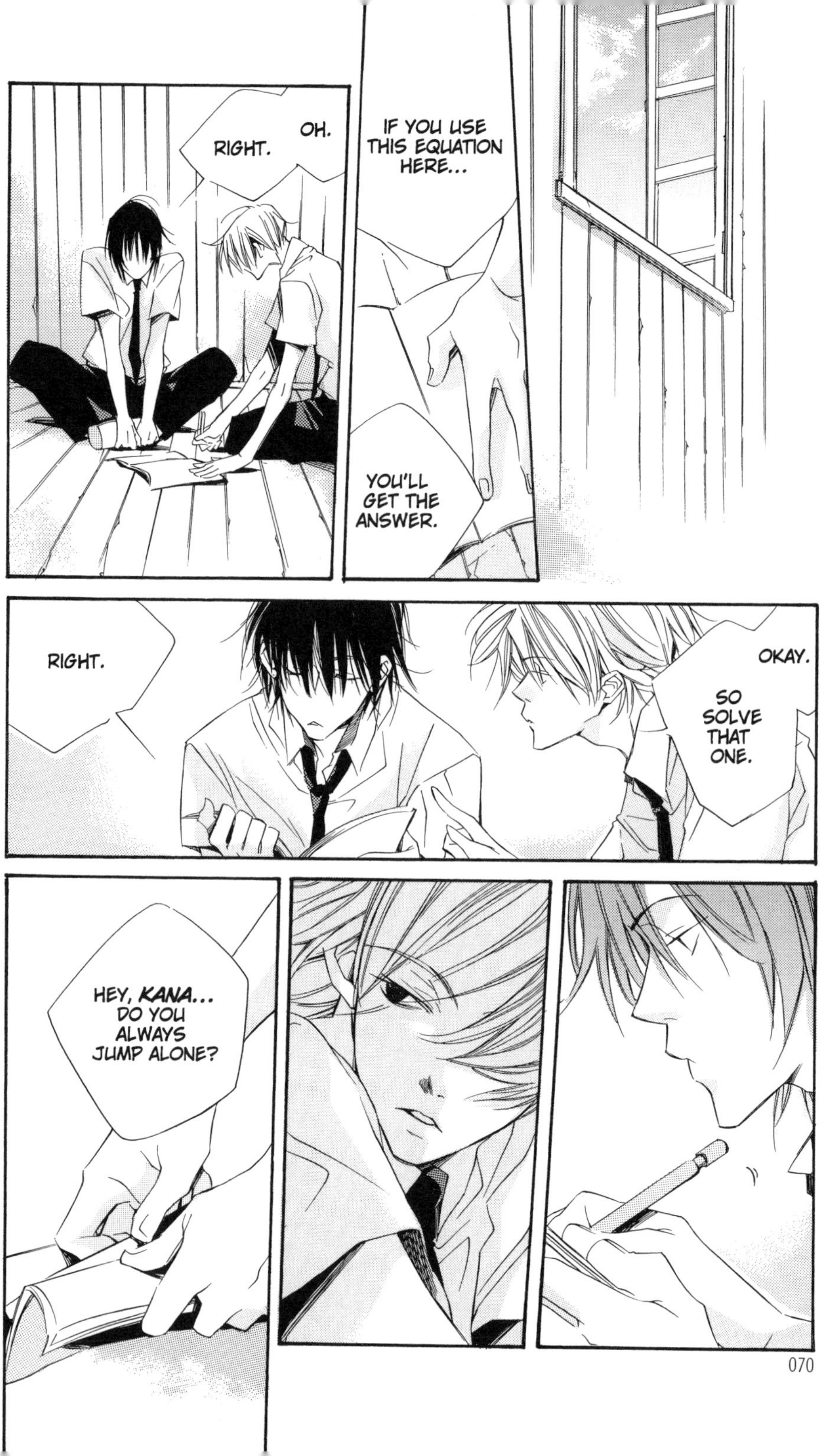
IF YOU USE THIS EQUATION HERE...
YOU'LL GET THE ANSWER.
OH. RIGHT.
OKAY.
SO SOLVE THAT ONE.
RIGHT.
HEY, *KANA*... DO YOU ALWAYS JUMP ALONE?

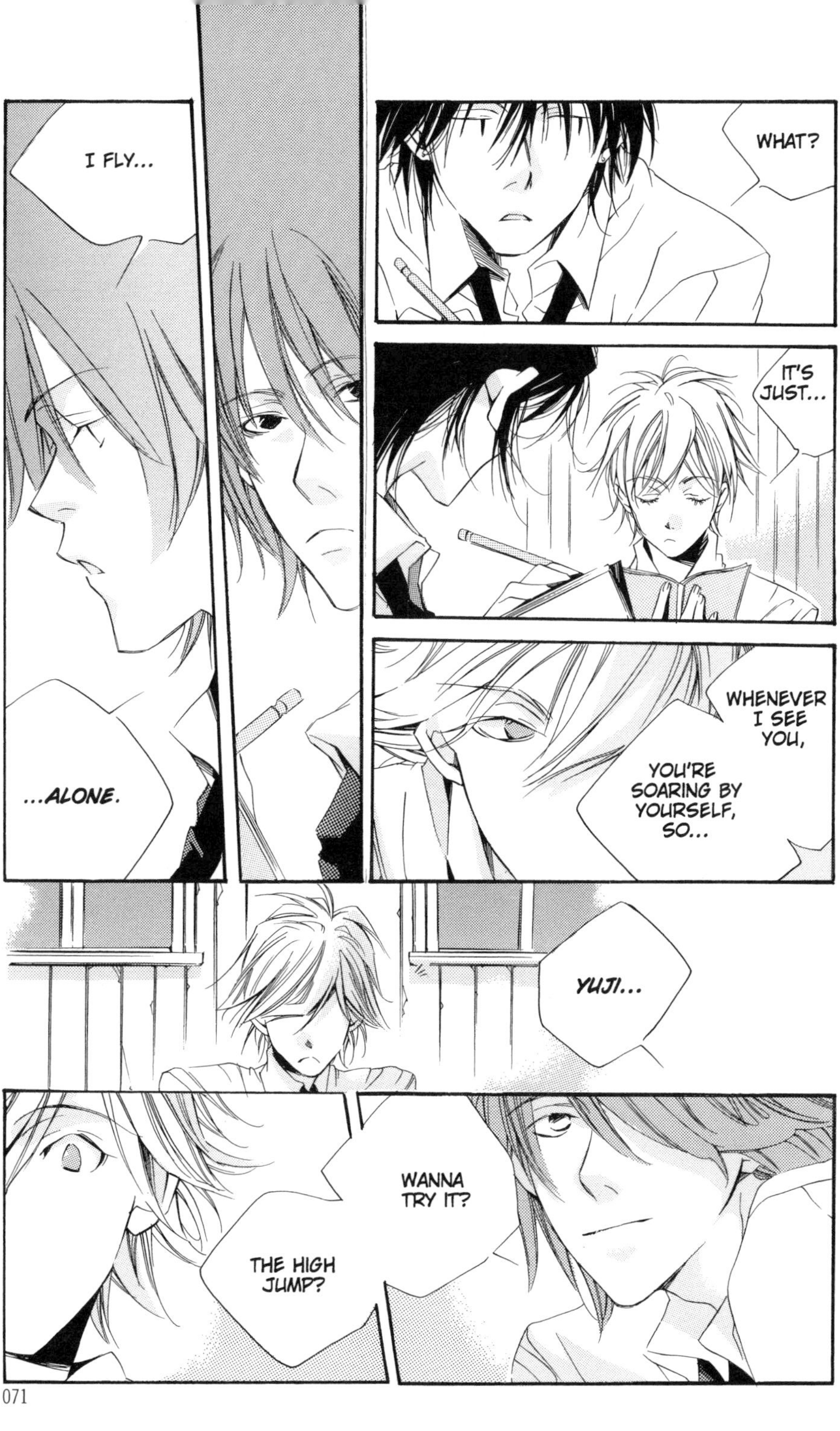
WHAT?
IT'S JUST...
WHENEVER I SEE YOU,
YOU'RE SOARING BY YOURSELF, SO...
I FLY...
...ALONE.
YUJI...
WANNA TRY IT?
THE HIGH JUMP?

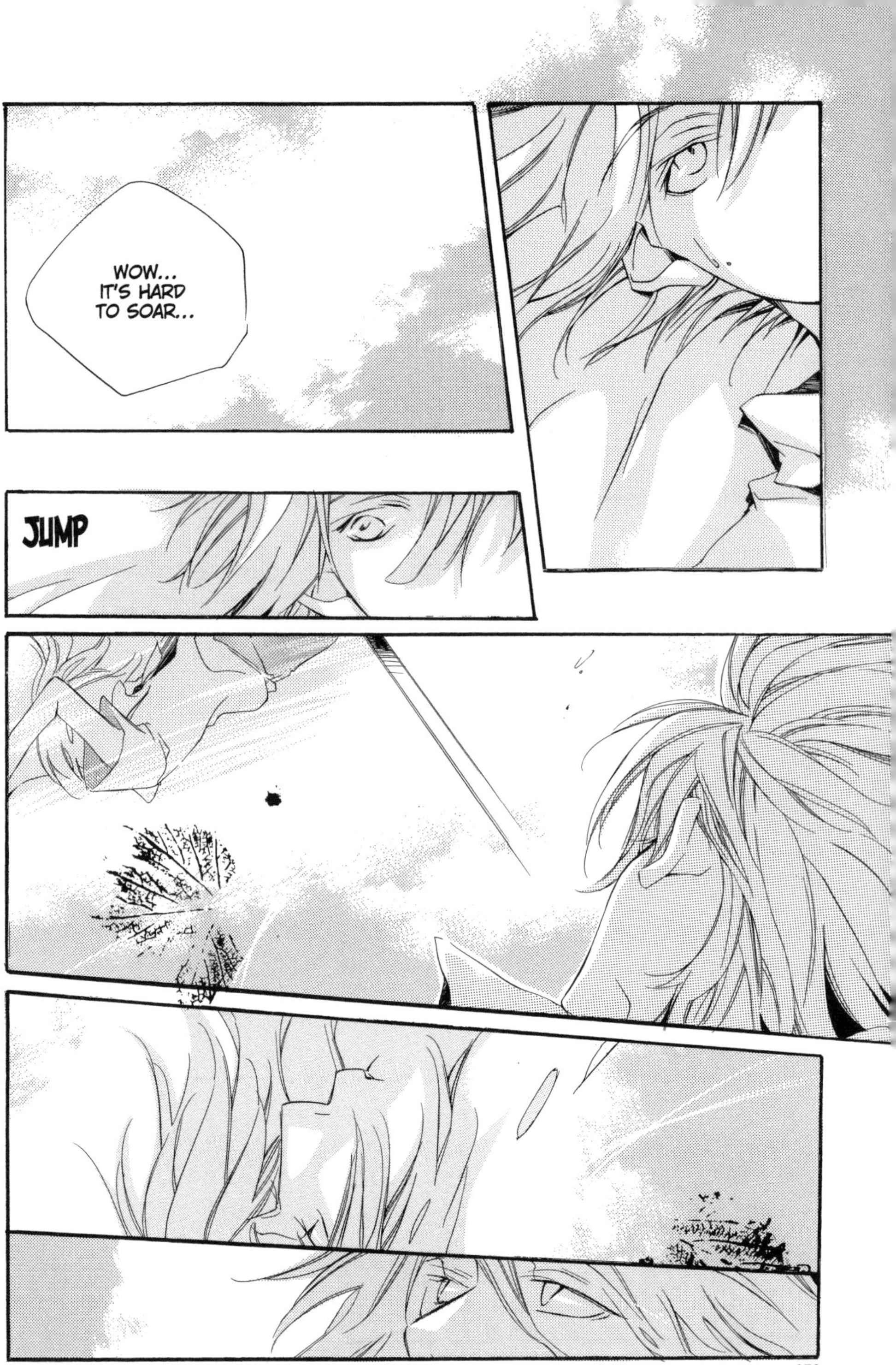
WOW...
IT'S HARD
TO SOAR...
JUMP

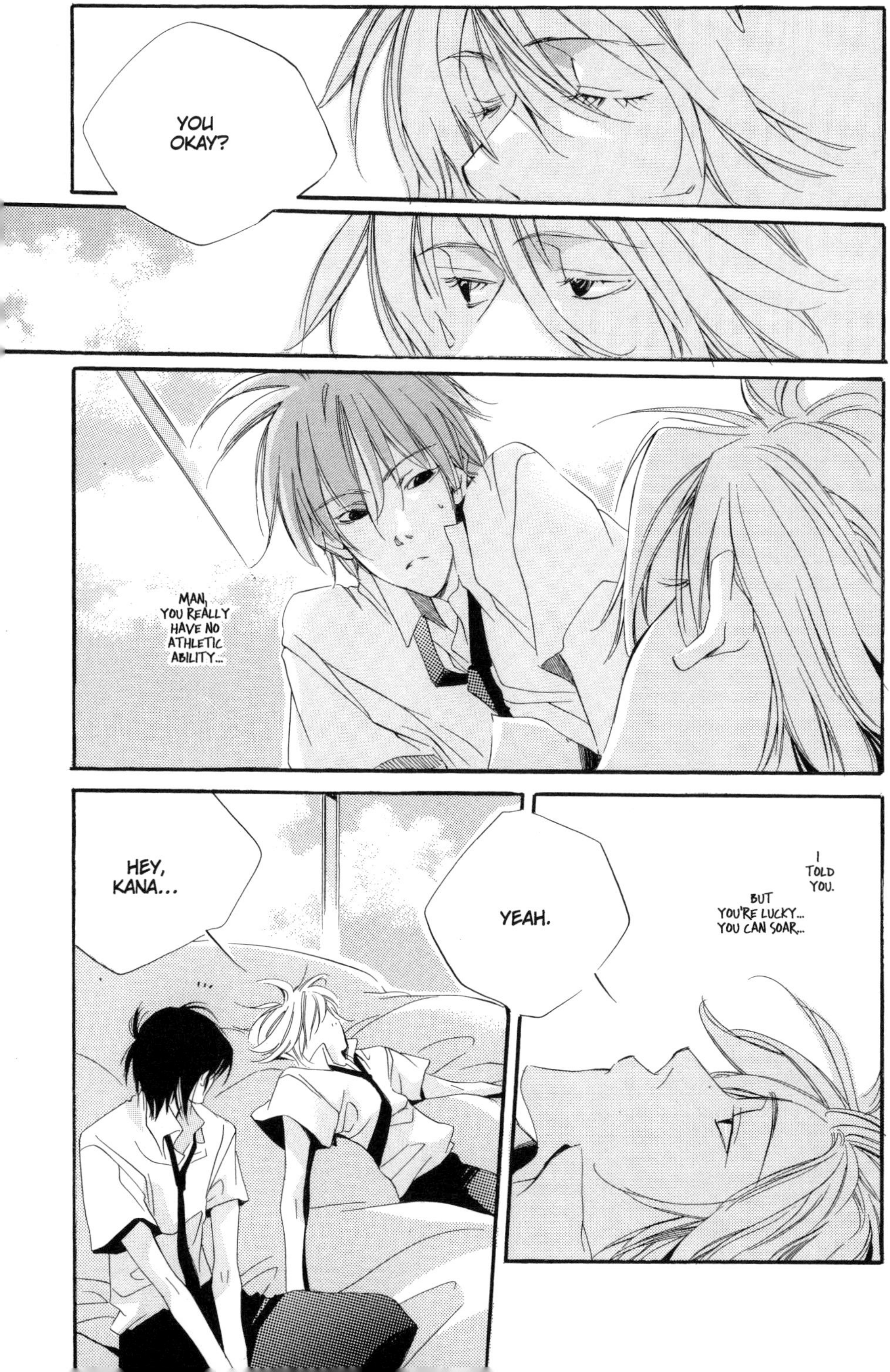
YOU OKAY?
MAN, YOU REALLY HAVE NO ATHLETIC ABILITY...
I TOLD YOU.
BUT YOU'RE LUCKY... YOU CAN SOAR...
YEAH.
HEY, KANA...
...

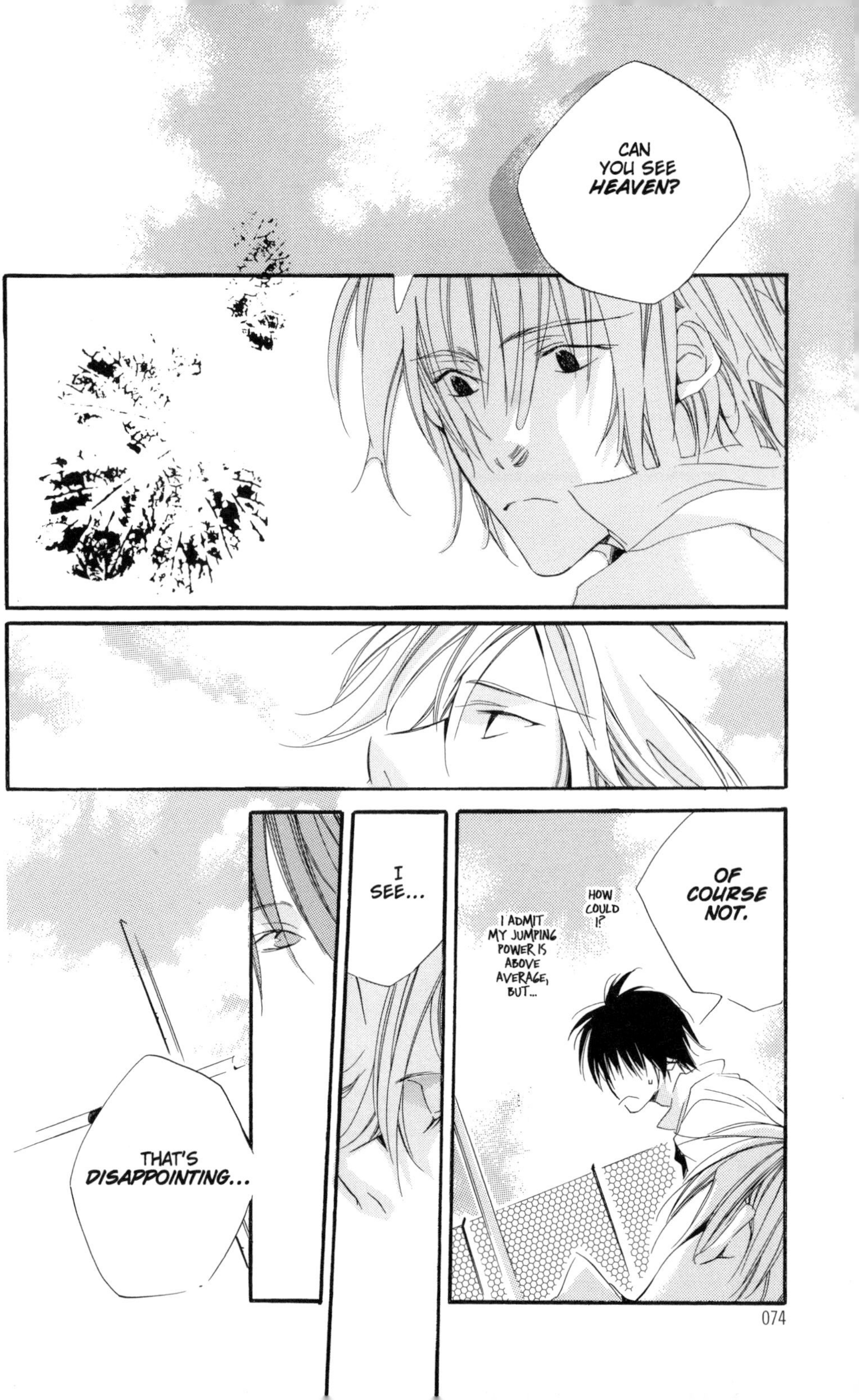
CAN YOU SEE HEAVEN?
OF COURSE NOT.
HOW COULD I?
I ADMIT MY JUMPING POWER IS ABOVE AVERAGE, BUT...
I SEE...
THAT'S DISAPPOINTING...

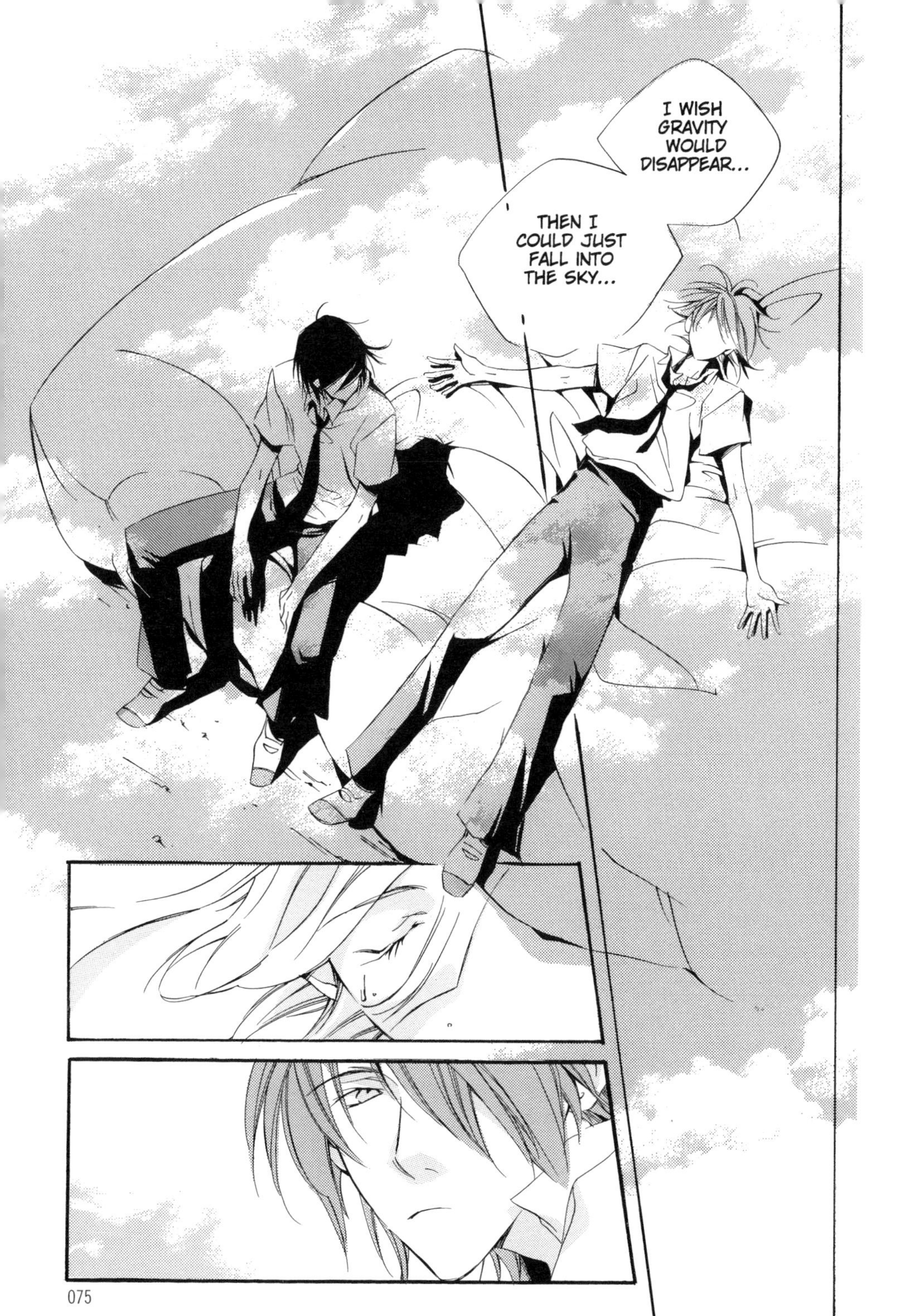
I WISH GRAVITY WOULD DISAPPEAR...
THEN I COULD JUST FALL INTO THE SKY...

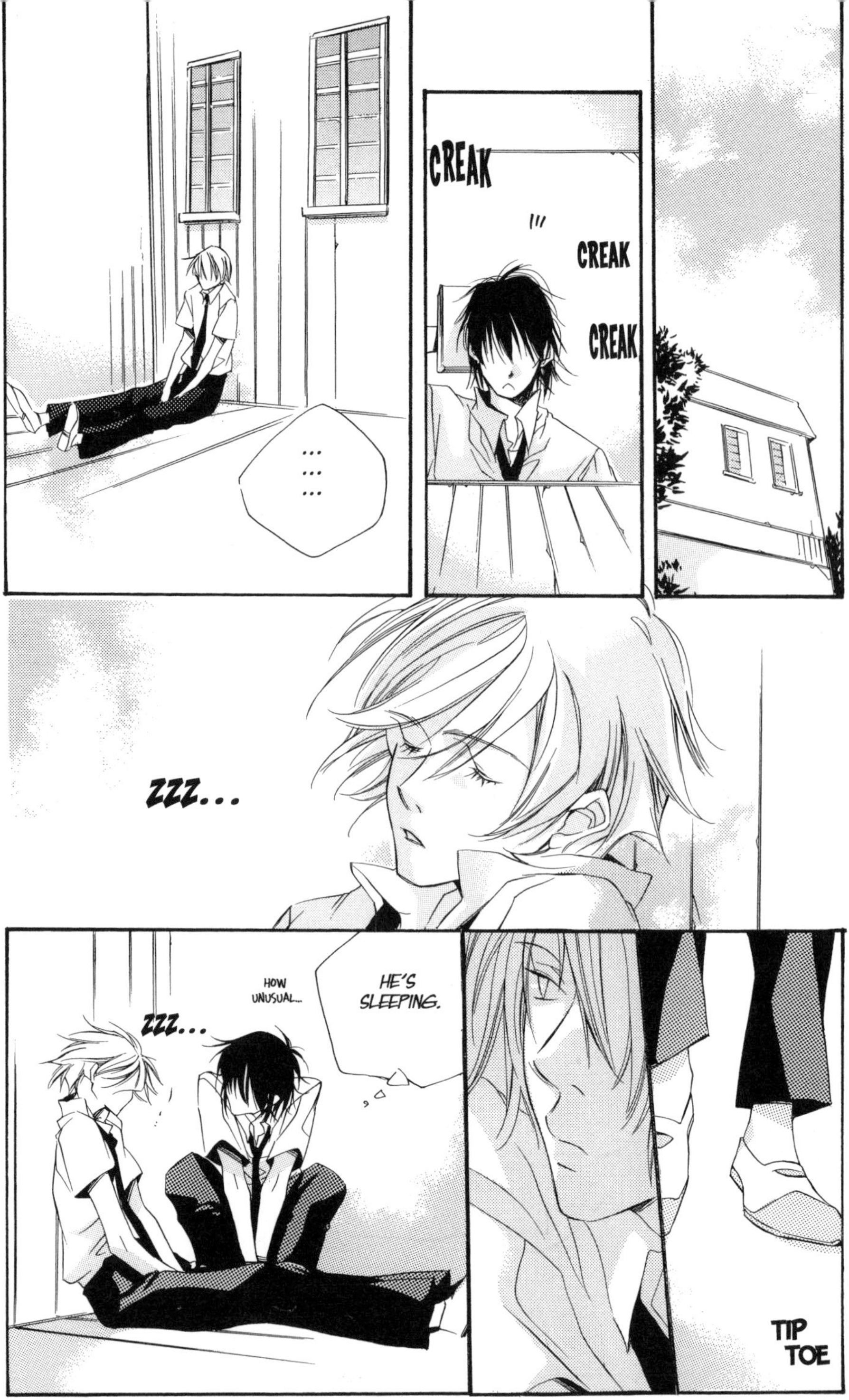
CREAK
CREAK
CREAK
...
...
...
ZZZ...
TIP TOE
HE'S SLEEPING.
HOW UNUSUAL...
ZZZ...

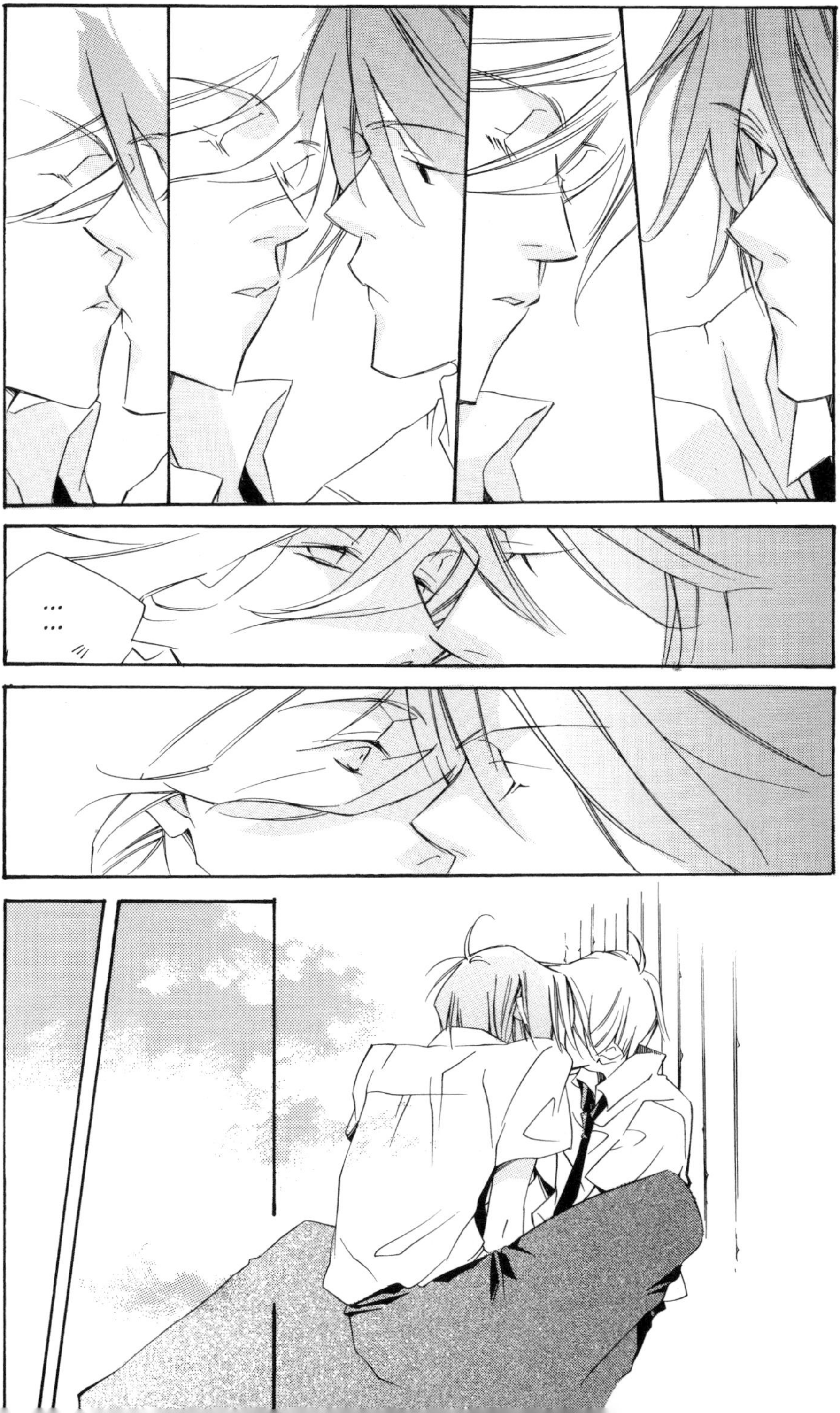
...
...

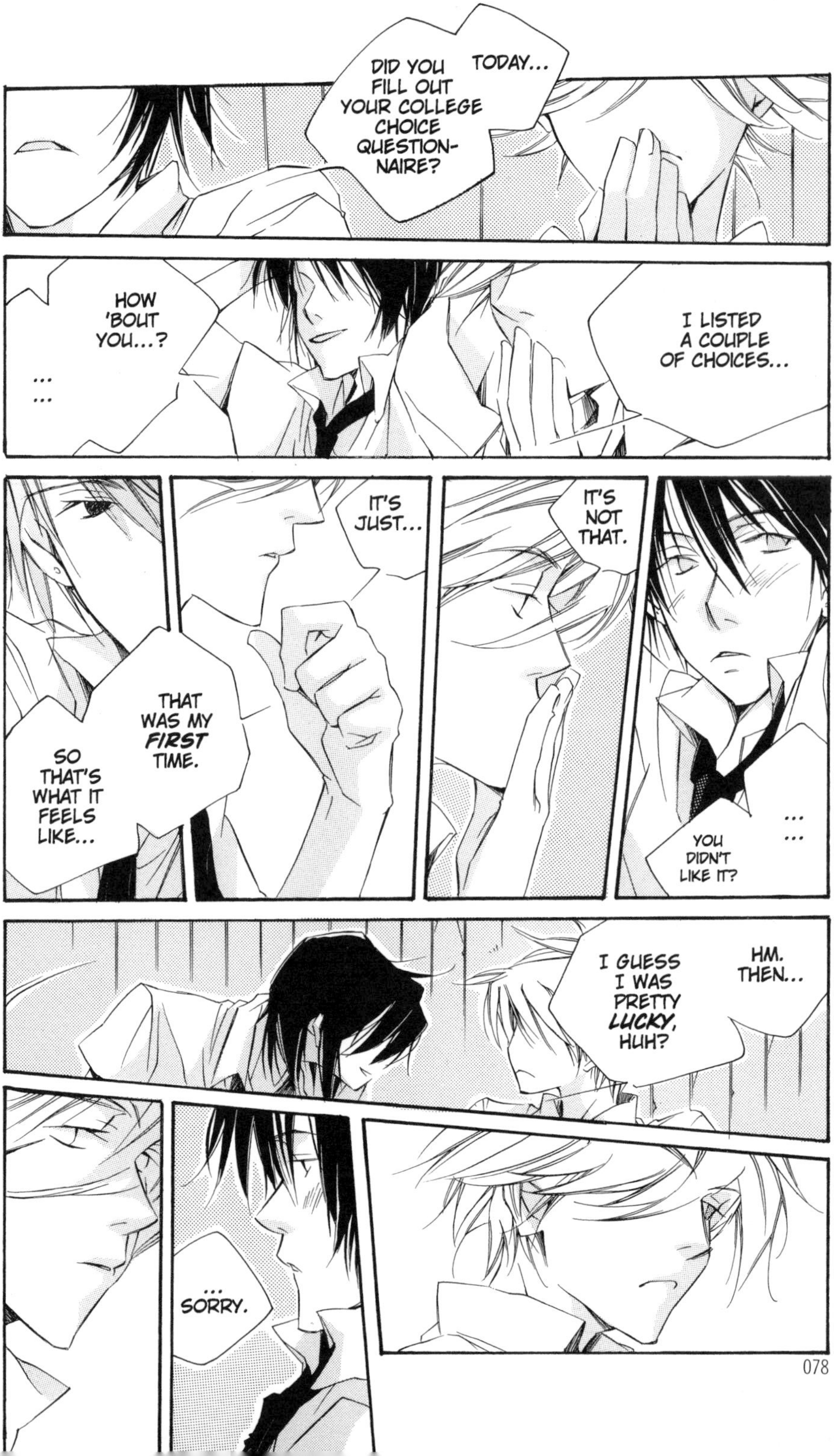
TODAY...
DID YOU FILL OUT YOUR COLLEGE CHOICE QUESTION-NAIRE?
I LISTED A COUPLE OF CHOICES...
HOW 'BOUT YOU...?
... ...
... ...
YOU DIDN'T LIKE IT?
IT'S NOT THAT.
IT'S JUST...
THAT WAS MY *FIRST* TIME.
SO THAT'S WHAT IT FEELS LIKE...
HM. THEN...
I GUESS I WAS PRETTY *LUCKY*, HUH?
... SORRY.

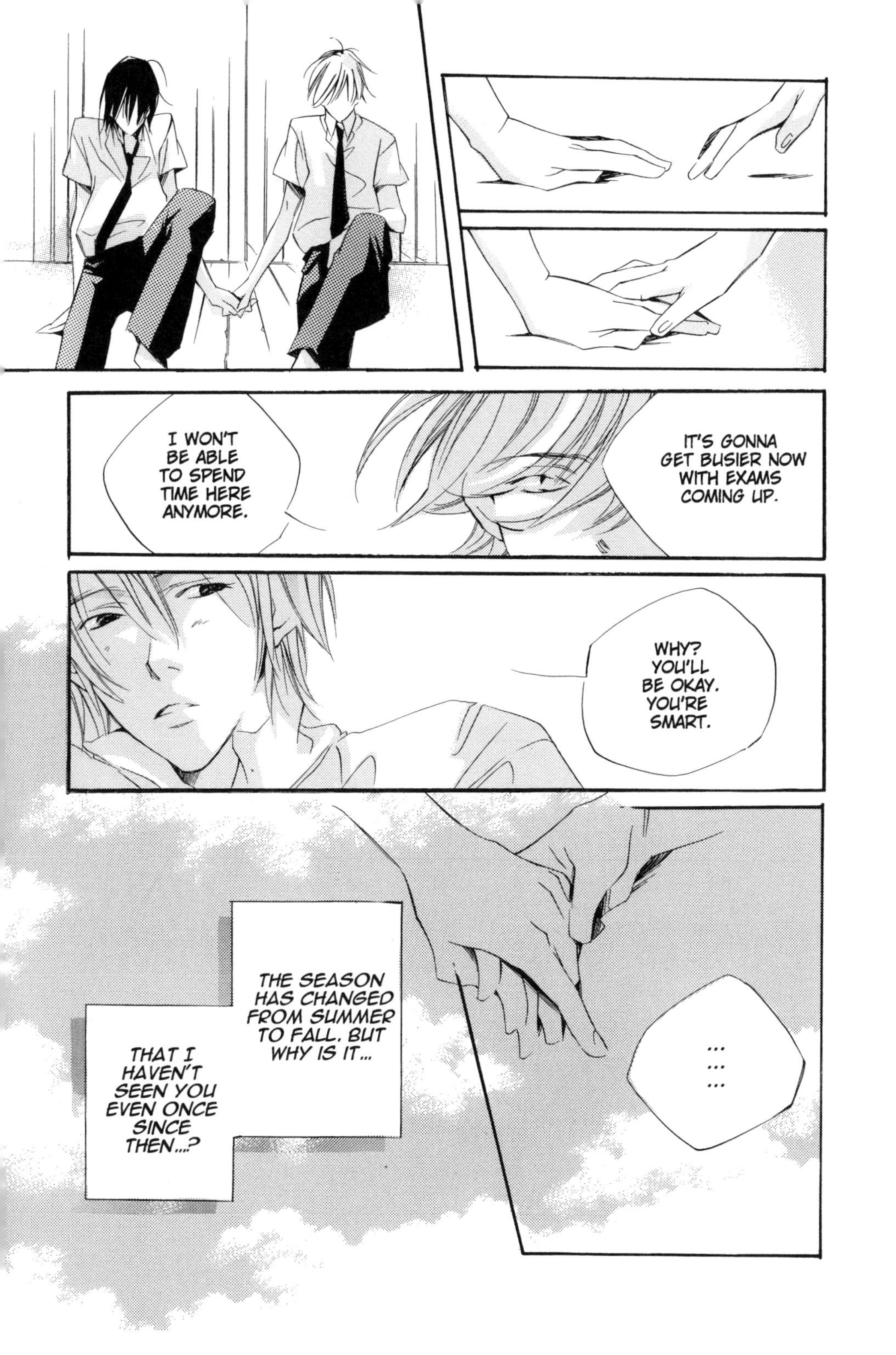

IT'S GONNA GET BUSIER NOW WITH EXAMS COMING UP.
I WON'T BE ABLE TO SPEND TIME HERE ANYMORE.
WHY? YOU'LL BE OKAY. YOU'RE SMART.
... ...
THE SEASON HAS CHANGED FROM SUMMER TO FALL. BUT WHY IS IT...
THAT I HAVEN'T SEEN YOU EVEN ONCE SINCE THEN...?

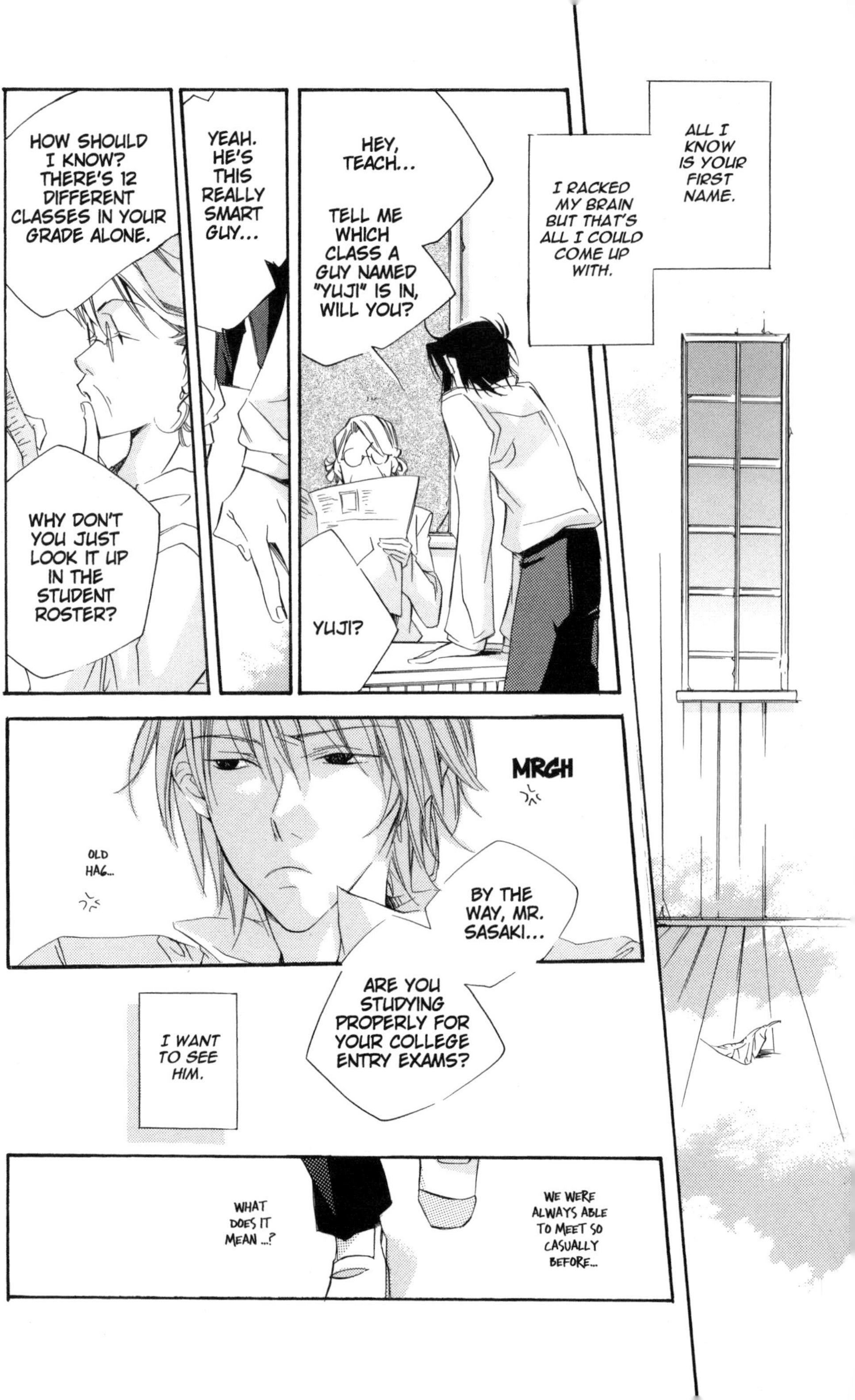
ALL I KNOW IS YOUR FIRST NAME.
I RACKED MY BRAIN BUT THAT'S ALL I COULD COME UP WITH.
HEY, TEACH...
TELL ME WHICH CLASS A GUY NAMED "YUJI" IS IN, WILL YOU?
YUJI?
YEAH. HE'S THIS REALLY SMART GUY...
HOW SHOULD I KNOW? THERE'S 12 DIFFERENT CLASSES IN YOUR GRADE ALONE.
WHY DON'T YOU JUST LOOK IT UP IN THE STUDENT ROSTER?
MRGH
BY THE WAY, MR. SASAKI...
ARE YOU STUDYING PROPERLY FOR YOUR COLLEGE ENTRY EXAMS?
OLD HAG...
I WANT TO SEE HIM.
WE WERE ALWAYS ABLE TO MEET SO CASUALLY BEFORE...
WHAT DOES IT MEAN ...?

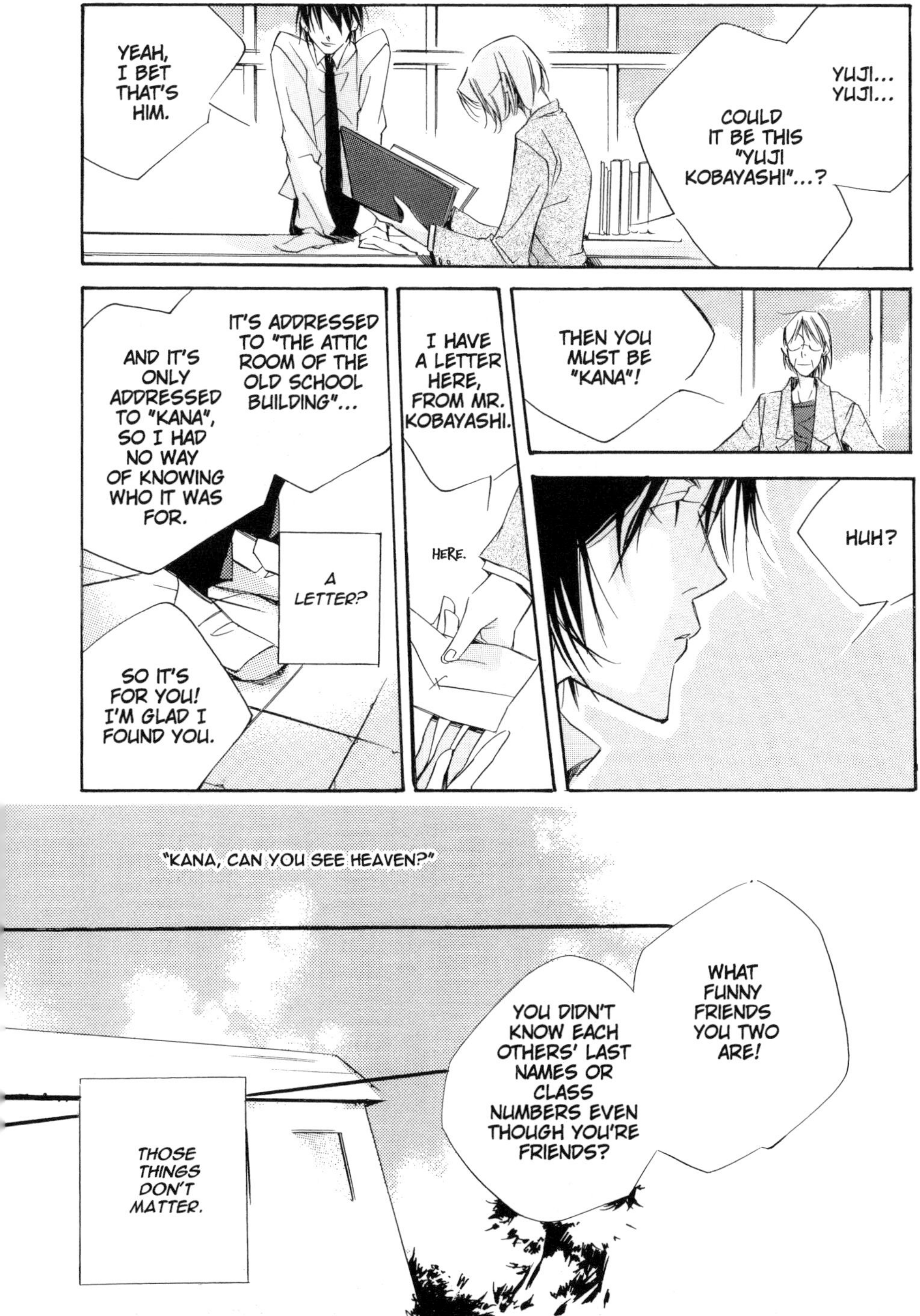
YUJI... YUJI...
COULD IT BE THIS "YUJI KOBAYASHI"...?
YEAH, I BET THAT'S HIM.
THEN YOU MUST BE "KANA"!
HUH?
I HAVE A LETTER HERE, FROM MR. KOBAYASHI.
HERE.
IT'S ADDRESSED TO "THE ATTIC ROOM OF THE OLD SCHOOL BUILDING"...
AND IT'S ONLY ADDRESSED TO "KANA", SO I HAD NO WAY OF KNOWING WHO IT WAS FOR.
A LETTER?
SO IT'S FOR YOU! I'M GLAD I FOUND YOU.
"KANA, CAN YOU SEE HEAVEN?"
WHAT FUNNY FRIENDS YOU TWO ARE!
YOU DIDN'T KNOW EACH OTHERS' LAST NAMES OR CLASS NUMBERS EVEN THOUGH YOU'RE FRIENDS?
THOSE THINGS DON'T MATTER.

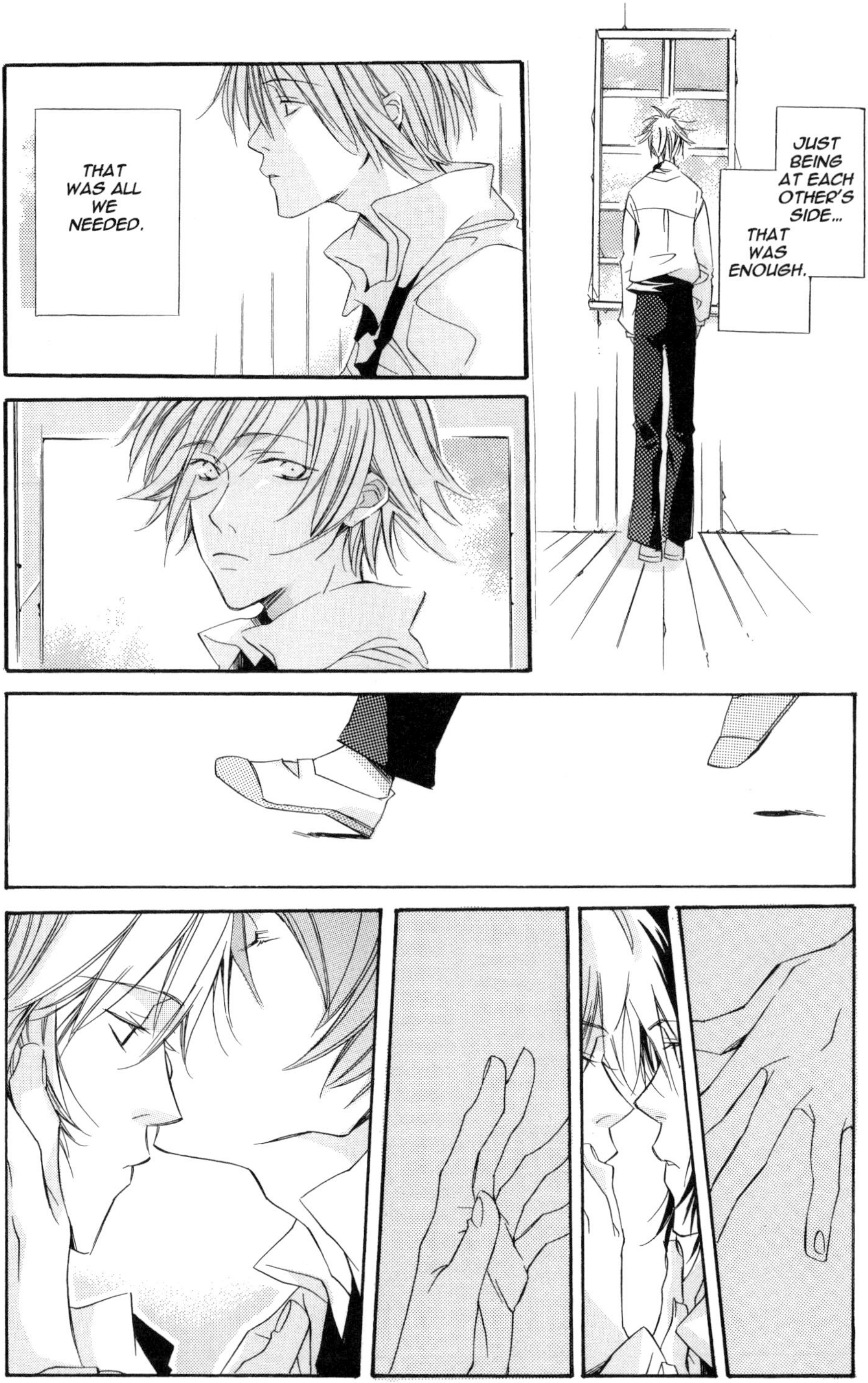
JUST BEING AT EACH OTHER'S SIDE...
THAT WAS ENOUGH.
THAT WAS ALL WE NEEDED.

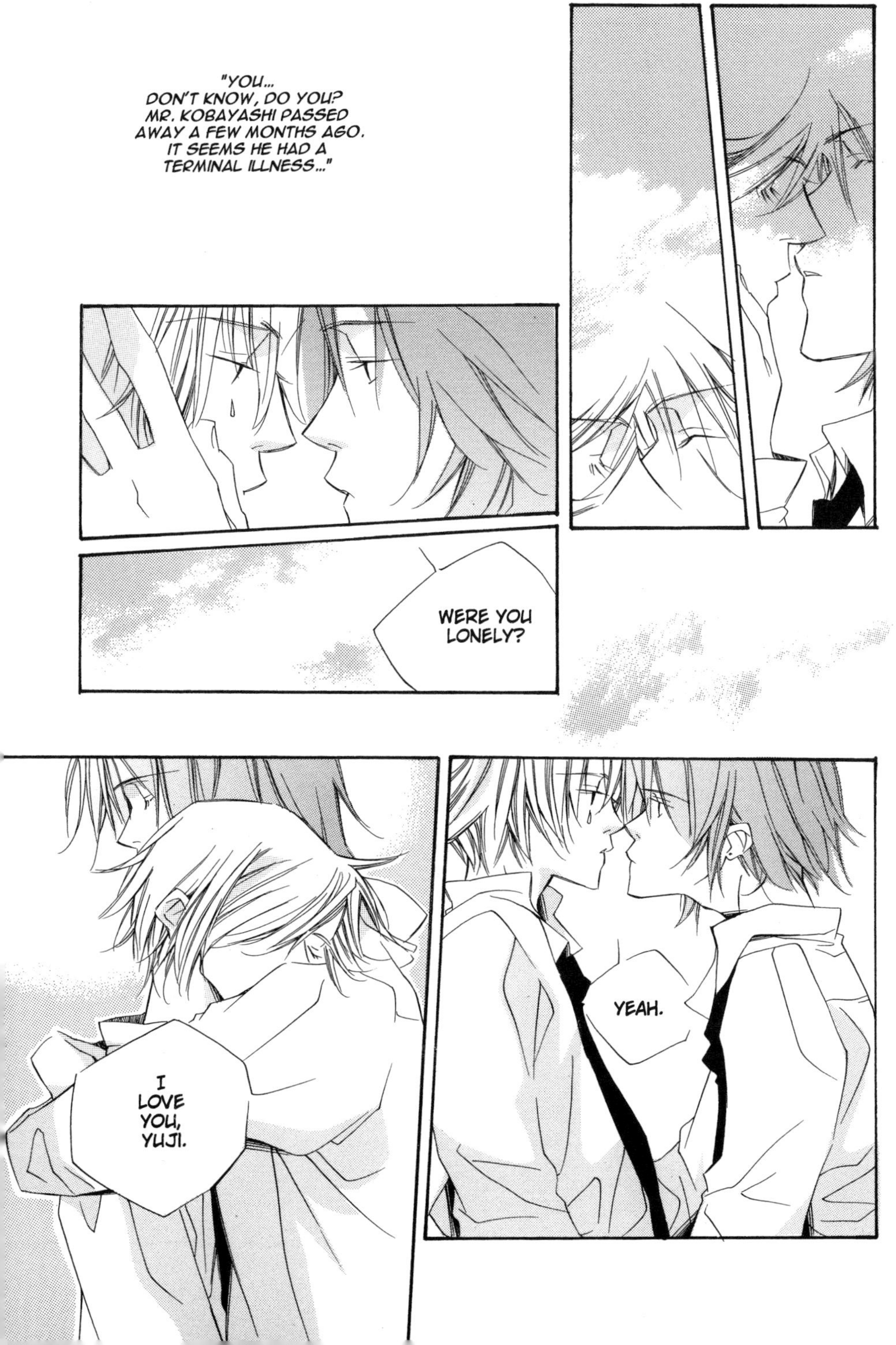
"YOU... DON'T KNOW, DO YOU? MR. KOBAYASHI PASSED AWAY A FEW MONTHS AGO. IT SEEMS HE HAD A TERMINAL ILLNESS..."
WERE YOU LONELY?
YEAH.
I LOVE YOU, YUJI.

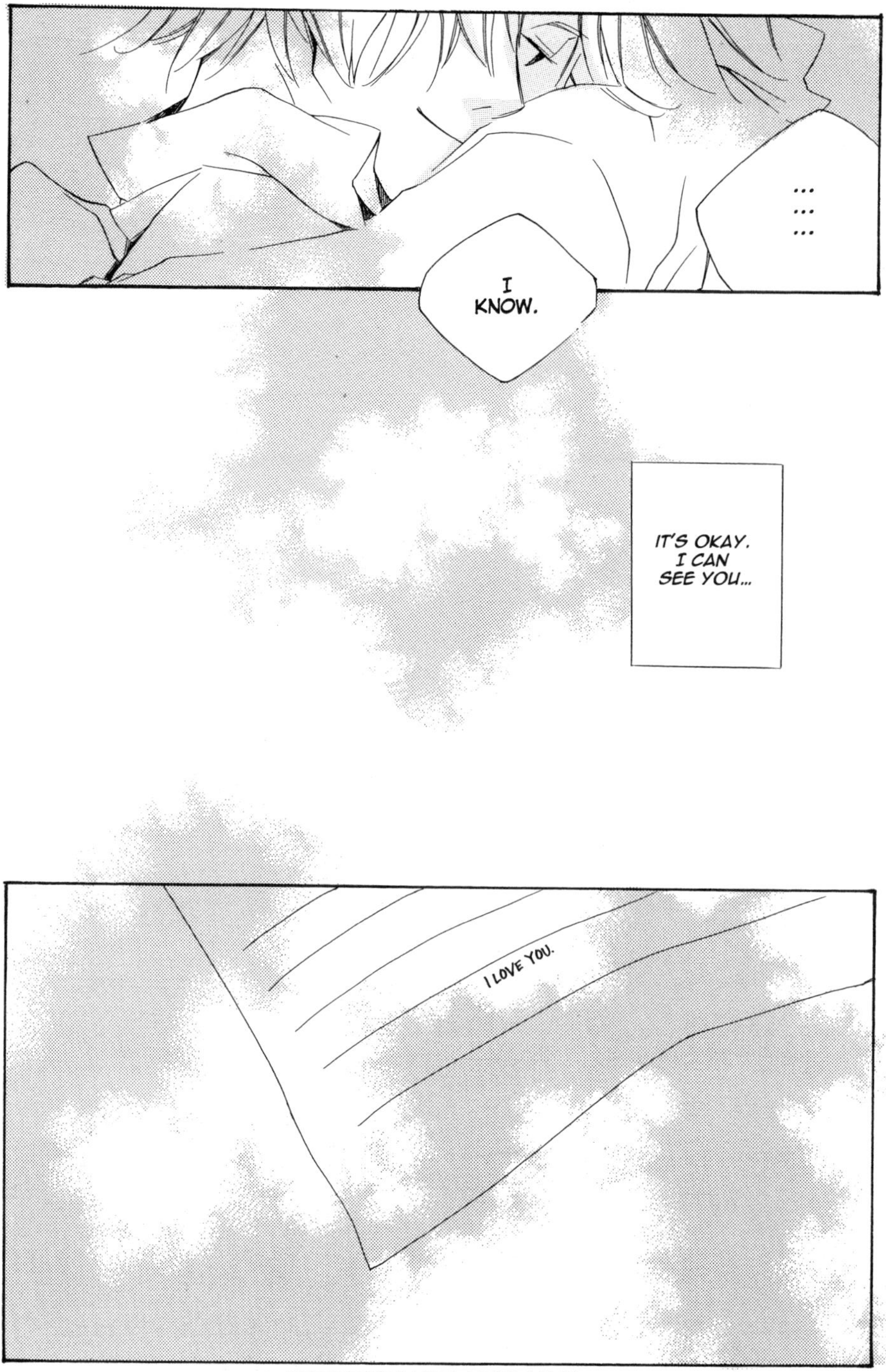
...
...
...
I KNOW.
IT'S OKAY. I CAN SEE YOU...
I LOVE YOU.

THE LETTER IN THE ATTIC / END

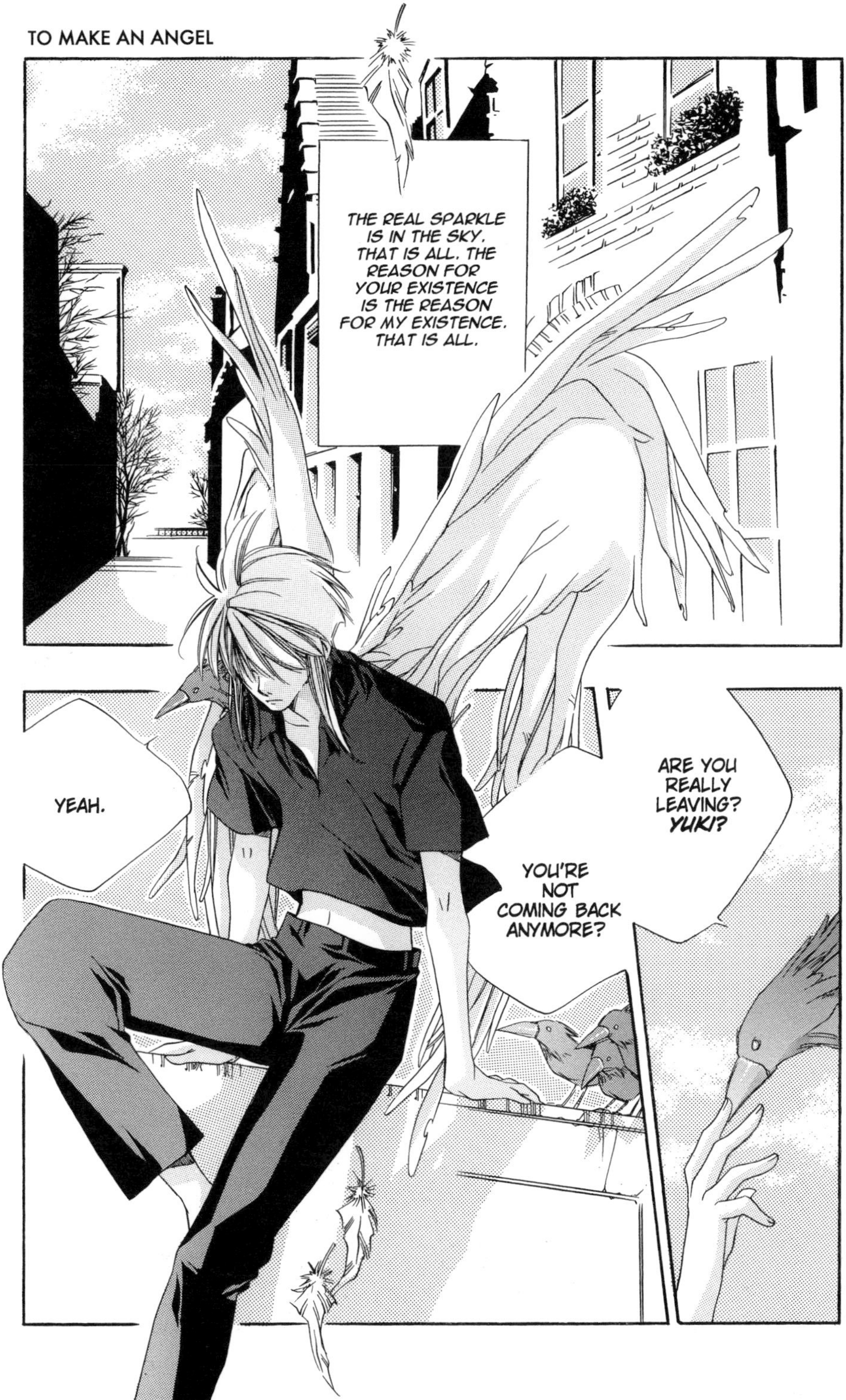
THE REAL SPARKLE IS IN THE SKY. THAT IS ALL. THE REASON FOR YOUR EXISTENCE IS THE REASON FOR MY EXISTENCE. THAT IS ALL.
ARE YOU REALLY LEAVING? *YUKI?*
YOU'RE NOT COMING BACK ANYMORE?
YEAH.

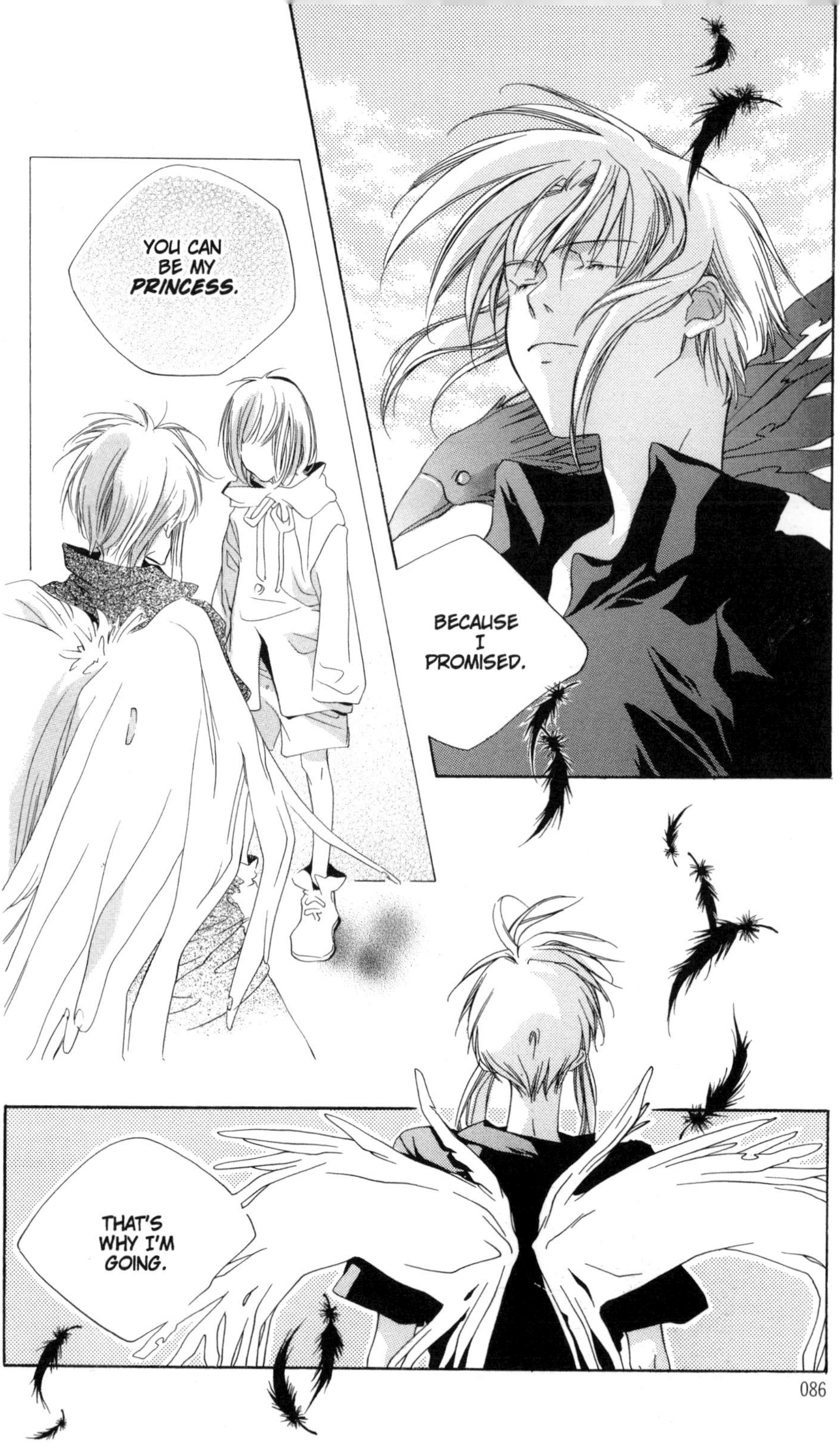
BECAUSE I PROMISED.
YOU CAN BE MY PRINCESS.
THAT'S WHY I'M GOING.

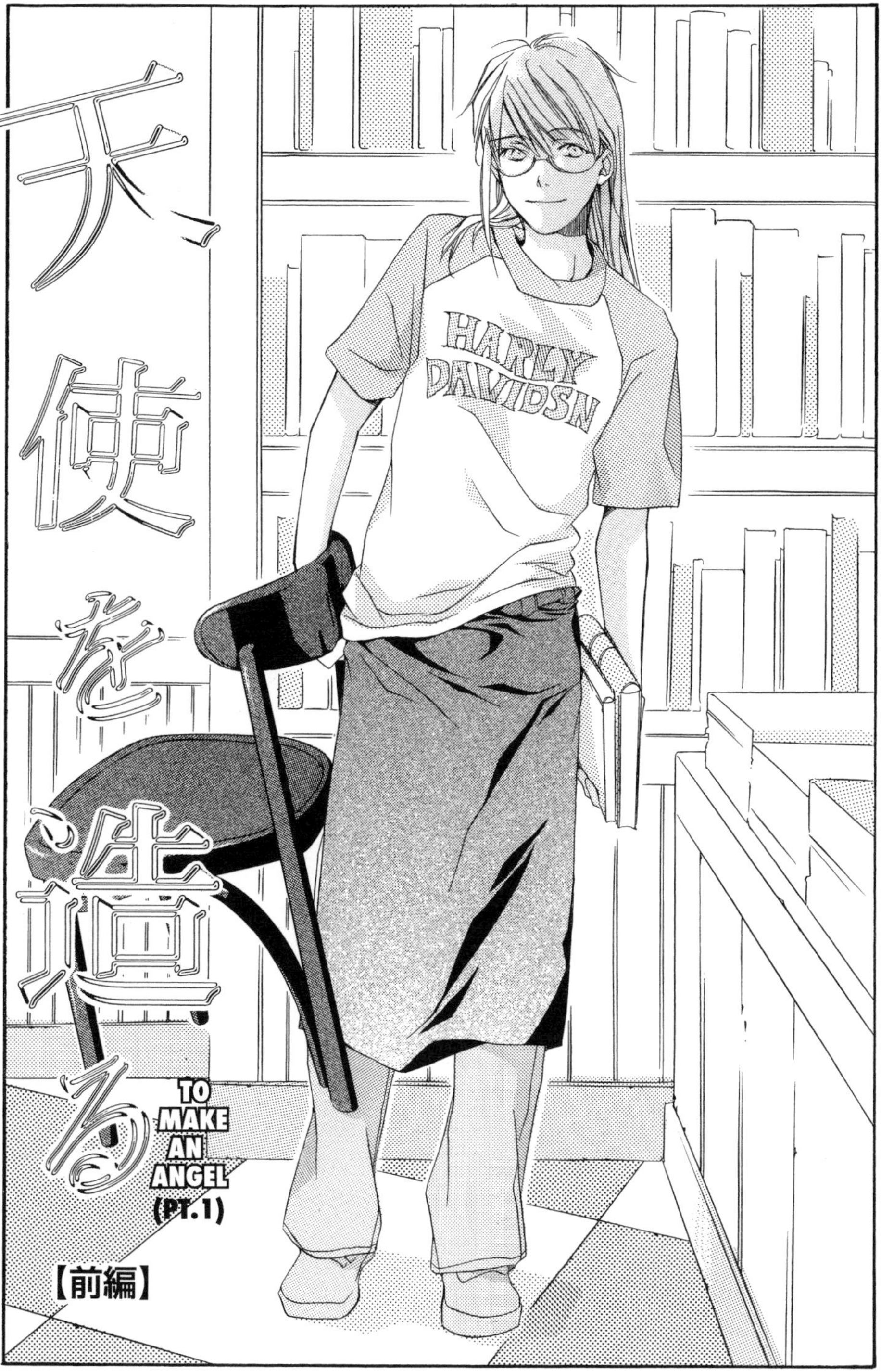
天使を造る
TO MAKE AN ANGEL (PT.1)
【前編】
HARLY DAVIDSN

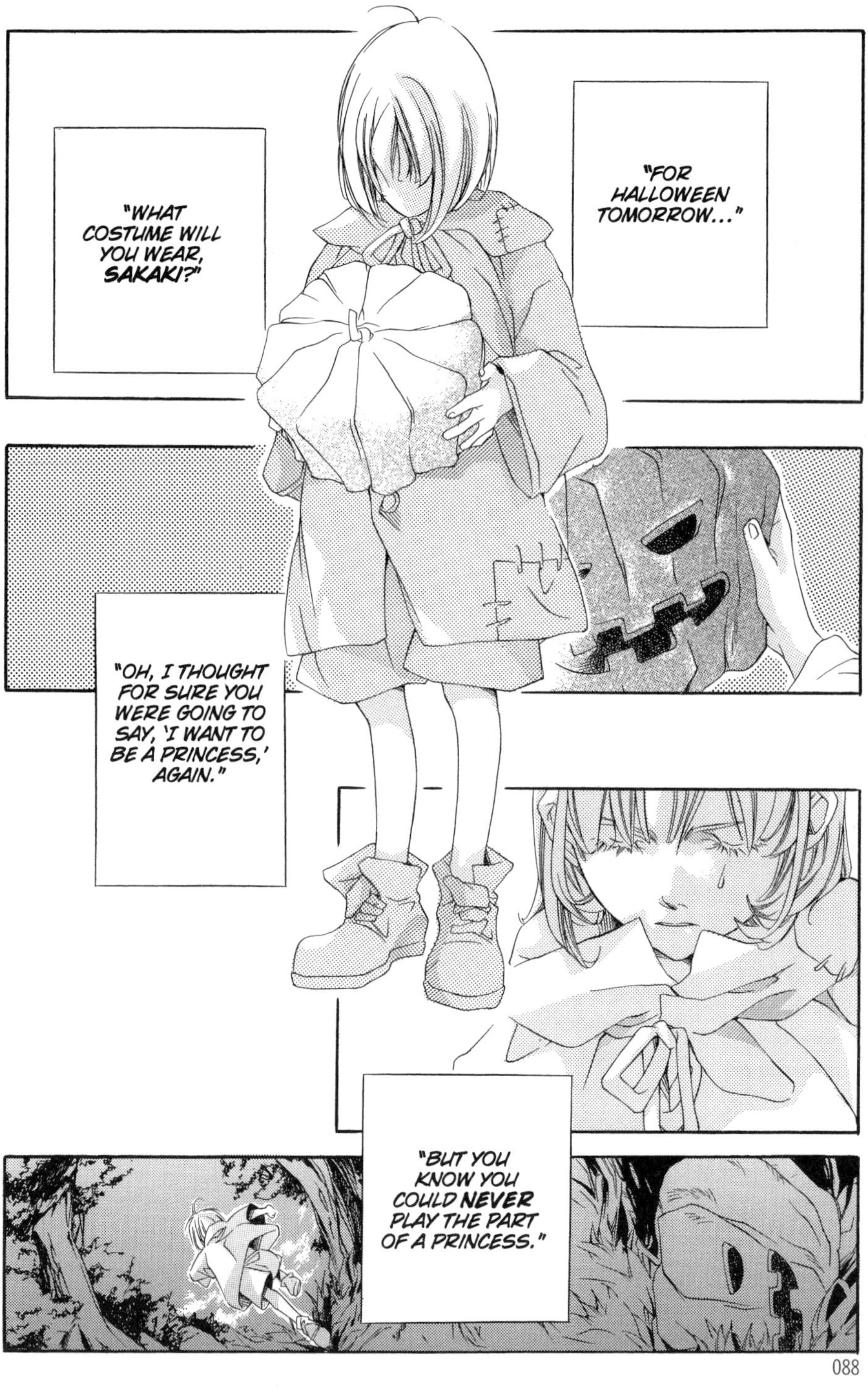
"FOR HALLOWEEN TOMORROW..."
"WHAT COSTUME WILL YOU WEAR, SAKAKI?"
"OH, I THOUGHT FOR SURE YOU WERE GOING TO SAY, 'I WANT TO BE A PRINCESS,' AGAIN."
"BUT YOU KNOW YOU COULD NEVER PLAY THE PART OF A PRINCESS."

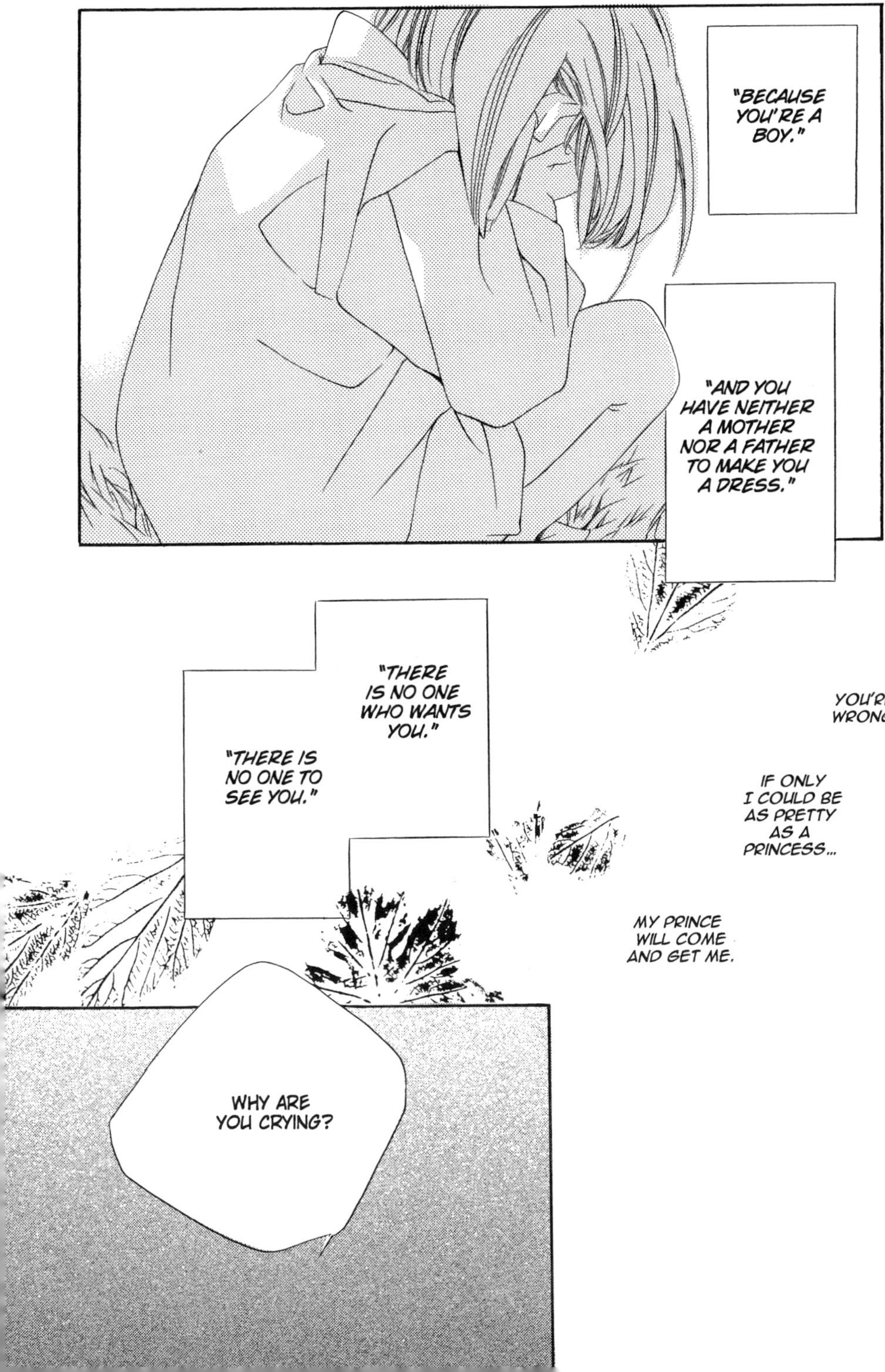
"BECAUSE YOU'RE A BOY."
"AND YOU HAVE NEITHER A MOTHER NOR A FATHER TO MAKE YOU A DRESS."
"THERE IS NO ONE WHO WANTS YOU."
"THERE IS NO ONE TO SEE YOU."
YOU'RE WRONG.
IF ONLY I COULD BE AS PRETTY AS A PRINCESS...
MY PRINCE WILL COME AND GET ME.
WHY ARE YOU CRYING?

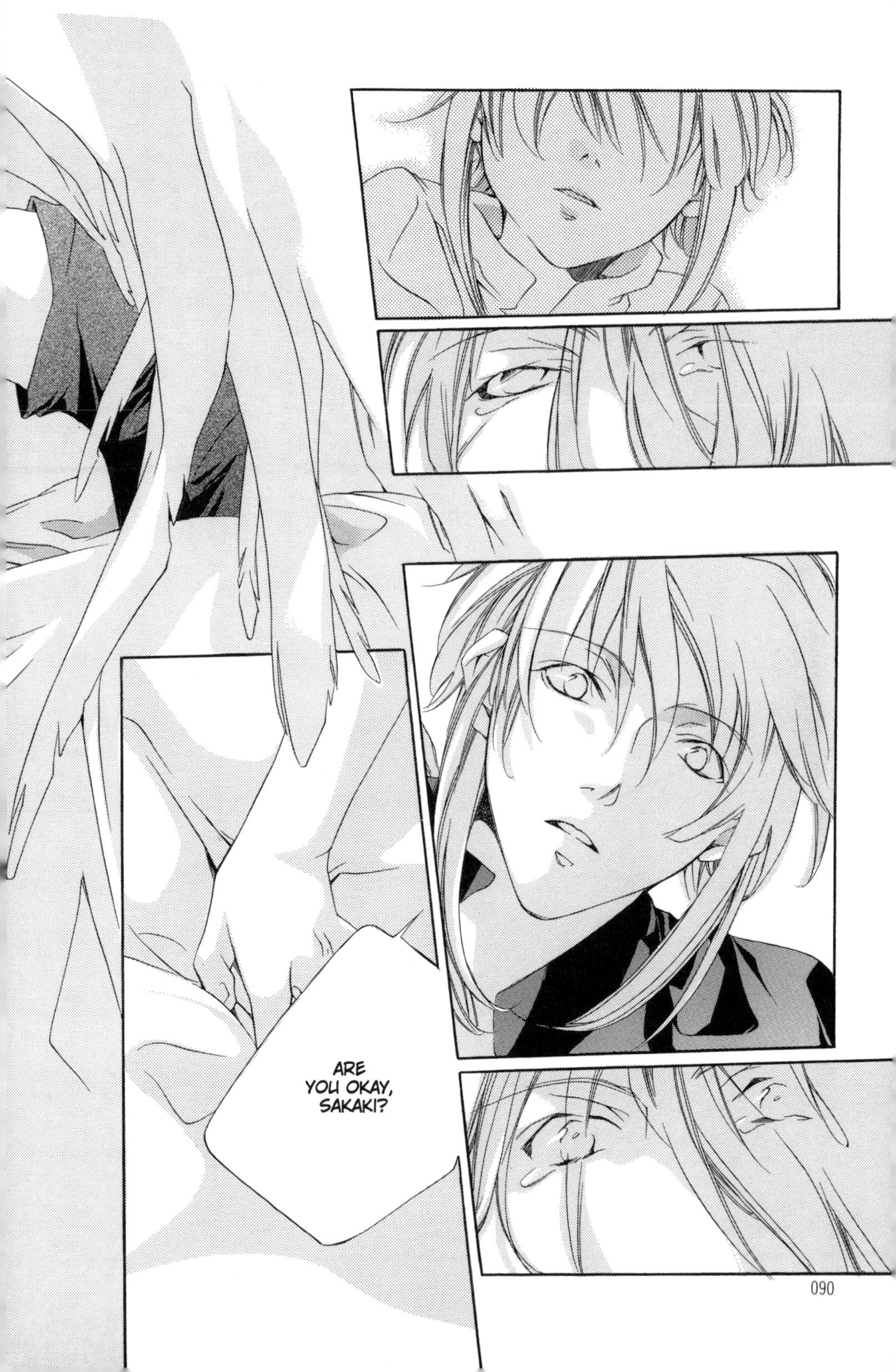
ARE YOU OKAY, SAKAKI?

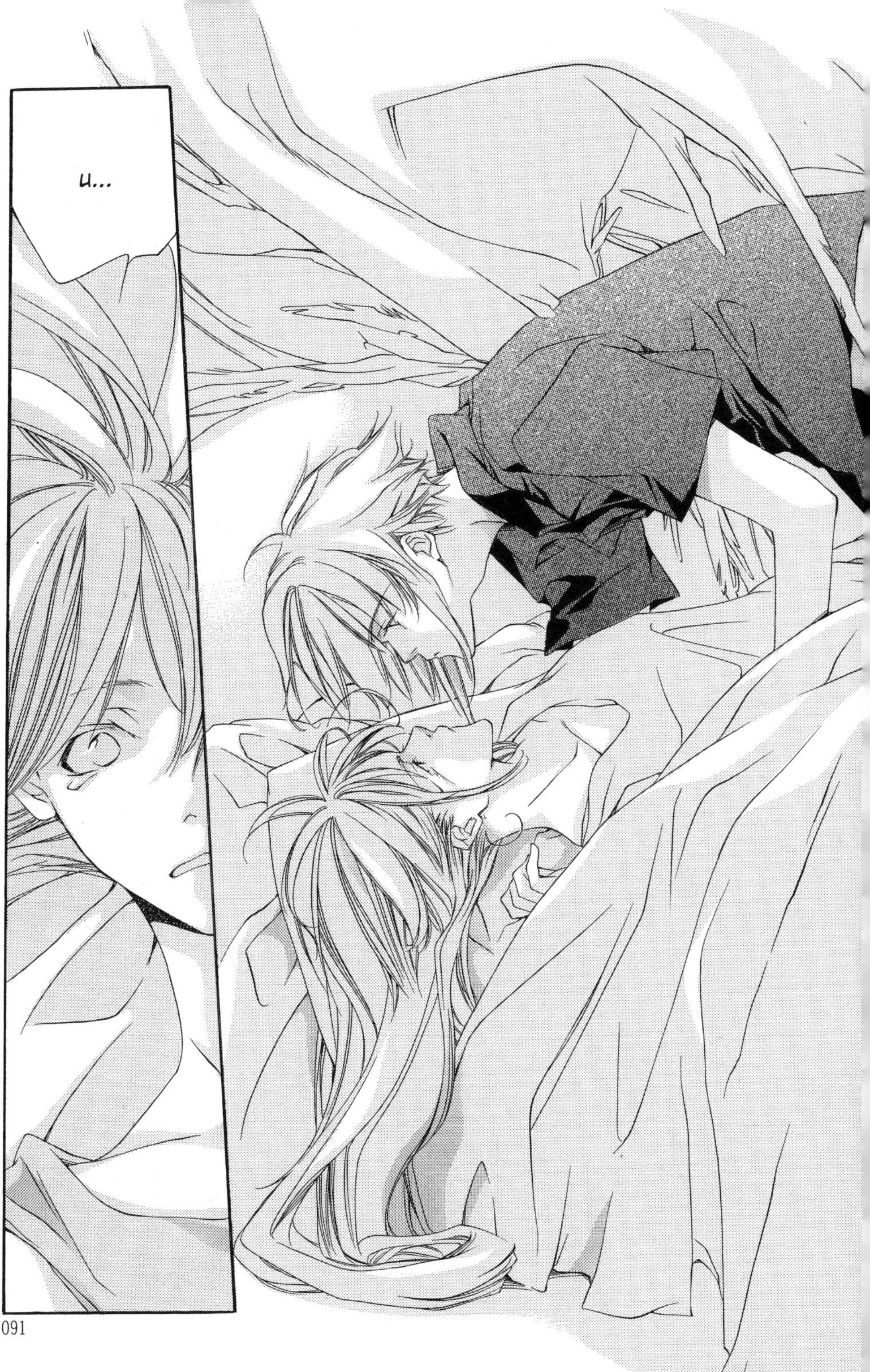
u...

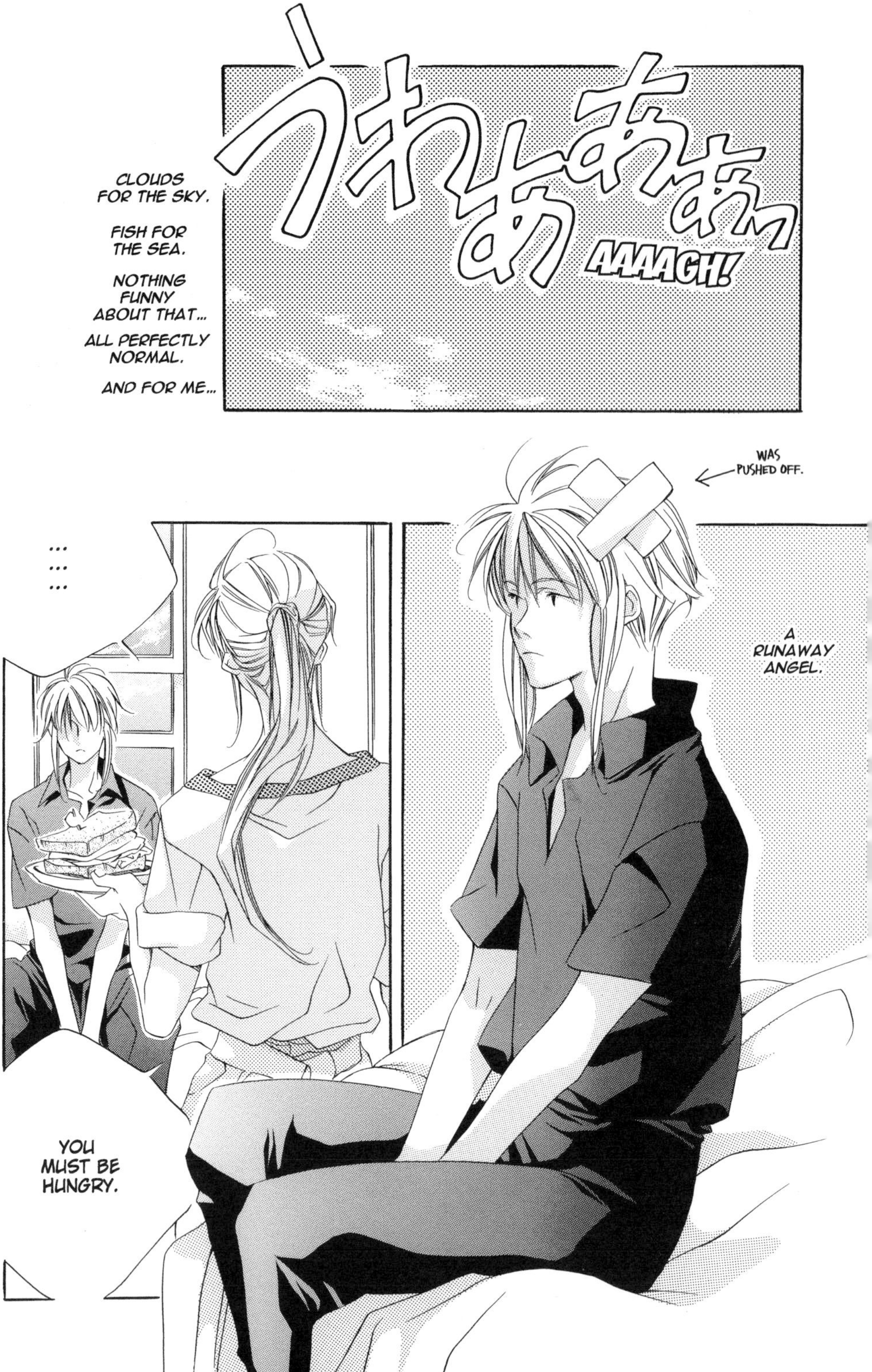

うわあああっ
AAAAGH!
CLOUDS FOR THE SKY.
FISH FOR THE SEA.
NOTHING FUNNY ABOUT THAT...
ALL PERFECTLY NORMAL.
AND FOR ME...
WAS PUSHED OFF.
A RUNAWAY ANGEL.
...
...
...
YOU MUST BE HUNGRY.

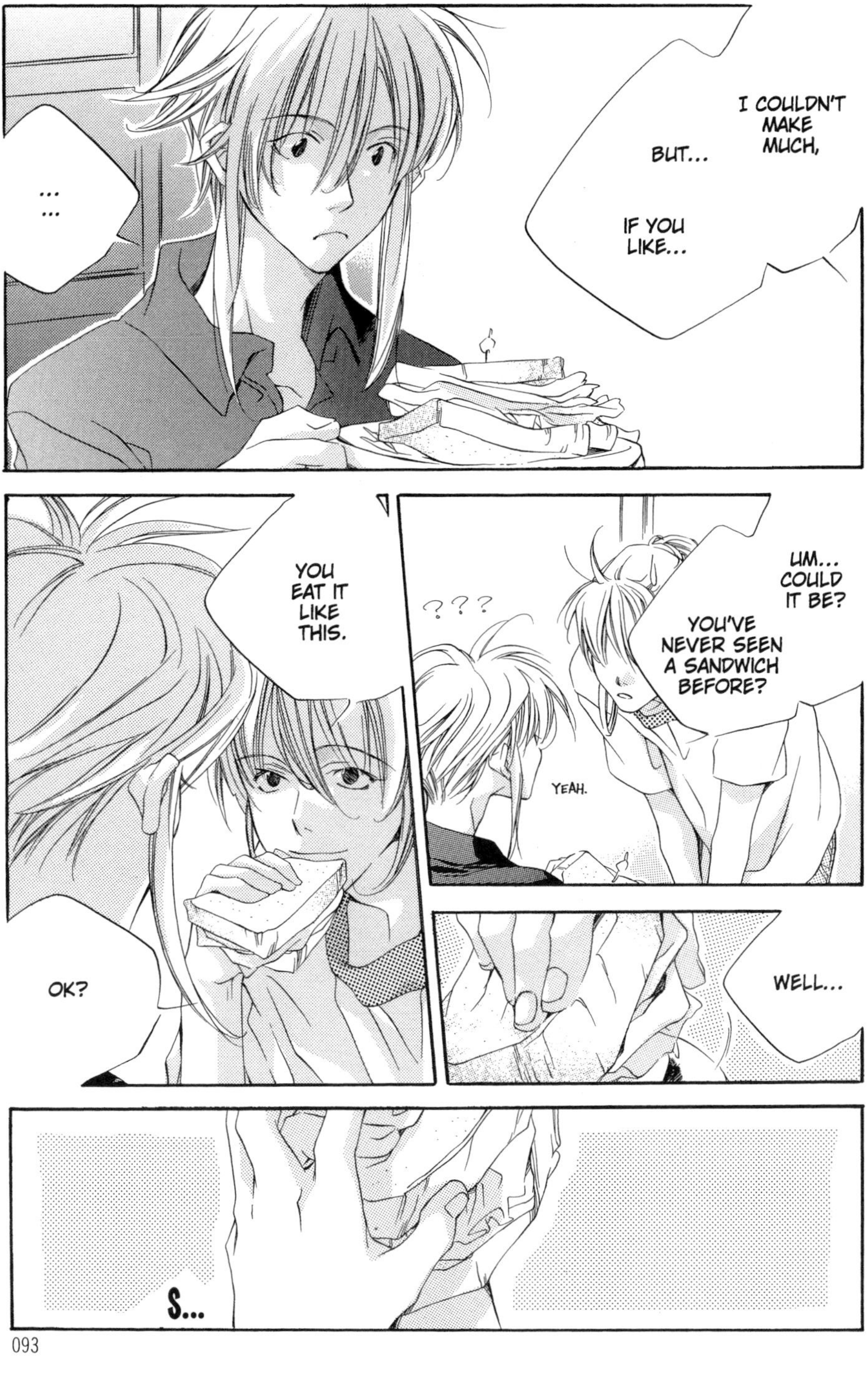
I COULDN'T MAKE MUCH,
BUT...
IF YOU LIKE...
......
UM... COULD IT BE?
YOU'VE NEVER SEEN A SANDWICH BEFORE?
???
YEAH.
WELL...
YOU EAT IT LIKE THIS.
OK?
S...

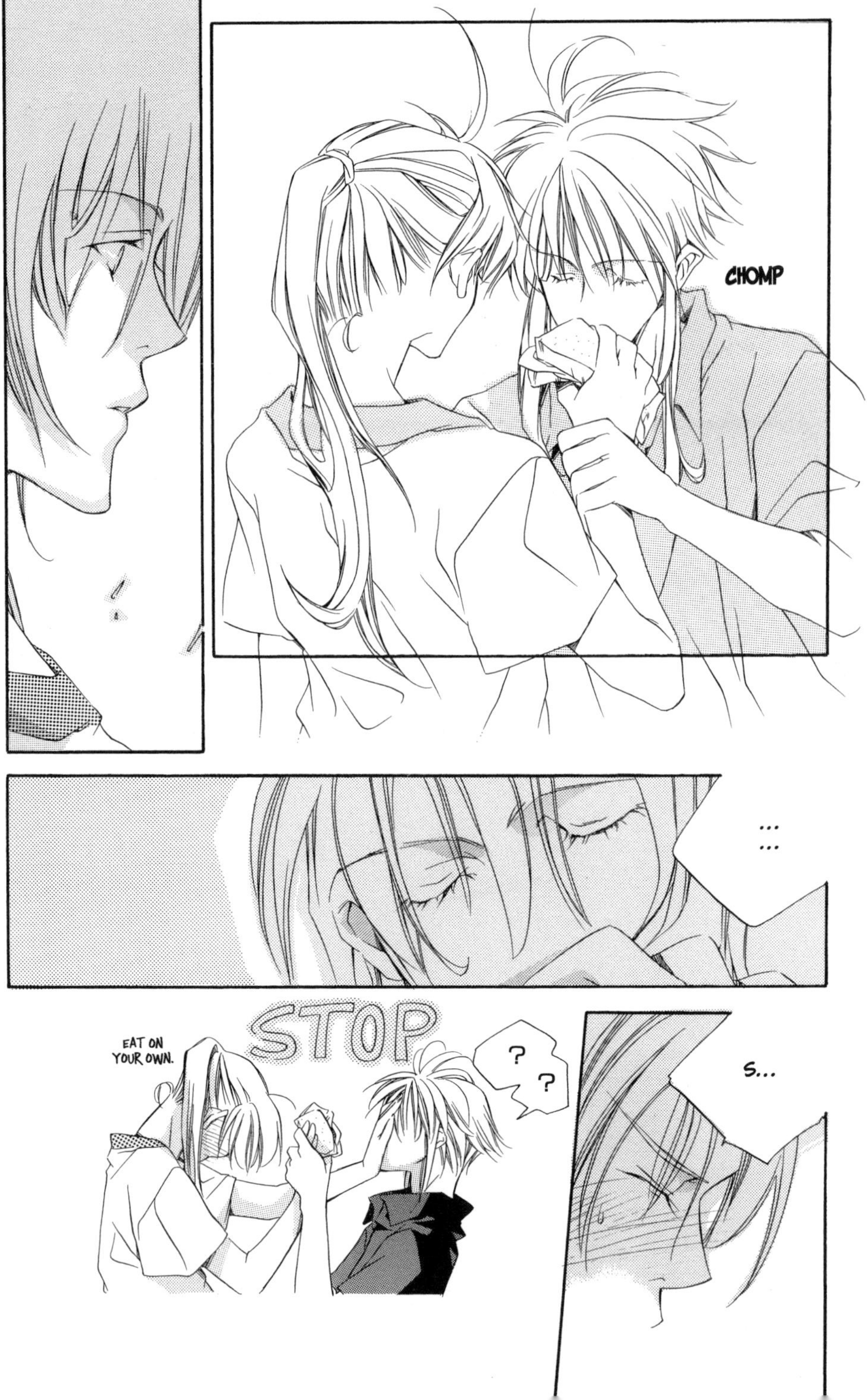
CHOMP
...
...
S...
? ?
STOP
EAT ON YOUR OWN.

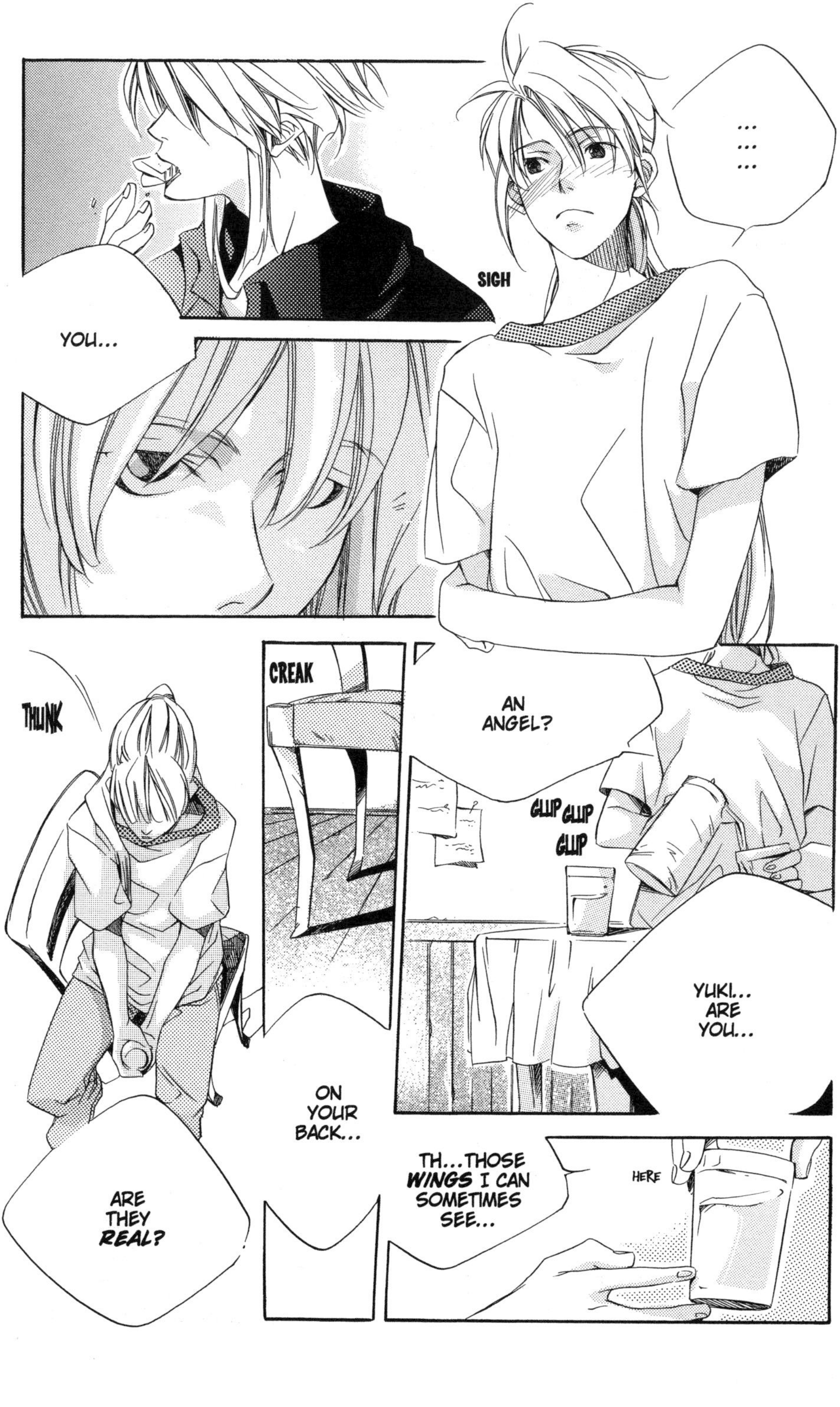

...
...
...
SIGH
YOU...
AN ANGEL?
GLUP GLUP GLUP
YUKI... ARE YOU...
CREAK
THUNK
HERE
TH...THOSE **WINGS** I CAN SOMETIMES SEE...
ON YOUR BACK...
ARE THEY **REAL**?

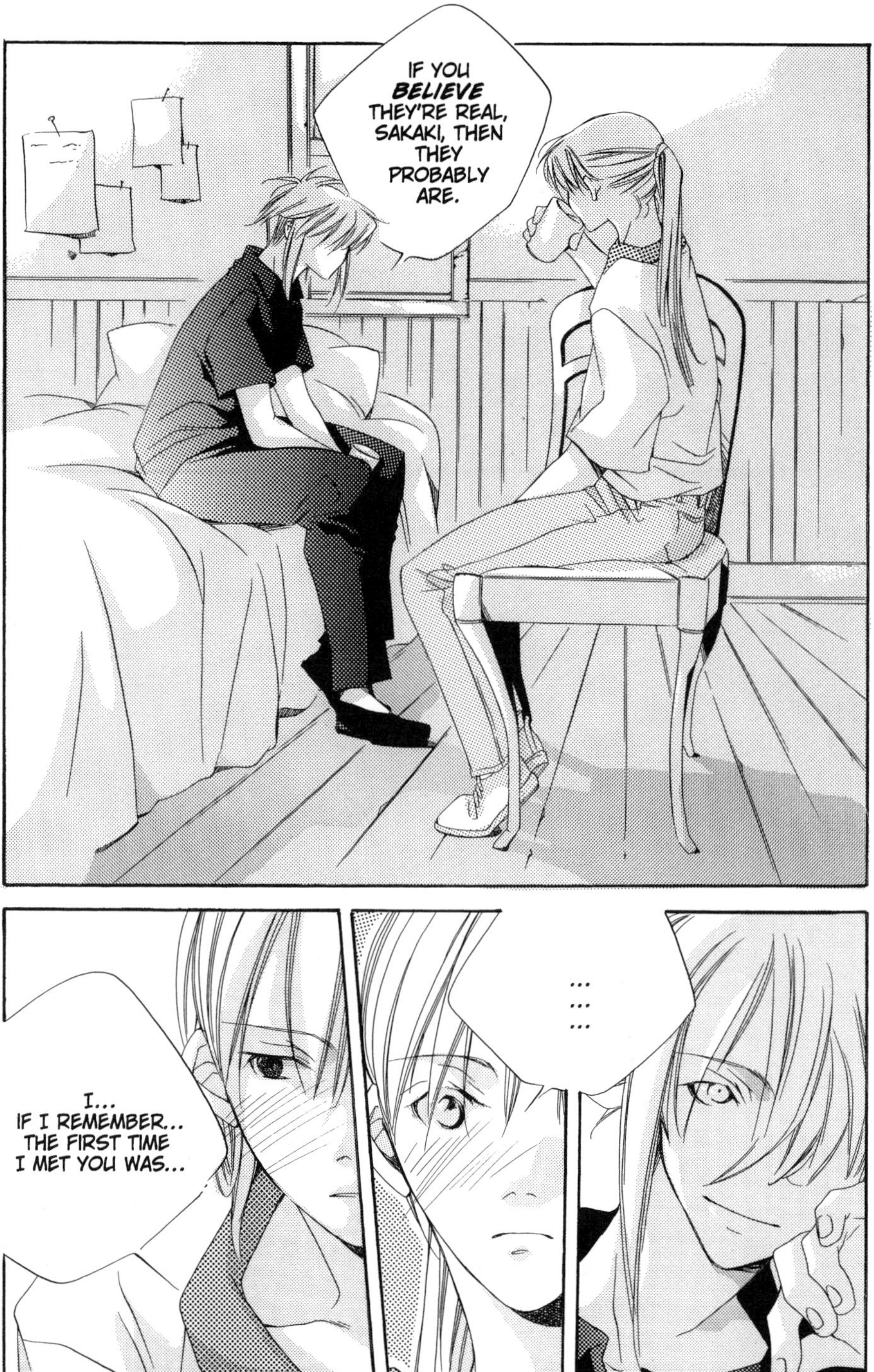
IF YOU **BELIEVE** THEY'RE REAL, SAKAKI, THEN THEY PROBABLY ARE.
... ...
I... IF I REMEMBER... THE FIRST TIME I MET YOU WAS...

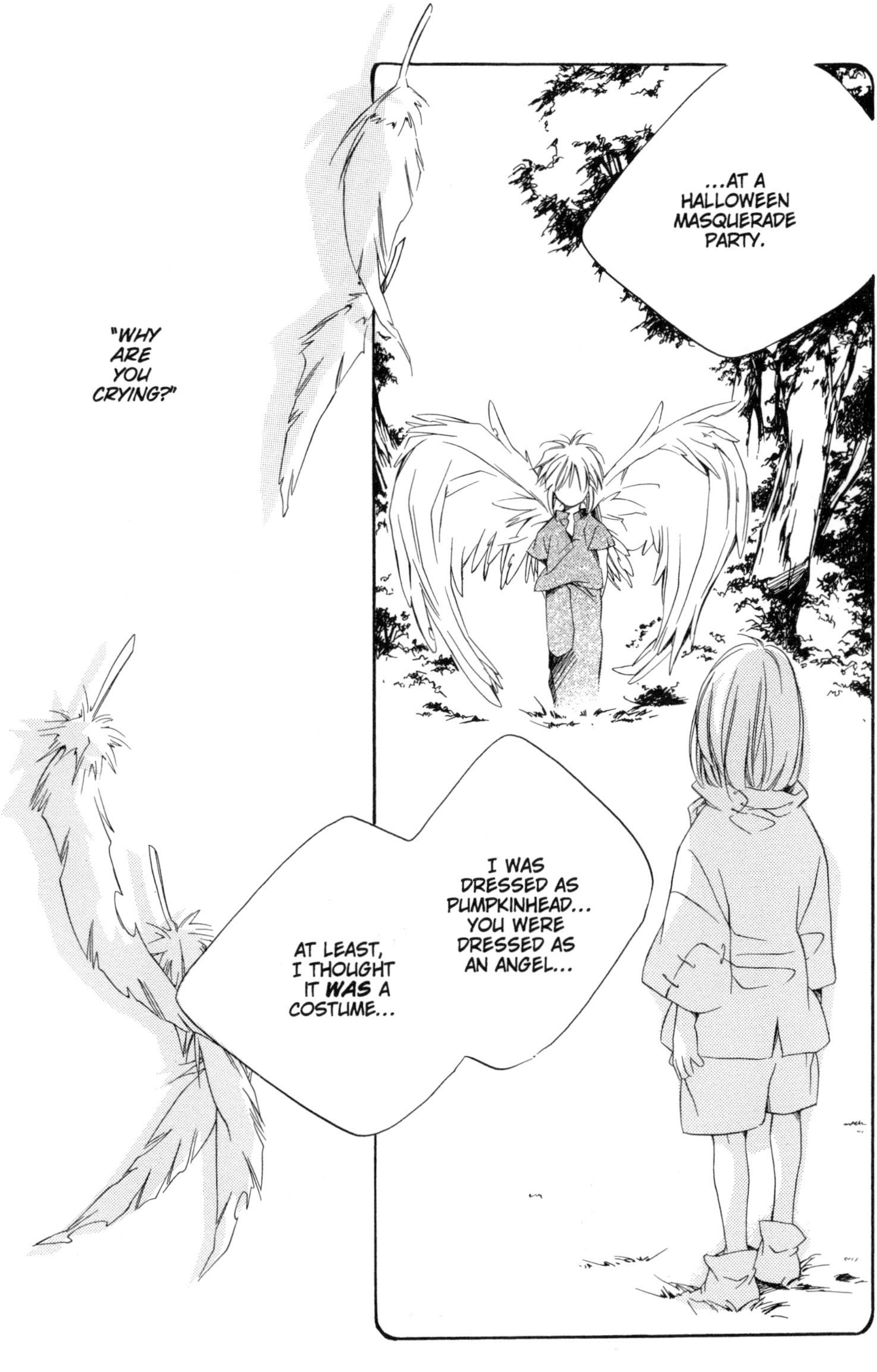
...AT A HALLOWEEN MASQUERADE PARTY.
I WAS DRESSED AS PUMPKINHEAD... YOU WERE DRESSED AS AN ANGEL...
AT LEAST, I THOUGHT IT **WAS** A COSTUME...
"WHY ARE YOU CRYING?"

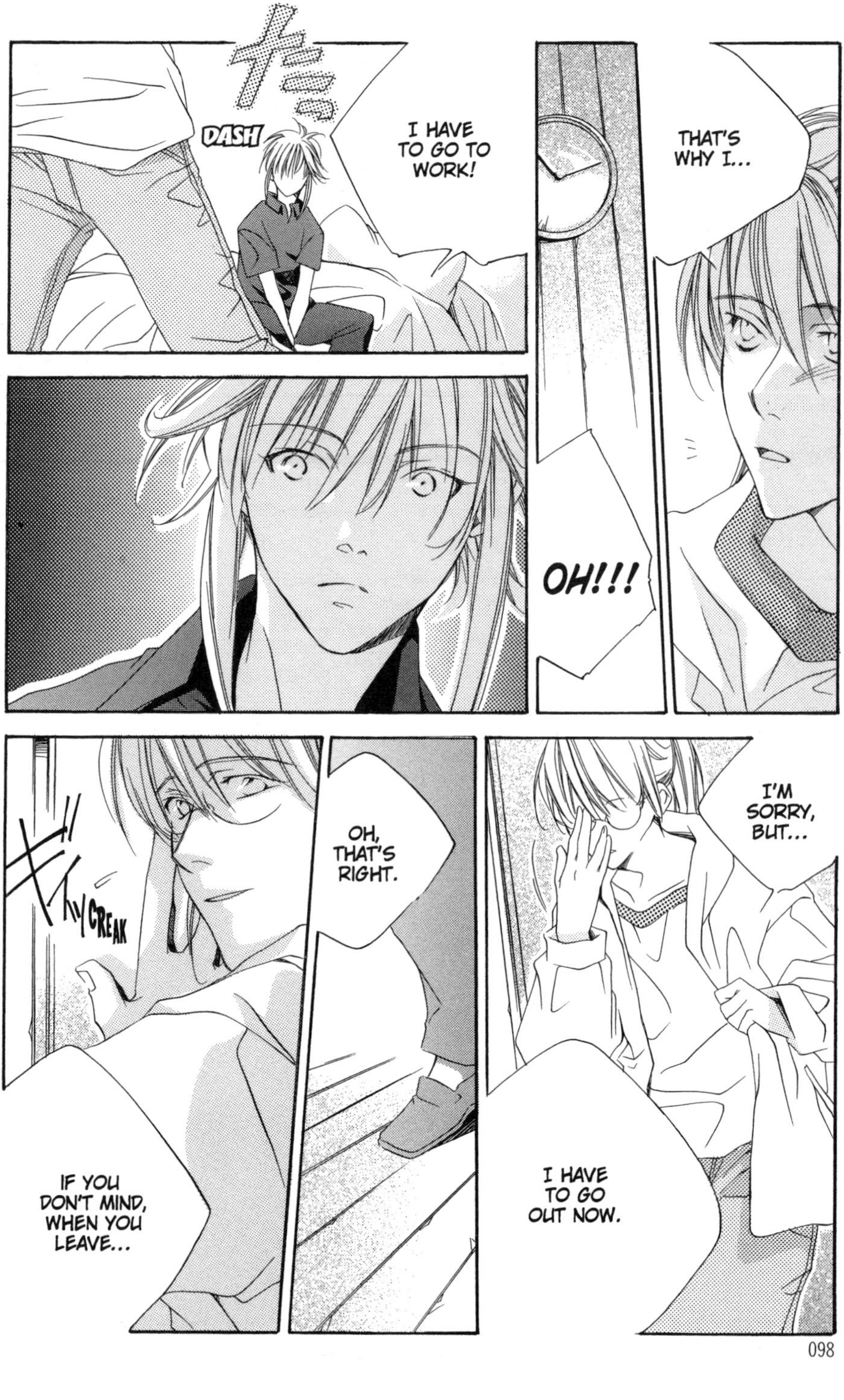
THAT'S WHY I...
I HAVE TO GO TO WORK!
DASH
OH!!!
I'M SORRY, BUT...
I HAVE TO GO OUT NOW.
OH, THAT'S RIGHT.
CREAK
IF YOU DON'T MIND, WHEN YOU LEAVE...

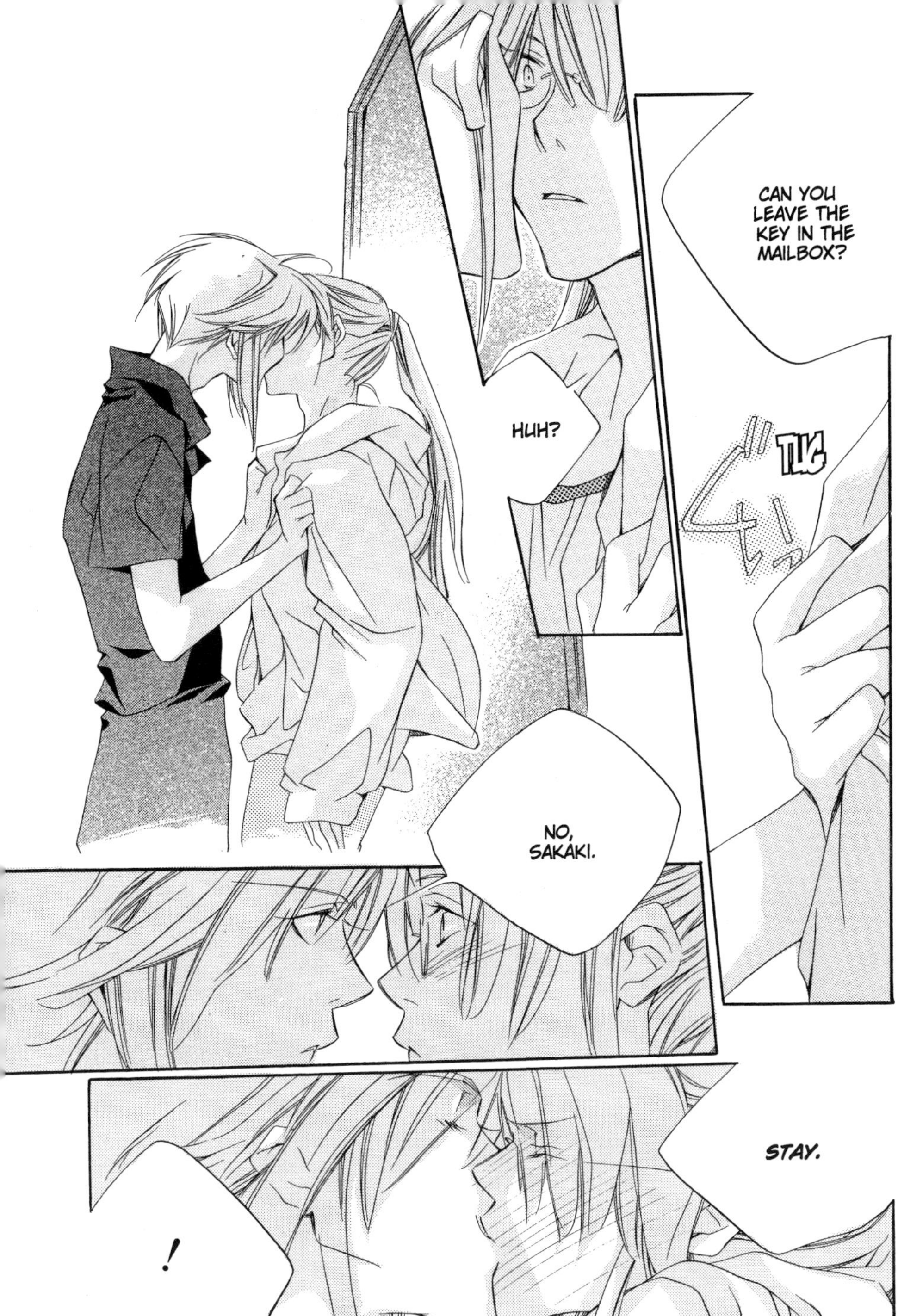
CAN YOU LEAVE THE KEY IN THE MAILBOX?
TUG
HUH?
NO, SAKAKI.
STAY.
!

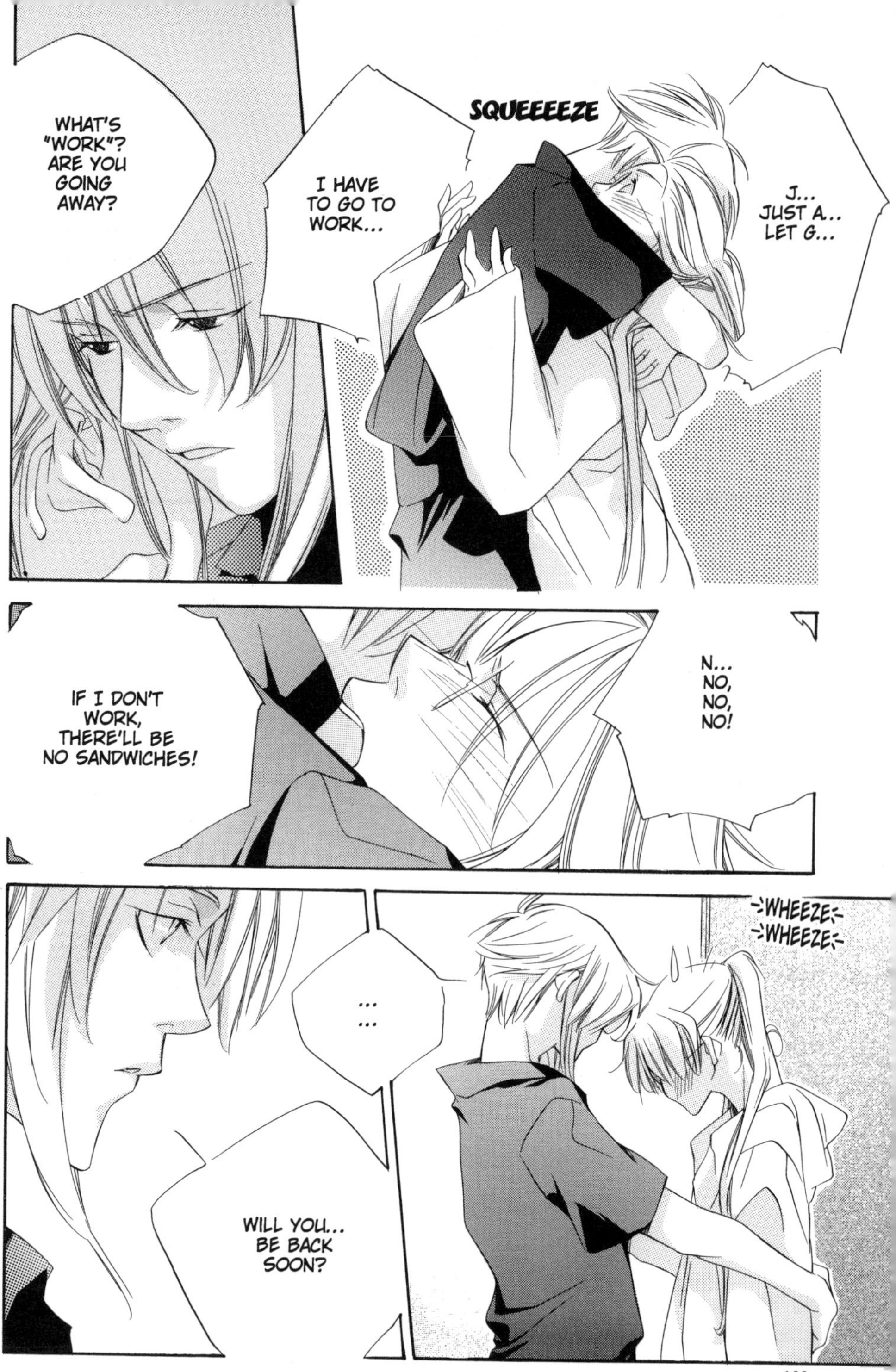
J... JUST A... LET G...
SQUEEEEZE
I HAVE TO GO TO WORK...
WHAT'S "WORK"? ARE YOU GOING AWAY?
N... NO, NO, NO!
IF I DON'T WORK, THERE'LL BE NO SANDWICHES!
WHEEZE
WHEEZE
... ...
WILL YOU... BE BACK SOON?

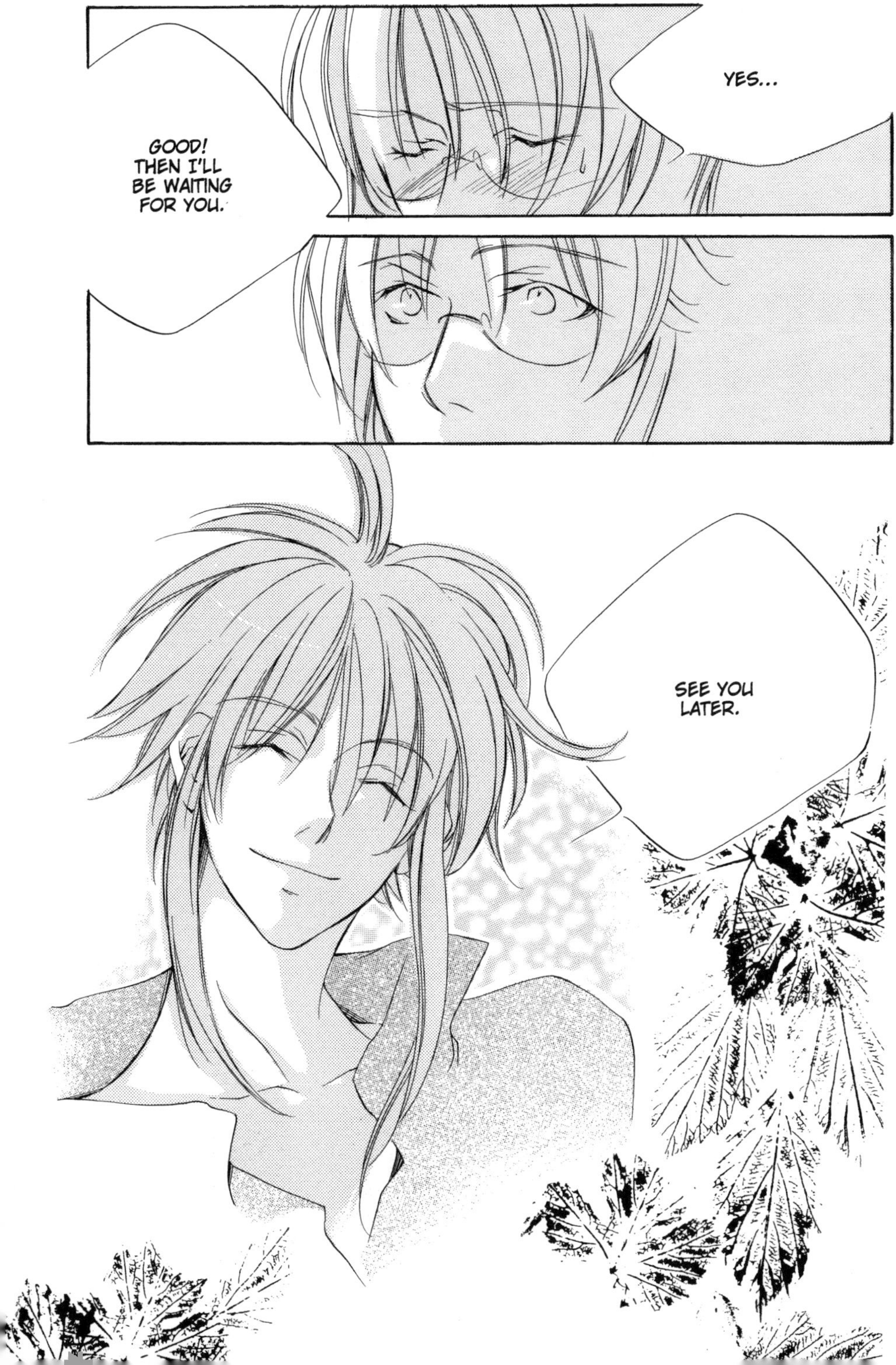
YES...
GOOD! THEN I'LL BE WAITING FOR YOU.
SEE YOU LATER.

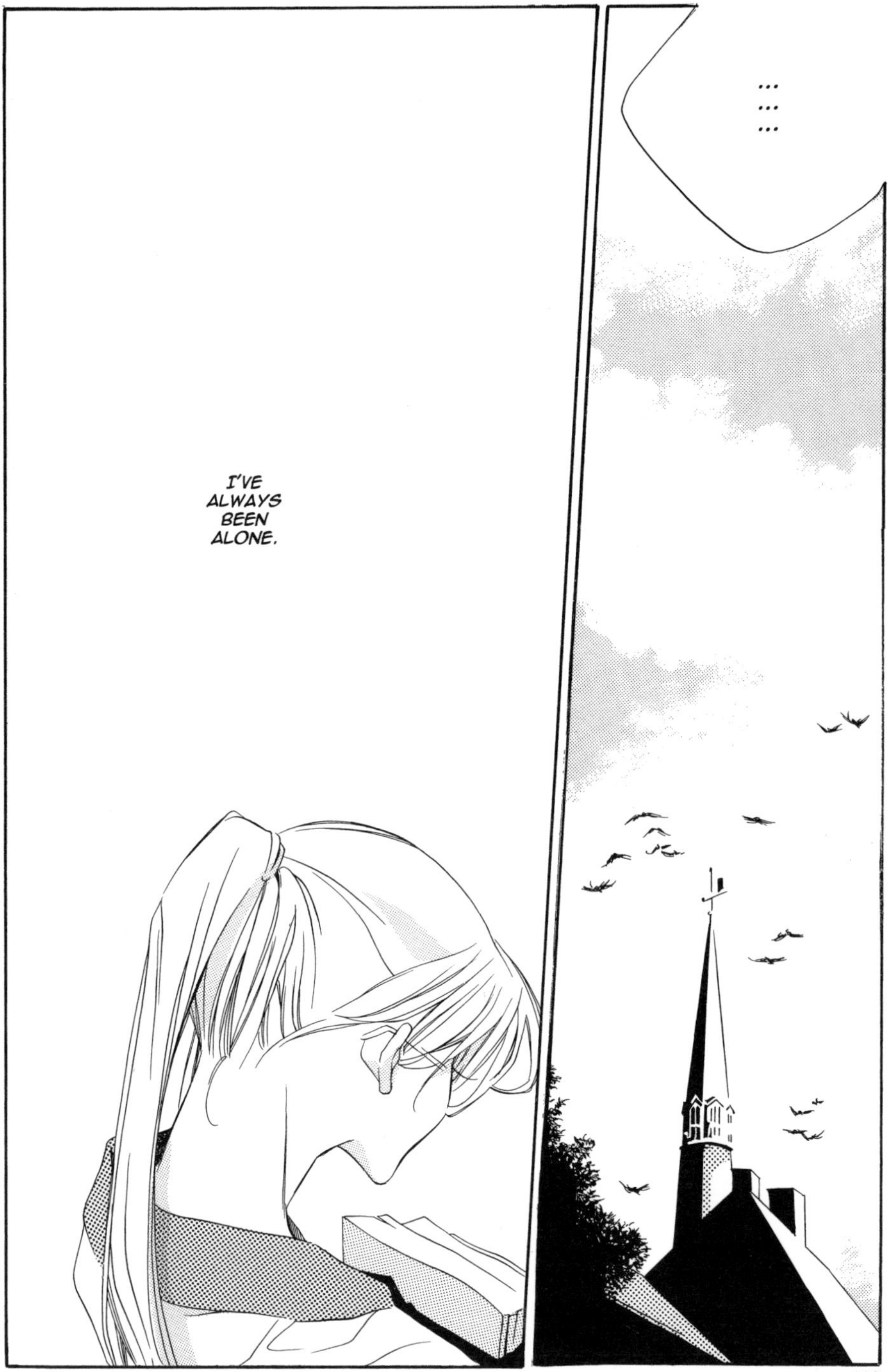
… … …
I'VE ALWAYS BEEN ALONE.

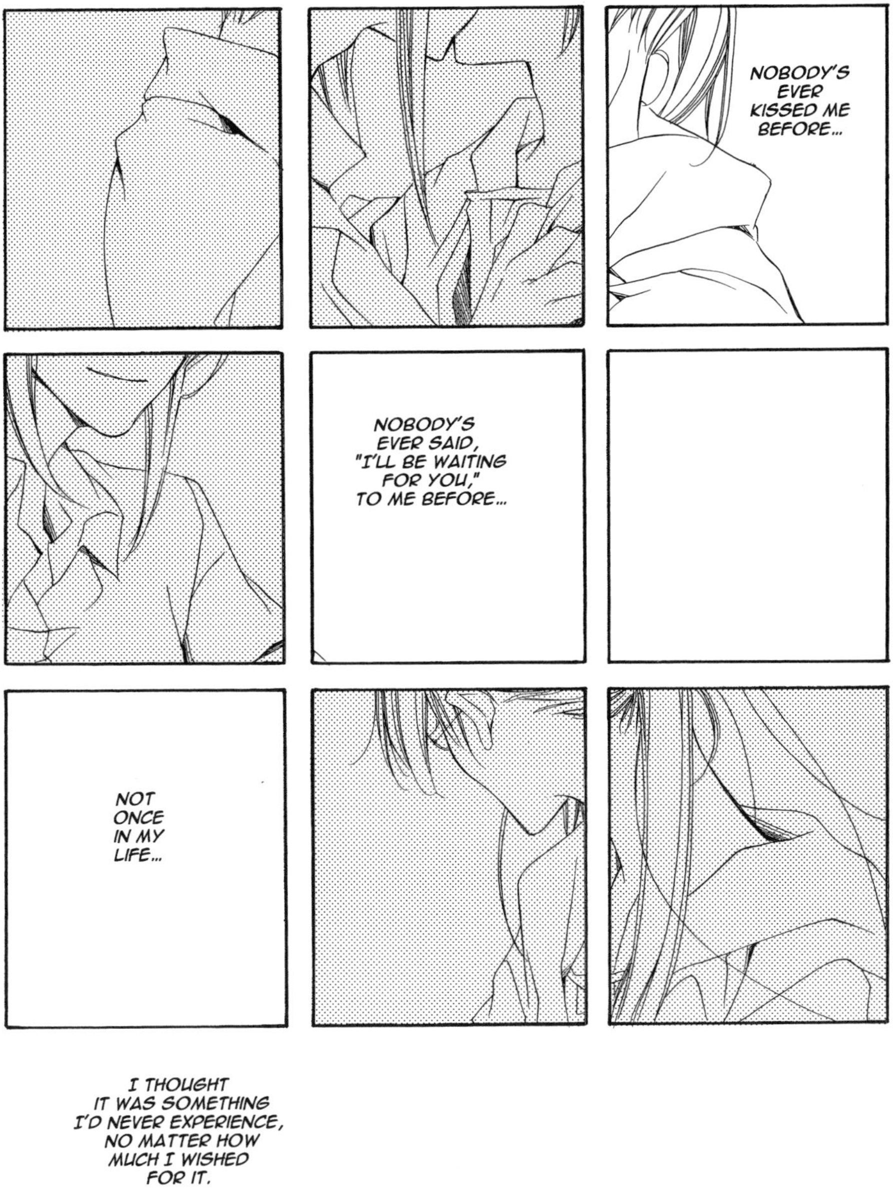
NOBODY'S EVER KISSED ME BEFORE...
NOBODY'S EVER SAID, "I'LL BE WAITING FOR YOU," TO ME BEFORE...
NOT ONCE IN MY LIFE...
I THOUGHT IT WAS SOMETHING I'D NEVER EXPERIENCE, NO MATTER HOW MUCH I WISHED FOR IT.

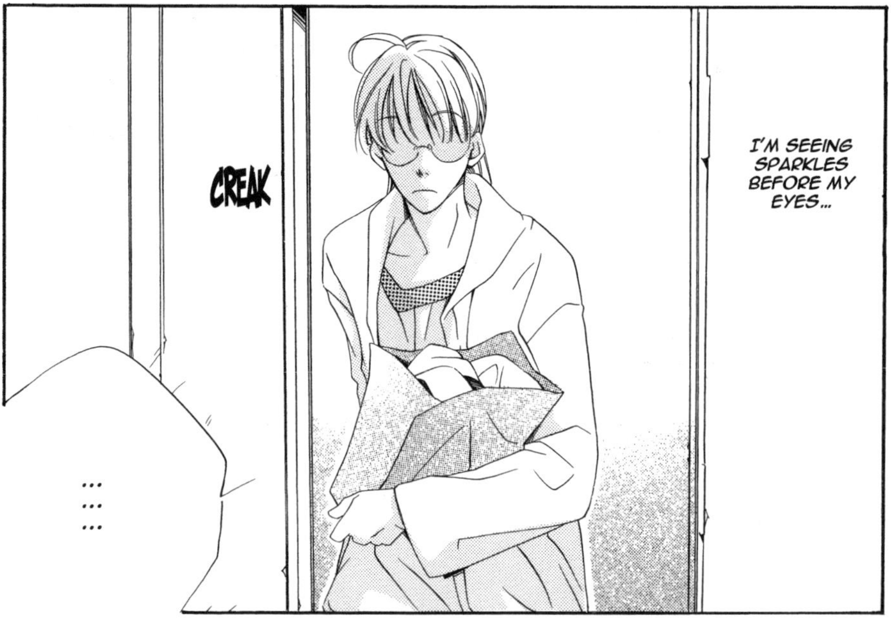
I'M SEEING SPARKLES BEFORE MY EYES...
CREAK
...
...
...

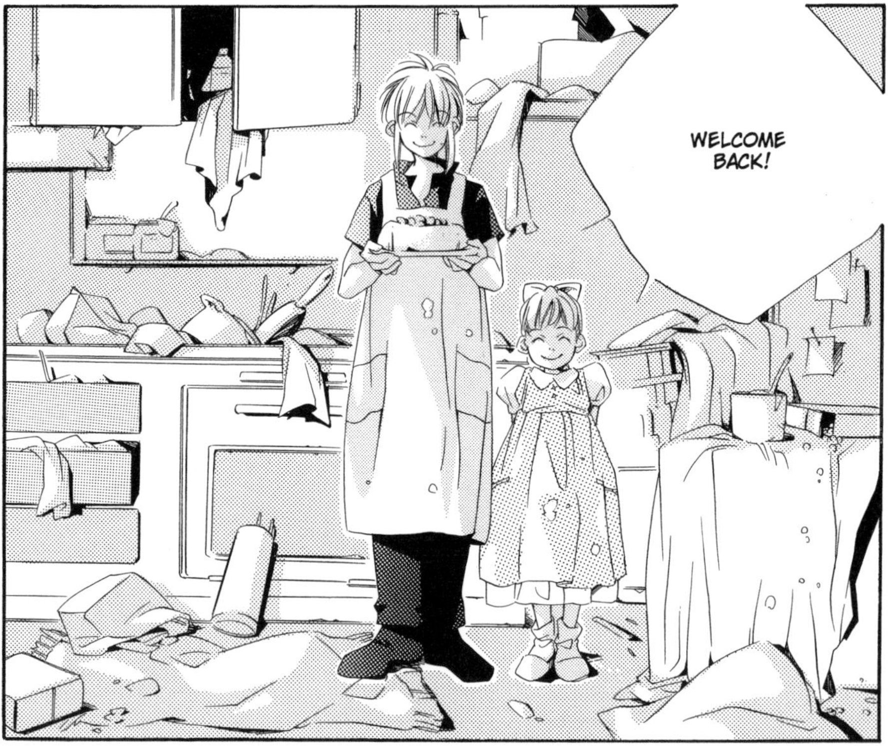
WELCOME BACK!

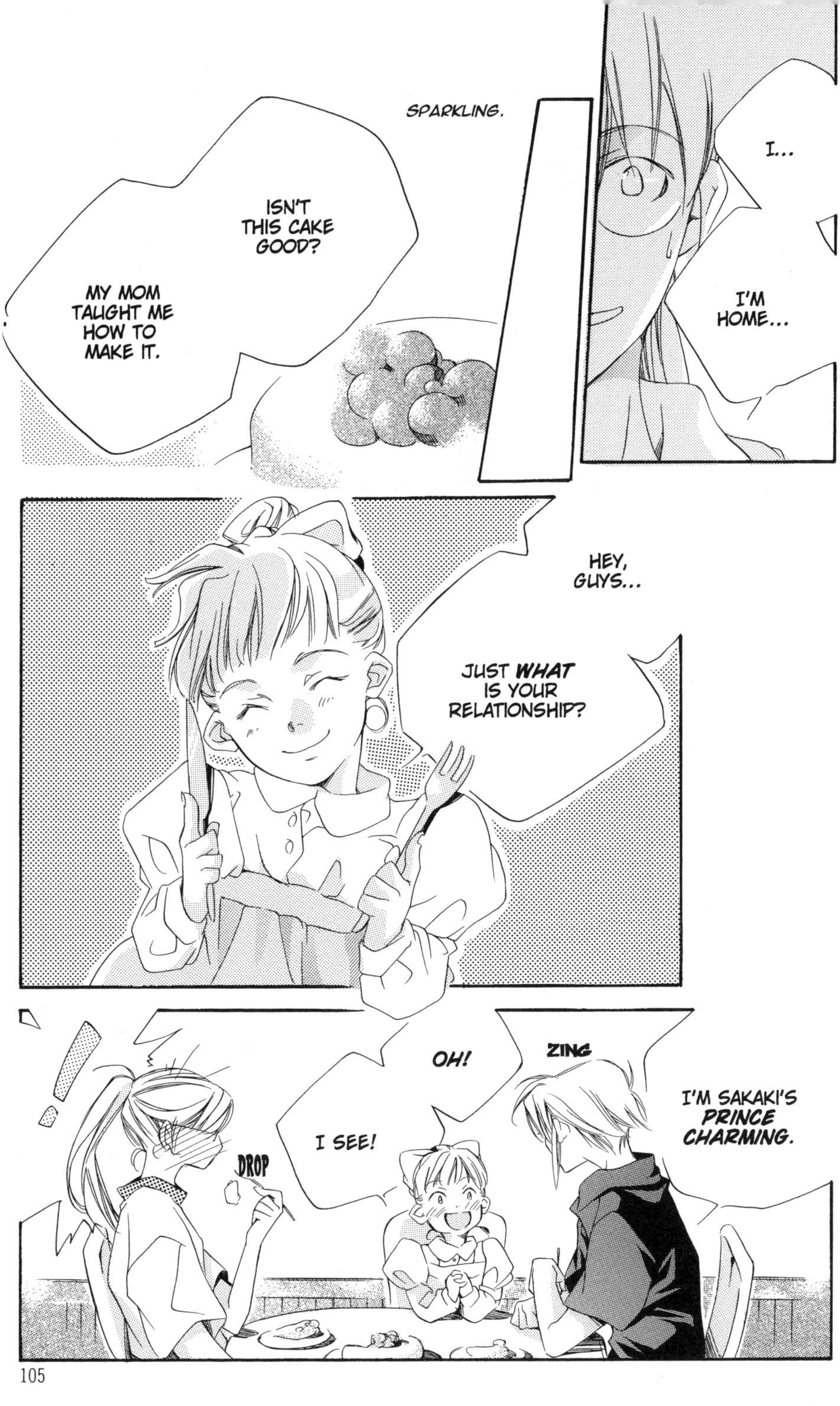
I...
I'M HOME...
SPARKLING.
ISN'T THIS CAKE GOOD?
MY MOM TAUGHT ME HOW TO MAKE IT.
HEY, GUYS...
JUST **WHAT** IS YOUR RELATIONSHIP?
I'M SAKAKI'S ***PRINCE CHARMING.***
ZING
OH!
I SEE!
DROP
!

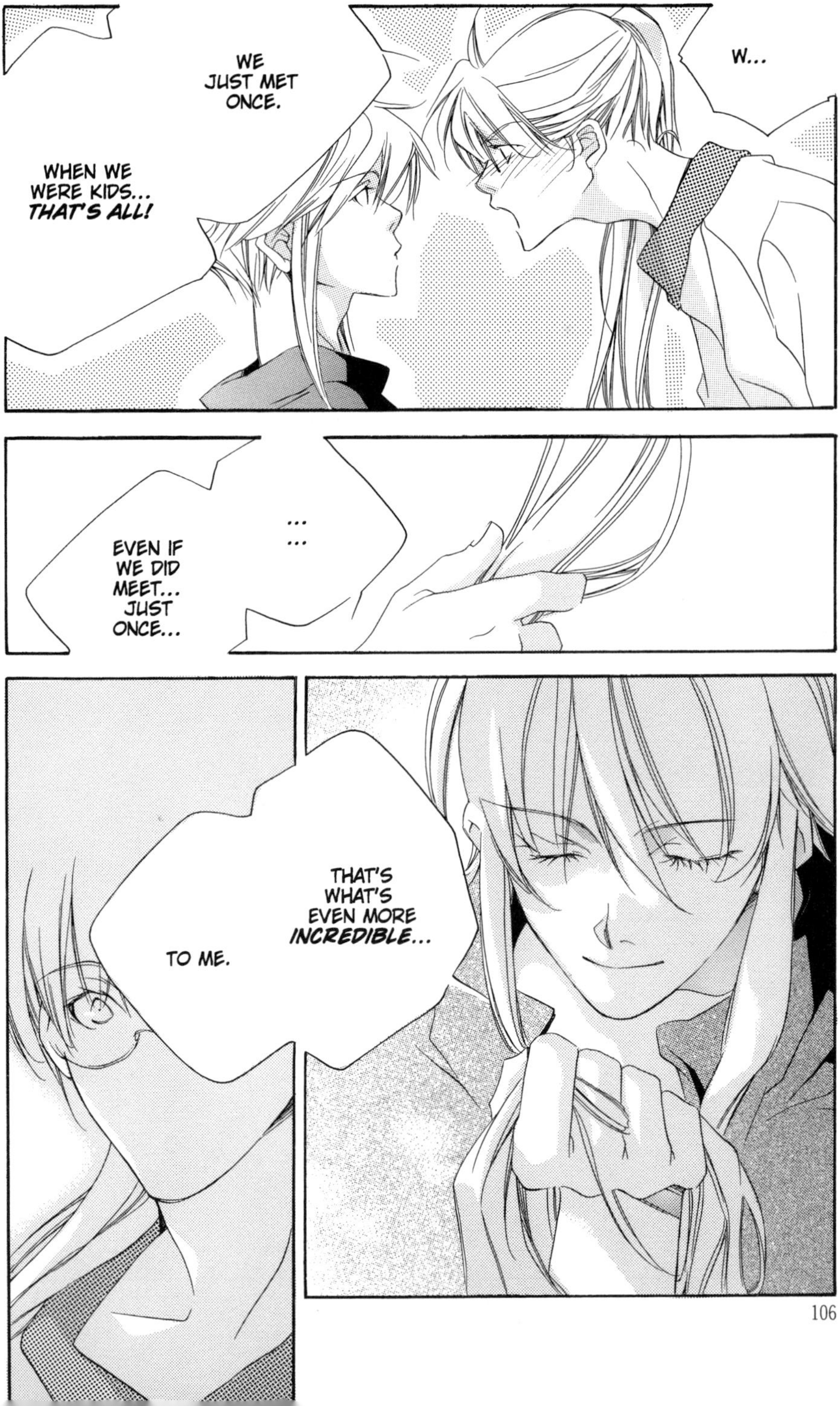
W...
WE JUST MET ONCE.
WHEN WE WERE KIDS... ***THAT'S ALL!***
......
EVEN IF WE DID MEET... JUST ONCE...
THAT'S WHAT'S EVEN MORE ***INCREDIBLE***...
TO ME.

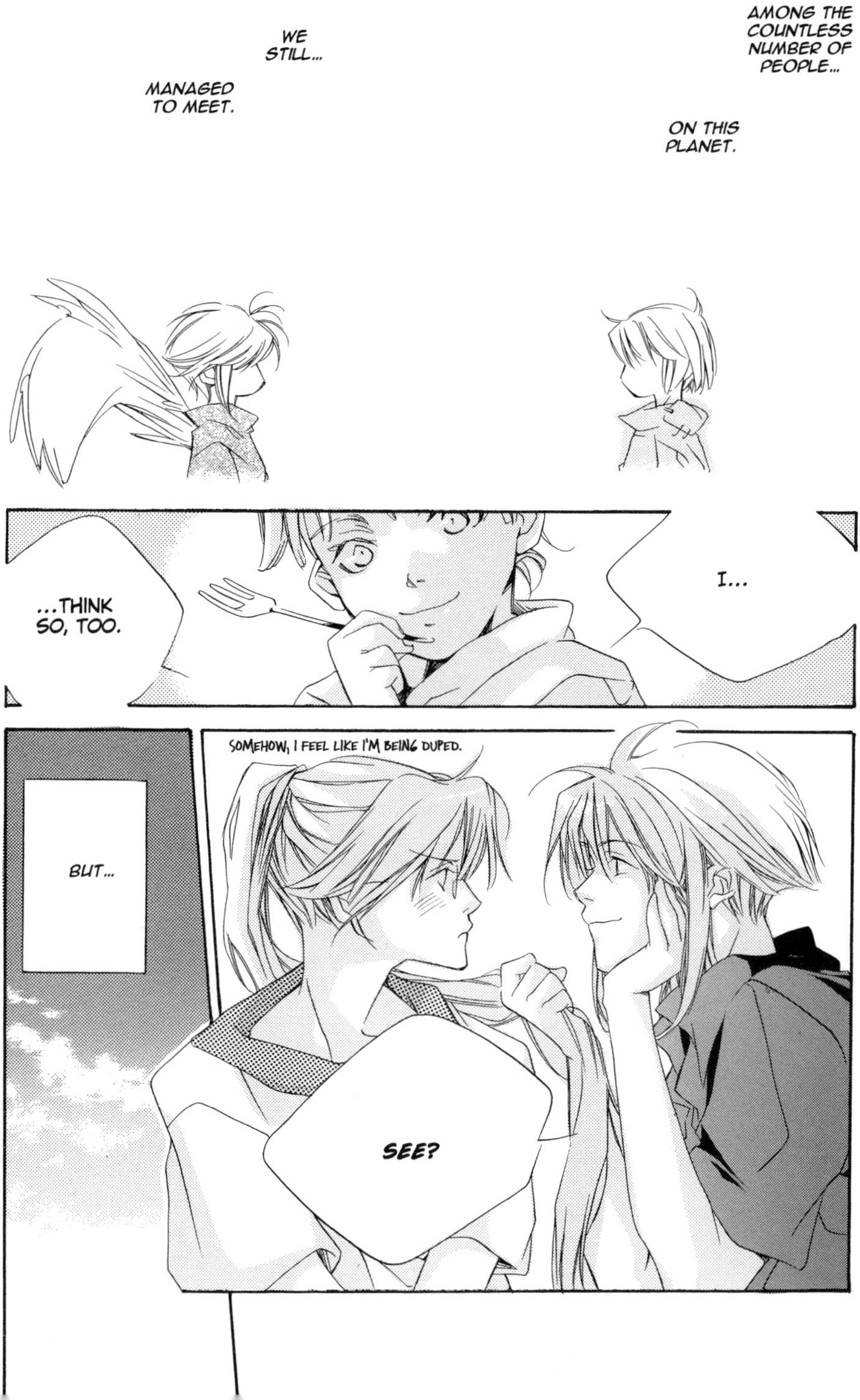
AMONG THE COUNTLESS NUMBER OF PEOPLE...
ON THIS PLANET.
WE STILL...
MANAGED TO MEET.
I...
...THINK SO, TOO.
SOMEHOW, I FEEL LIKE I'M BEING DUPED.
SEE?
BUT...

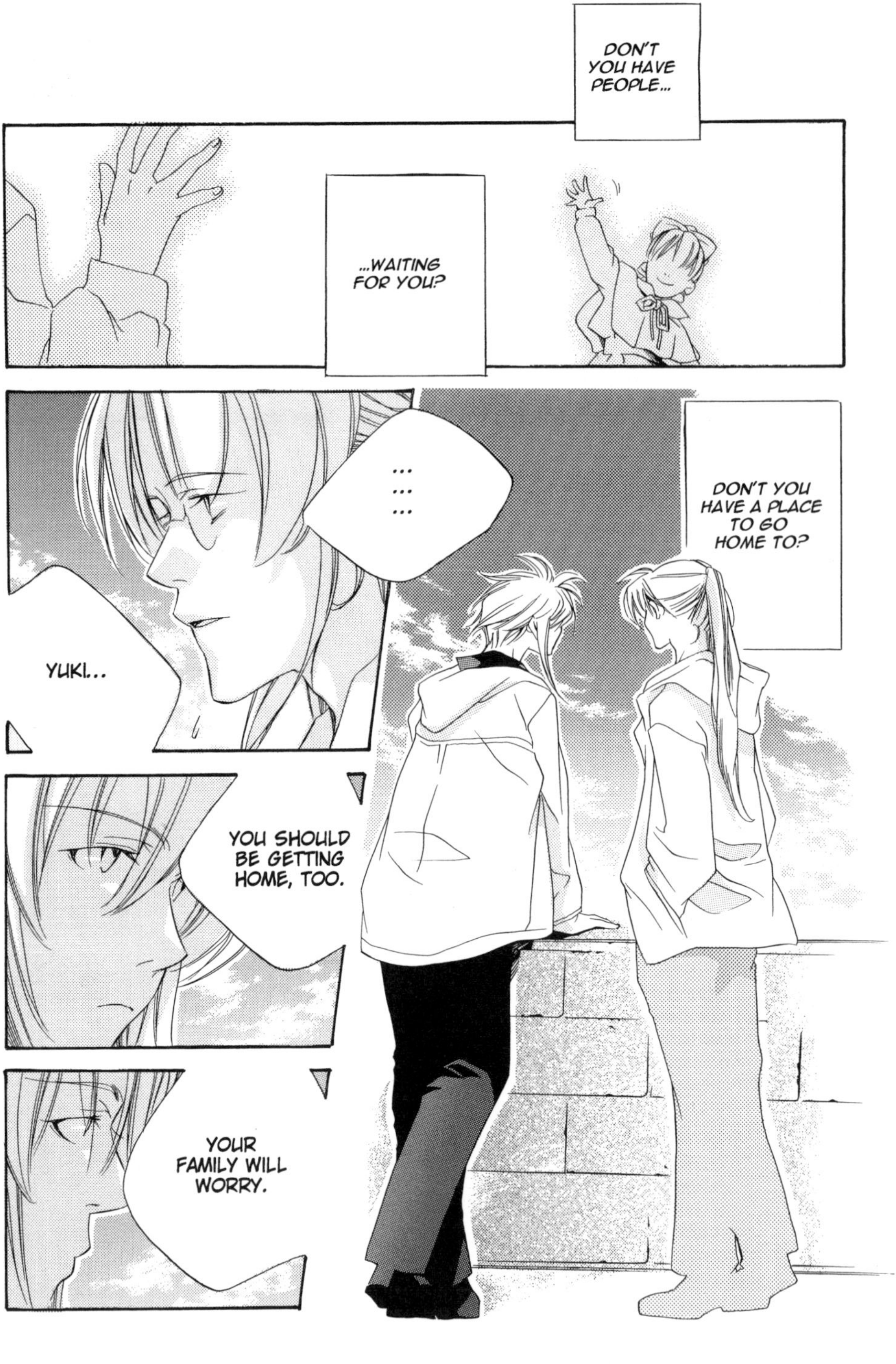
DON'T YOU HAVE PEOPLE...
...WAITING FOR YOU?
DON'T YOU HAVE A PLACE TO GO HOME TO?
...
...
...
YUKI...
YOU SHOULD BE GETTING HOME, TOO.
YOUR FAMILY WILL WORRY.

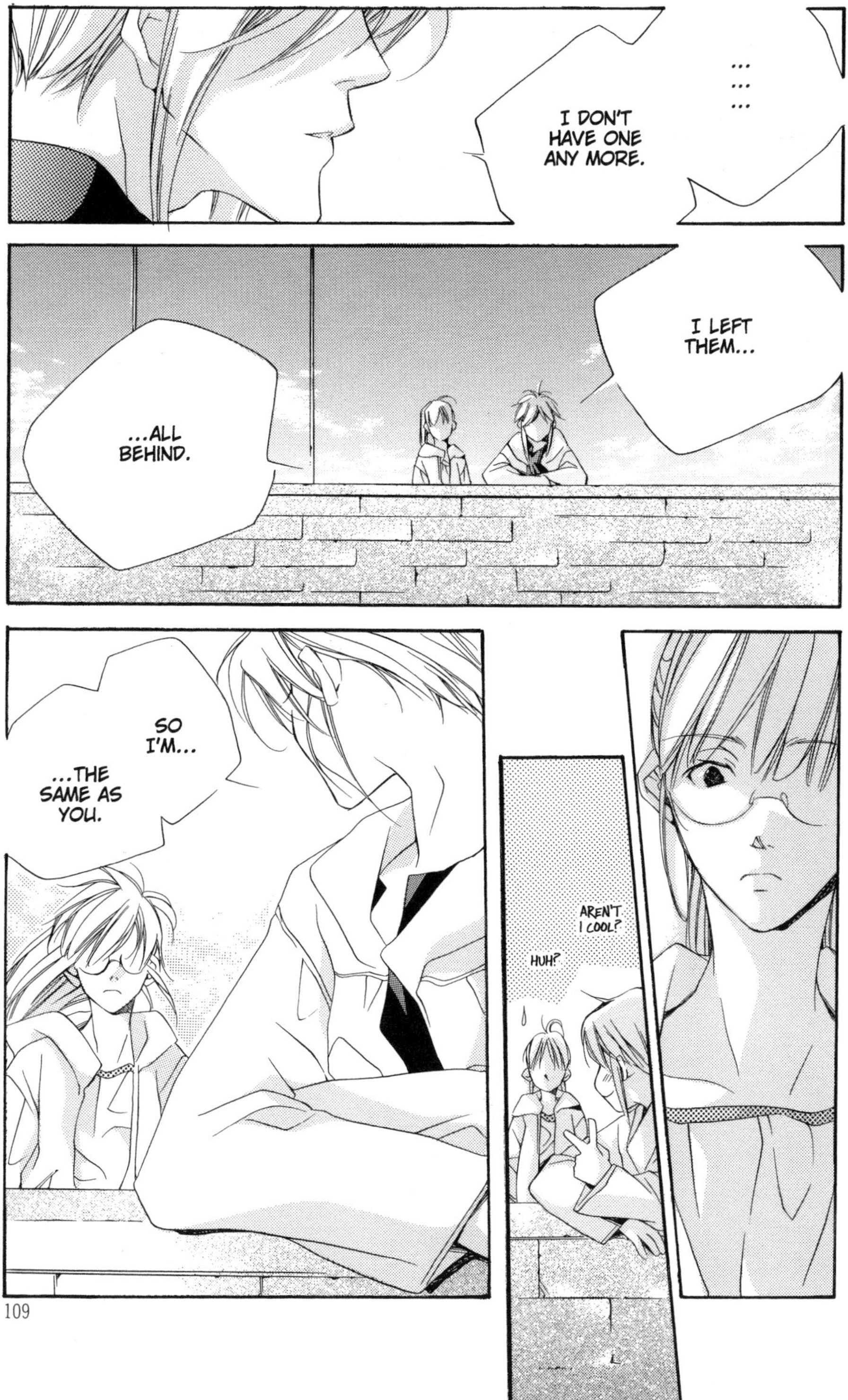
...
...
...
I DON'T HAVE ONE ANY MORE.
I LEFT THEM...
...ALL BEHIND.
AREN'T I COOL?
HUH?
SO I'M...
...THE SAME AS YOU.

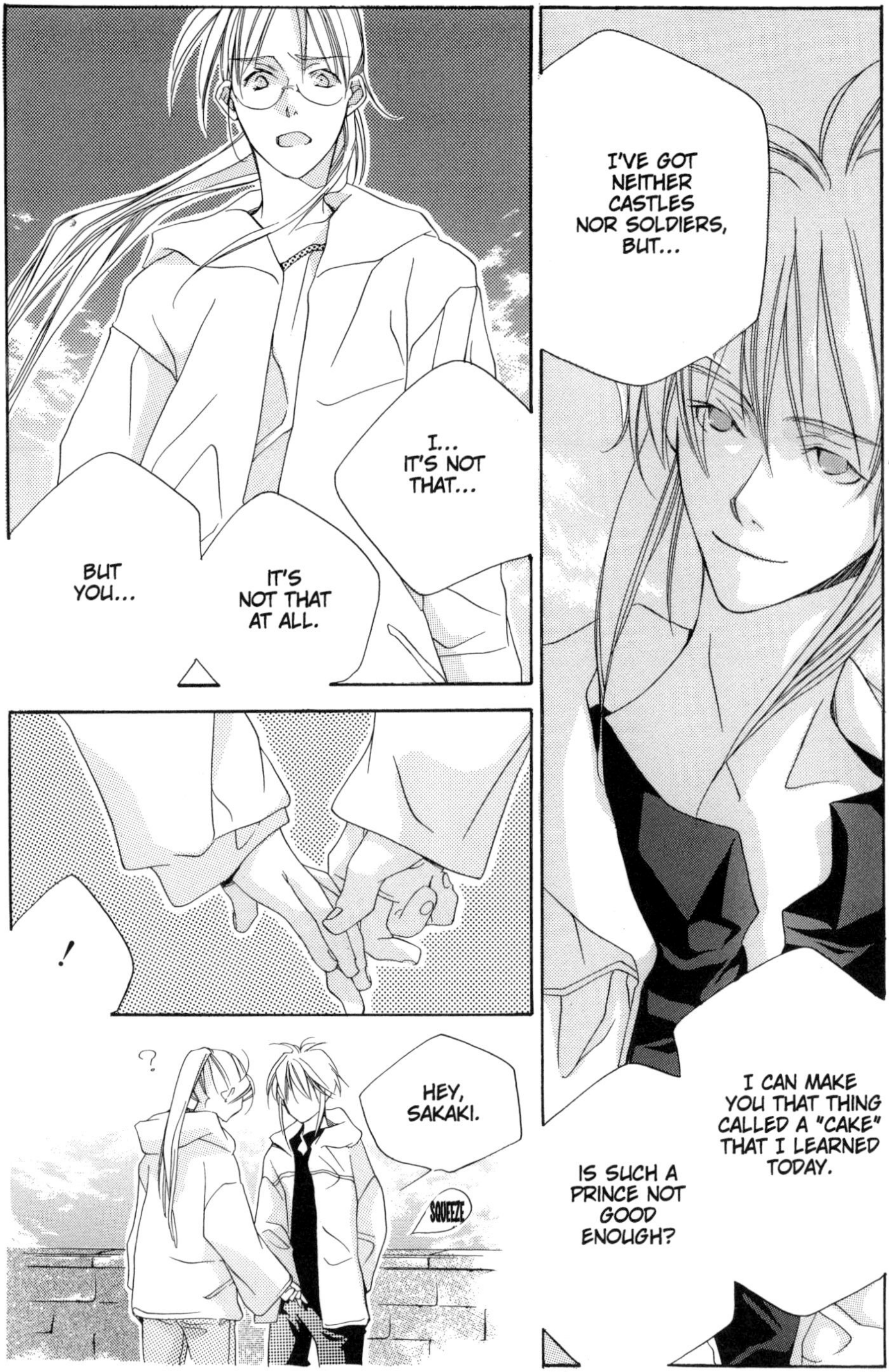
I'VE GOT NEITHER CASTLES NOR SOLDIERS, BUT...
I CAN MAKE YOU THAT THING CALLED A "CAKE" THAT I LEARNED TODAY.
IS SUCH A PRINCE NOT GOOD ENOUGH?
I... IT'S NOT THAT...
IT'S NOT THAT AT ALL.
BUT YOU...
!
HEY, SAKAKI.
?
SQUEEZE

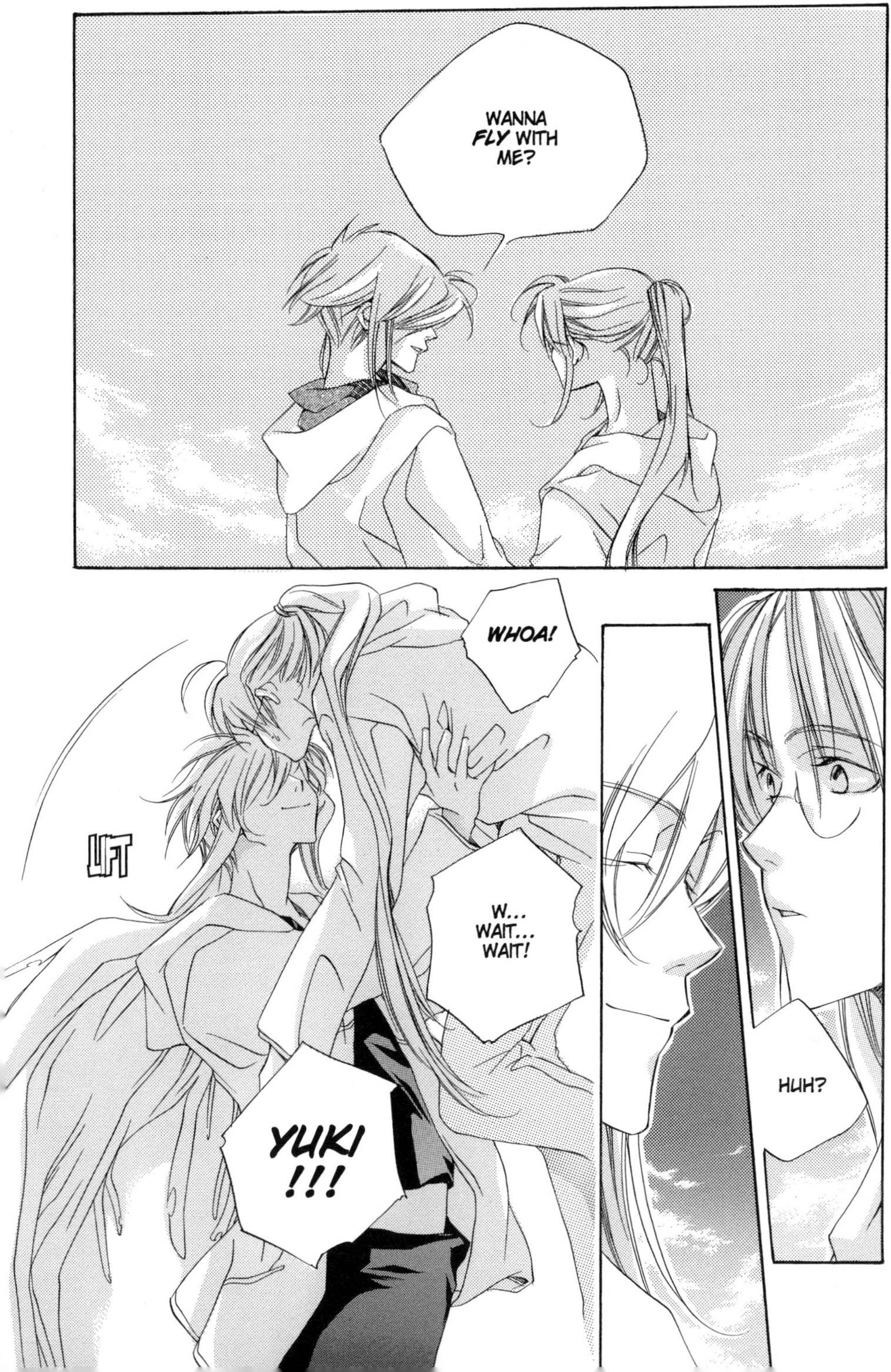
WANNA *FLY* WITH ME?
HUH?
WHOA!
W... WAIT... WAIT!
LIFT
YUKI !!!

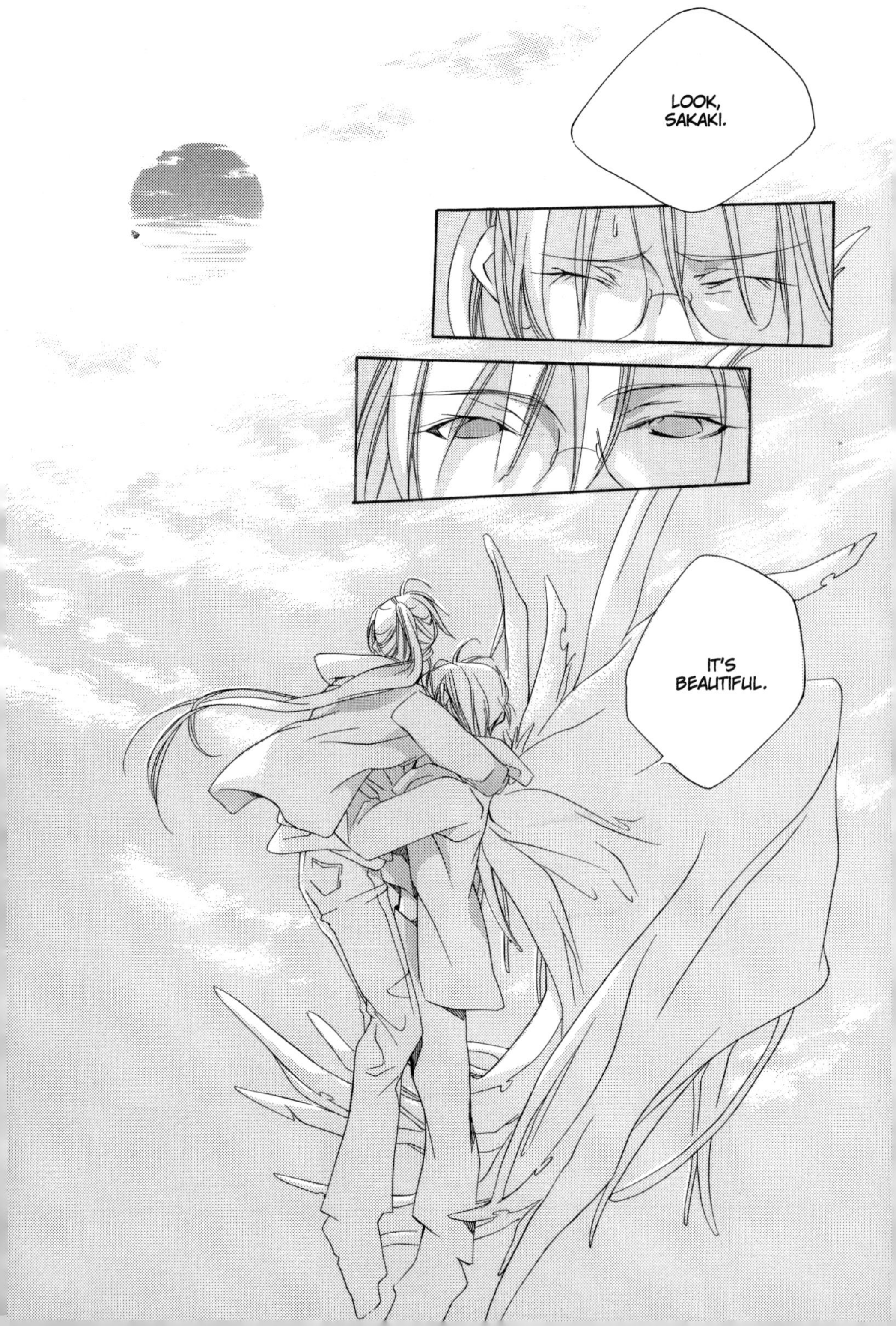
LOOK, SAKAKI.
IT'S BEAUTIFUL.

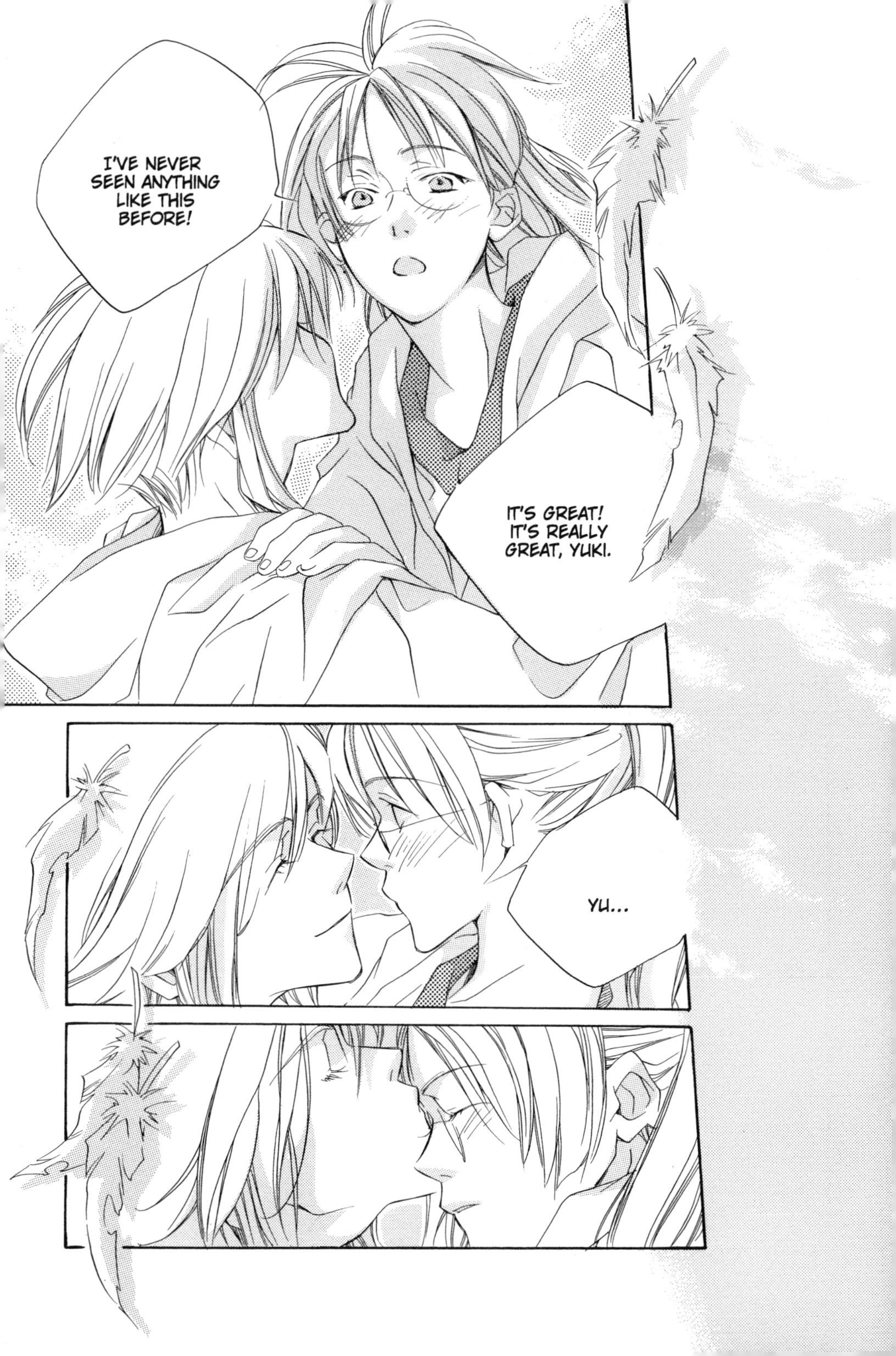
I'VE NEVER SEEN ANYTHING LIKE THIS BEFORE!
IT'S GREAT! IT'S REALLY GREAT, YUKI.
YU...

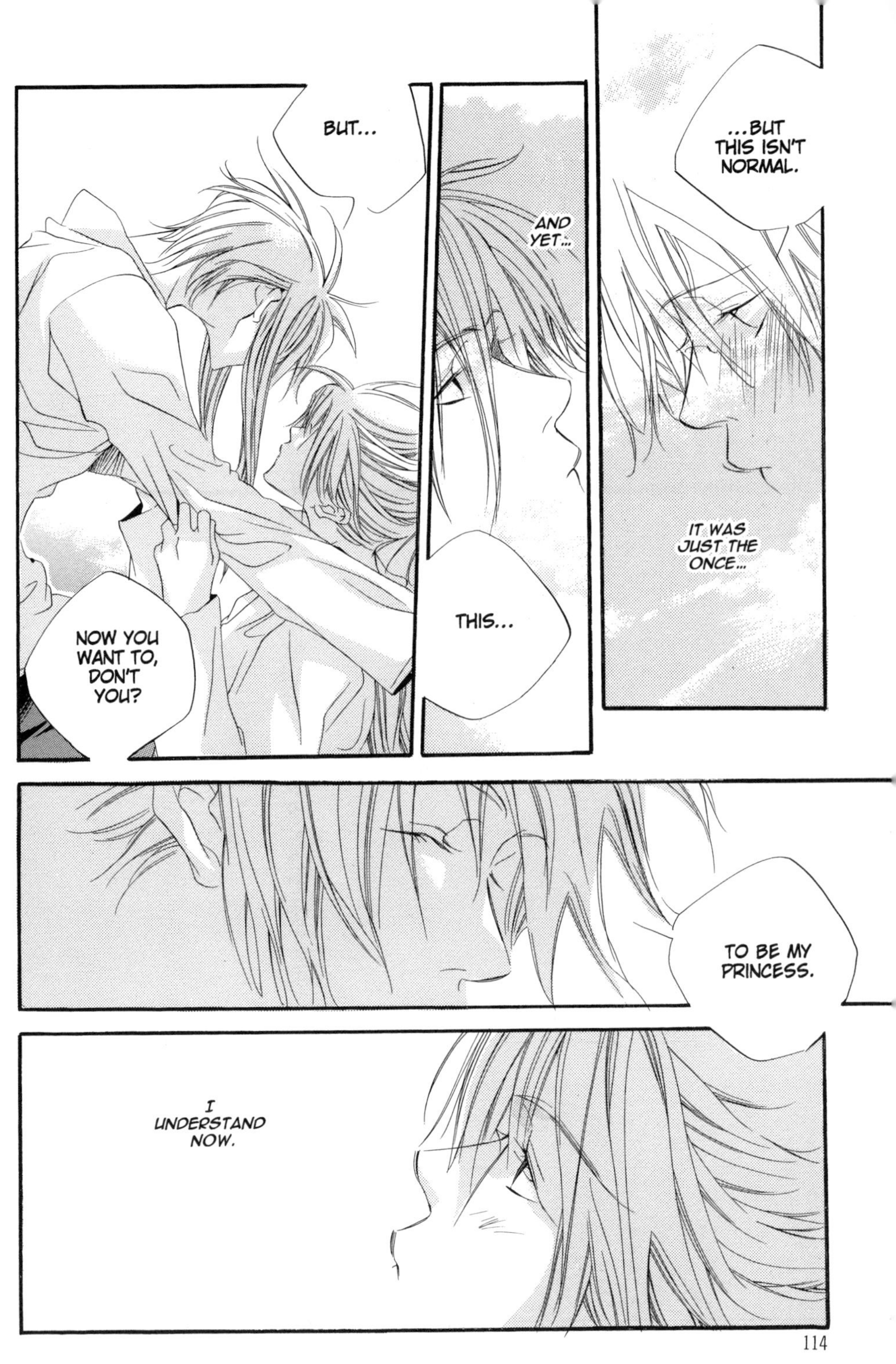
...BUT THIS ISN'T NORMAL.
IT WAS JUST THE ONCE...
AND YET...
THIS...
BUT...
NOW YOU WANT TO, DON'T YOU?
TO BE MY PRINCESS.
I UNDERSTAND NOW.

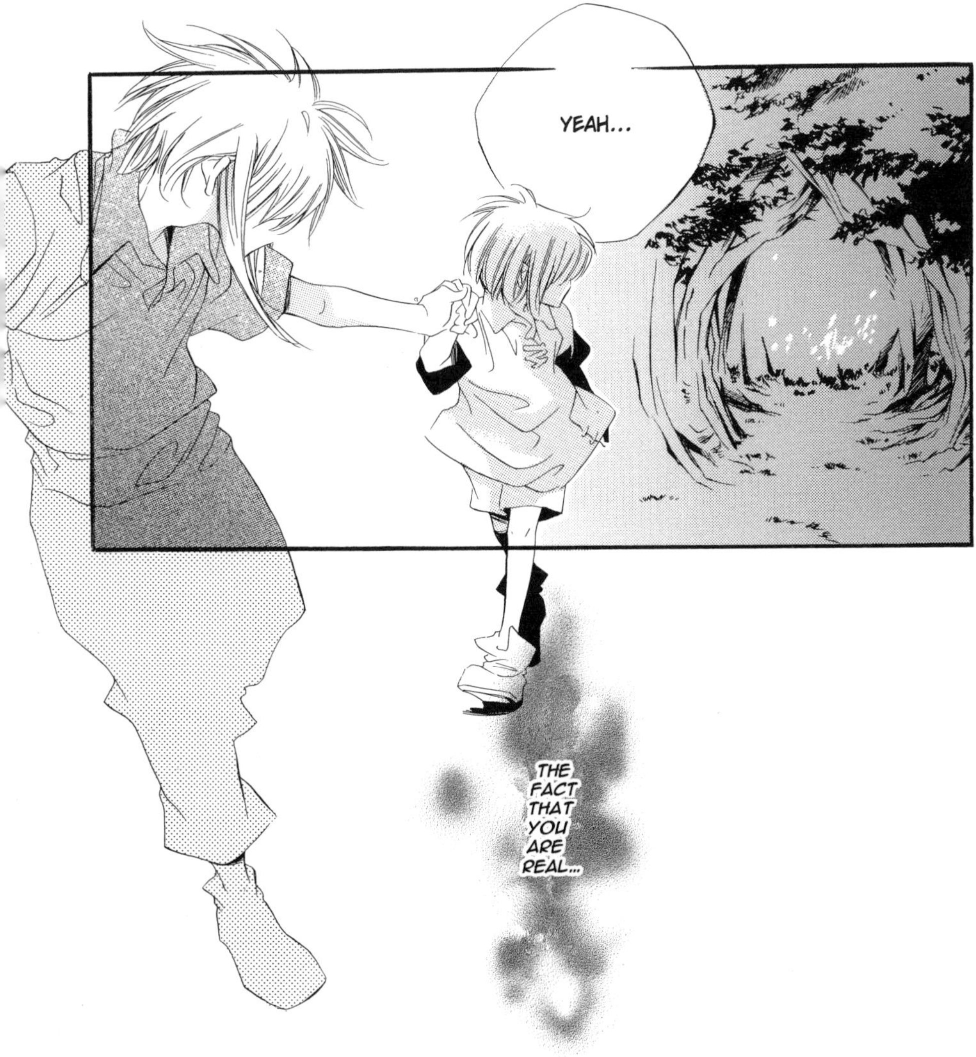
YEAH...
THE FACT THAT YOU ARE REAL...
NO MATTER HOW MANY OTHER SPARKLY OBJECTS I POSSESSED...

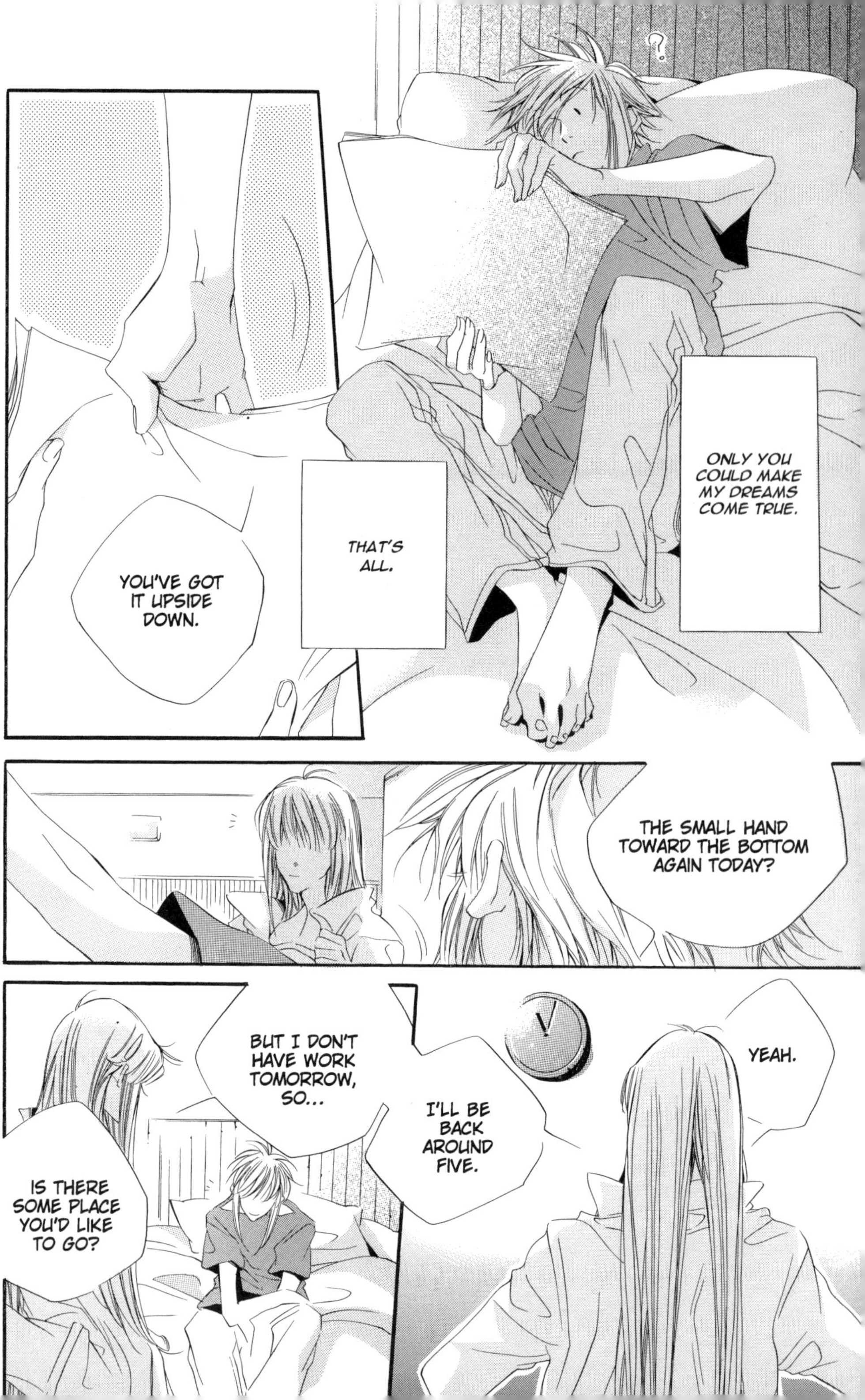
?
ONLY YOU COULD MAKE MY DREAMS COME TRUE.
THAT'S ALL.
YOU'VE GOT IT UPSIDE DOWN.
THE SMALL HAND TOWARD THE BOTTOM AGAIN TODAY?
YEAH.
I'LL BE BACK AROUND FIVE.
BUT I DON'T HAVE WORK TOMORROW, SO...
IS THERE SOME PLACE YOU'D LIKE TO GO?

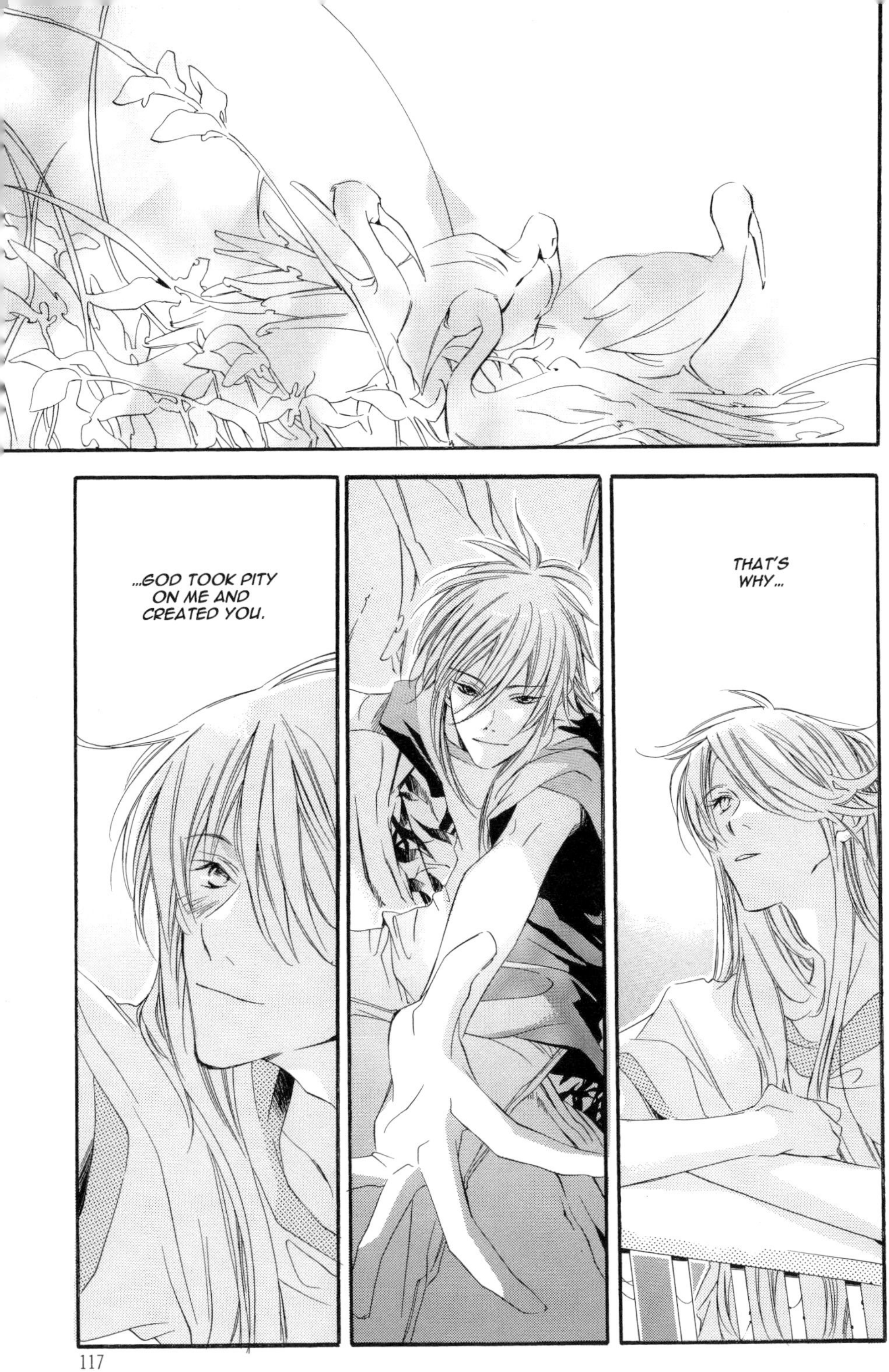
THAT'S WHY...
...GOD TOOK PITY ON ME AND CREATED YOU.

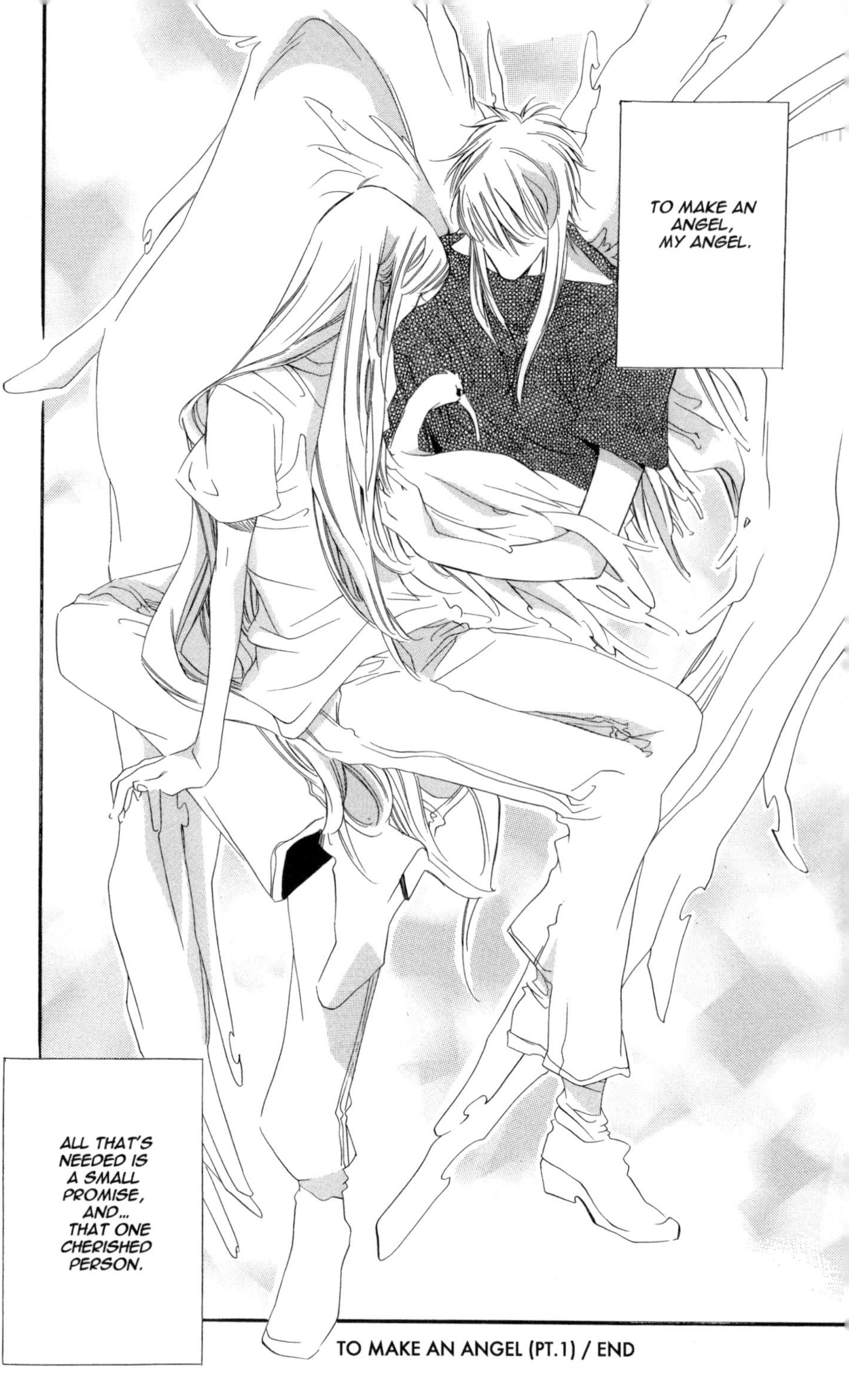
TO MAKE AN ANGEL, MY ANGEL.
ALL THAT'S NEEDED IS A SMALL PROMISE, AND... THAT ONE CHERISHED PERSON.

TO MAKE AN ANGEL (PT.1) / END

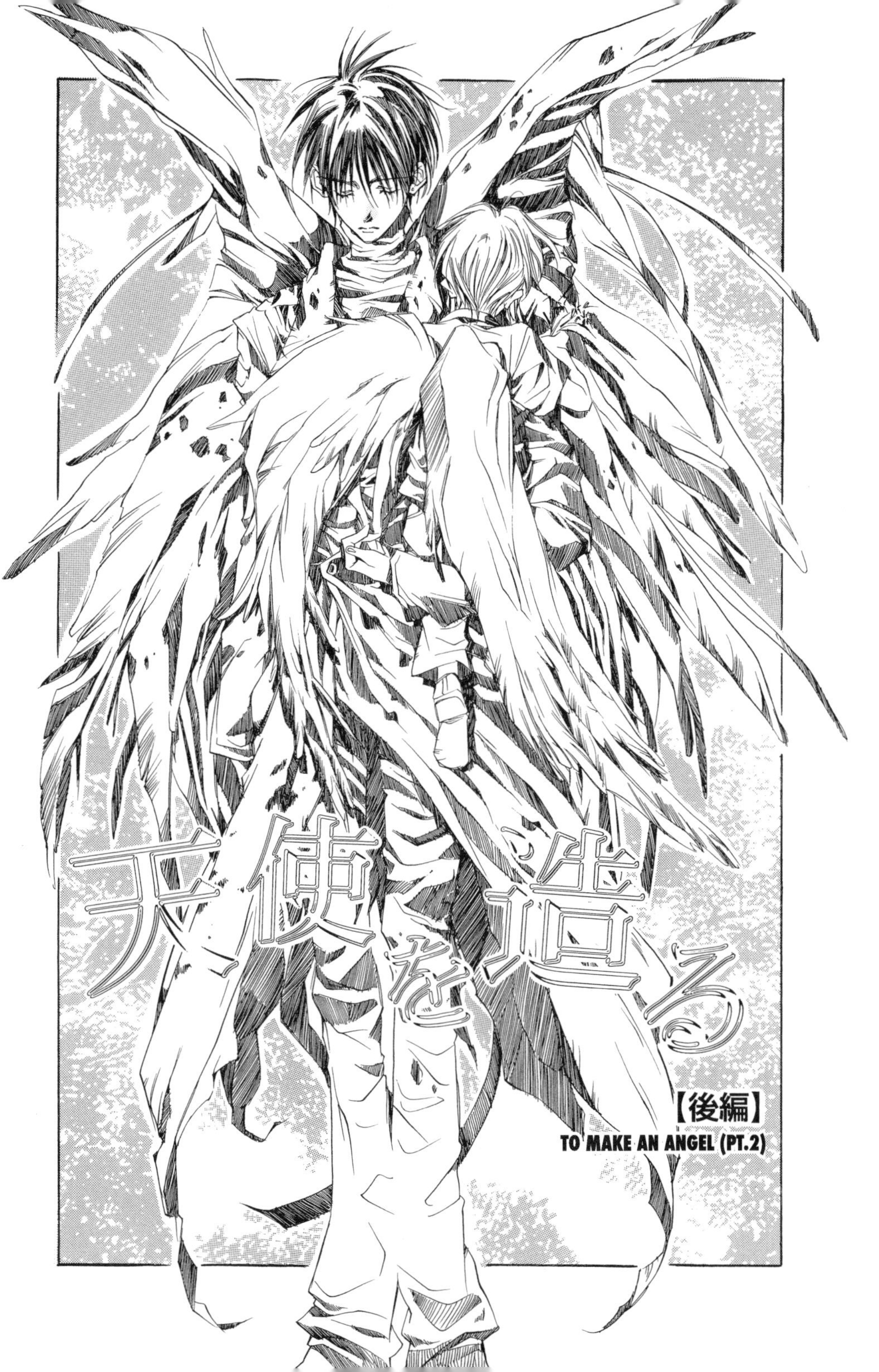
天使を造る
【後編】
TO MAKE AN ANGEL (PT.2)

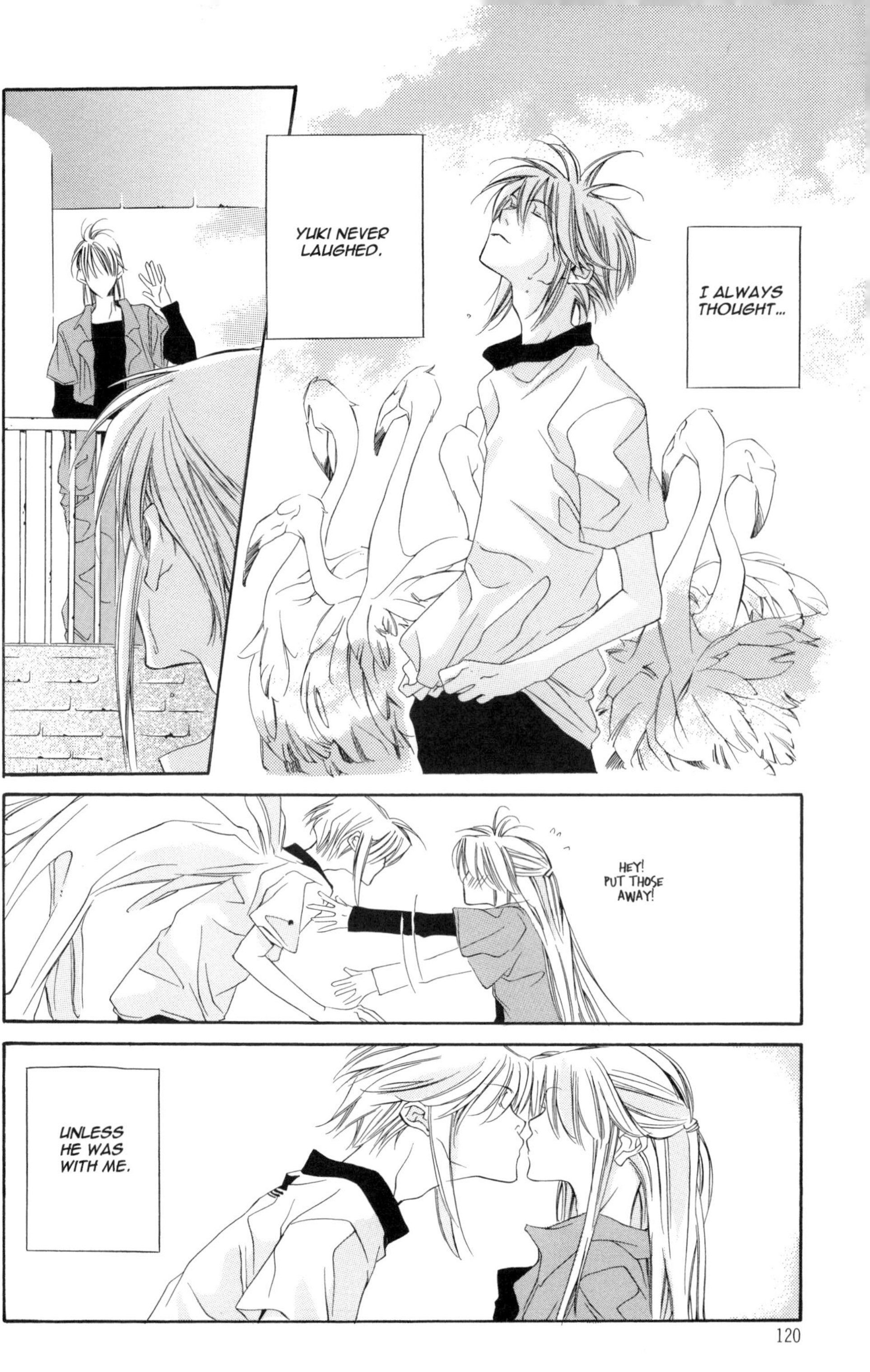
I ALWAYS THOUGHT...
YUKI NEVER LAUGHED.
HEY! PUT THOSE AWAY!
UNLESS HE WAS WITH ME.

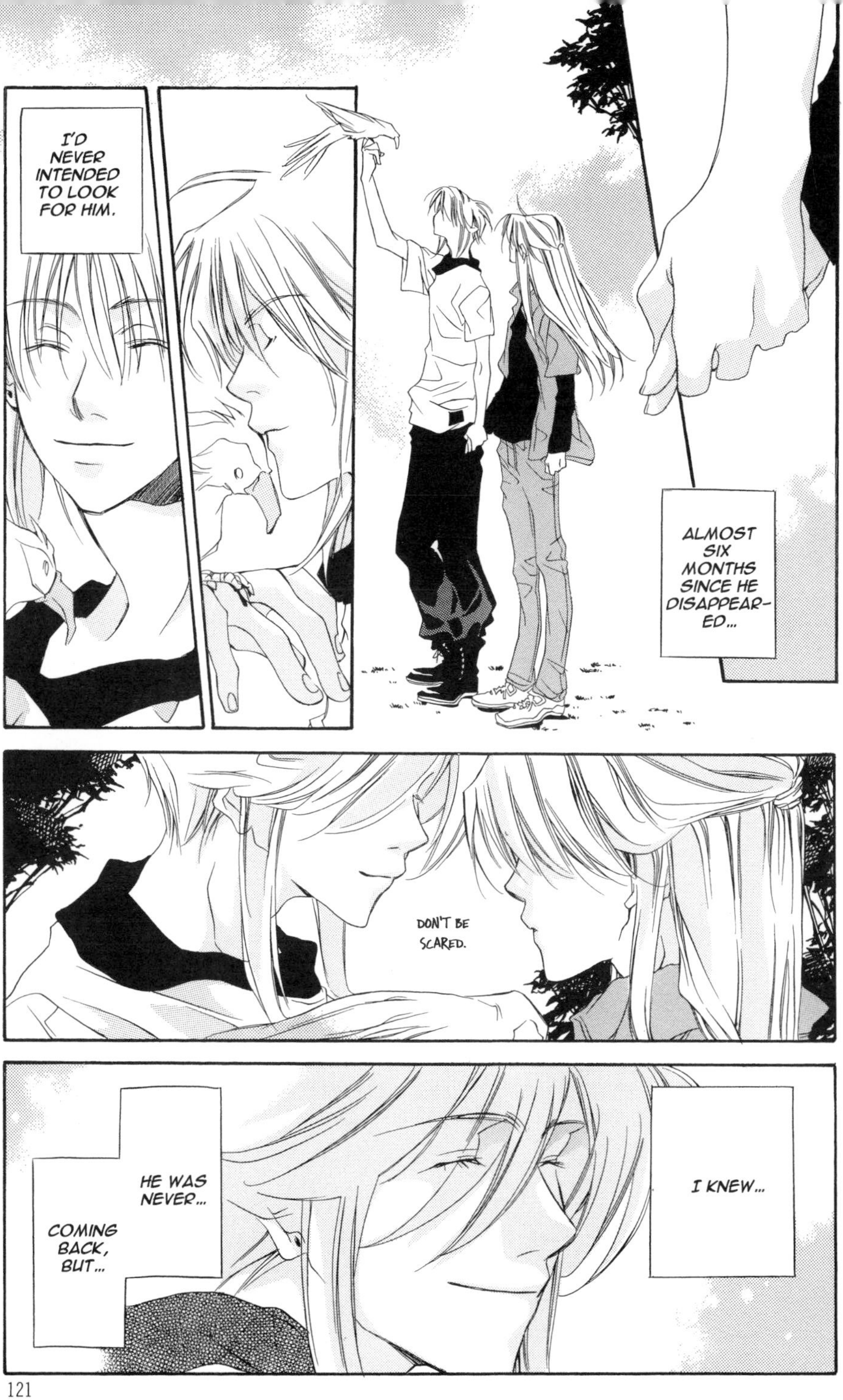
ALMOST SIX MONTHS SINCE HE DISAPPEARED-ED...
I'D NEVER INTENDED TO LOOK FOR HIM.
DON'T BE SCARED.
I KNEW...
HE WAS NEVER...
COMING BACK, BUT...

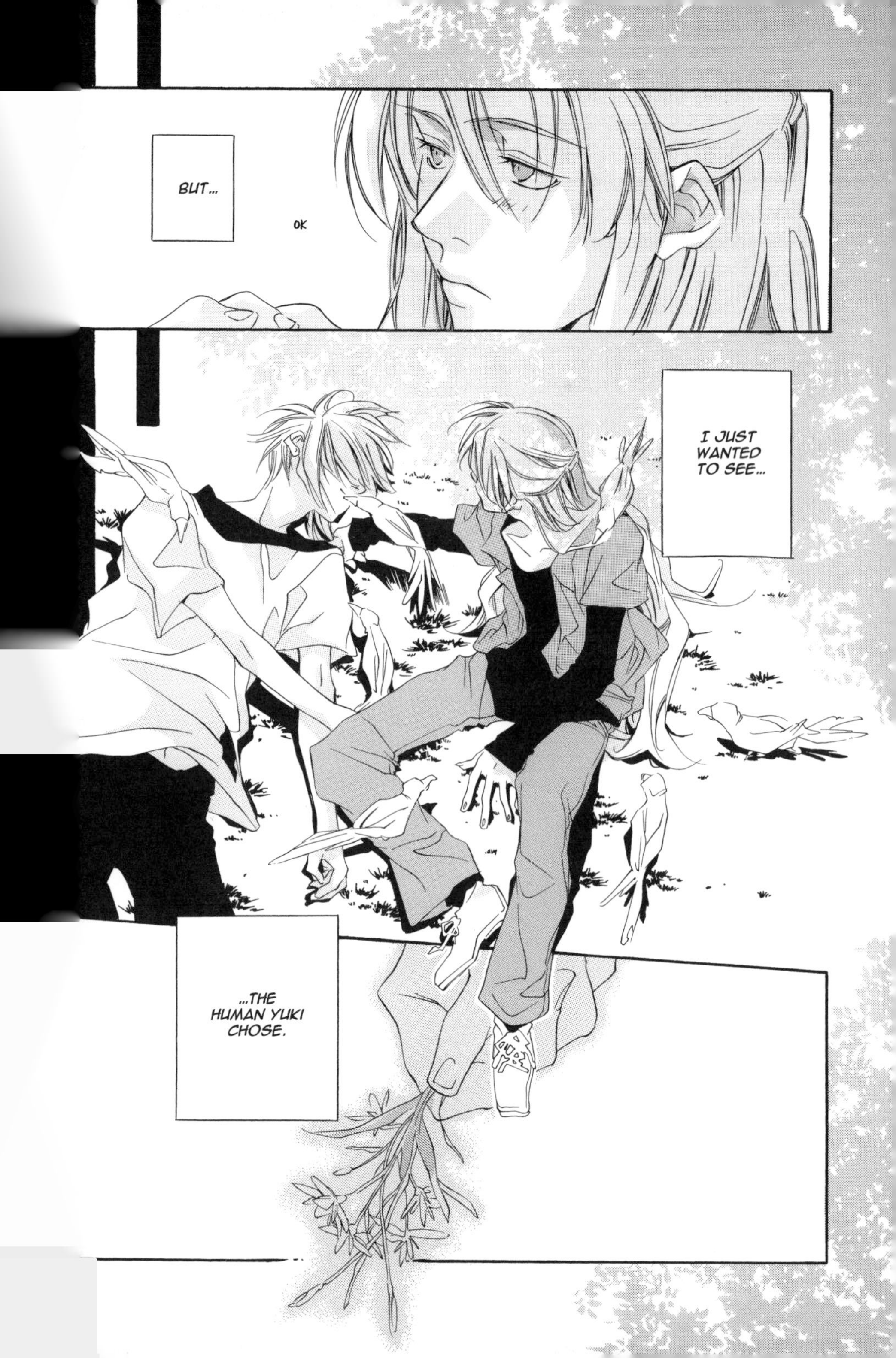
BUT...
OK
I JUST WANTED TO SEE...
...THE HUMAN YUKI CHOSE.

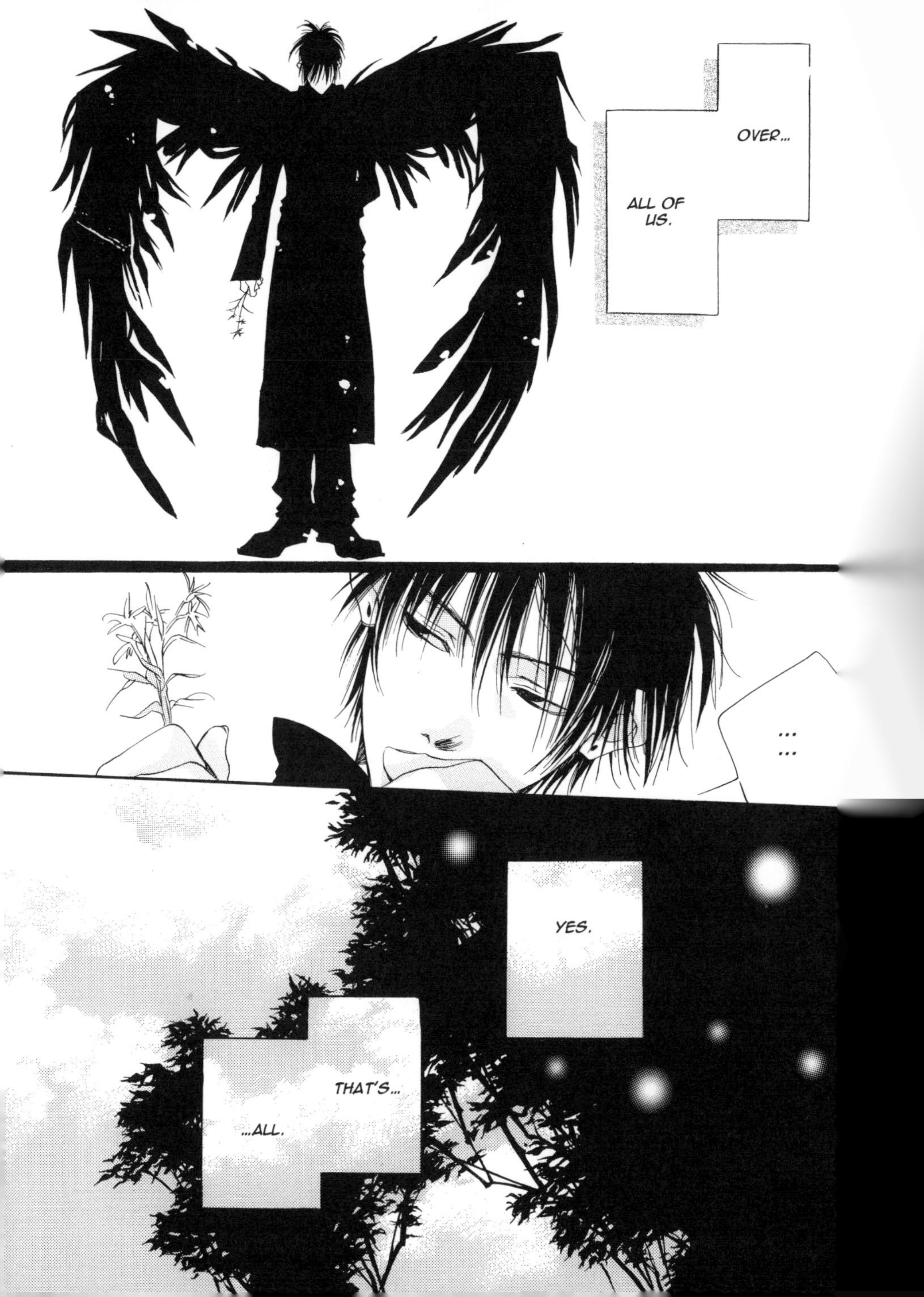

OVER...
ALL OF US.
...
...
YES.
THAT'S...
...ALL.

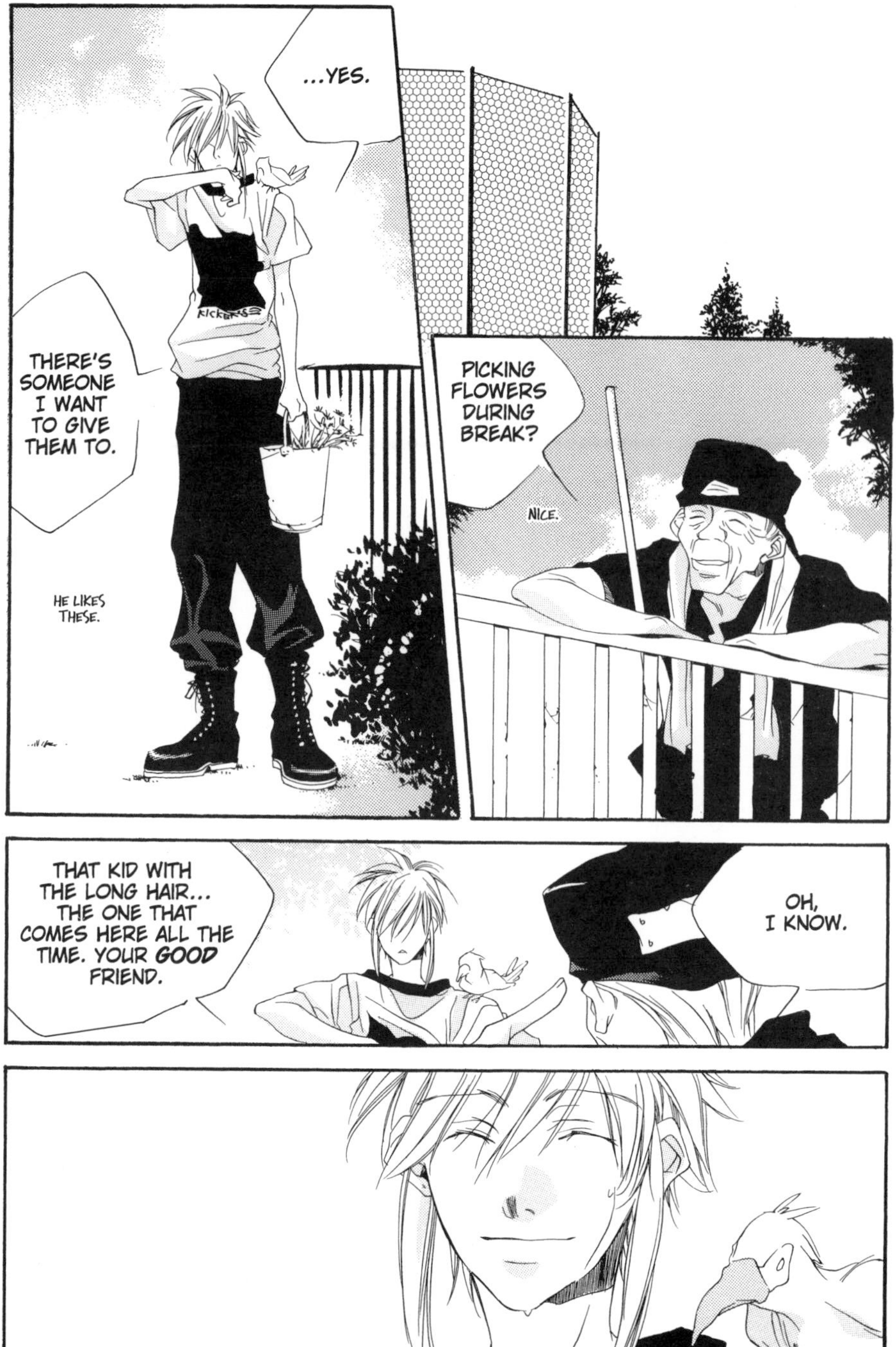
PICKING FLOWERS DURING BREAK?
NICE.
...YES.
THERE'S SOMEONE I WANT TO GIVE THEM TO.
HE LIKES THESE.
OH, I KNOW.
THAT KID WITH THE LONG HAIR... THE ONE THAT COMES HERE ALL THE TIME. YOUR GOOD FRIEND.

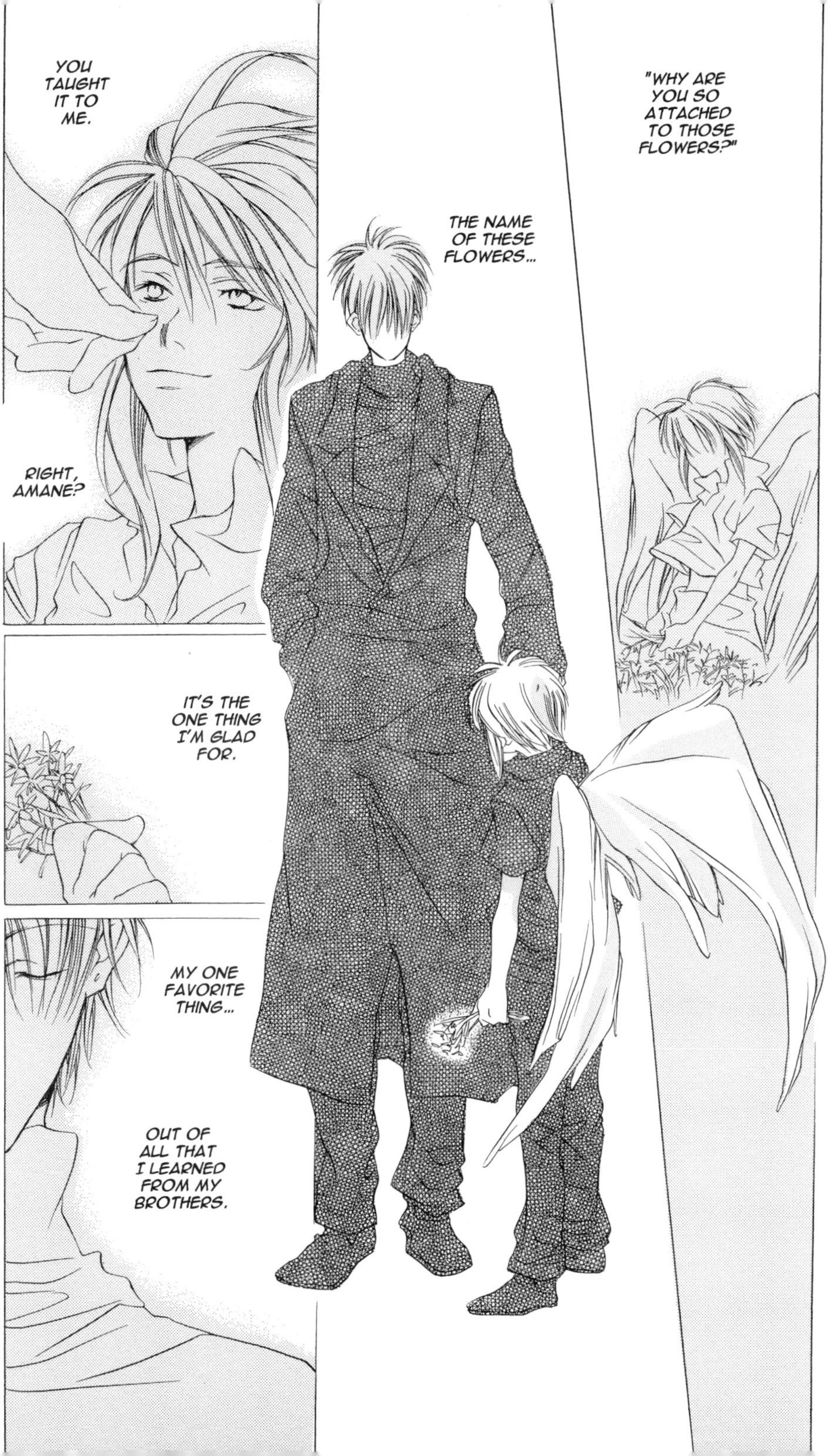
"WHY ARE YOU SO ATTACHED TO THOSE FLOWERS?"
THE NAME OF THESE FLOWERS...
YOU TAUGHT IT TO ME.
RIGHT, AMANE?
IT'S THE ONE THING I'M GLAD FOR.
MY ONE FAVORITE THING...
OUT OF ALL THAT I LEARNED FROM MY BROTHERS.

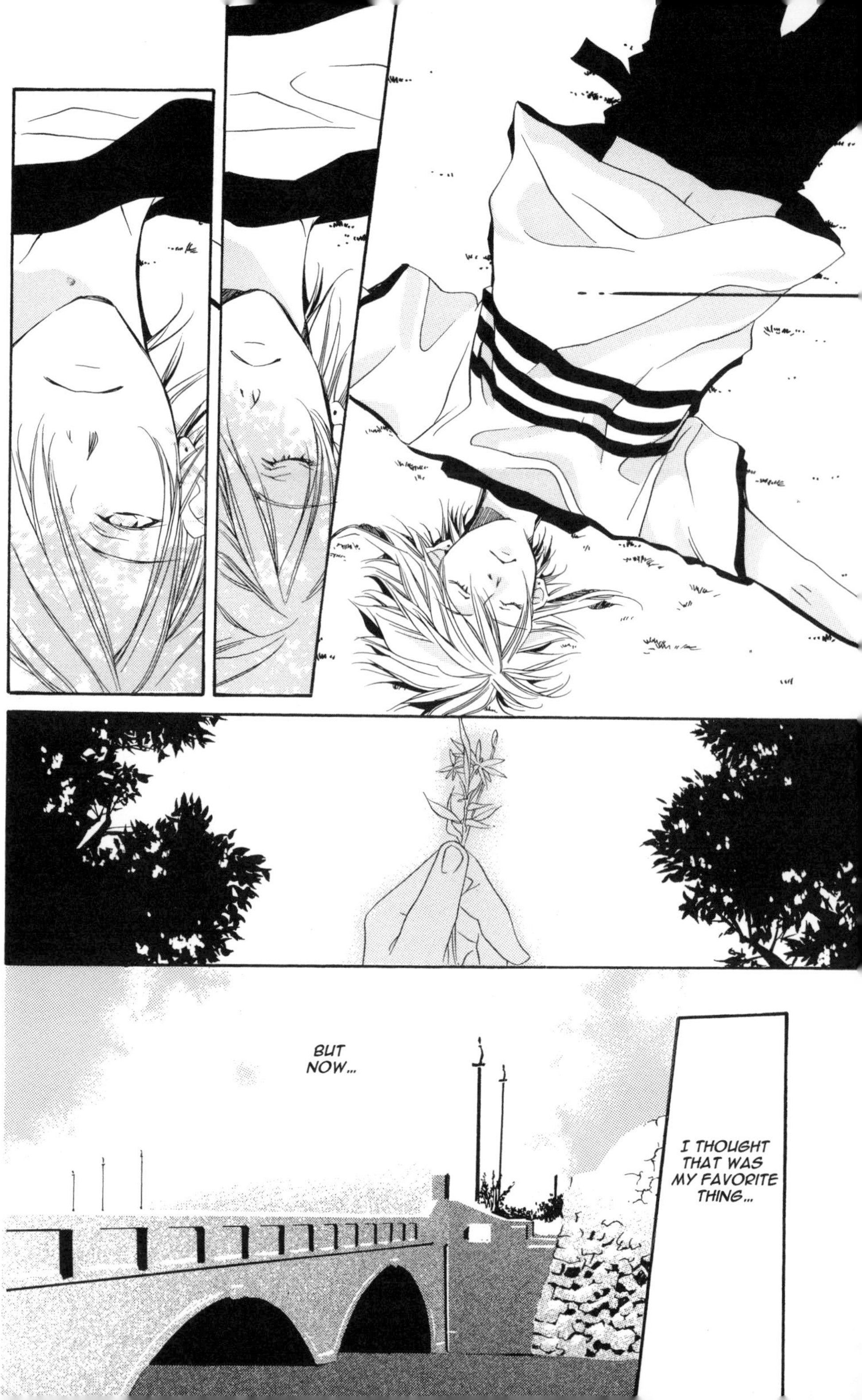
I THOUGHT THAT WAS MY FAVORITE THING...
BUT NOW...

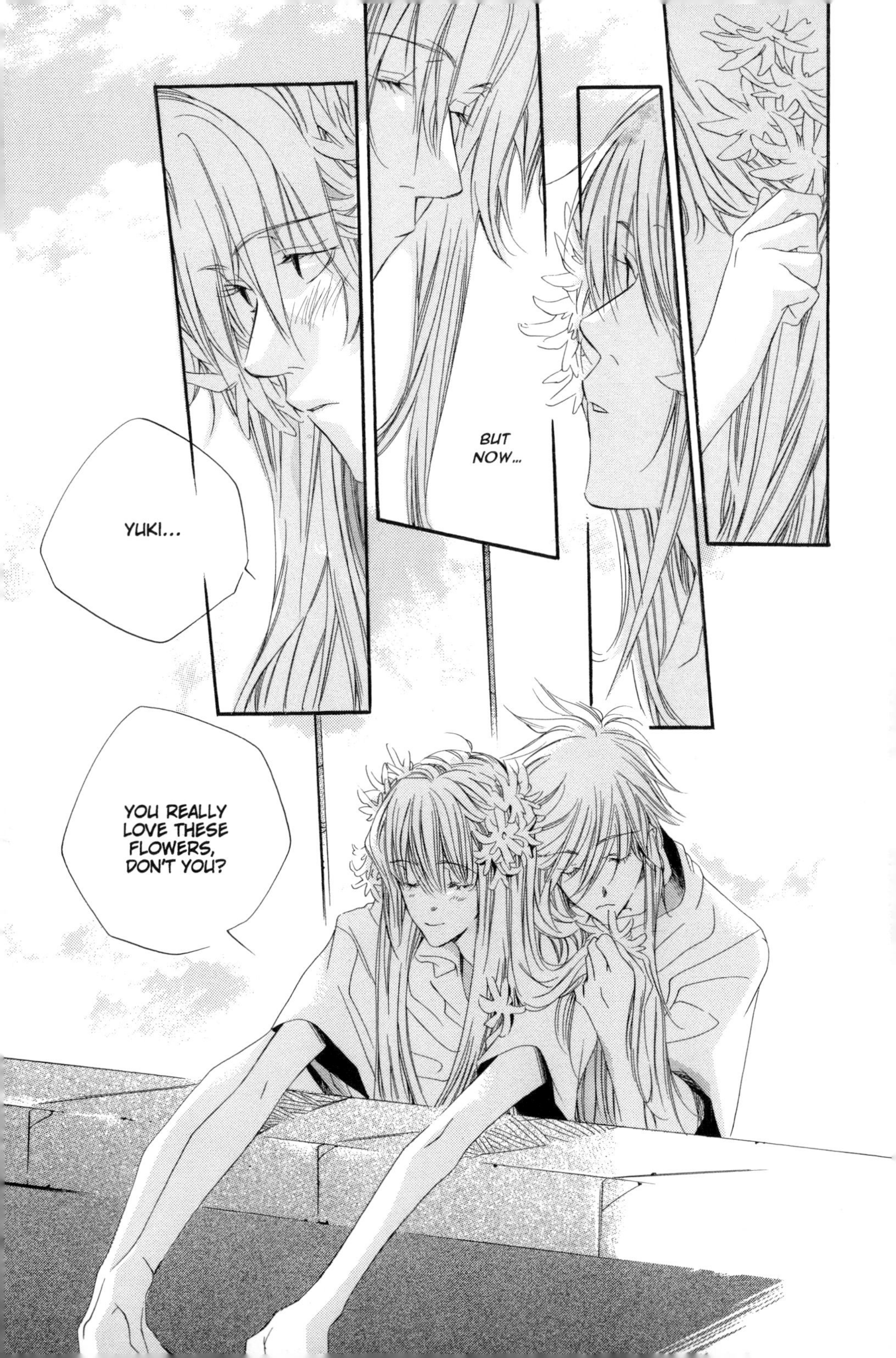
BUT NOW...
YUKI...
YOU REALLY LOVE THESE FLOWERS, DON'T YOU?

GRIN

YEAH.
AFTER
YOU,
SAKAKI.

AND THEN
HE SAID
HE WASN'T
LONELY.

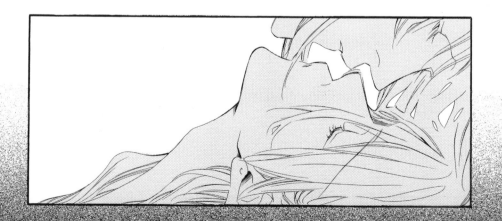

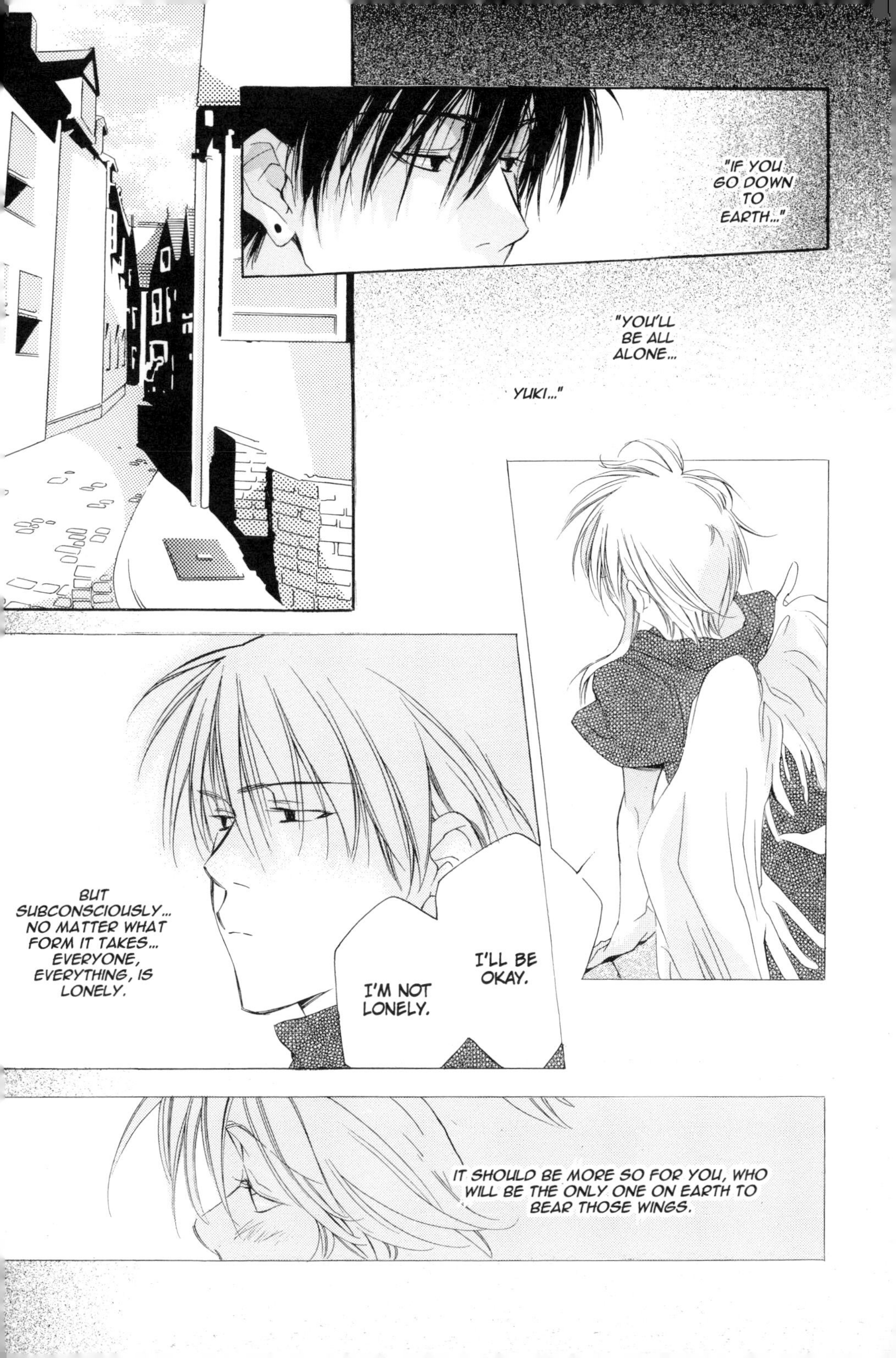
"IF YOU GO DOWN TO EARTH..."
"YOU'LL BE ALL ALONE...
YUKI..."
I'LL BE OKAY.
I'M NOT LONELY.
BUT SUBCONSCIOUSLY... NO MATTER WHAT FORM IT TAKES... EVERYONE, EVERYTHING, IS LONELY.
IT SHOULD BE MORE SO FOR YOU, WHO WILL BE THE ONLY ONE ON EARTH TO BEAR THOSE WINGS.

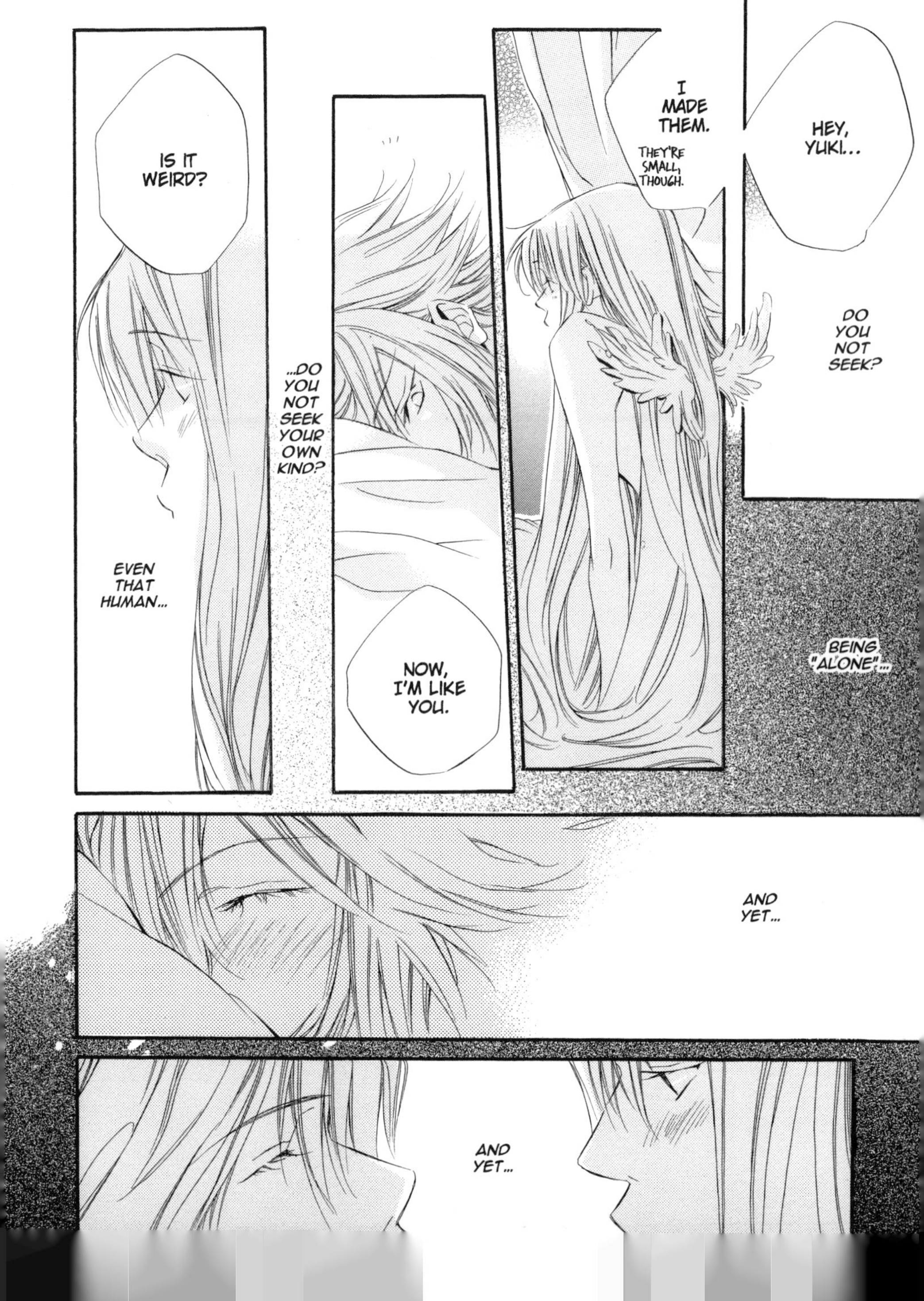
HEY, YUKI...
DO YOU NOT SEEK?
BEING "ALONE"...
I MADE THEM.
THEY'RE SMALL, THOUGH.
NOW, I'M LIKE YOU.
...DO YOU NOT SEEK YOUR OWN KIND?
IS IT WEIRD?
EVEN THAT HUMAN...
AND YET...
AND YET...

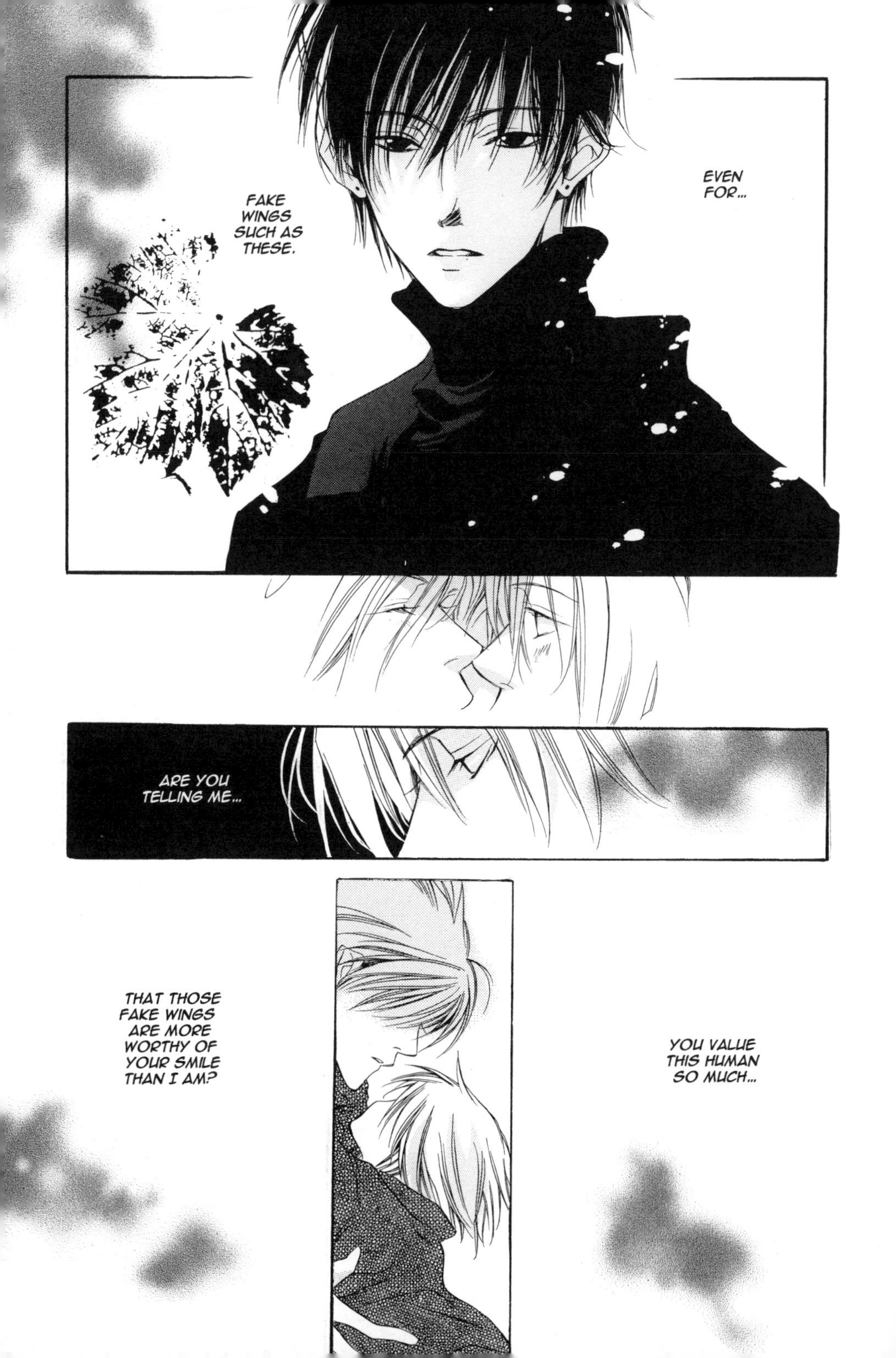
EVEN FOR...
FAKE WINGS SUCH AS THESE.
ARE YOU TELLING ME...
YOU VALUE THIS HUMAN SO MUCH...
THAT THOSE FAKE WINGS ARE MORE WORTHY OF YOUR SMILE THAN I AM?

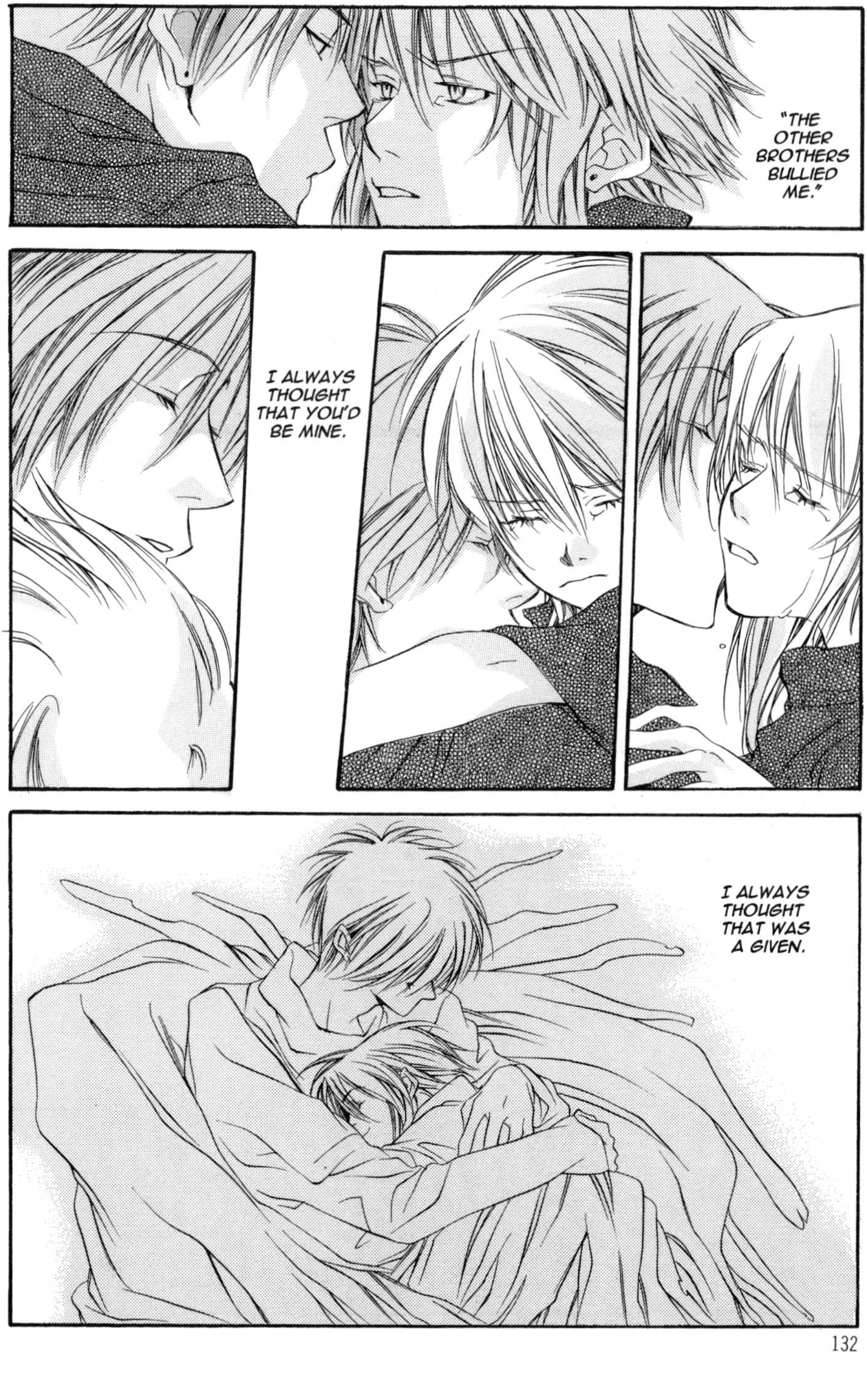
"THE OTHER BROTHERS BULLIED ME."
I ALWAYS THOUGHT THAT YOU'D BE MINE.
I ALWAYS THOUGHT THAT WAS A GIVEN.

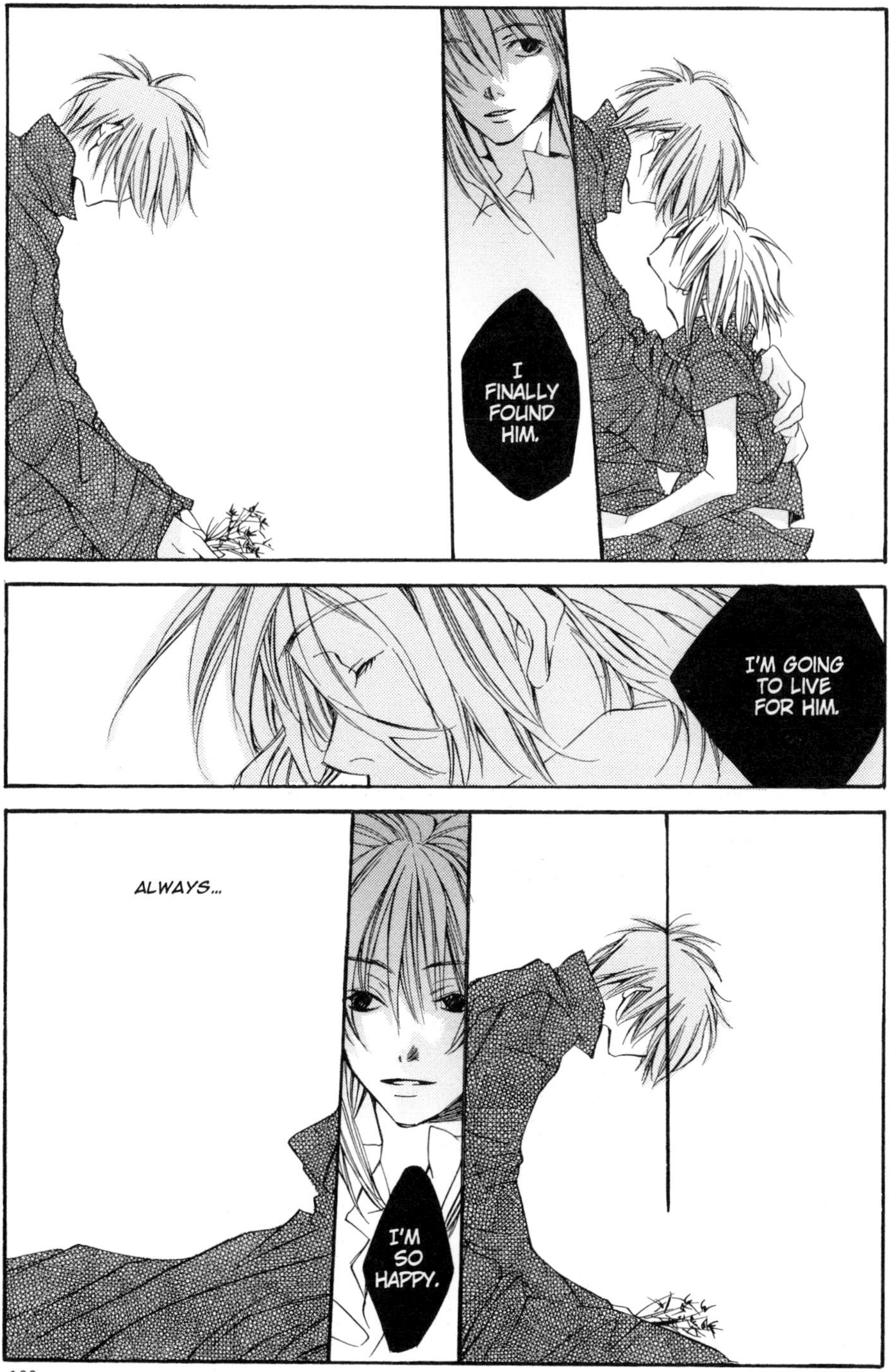
I FINALLY FOUND HIM.
I'M GOING TO LIVE FOR HIM.
I'M SO HAPPY.
ALWAYS...

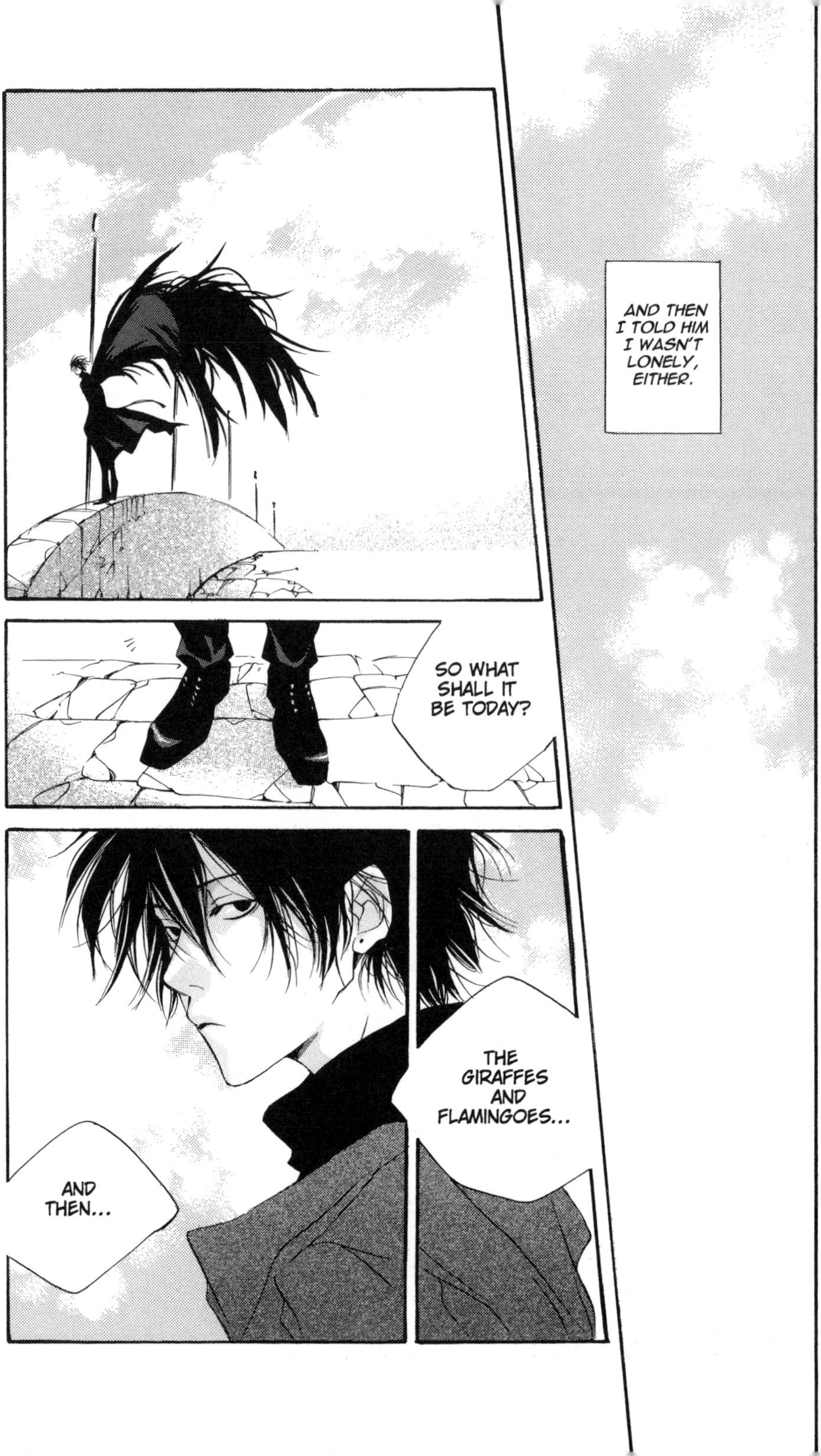
AND THEN I TOLD HIM I WASN'T LONELY, EITHER.
SO WHAT SHALL IT BE TODAY?
THE GIRAFFES AND FLAMINGOES...
AND THEN...

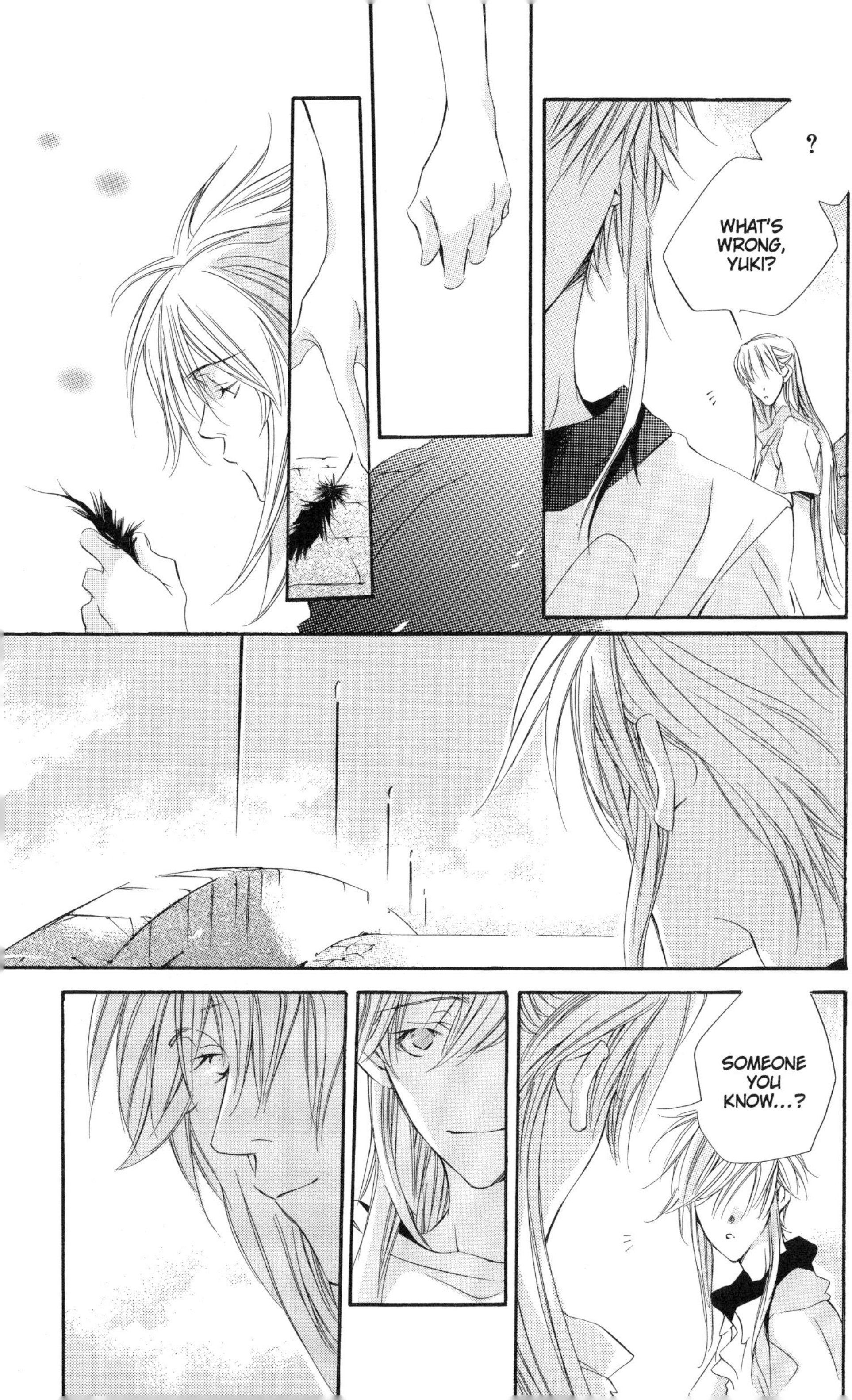
?
WHAT'S WRONG, YUKI?
SOMEONE YOU KNOW...?

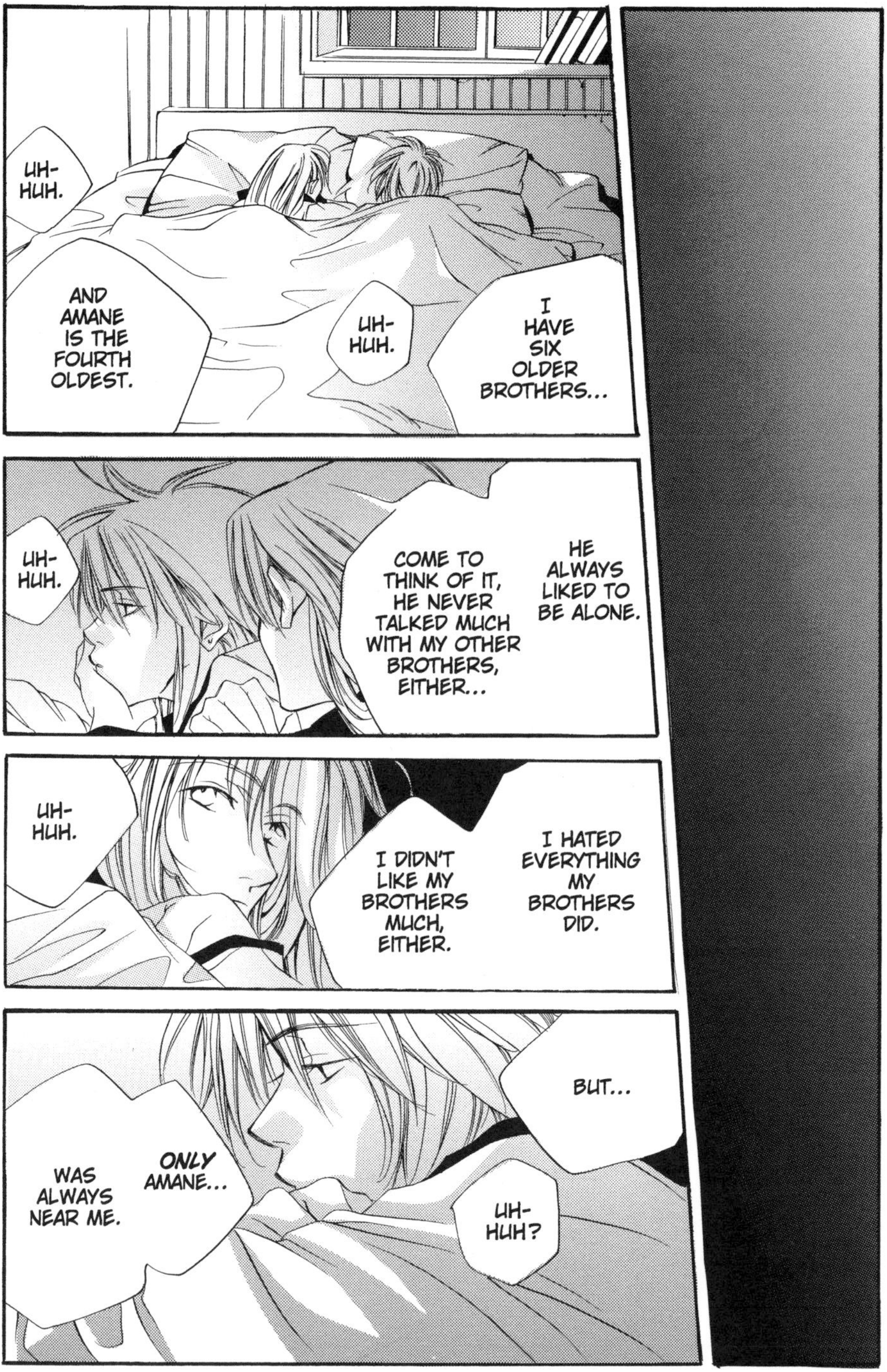
I HAVE SIX OLDER BROTHERS...
UH-HUH.
AND AMANE IS THE FOURTH OLDEST.
UH-HUH.
HE ALWAYS LIKED TO BE ALONE.
COME TO THINK OF IT, HE NEVER TALKED MUCH WITH MY OTHER BROTHERS, EITHER...
UH-HUH.
I HATED EVERYTHING MY BROTHERS DID.
I DIDN'T LIKE MY BROTHERS MUCH, EITHER.
UH-HUH.
BUT...
UH-HUH?
ONLY AMANE...
WAS ALWAYS NEAR ME.

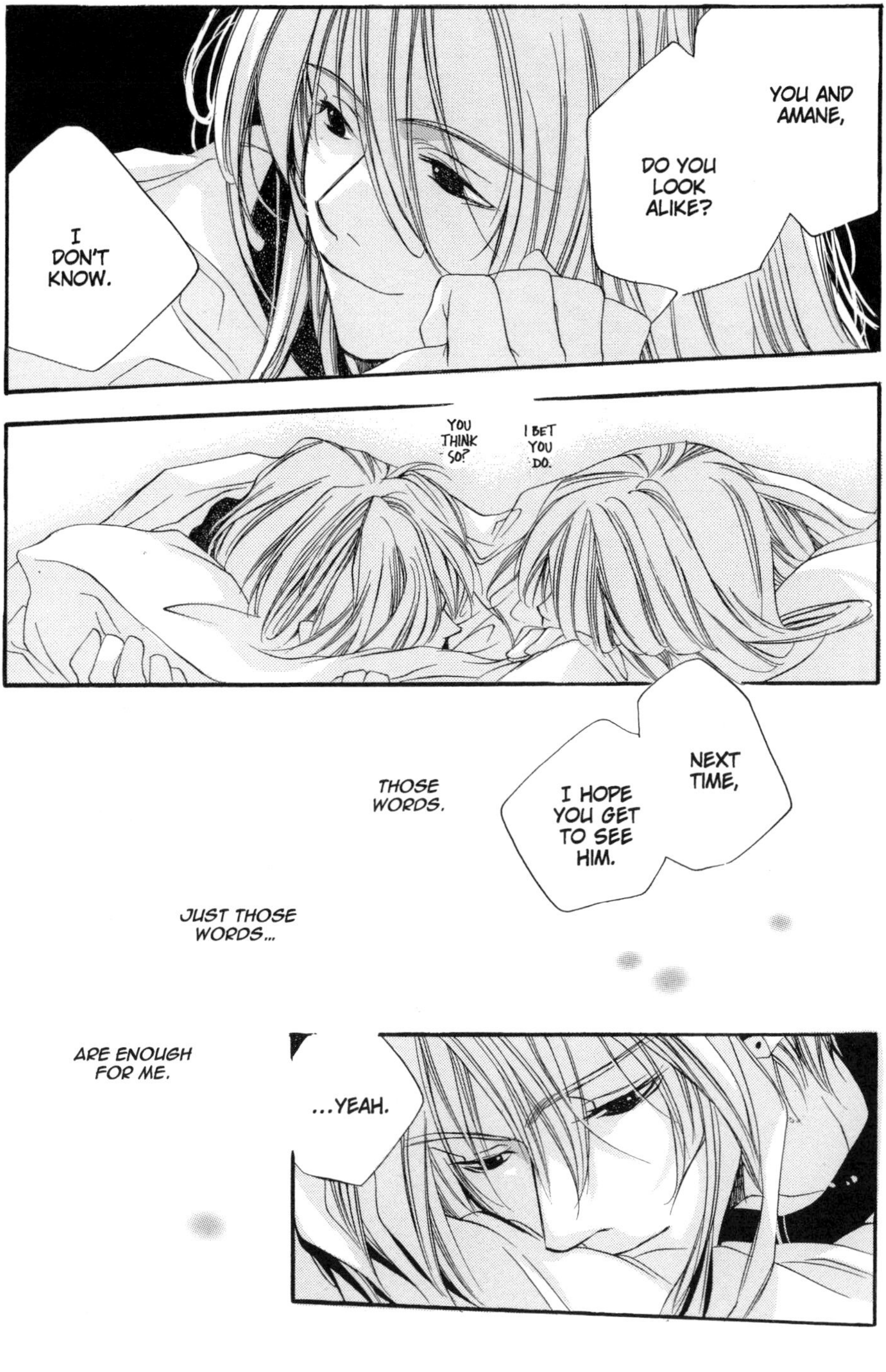
YOU AND AMANE,
DO YOU LOOK ALIKE?
I DON'T KNOW.
I BET YOU DO.
YOU THINK SO?
NEXT TIME,
I HOPE YOU GET TO SEE HIM.
THOSE WORDS.
JUST THOSE WORDS...
...YEAH.
ARE ENOUGH FOR ME.

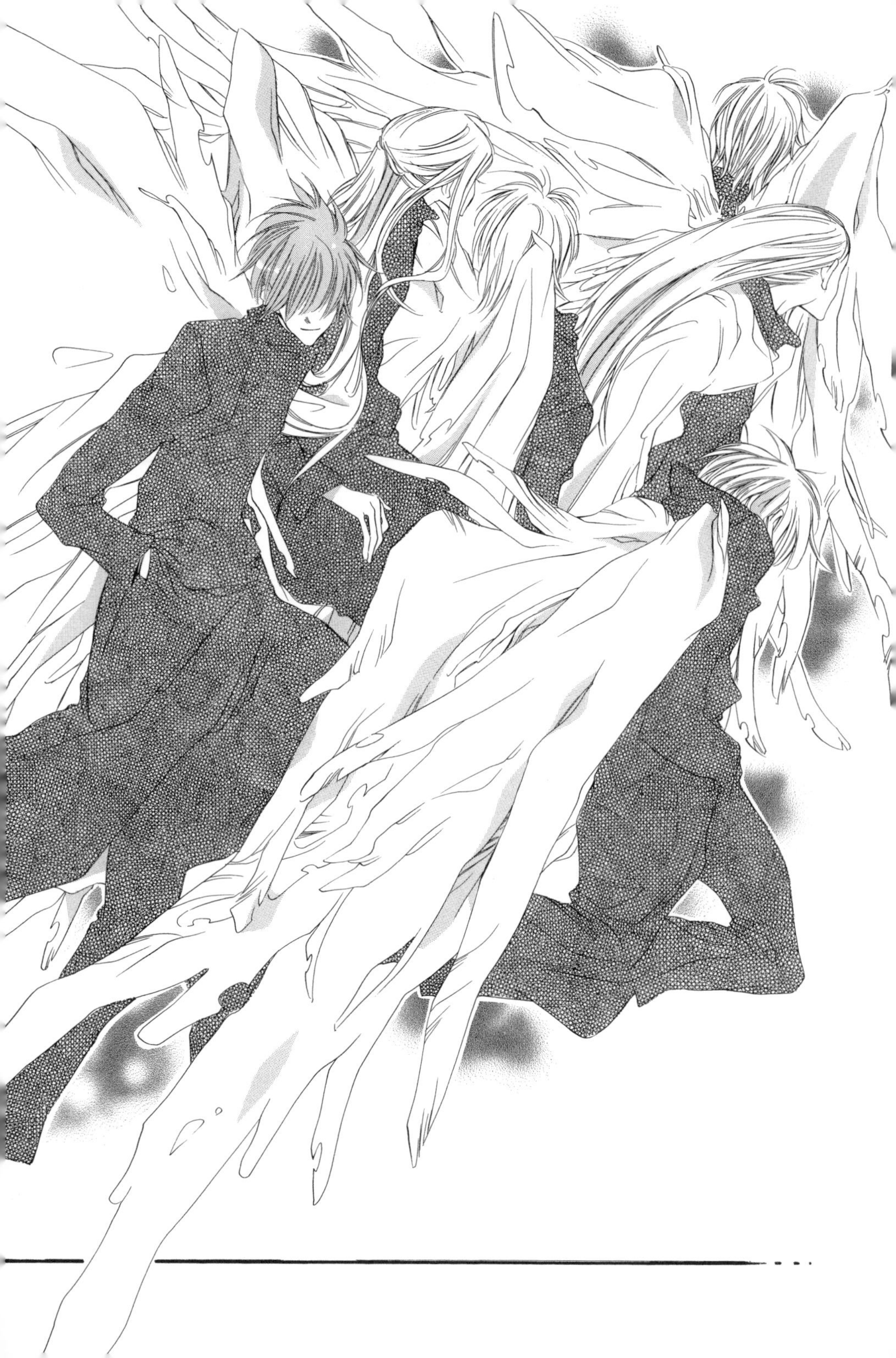

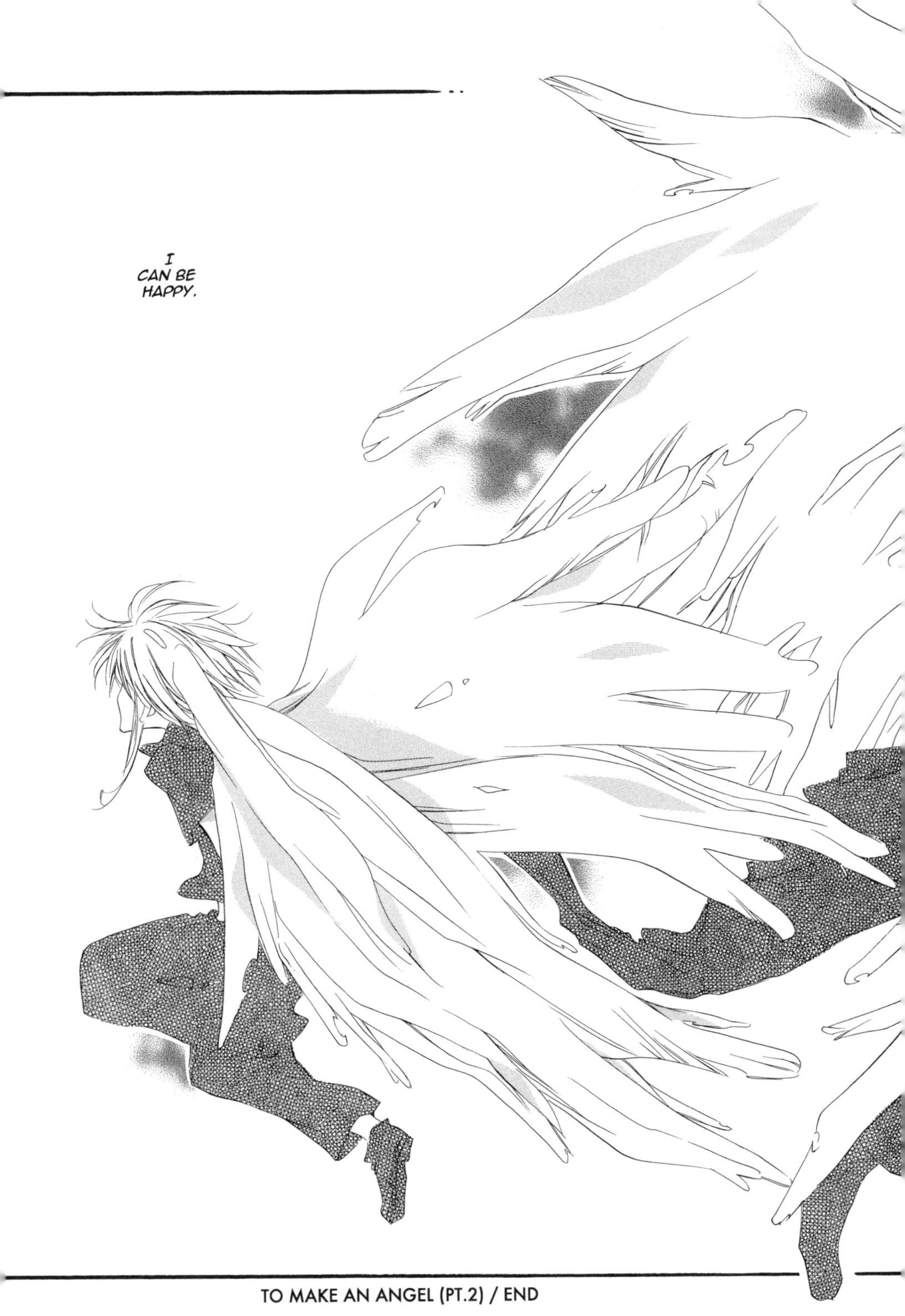
I CAN BE HAPPY.

TO MAKE AN ANGEL (PT.2) / END

SAME-CELL ORGANISM

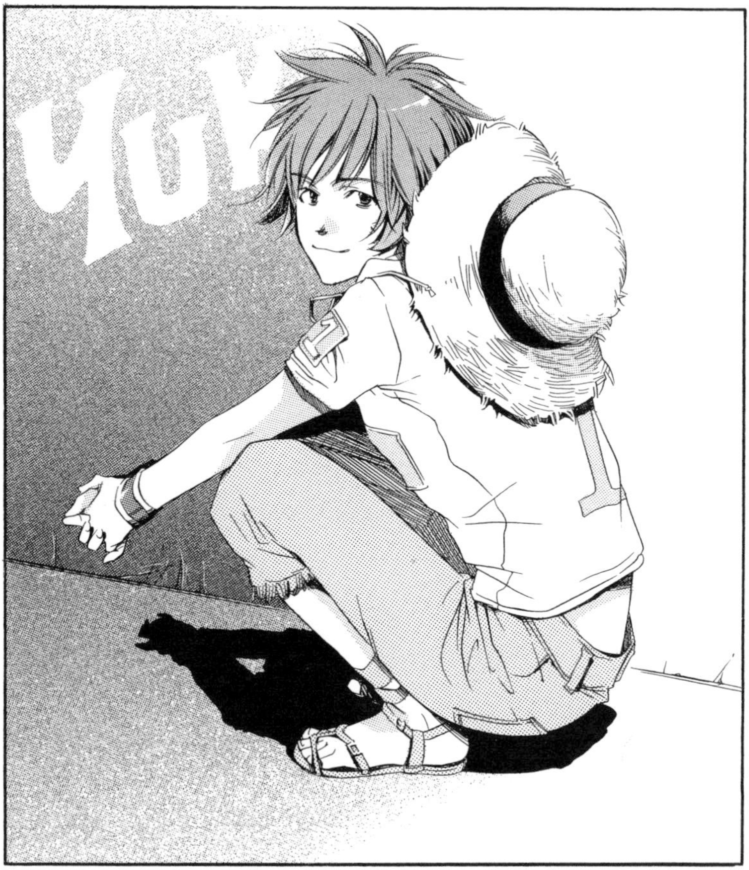

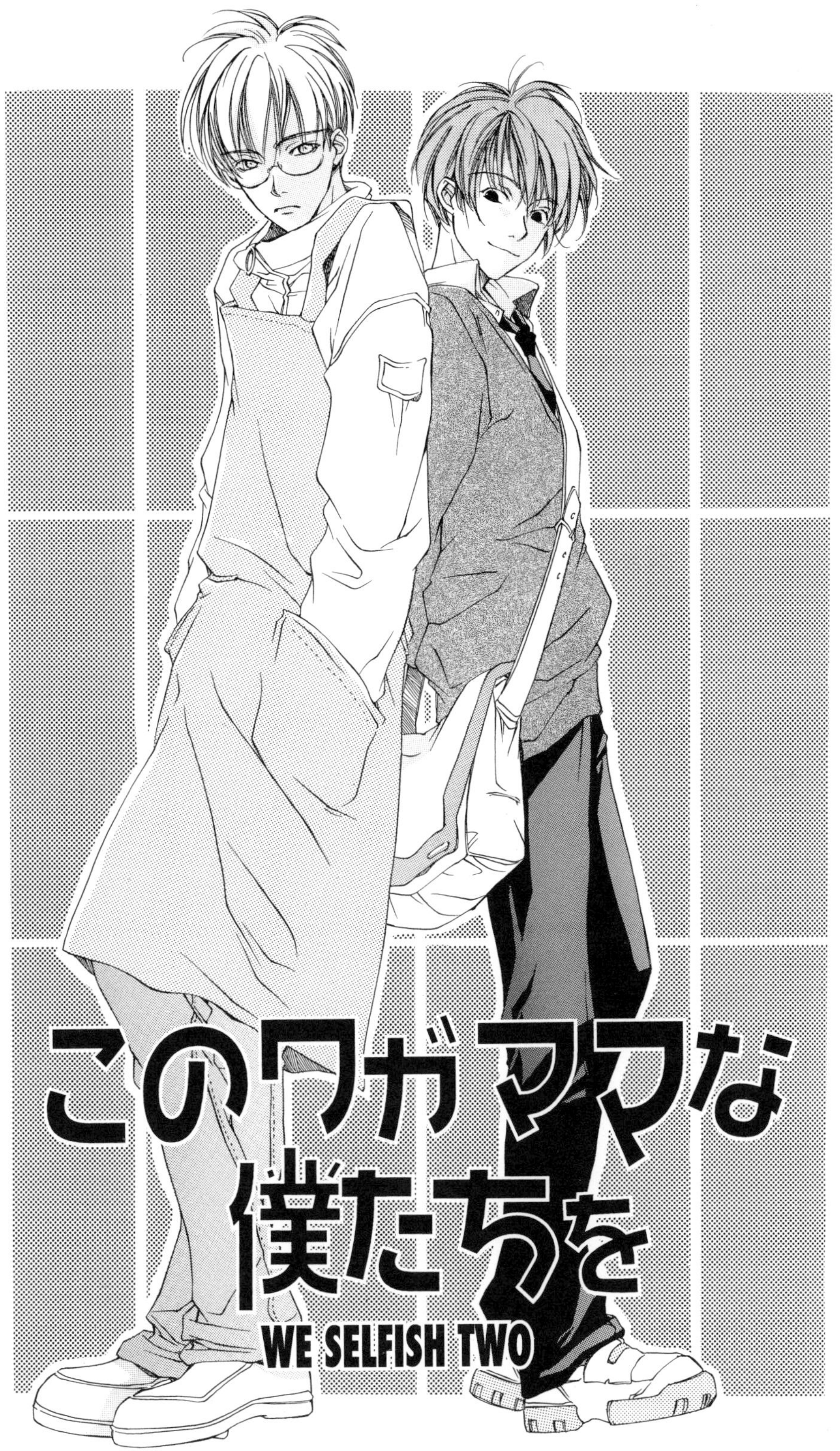
このワガママな
僕たちを
WE SELFISH TWO

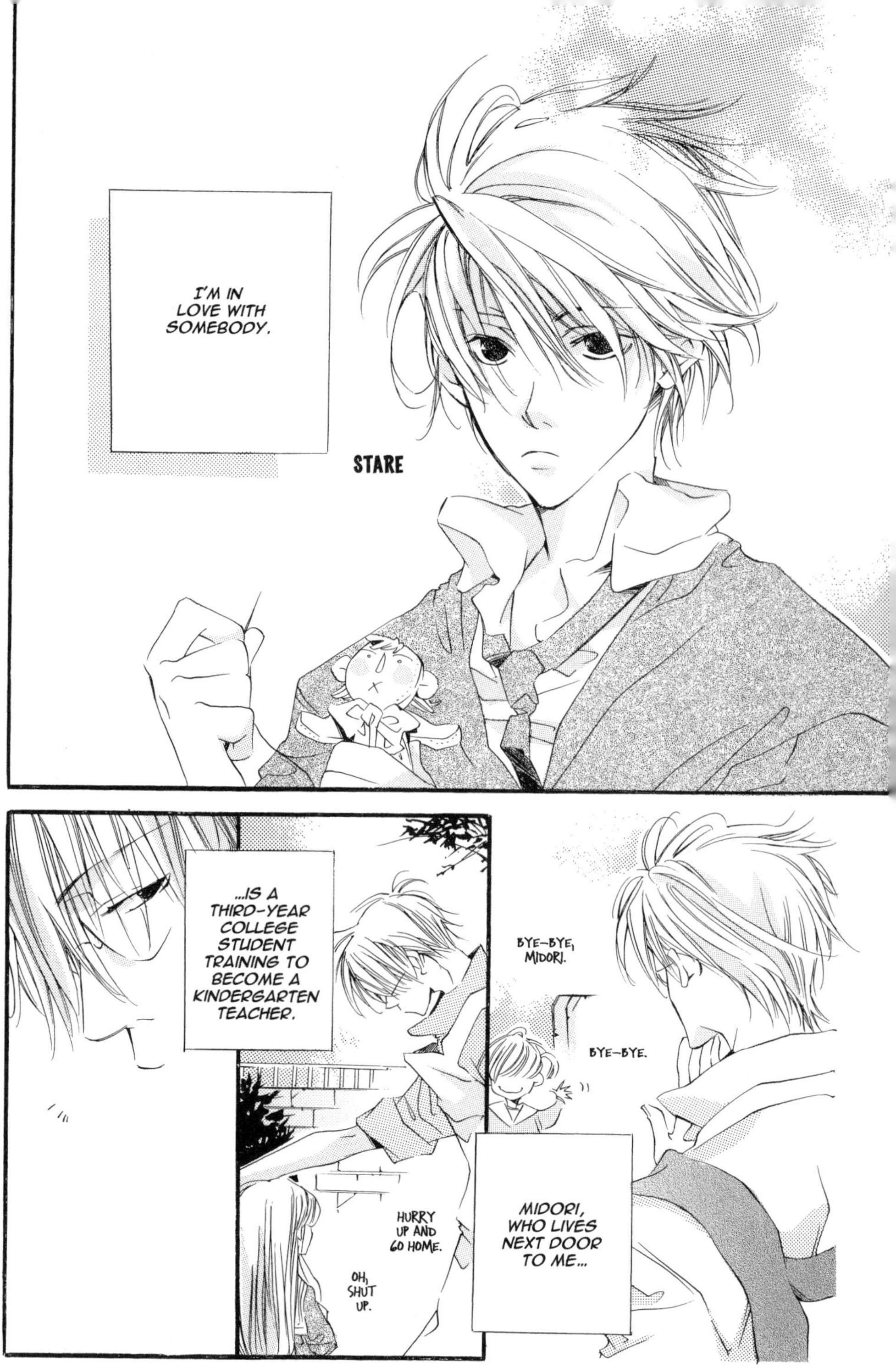
I'M IN LOVE WITH SOMEBODY.
STARE
BYE-BYE, MIDORI.
BYE-BYE.
MIDORI, WHO LIVES NEXT DOOR TO ME...
...IS A THIRD-YEAR COLLEGE STUDENT TRAINING TO BECOME A KINDERGARTEN TEACHER.
HURRY UP AND GO HOME.
OH, SHUT UP.

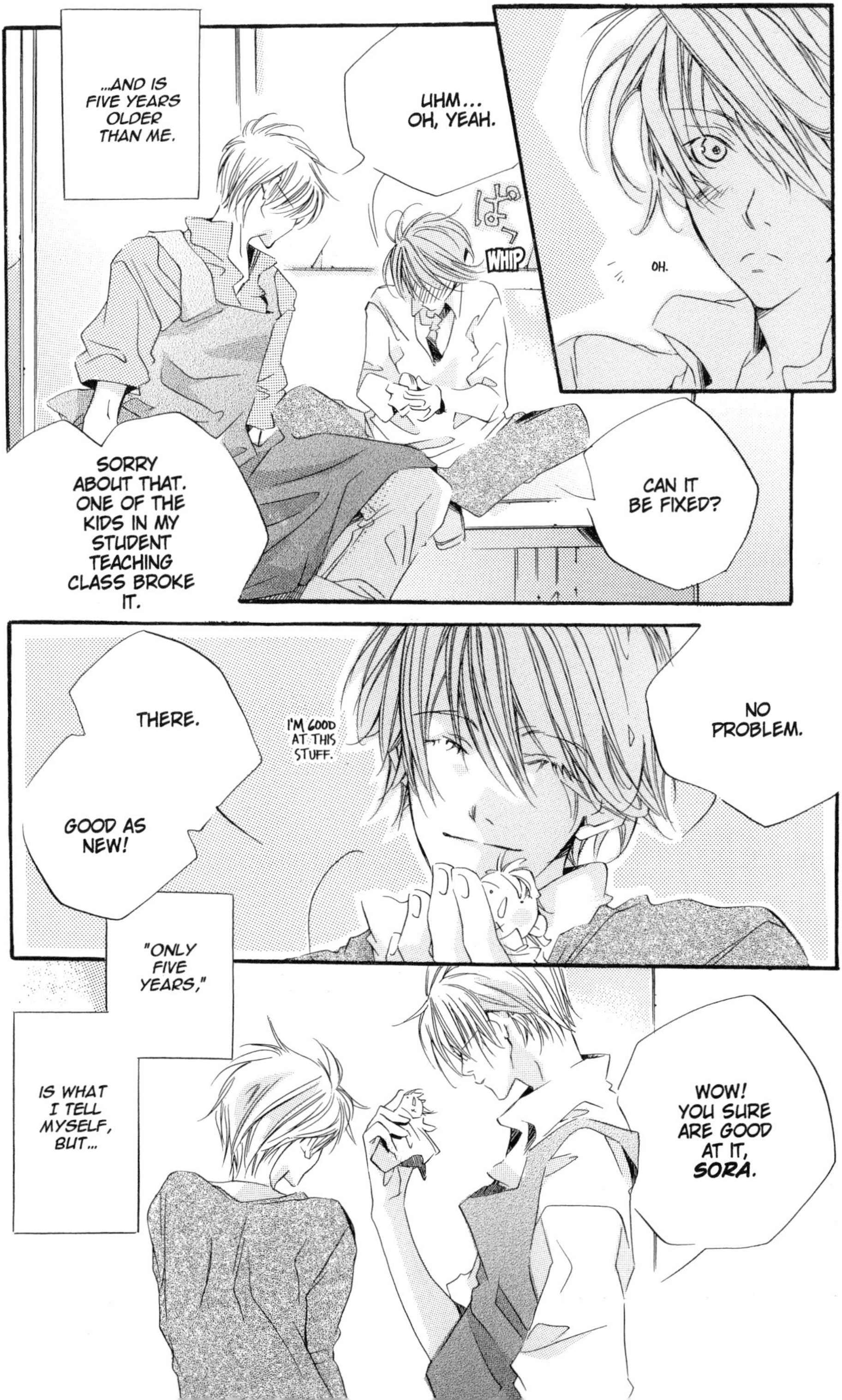
...AND IS FIVE YEARS OLDER THAN ME.
UHM... OH, YEAH.
WHIP
OH.
CAN IT BE FIXED?
SORRY ABOUT THAT. ONE OF THE KIDS IN MY STUDENT TEACHING CLASS BROKE IT.
NO PROBLEM.
I'M GOOD AT THIS STUFF.
THERE.
GOOD AS NEW!
WOW! YOU SURE ARE GOOD AT IT, **SORA**.
"ONLY FIVE YEARS,"
IS WHAT I TELL MYSELF, BUT...

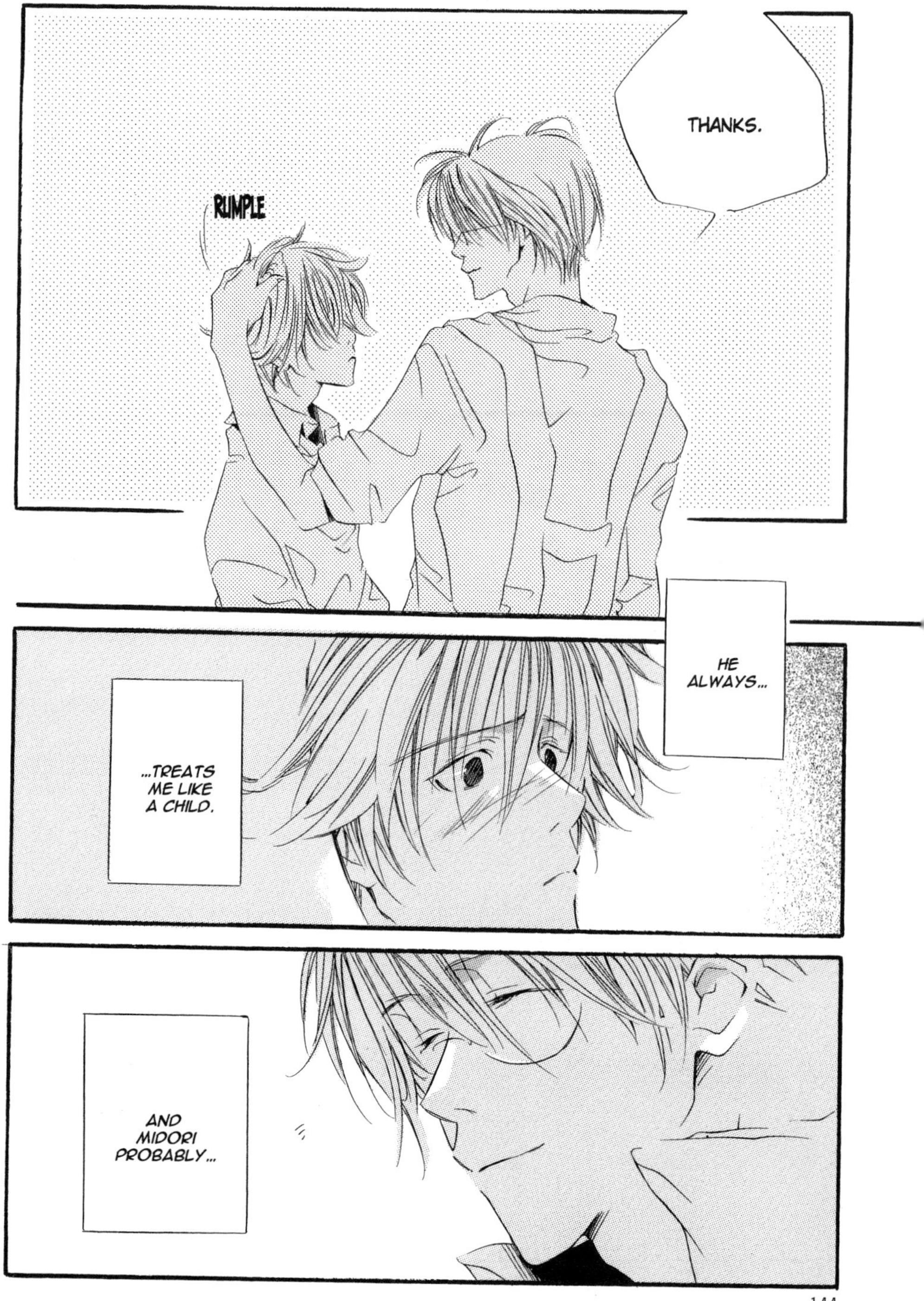
THANKS.
RUMPLE
HE ALWAYS...
...TREATS ME LIKE A CHILD.
AND MIDORI PROBABLY...

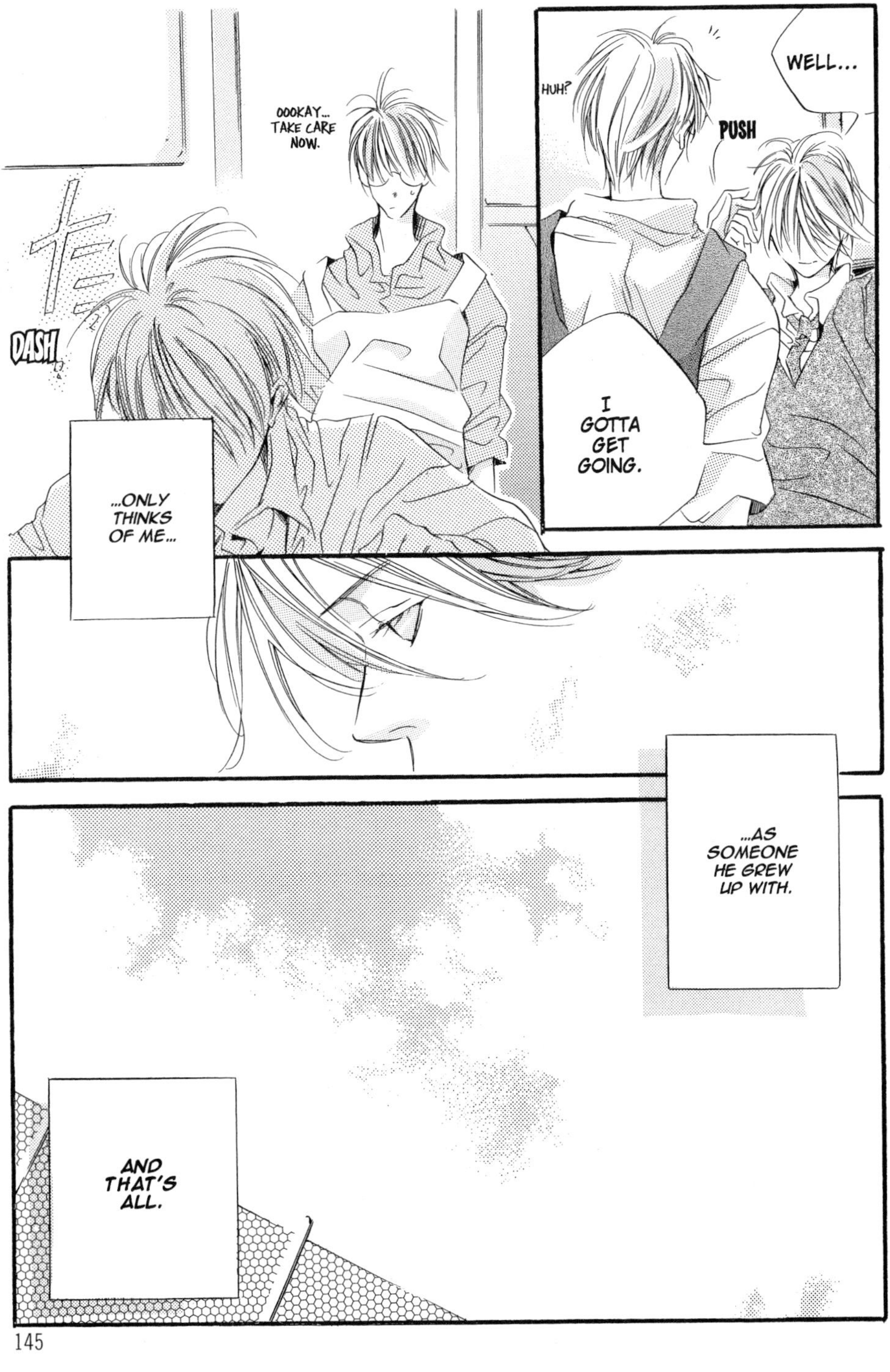
WELL...
HUH?
PUSH
I GOTTA GET GOING.
OOOKAY... TAKE CARE NOW.
DASH
...ONLY THINKS OF ME...
...AS SOMEONE HE GREW UP WITH.
AND THAT'S ALL.

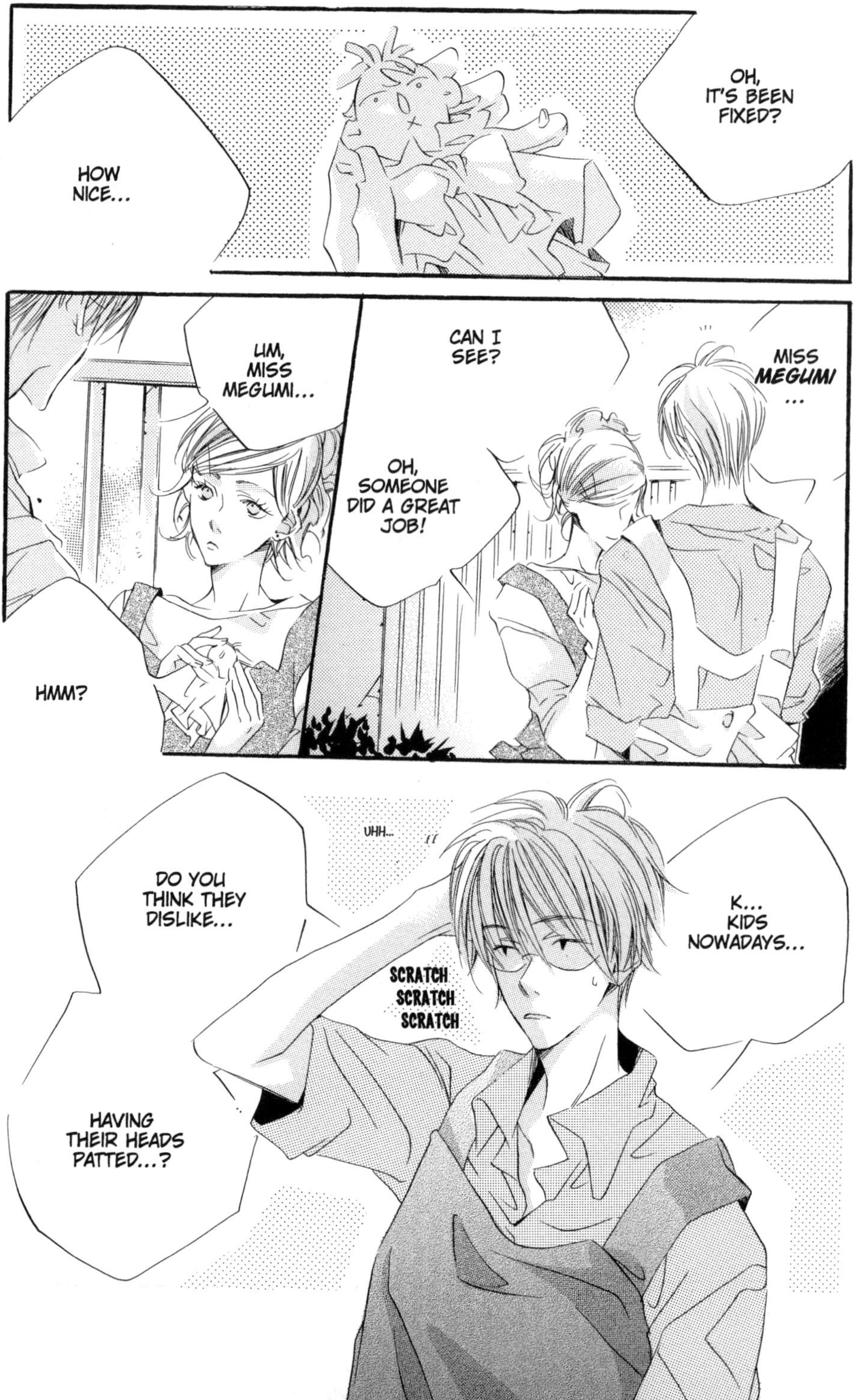
OH, IT'S BEEN FIXED?
HOW NICE...
MISS MEGUMI ...
CAN I SEE?
OH, SOMEONE DID A GREAT JOB!
UM, MISS MEGUMI...
HMM?
K... KIDS NOWADAYS...
UHH...
SCRATCH SCRATCH SCRATCH
DO YOU THINK THEY DISLIKE...
HAVING THEIR HEADS PATTED...?

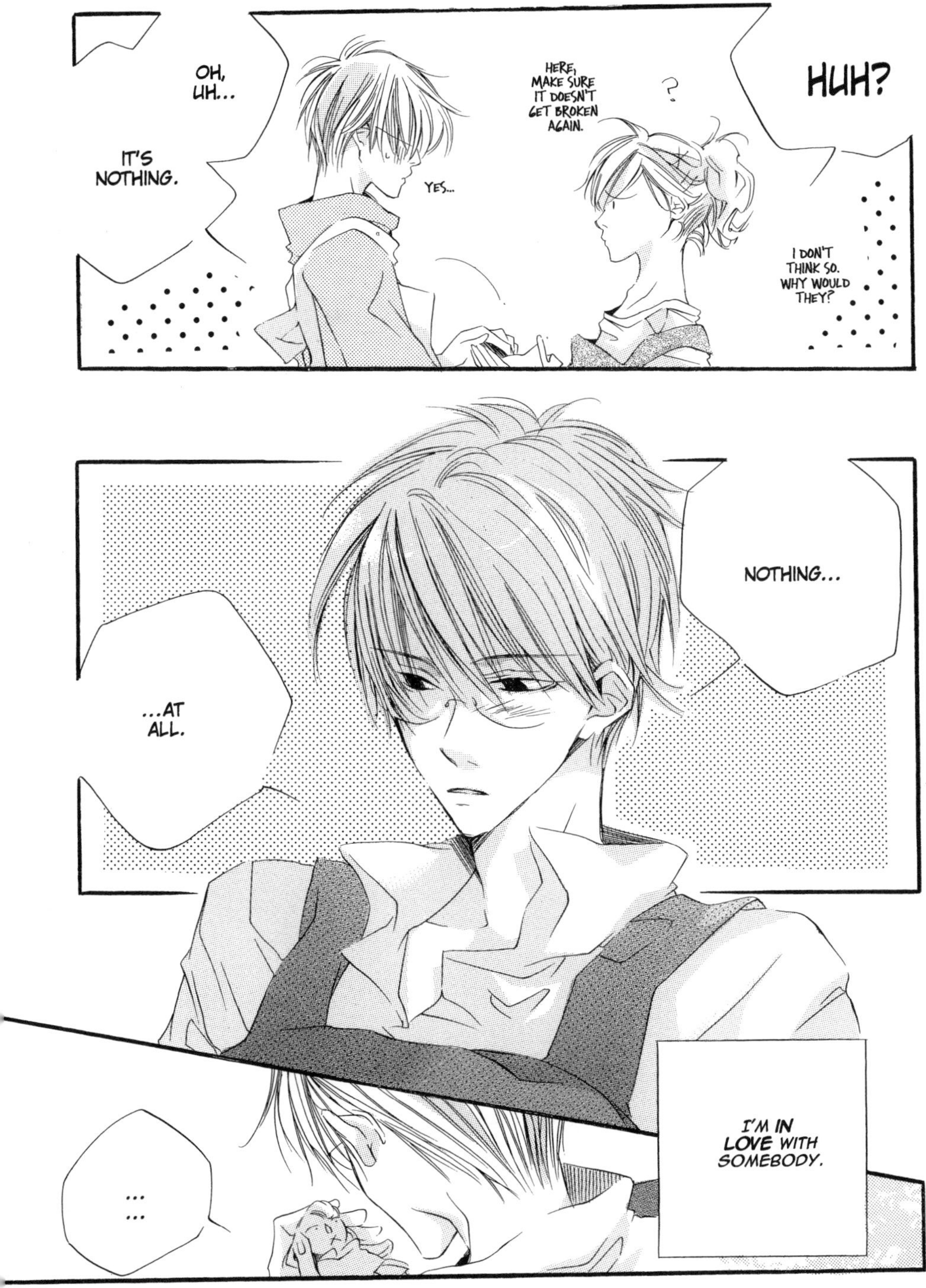
HUH?
I DON'T THINK SO. WHY WOULD THEY?
HERE, MAKE SURE IT DOESN'T GET BROKEN AGAIN.
?
YES...
OH, UH...
IT'S NOTHING.
NOTHING...
...AT ALL.
I'M IN LOVE WITH SOMEBODY.
... ...

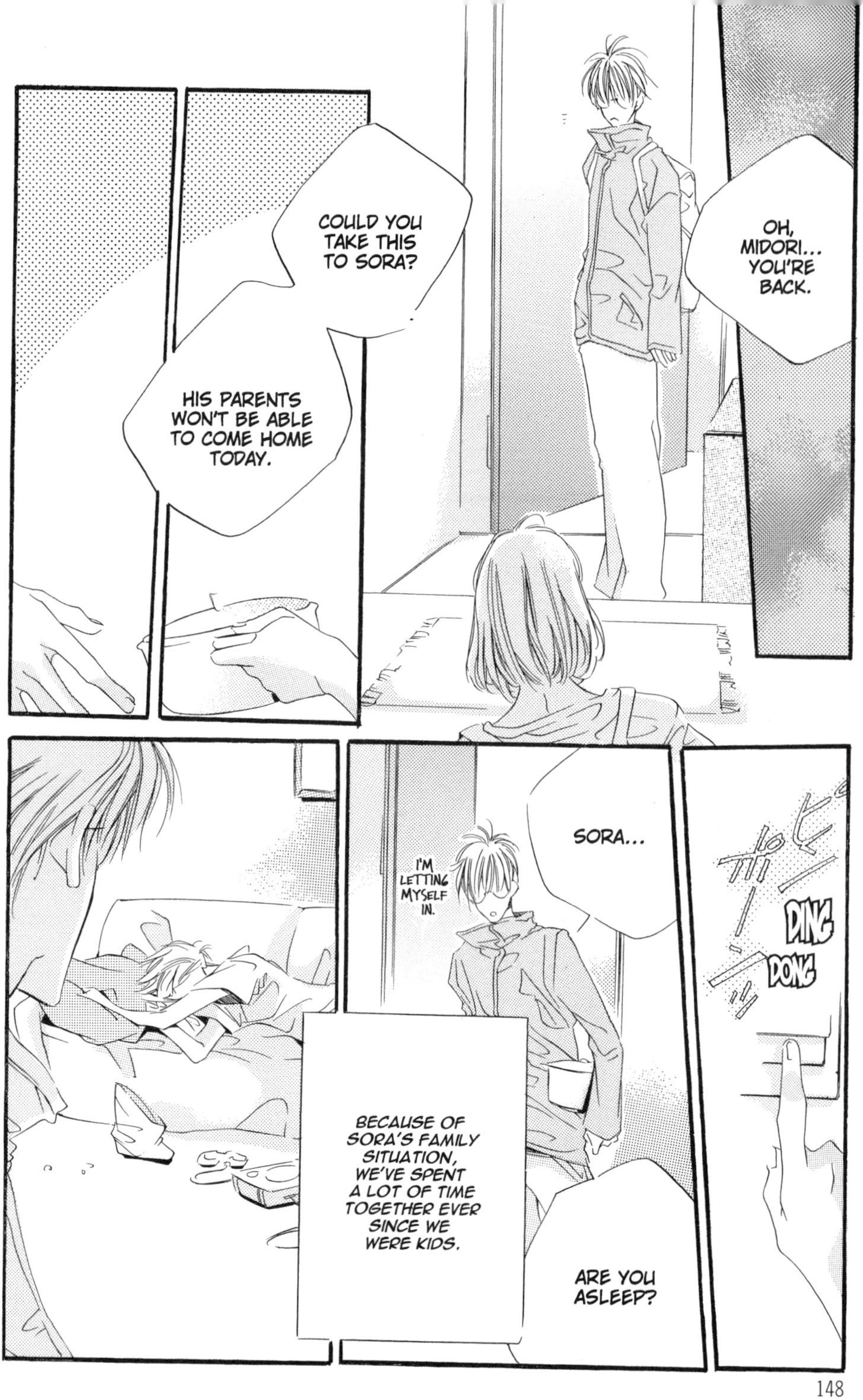
OH, MIDORI... YOU'RE BACK.
COULD YOU TAKE THIS TO SORA?
HIS PARENTS WON'T BE ABLE TO COME HOME TODAY.
DING
DONG
SORA...
I'M LETTING MYSELF IN.
ARE YOU ASLEEP?
BECAUSE OF SORA'S FAMILY SITUATION, WE'VE SPENT A LOT OF TIME TOGETHER EVER SINCE WE WERE KIDS.

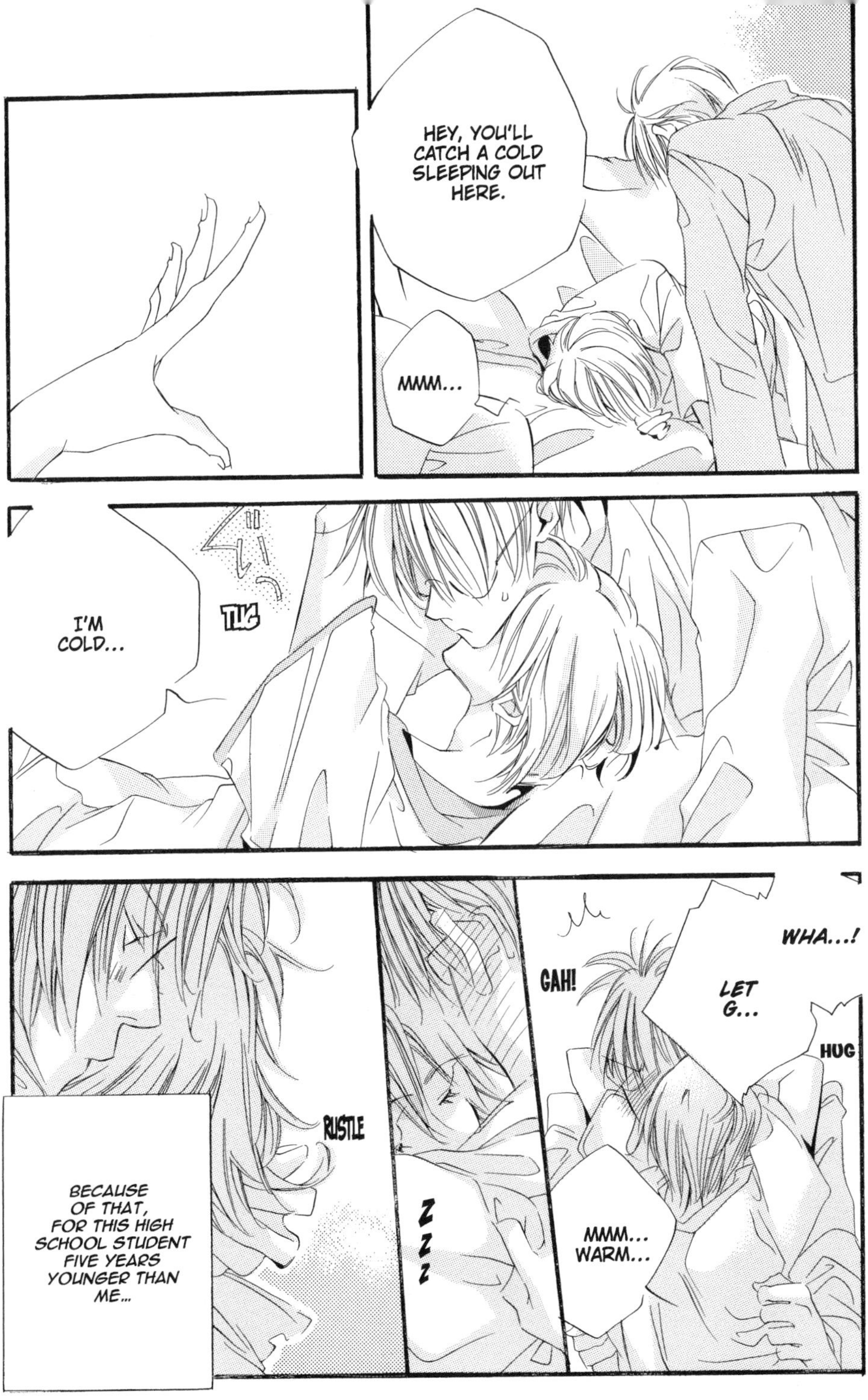
HEY, YOU'LL CATCH A COLD SLEEPING OUT HERE.
MMM...
TUG
I'M COLD...
WHA...!
LET G...
GAH!
HUG
MMM... WARM...
Z Z Z
RUSTLE
BECAUSE OF THAT, FOR THIS HIGH SCHOOL STUDENT FIVE YEARS YOUNGER THAN ME...

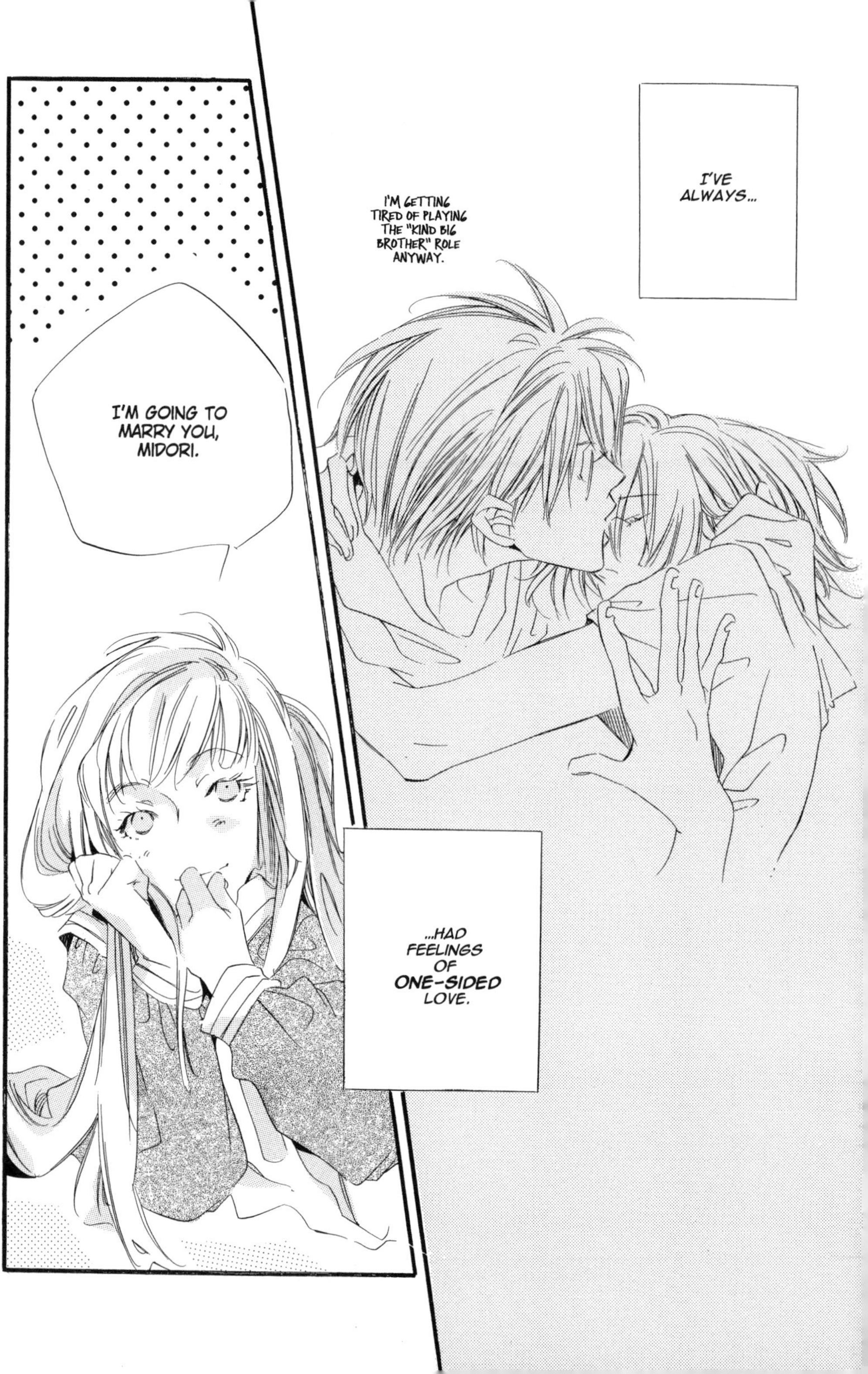
I'VE ALWAYS...
I'M GETTING TIRED OF PLAYING THE "KIND BIG BROTHER" ROLE ANYWAY.
...HAD FEELINGS OF ONE-SIDED LOVE.
I'M GOING TO MARRY YOU, MIDORI.

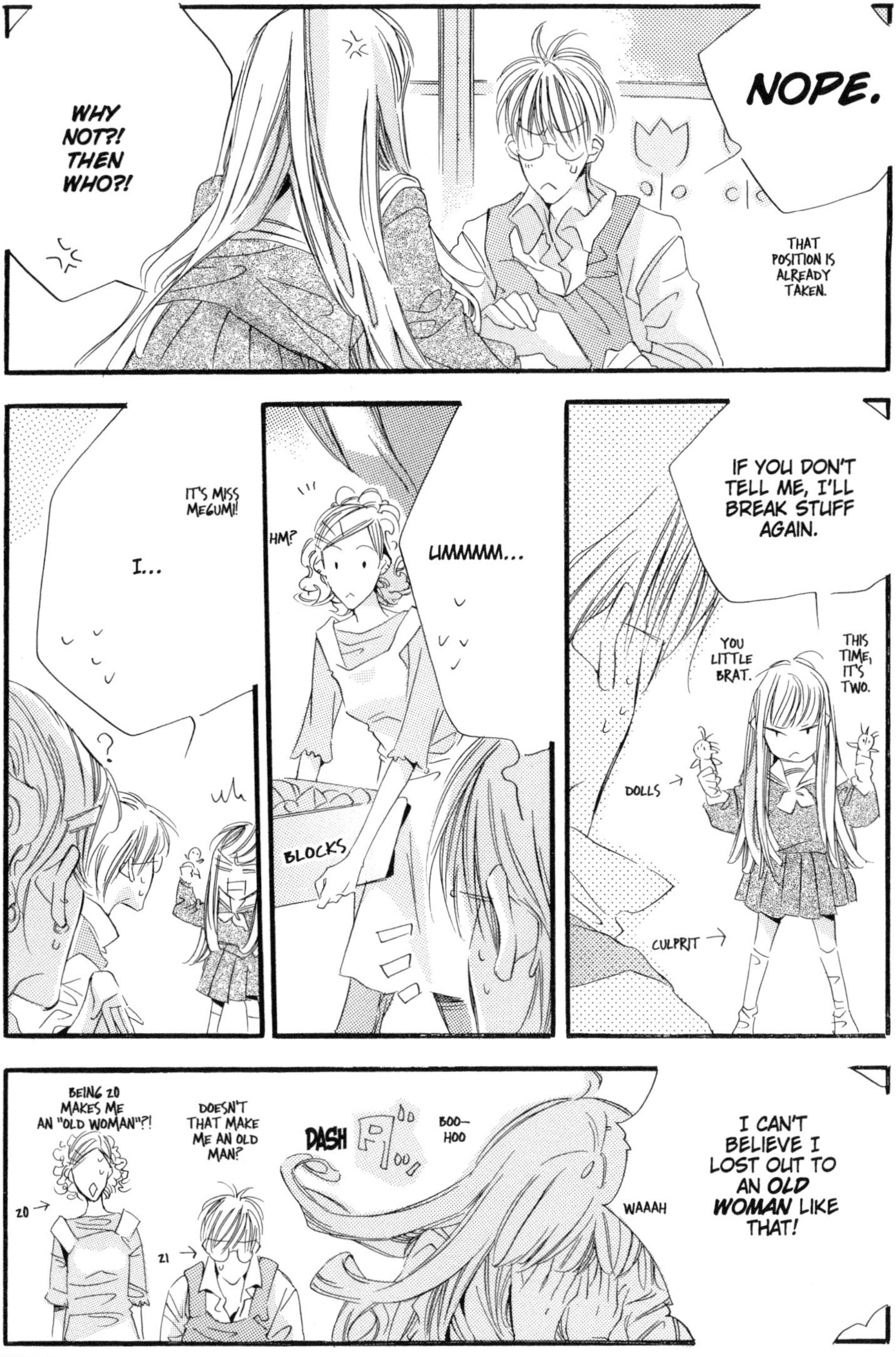
NOPE.
THAT POSITION IS ALREADY TAKEN.
WHY NOT?! THEN WHO?!
IF YOU DON'T TELL ME, I'LL BREAK STUFF AGAIN.
THIS TIME, IT'S TWO.
YOU LITTLE BRAT.
DOLLS
CULPRIT
UMMMMM...
HM?
BLOCKS
IT'S MISS MEGUMI!
I...
I CAN'T BELIEVE I LOST OUT TO AN *OLD WOMAN* LIKE THAT!
WAAAH
BOO-HOO
DASH
DOESN'T THAT MAKE ME AN OLD MAN?
21
BEING 20 MAKES ME AN "OLD WOMAN"?!
20

IN SHOCK.

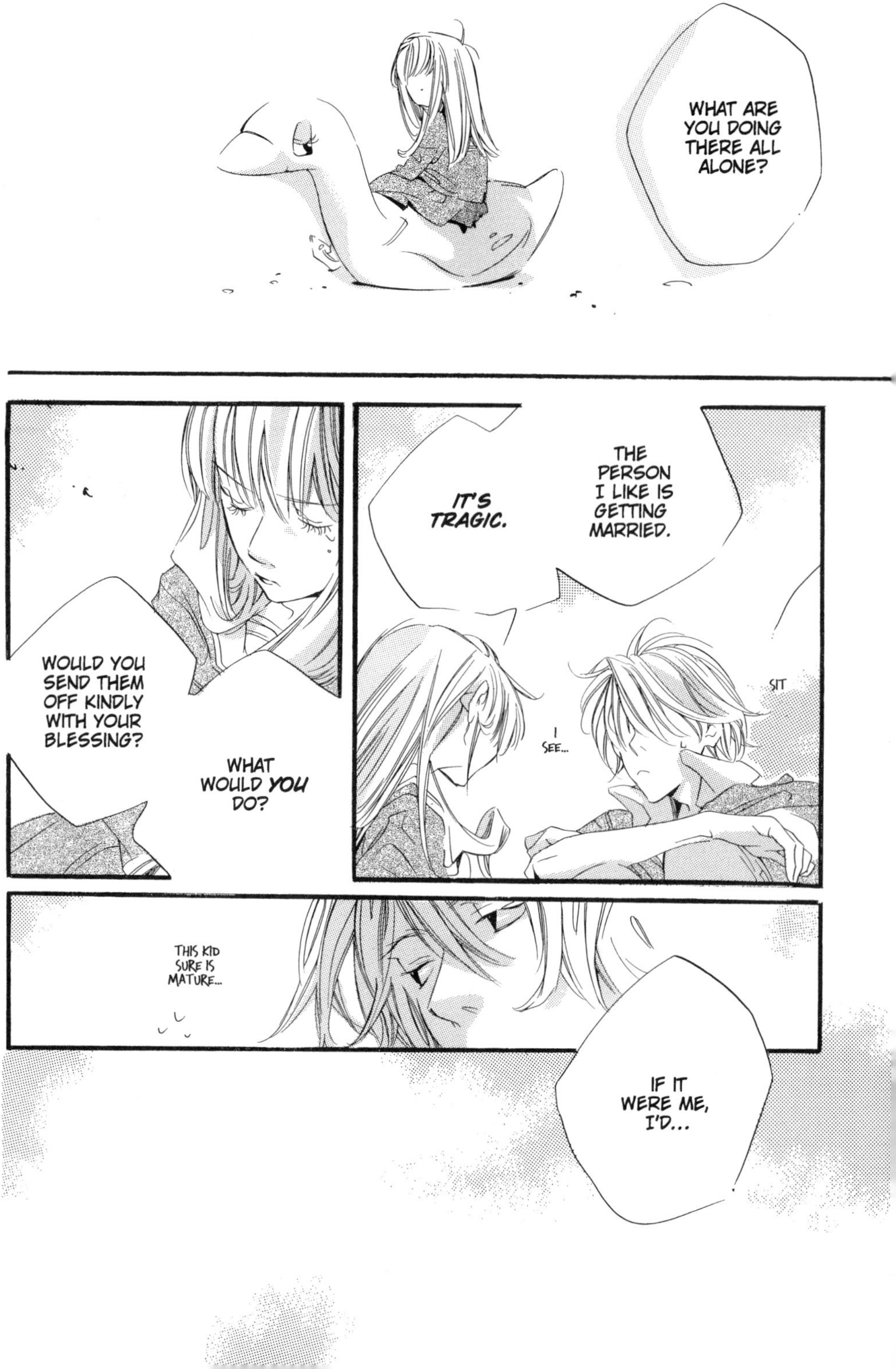
WHAT ARE YOU DOING THERE ALL ALONE?
THE PERSON I LIKE IS GETTING MARRIED.
IT'S TRAGIC.
SIT
I SEE...
WOULD YOU SEND THEM OFF KINDLY WITH YOUR BLESSING?
WHAT WOULD *YOU* DO?
THIS KID SURE IS MATURE...
IF IT WERE ME, I'D...

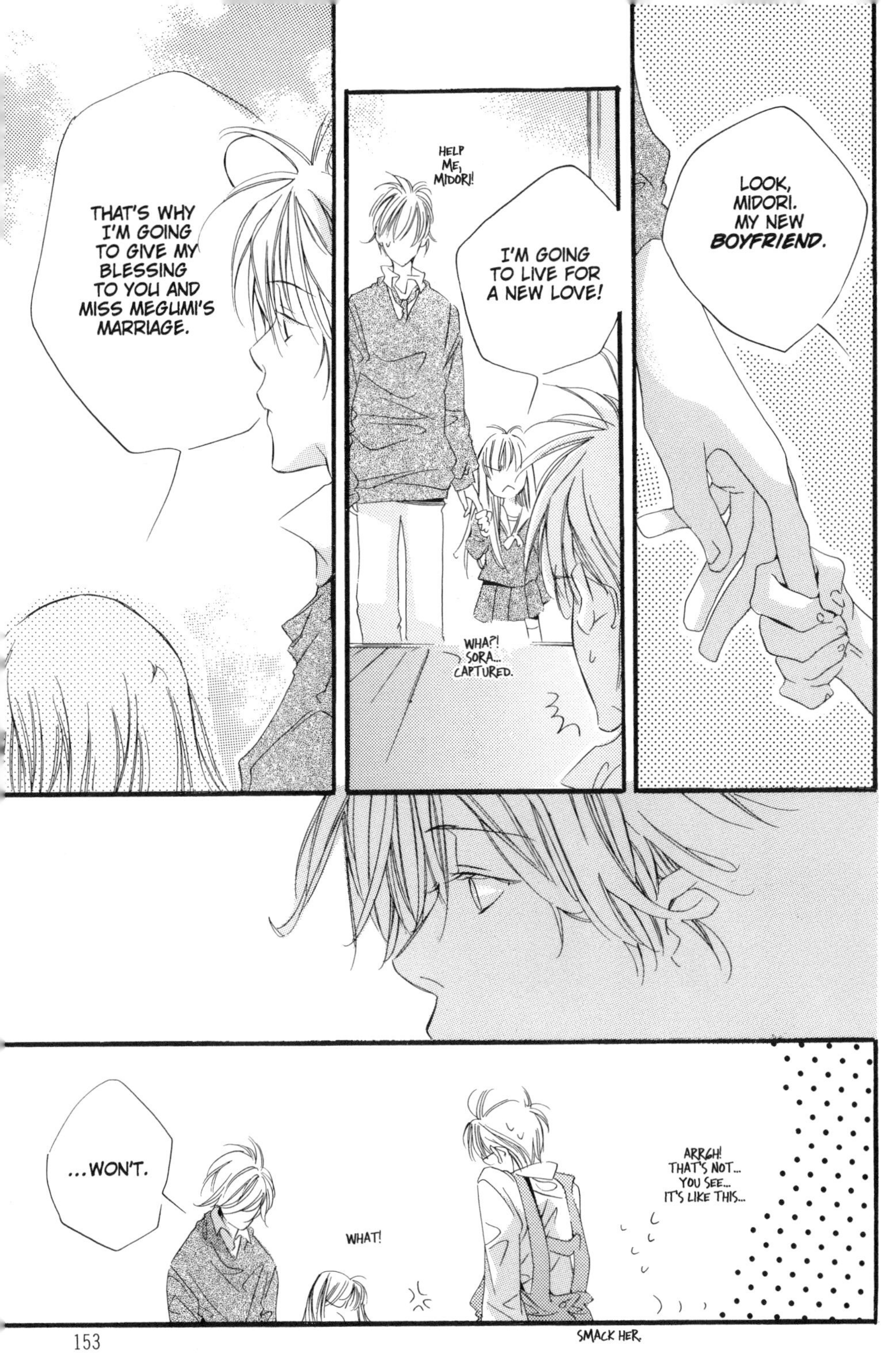
LOOK, MIDORI. MY NEW BOYFRIEND.
I'M GOING TO LIVE FOR A NEW LOVE!
HELP ME, MIDORI!
WHA?! SORA... CAPTURED.
THAT'S WHY I'M GOING TO GIVE MY BLESSING TO YOU AND MISS MEGUMI'S MARRIAGE.
ARRGH! THAT'S NOT... YOU SEE... IT'S LIKE THIS...
WHAT!
...WON'T.
SMACK HER.

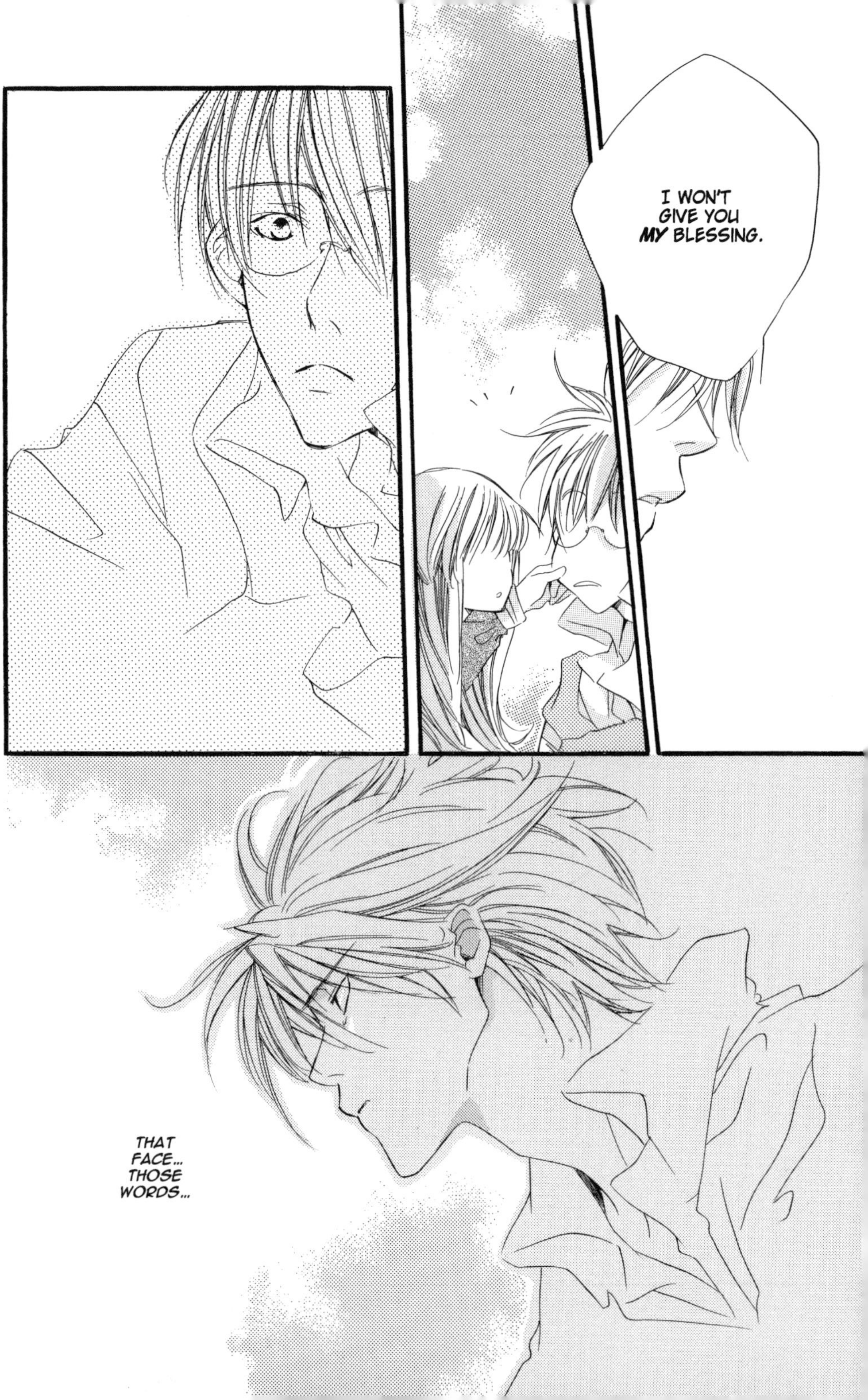
I WON'T GIVE YOU MY BLESSING.
THAT FACE... THOSE WORDS...

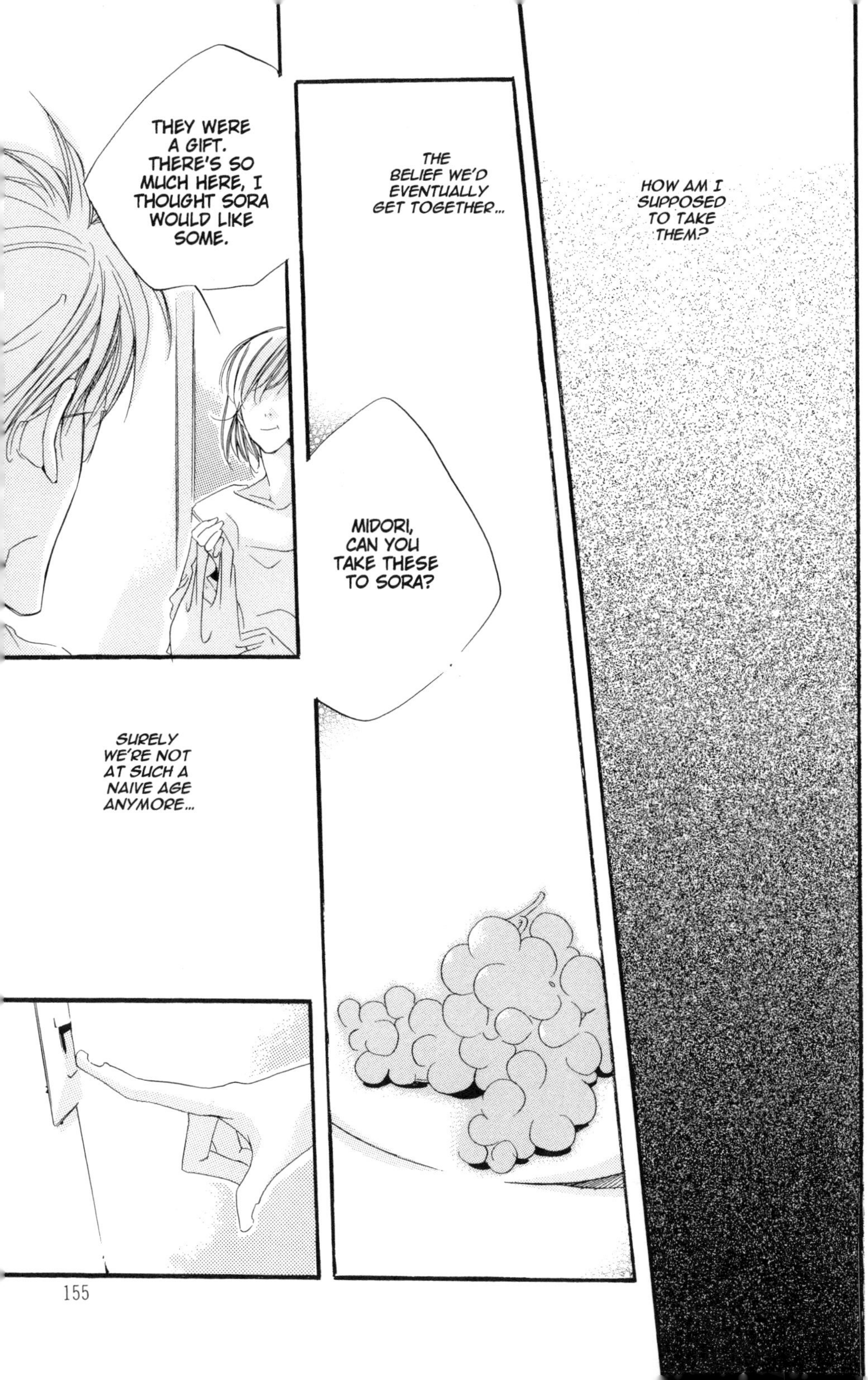
HOW AM I SUPPOSED TO TAKE THEM?
THE BELIEF WE'D EVENTUALLY GET TOGETHER...
MIDORI, CAN YOU TAKE THESE TO SORA?
THEY WERE A GIFT. THERE'S SO MUCH HERE, I THOUGHT SORA WOULD LIKE SOME.
SURELY WE'RE NOT AT SUCH A NAIVE AGE ANYMORE...

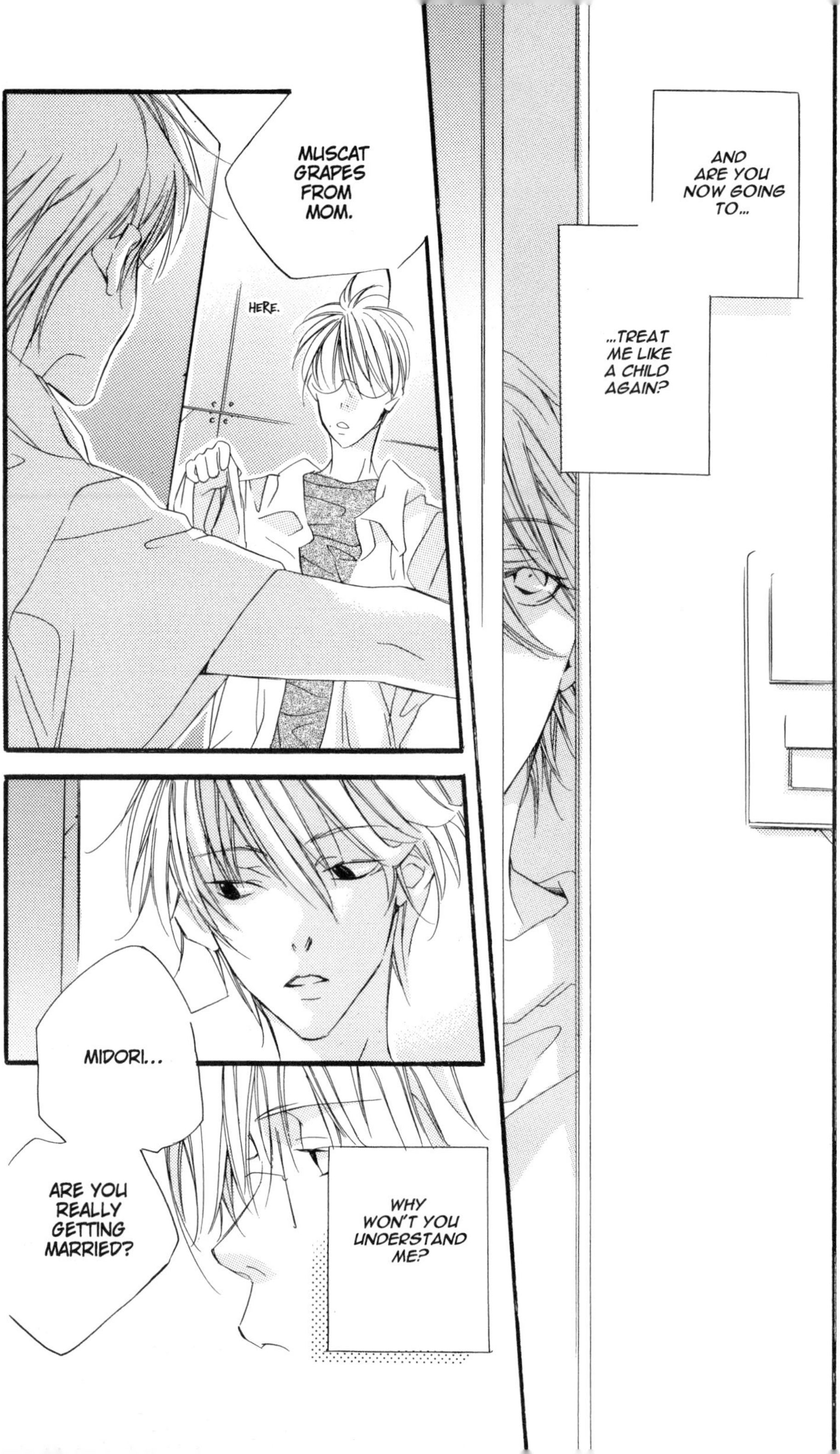
AND ARE YOU NOW GOING TO...
...TREAT ME LIKE A CHILD AGAIN?
MUSCAT GRAPES FROM MOM.
HERE.
MIDORI... ARE YOU REALLY GETTING MARRIED?
WHY WON'T YOU UNDERSTAND ME?

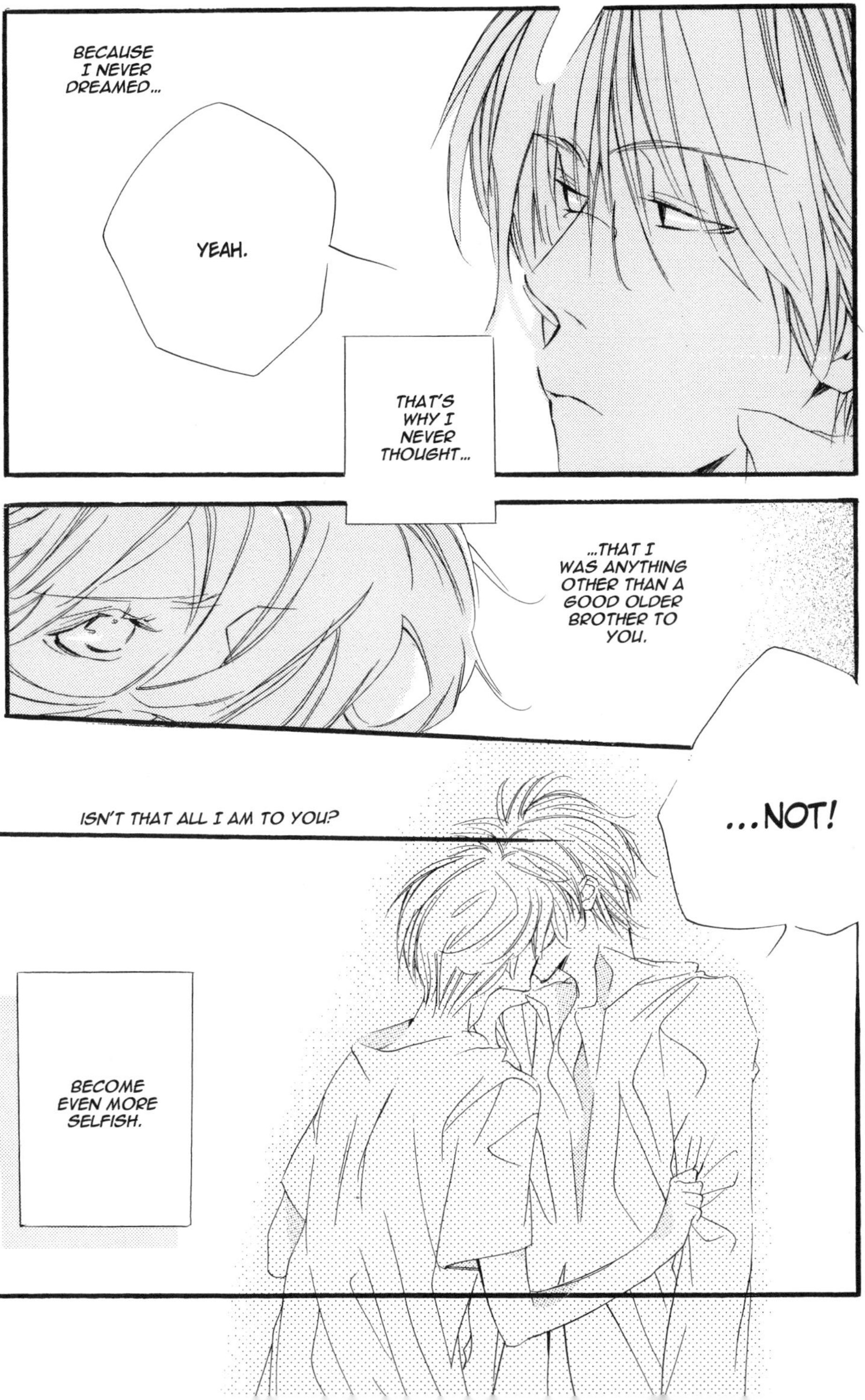
BECAUSE I NEVER DREAMED...
YEAH.
THAT'S WHY I NEVER THOUGHT...
...THAT I WAS ANYTHING OTHER THAN A GOOD OLDER BROTHER TO YOU.
ISN'T THAT ALL I AM TO YOU?
...NOT!
BECOME EVEN MORE SELFISH.

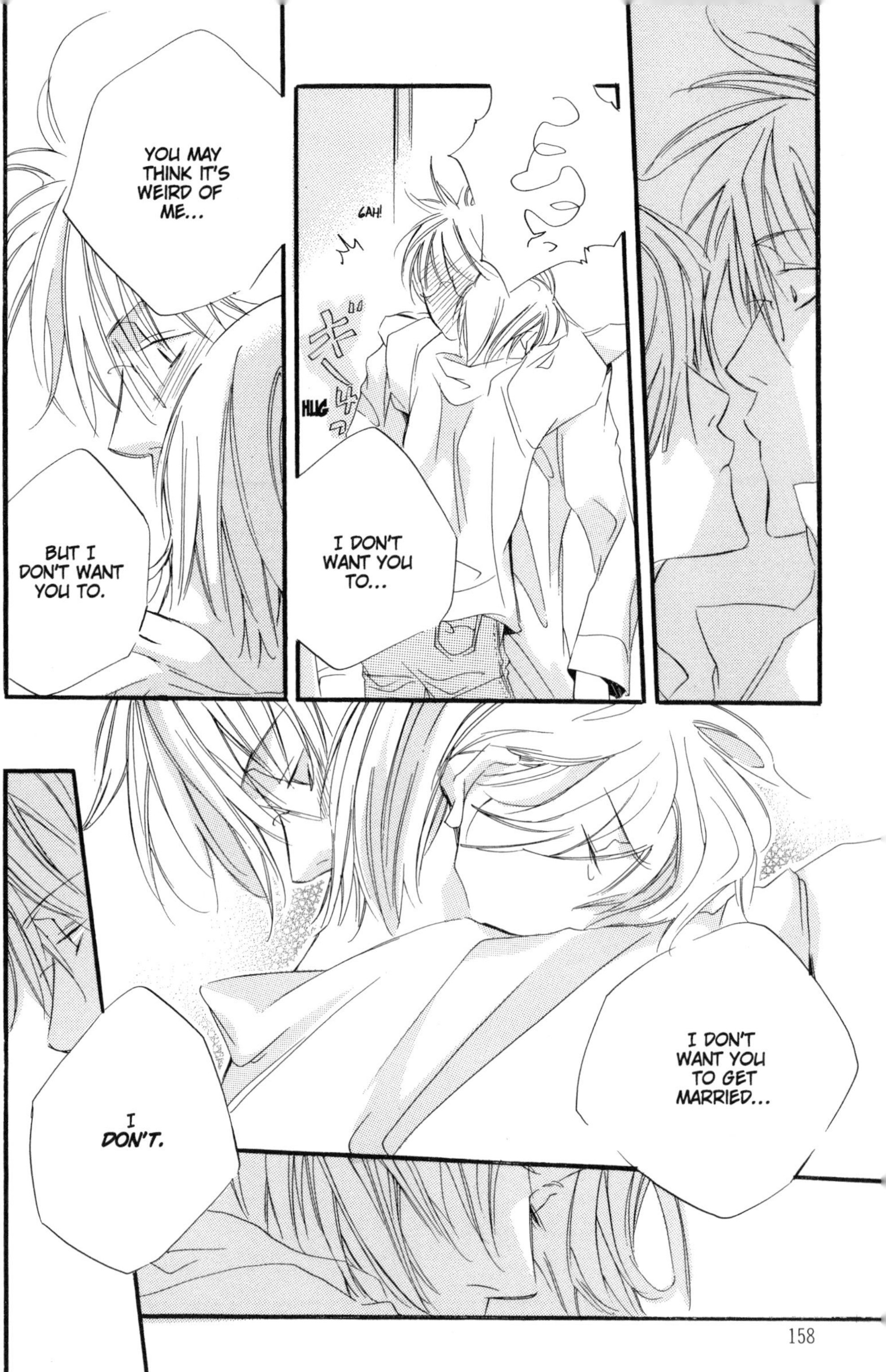
GAH!
HUG
I DON'T WANT YOU TO...
YOU MAY THINK IT'S WEIRD OF ME...
BUT I DON'T WANT YOU TO.
I DON'T WANT YOU TO GET MARRIED...
I DON'T.

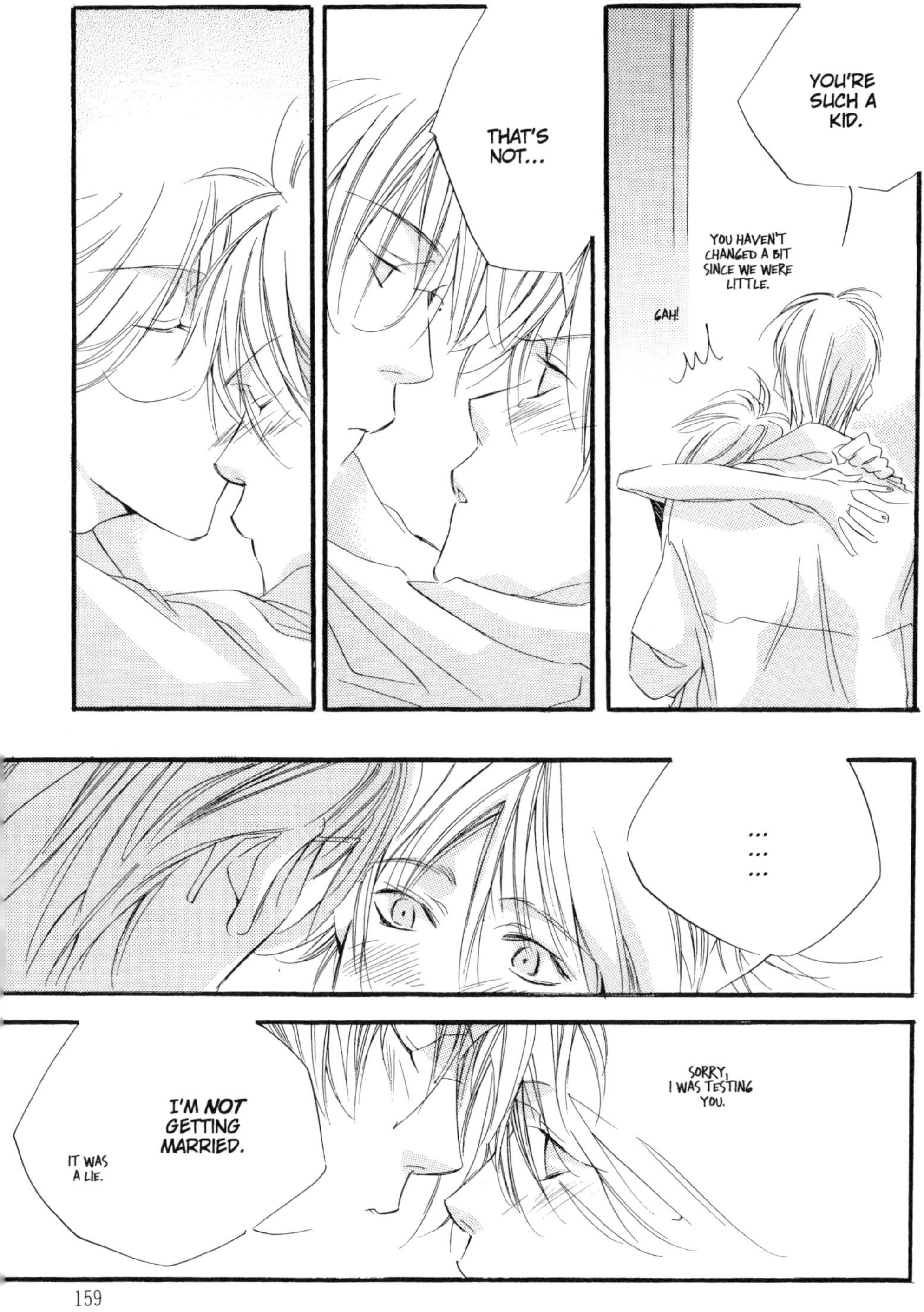
YOU'RE SUCH A KID.
YOU HAVEN'T CHANGED A BIT SINCE WE WERE LITTLE.
GAH!
THAT'S NOT...
...
...
...
SORRY, I WAS TESTING YOU.
I'M NOT GETTING MARRIED.
IT WAS A LIE.

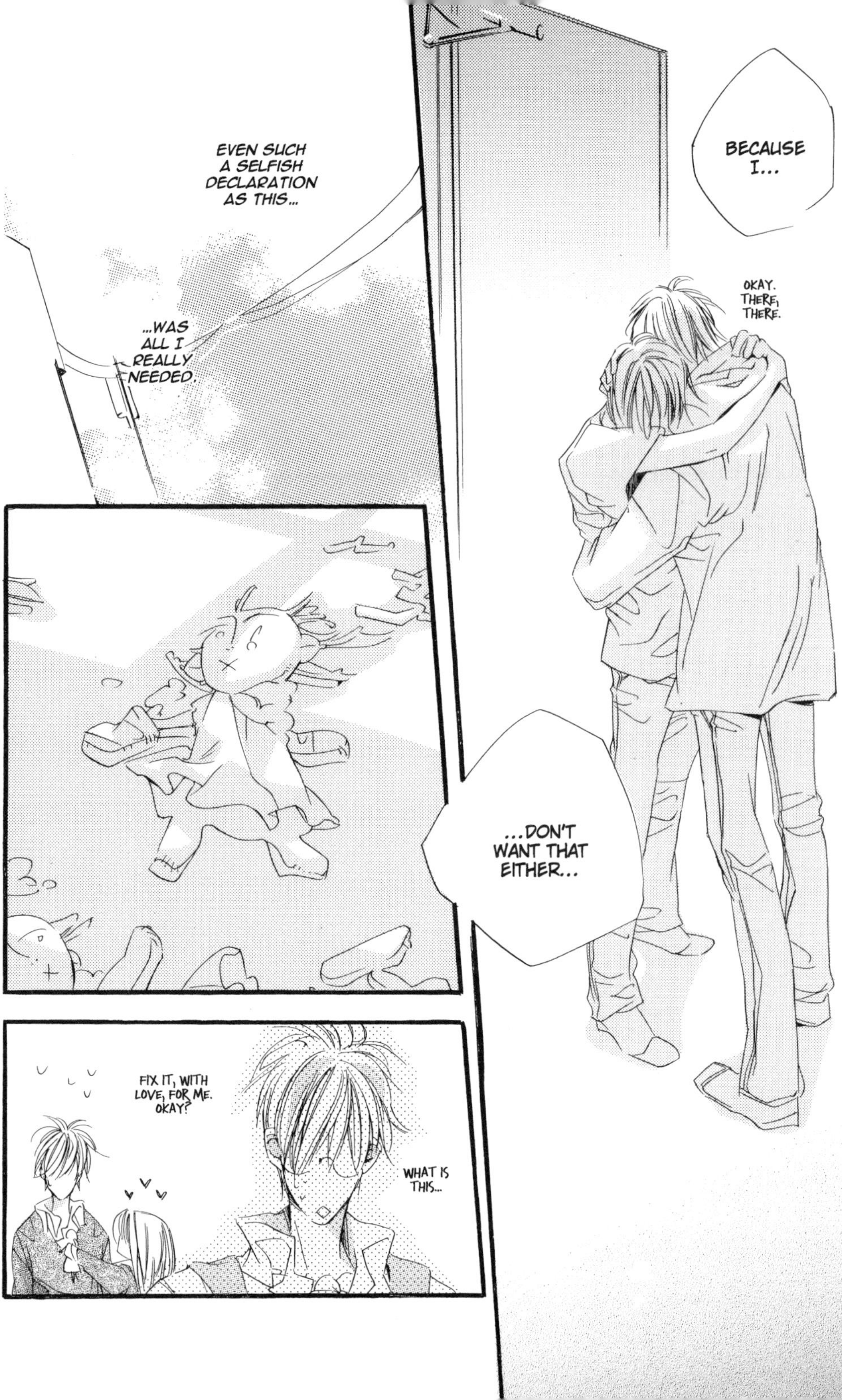
BECAUSE I...
OKAY. THERE, THERE.
...DON'T WANT THAT EITHER...
EVEN SUCH A SELFISH DECLARATION AS THIS...
...WAS ALL I REALLY NEEDED.
FIX IT, WITH LOVE, FOR ME. OKAY?
WHAT IS THIS...

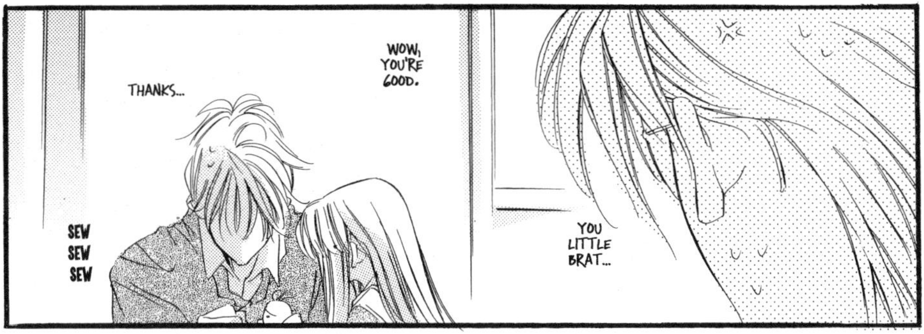
YOU LITTLE BRAT...
WOW, YOU'RE GOOD.
THANKS...
SEW SEW SEW

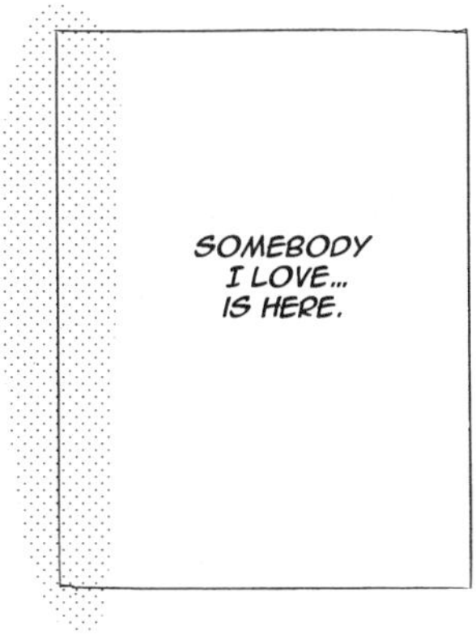
SOMEBODY I LOVE... IS HERE.

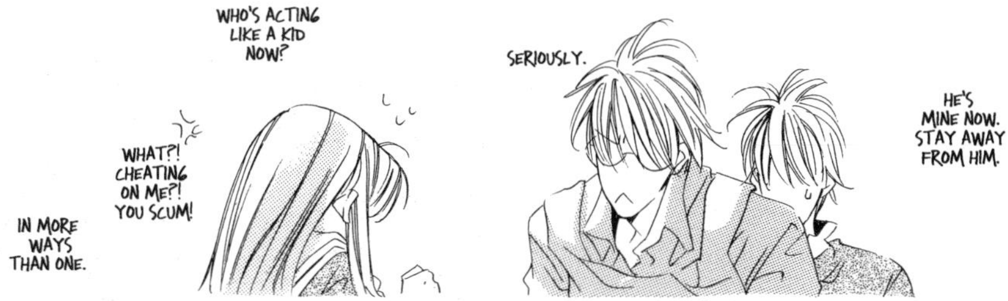
HE'S MINE NOW. STAY AWAY FROM HIM.
SERIOUSLY.
WHO'S ACTING LIKE A KID NOW?
WHAT?! CHEATING ON ME?! YOU SCUM!
IN MORE WAYS THAN ONE.

WE SELFISH TWO / END

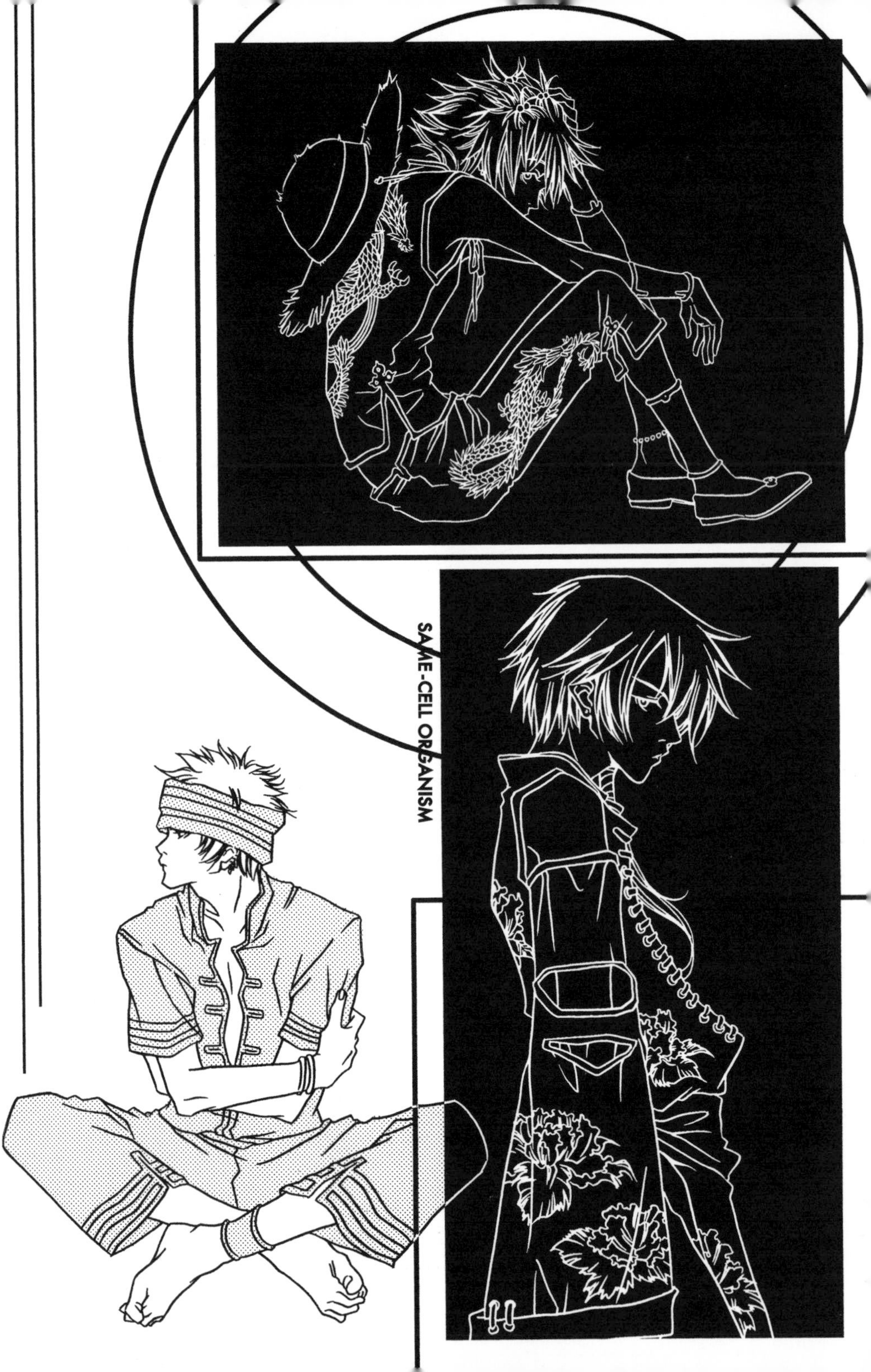
SAME-CELL ORGANISM

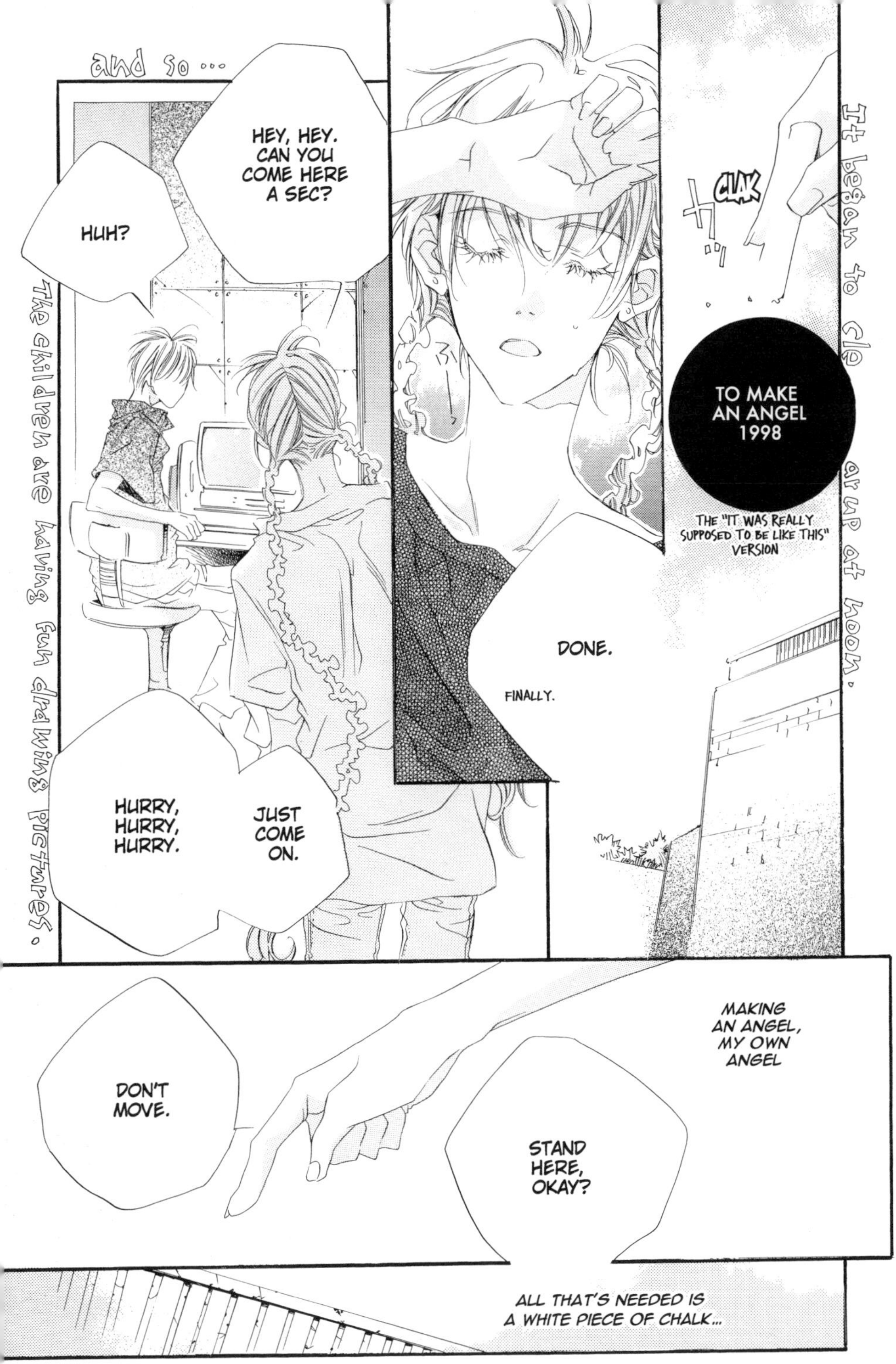
It began to clear up at noon.
CLAK
TO MAKE AN ANGEL 1998
THE "IT WAS REALLY SUPPOSED TO BE LIKE THIS" VERSION
DONE.
FINALLY.
and so...
HEY, HEY. CAN YOU COME HERE A SEC?
HUH?
The children are having fun drawing pictures.
JUST COME ON.
HURRY, HURRY, HURRY.
MAKING AN ANGEL, MY OWN ANGEL
STAND HERE, OKAY?
DON'T MOVE.
ALL THAT'S NEEDED IS A WHITE PIECE OF CHALK...

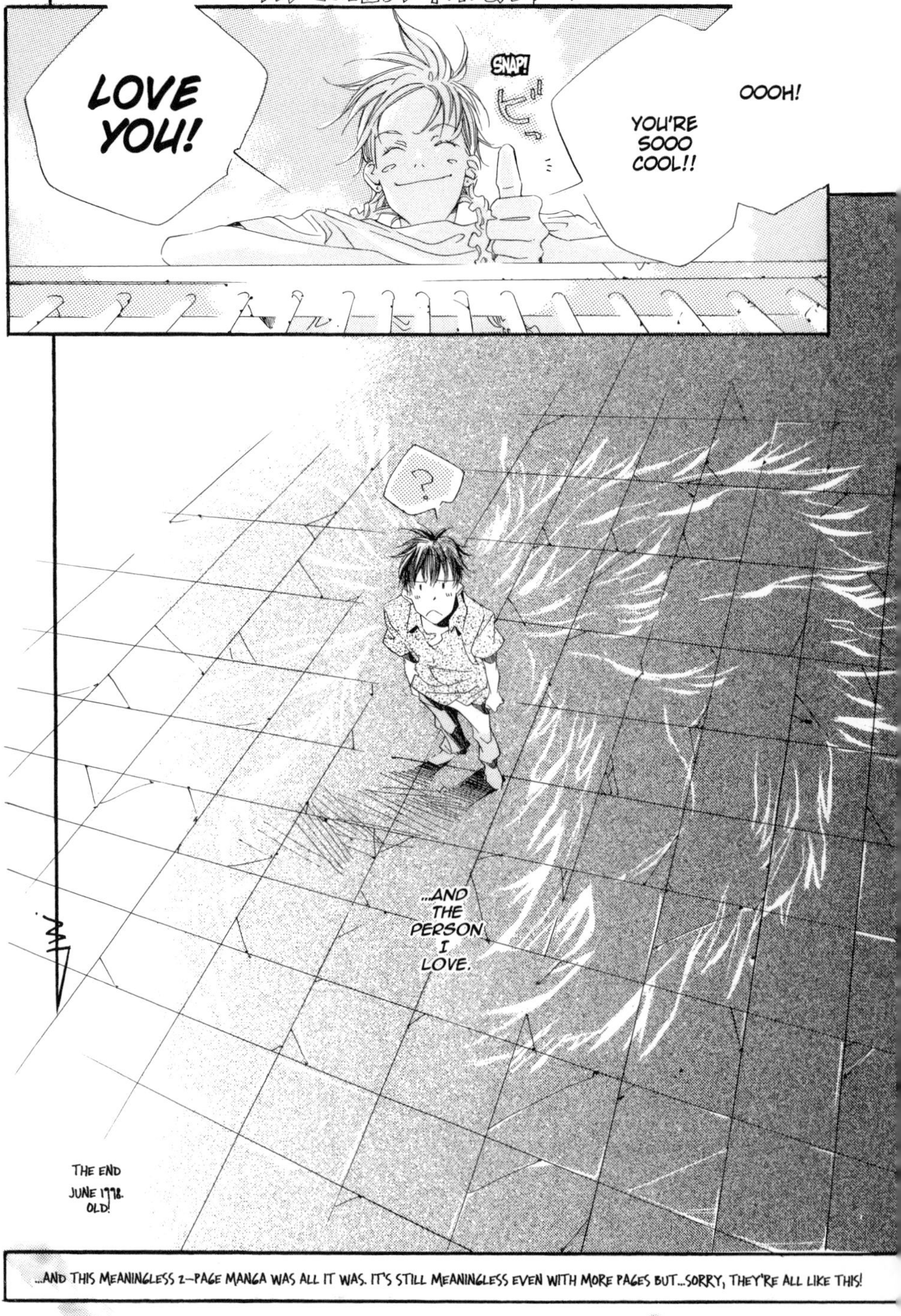
OOOH!
YOU'RE SOOO COOL!!
SNAP!
LOVE YOU!
?
...AND THE PERSON I LOVE.
THE END
JUNE 1998. OLD!

...AND THIS MEANINGLESS 2-PAGE MANGA WAS ALL IT WAS. IT'S STILL MEANINGLESS EVEN WITH MORE PAGES BUT...SORRY, THEY'RE ALL LIKE THIS!

ENDING

SAME-CELL ORGANISM

SUMOMO YUMEKA

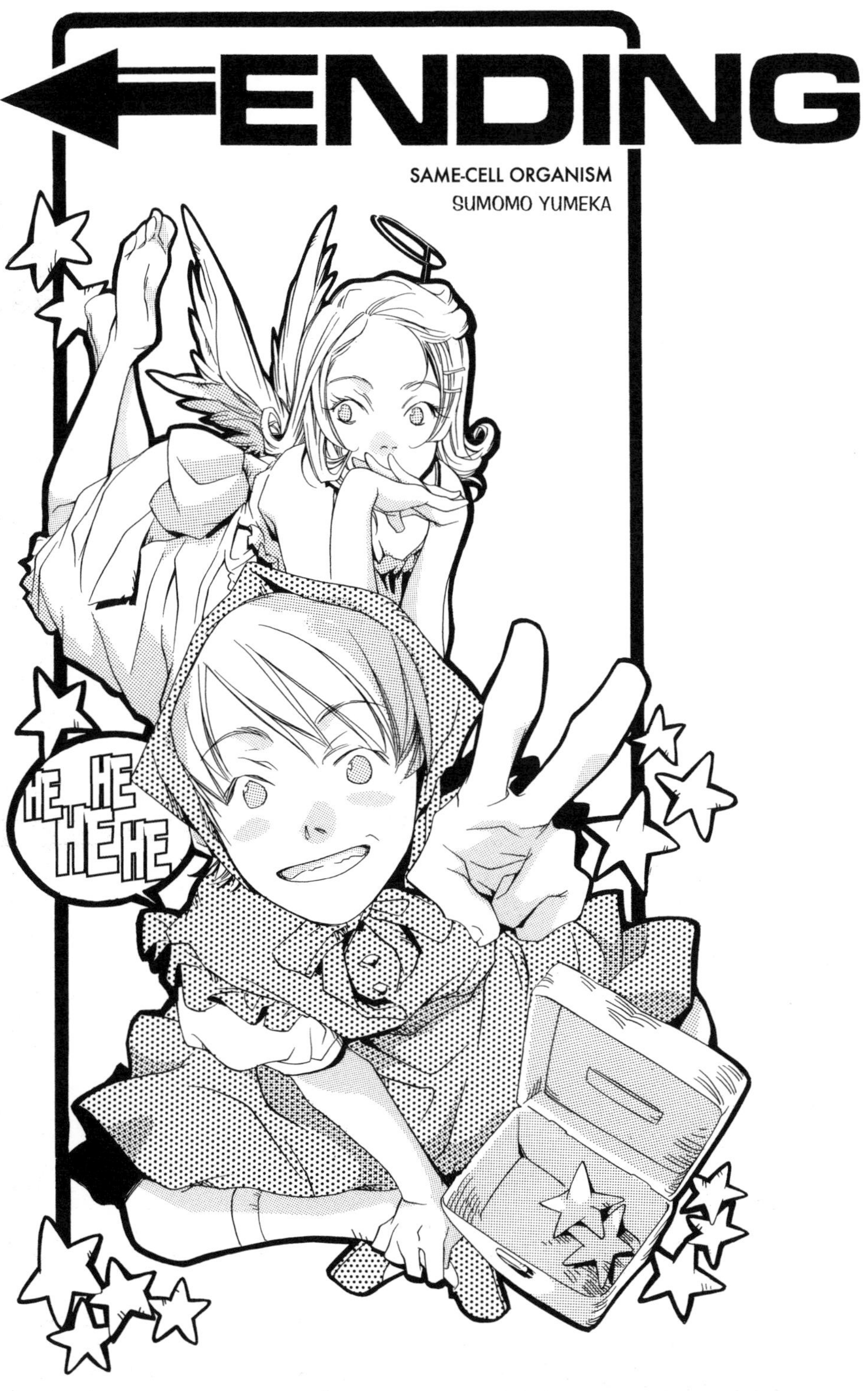
HE HE HE HE

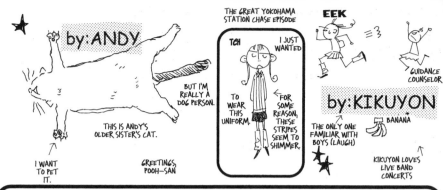

THE GREAT YOKOHAMA STATION CHASE EPISODE
EEK
≡3
GUIDANCE COUNSELOR
by:KIKUYON
THE ONLY ONE FAMILIAR WITH BOYS (LAUGH)
BANANA
KIKUYON LOVES LIVE BAND CONCERTS
TCH
I JUST WANTED
TO WEAR THIS UNIFORM.
FOR SOME REASON, THESE STRIPES SEEM TO SHIMMER.
by:ANDY
BUT I'M REALLY A DOG PERSON.
THIS IS ANDY'S OLDER SISTER'S CAT.
I WANT TO PET IT.
GREETINGS, POOH-SAN

I AM DEEPLY GRATEFUL THAT SUCH A WORK AS THIS, INCOMPLETE AS IT IS ON SO MANY LEVELS, HAS BEEN PUBLISHED. SINCE I LACK CONCENTRATION MORE THAN MOST PEOPLE, I AM ONLY ABLE TO PRODUCE WORKS THAT ARE SUB-AMATEUR AT BEST...I LEARNED THAT DRAWING A MANGA IS VERY HARD. I'M HUMBLED.

WITH REGARDS TO "SAME-CELL ORGANISM," "I LOVE YOU," AND "LULLABY IN MY HAND" - I HAVE PERSONAL EXPERIENCE WORKING PART-TIME IN A CONVENIENCE STORE. BUT I HAVE UNPLEASANT MEMORIES OF BEING FOUND OUT BY A TEACHER AND HAVING TO SPEND MY WINTER VACATIONS IN LONELY EXTRA STUDY SESSIONS.
(NOTE: IN JAPAN, HIGH SCHOOL STUDENTS ARE NOT ALLOWED TO HAVE JOBS, AS IT INTERFERES WITH THEIR STUDIES.)

AS FOR "TO MAKE AN ANGEL" (FORMERLY ENTITLED "TRAVELER OF SION") - AT FIRST, IT WAS OMITTED BECAUSE OF ITS INCOMPLETENESS. IN ITS PLACE, THERE WAS A PLAN TO INCLUDE A DIFFERENT WORK OF MINE CALLED "MAKING AN ANGEL" (OF WHICH I HAVE PAINFUL MEMORIES, SINCE WORKING ON IT DURING EXAM SEASON RESULTED IN MY LOWERED GRADES) THAT I HAD DONE FOR ANOTHER PUBLISHER...BUT IN THE END, THE RESULT IS AS YOU SEE IT HERE. TO PUT IT CLEARLY, I DIDN'T FINISH IN TIME. YES, I AM A FOOL.

I USED TO HAVE A WHITE BIRD THAT WOULD SIT ON MY HAND. I THINK IT LIVED PRETTY LONG FOR A BIRD. MY FATHER BOUGHT IT FOR ME WHEN I WAS IN ELEMENTARY SCHOOL, AND IT WAS FAIRLY LIVELY UP UNTIL AROUND THE TIME I WAS WORKING ON (FORMERLY ENTITLED) "TRAVELER OF SION"...
NOW? YES, IT'S TAKEN ITS PLACE AMONG THE STARS IN THE SKY...

FOR "WE SELFISH TWO," THE ONLY MEMORY I HAVE REMAINING OF IT IS THAT I DECIDED ON THE MAIN CHARACTERS' NAMES AS "MIDORI MORI (GREEN FOREST)" AND "SORA AOKI (BLUE SKY)" - SO CLICHÉ. SORRY.

"DOODLES ON THE BACK OF RECEIPTS" (THE VARIOUS DRAWINGS YOU SEE SCATTERED HERE)
THESE ARE BY THE WARM, KIND PEOPLE WHO UNDERSTAND ME BEST (OR SO I'D LIKE TO BELIEVE), AND YET ARE STILL WILLING TO HANG OUT WITH ME!

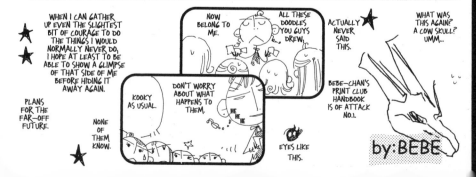

WHAT WAS THIS AGAIN? A COW SKULL? UMM...
ACTUALLY NEVER SAID THIS.
BEBE-CHAN'S PRINT CLUB HANDBOOK IS OF ATTACK NO.1.
by:BEBE
EYES LIKE THIS.
ALL THESE DOODLES YOU GUYS DREW,
NOW BELONG TO ME.
DON'T WORRY ABOUT WHAT HAPPENS TO THEM.
HE HE HE
KOOKY AS USUAL.
NONE OF THEM KNOW.
WHEN I CAN GATHER UP EVEN THE SLIGHTEST BIT OF COURAGE TO DO THE THINGS I WOULD NORMALLY NEVER DO, I HOPE AT LEAST TO BE ABLE TO SHOW A GLIMPSE OF THAT SIDE OF ME BEFORE HIDING IT AWAY AGAIN.
PLANS FOR THE FAR-OFF FUTURE.

ENDING*ENDING*ENDING*ENDING

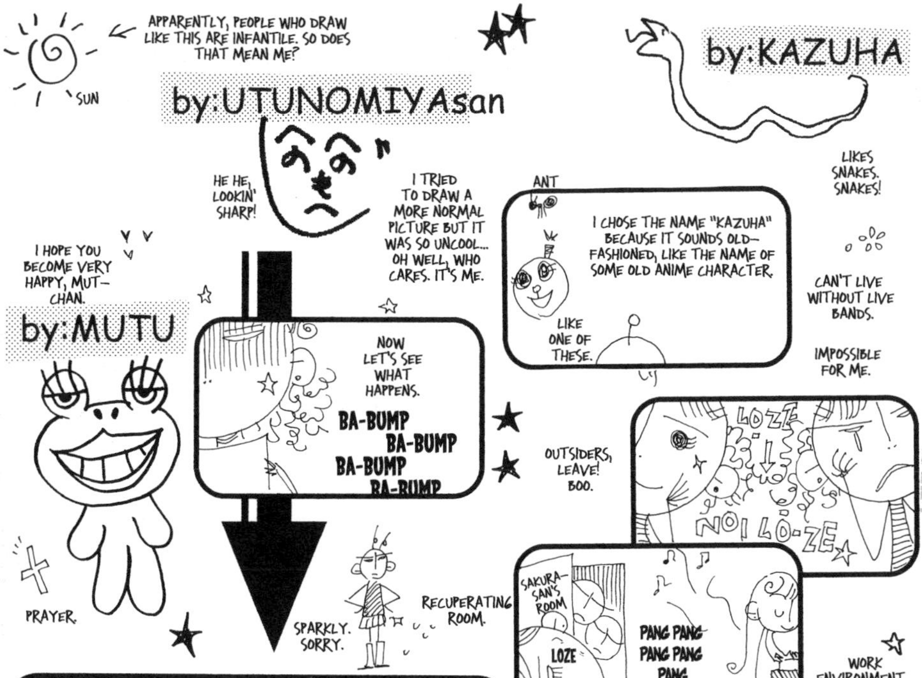
by:KAZUHA
LIKES SNAKES. SNAKES!
ANT
I CHOSE THE NAME "KAZUHA" BECAUSE IT SOUNDS OLD-FASHIONED, LIKE THE NAME OF SOME OLD ANIME CHARACTER.
LIKE ONE OF THESE.
CAN'T LIVE WITHOUT LIVE BANDS.
IMPOSSIBLE FOR ME.
APPARENTLY, PEOPLE WHO DRAW LIKE THIS ARE INFANTILE. SO DOES THAT MEAN ME?
SUN
by:UTUNOMIYAsan
I TRIED TO DRAW A MORE NORMAL PICTURE BUT IT WAS SO UNCOOL... OH WELL, WHO CARES. IT'S ME.
HE HE LOOKIN' SHARP!
I HOPE YOU BECOME VERY HAPPY, MUT-CHAN.
by:MUTU
NOW LET'S SEE WHAT HAPPENS.
BA-BUMP BA-BUMP BA-BUMP BA-BUMP
PRAYER.
SPARKLY. SORRY.
RECUPERATING ROOM.
OUTSIDERS, LEAVE! BOO.
LOZE
NOI LO-ZE
SAKURA-SAN'S ROOM
LOZE
PANG PANG PANG PANG PANG
WORK ENVIRONMENT AT THE TIME THIS WAS BEING DRAWN
SHUT UP. IF YOU'RE GONNA FLIRT, GO SOMEWHERE ELSE.

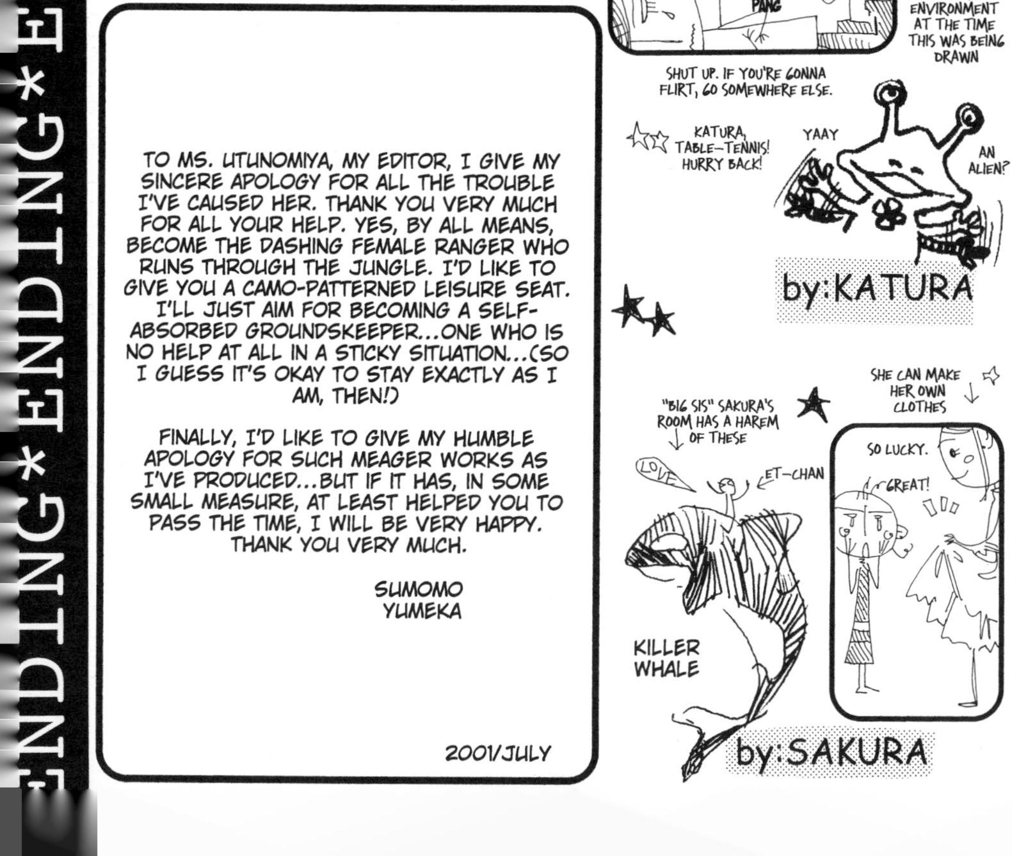
KATURA, TABLE-TENNIS! HURRY BACK!
YAAY
AN ALIEN?
by:KATURA
SHE CAN MAKE HER OWN CLOTHES
"BIG SIS" SAKURA'S ROOM HAS A HAREM OF THESE
LOVE
ET-CHAN
SO LUCKY.
GREAT!
KILLER WHALE
by:SAKURA

TO MS. UTUNOMIYA, MY EDITOR, I GIVE MY SINCERE APOLOGY FOR ALL THE TROUBLE I'VE CAUSED HER. THANK YOU VERY MUCH FOR ALL YOUR HELP. YES, BY ALL MEANS, BECOME THE DASHING FEMALE RANGER WHO RUNS THROUGH THE JUNGLE. I'D LIKE TO GIVE YOU A CAMO-PATTERNED LEISURE SEAT. I'LL JUST AIM FOR BECOMING A SELF-ABSORBED GROUNDSKEEPER...ONE WHO IS NO HELP AT ALL IN A STICKY SITUATION...(SO I GUESS IT'S OKAY TO STAY EXACTLY AS I AM, THEN!)

FINALLY, I'D LIKE TO GIVE MY HUMBLE APOLOGY FOR SUCH MEAGER WORKS AS I'VE PRODUCED...BUT IF IT HAS, IN SOME SMALL MEASURE, AT LEAST HELPED YOU TO PASS THE TIME, I WILL BE VERY HAPPY. THANK YOU VERY MUCH.

SUMOMO YUMEKA

2001/JULY

SAME CELL ORGANISM

Translation	**Sachiko Sato**
Lettering	**Jennifer Baker**
Graphic Design	**Wendy Lee / Fred Lui**
Editing	**Bambi Eloriaga**
Editor in Chief	**Fred Lui**
Publisher	**Hikaru Sasahara**

English Edition Published by
DIGITAL MANGA PUBLISHING
A division of DIGITAL MANGA, Inc.
1487 W 178th Street, Suite 300
Gardena, CA 90248

www.dmpbooks.com

First Edition: May 2006
ISBN: 1-56970-926-2

1 3 5 7 9 10 8 6 4 2

Printed in China

When the music stops...
love begins.

Il gatto sul G

Kind-hearted Atsushi finds Riya injured on his doorstep and offers him a safe haven from the demons pursuing him.

By Tooko Miyagi

Vol. 1 ISBN# 1-56970-923-8 $12.95
Vol. 2 ISBN# 1-56970-893-2 $12.95

DMP
DIGITAL MANGA
PUBLISHING

yaoi-manga.com
The girls only sanctuary

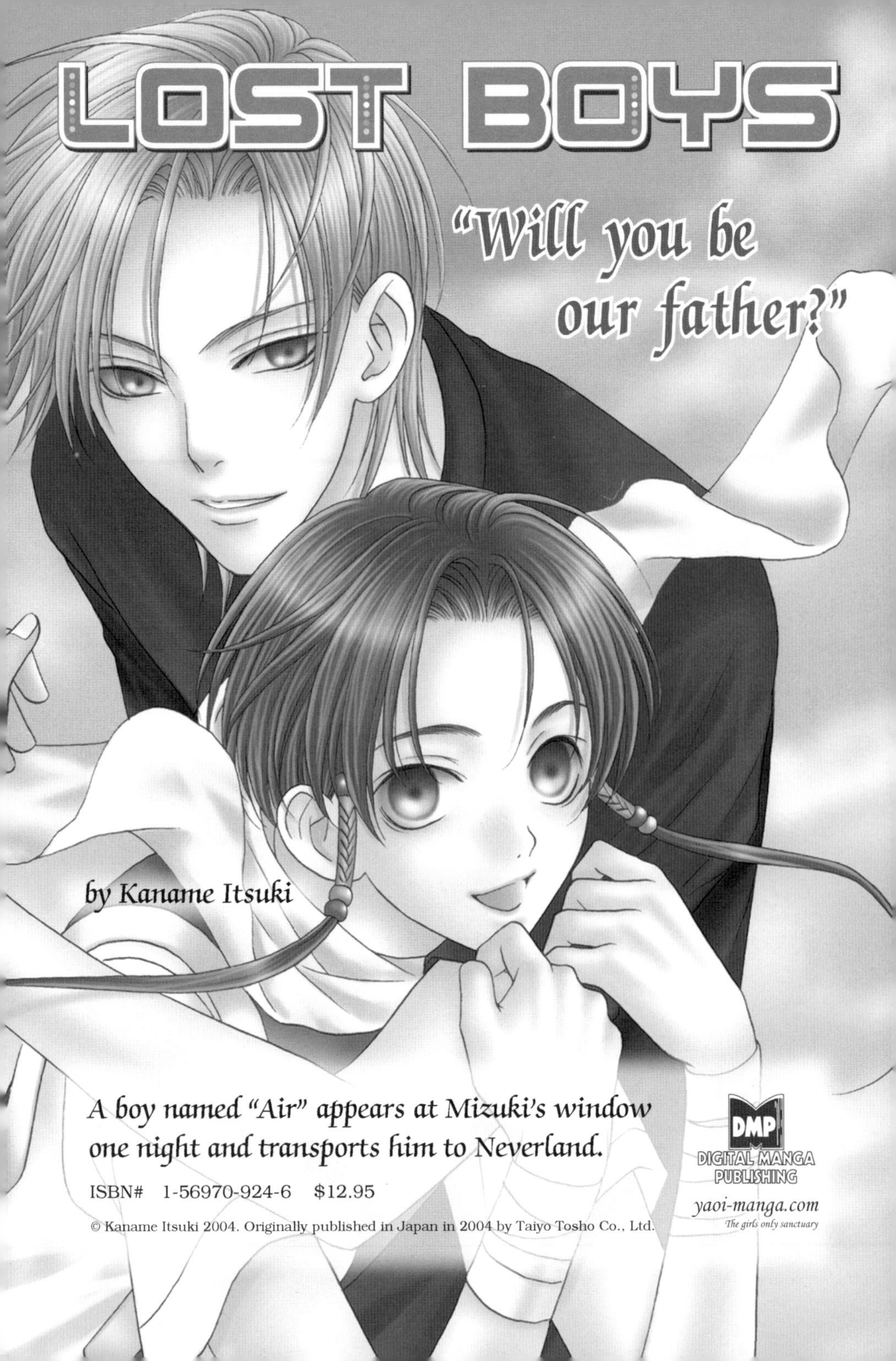
LOST BOYS
"Will you be our father?"
by Kaname Itsuki
A boy named "Air" appears at Mizuki's window one night and transports him to Neverland.
ISBN# 1-56970-924-6 $12.95
© Kaname Itsuki 2004. Originally published in Japan in 2004 by Taiyo Tosho Co., Ltd.
DMP
DIGITAL MANGA PUBLISHING
yaoi-manga.com
The girls only sanctuary

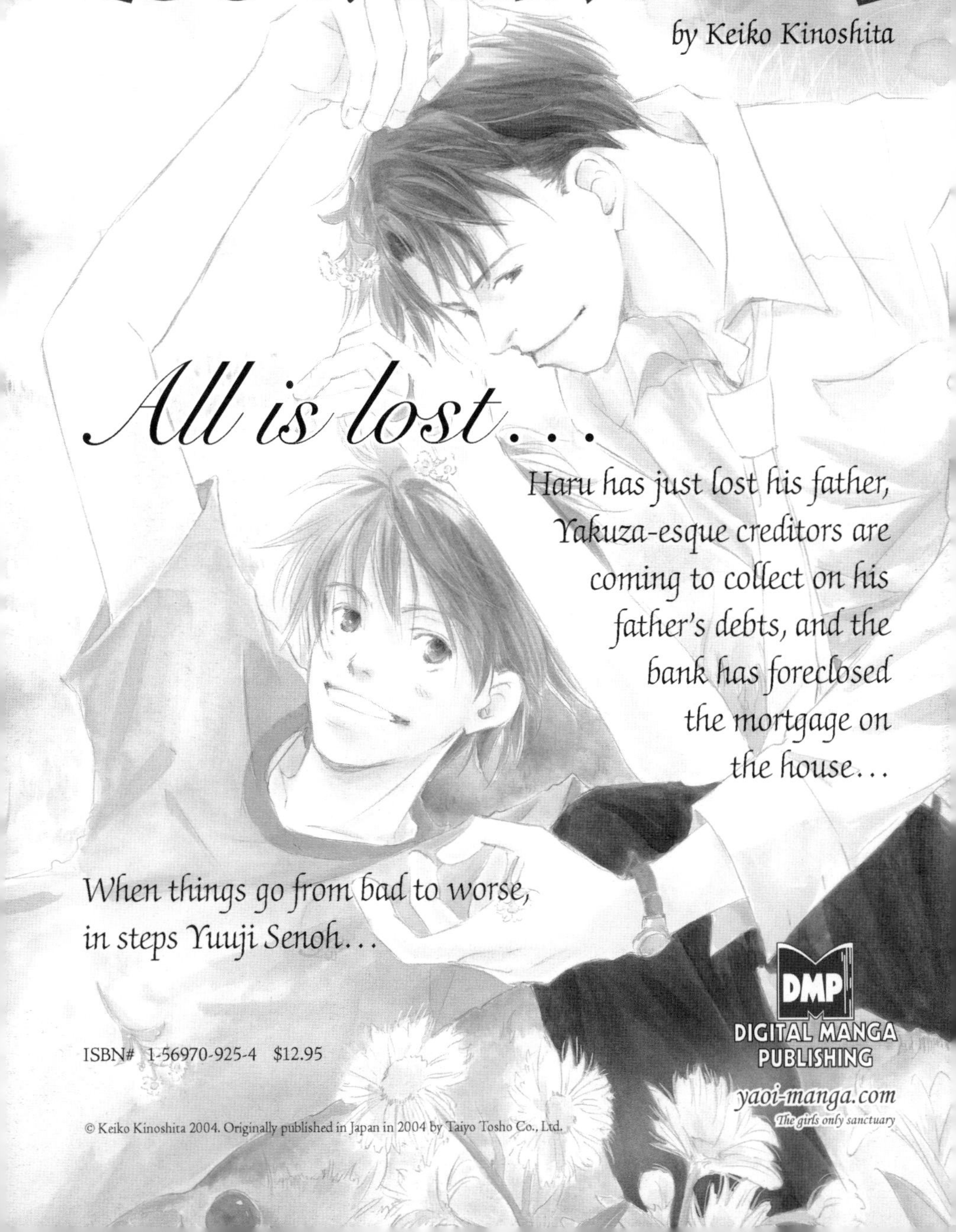

You & Harujion

by Keiko Kinoshita

All is lost . . .

Haru has just lost his father, Yakuza-esque creditors are coming to collect on his father's debts, and the bank has foreclosed the mortgage on the house…

When things go from bad to worse, in steps Yuuji Senoh…

ISBN# 1-56970-925-4 $12.95

DMP
DIGITAL MANGA PUBLISHING
yaoi-manga.com
The girls only sanctuary

Evil Nobunaga possess the scroll of the Heavens and will stop at nothing to find the scroll of the Earth, because when the two scrolls meet they form the Tenka Musō a near infinite source of power!

**Just one small problem...
The scroll of the Earth
is located inside
13 year old
Hattori Hanzou!**

Vol. 1 ISBN# 1-56970-955-6 $12.95
Vol. 2 ISBN# 1-56970-954-8 $12.95

An epic fictional adventure inspired by the true life stories of Hattori Hanzou

PRINCESS NINJA SCROLL

TENKA MUSŌ